DOING CHRISTIAN ETHICS
FROM THE MARGINS

DOING CHRISTIAN ETHICS
FROM THE MARGINS

SECOND EDITION
REVISED AND EXPANDED

Miguel A. De La Torre

ORBIS BOOKS

Maryknoll, New York 10545

ORBIS BOOKS
Maryknoll, New York 10545

Fathers and Brothers
MARYKNOLL™

Founded in 1970, Orbis Books endeavors to publish works that enlighten the mind, nourish the spirit, and challenge the conscience. The publishing arm of the Maryknoll Fathers and Brothers, Orbis seeks to explore the global dimensions of the Christian faith and mission, to invite dialogue with diverse cultures and religious traditions, and to serve the cause of reconciliation and peace. The books published reflect the views of their authors and do not represent the official position of the Maryknoll Society. To learn more about Maryknoll and Orbis Books, please visit our website at www.maryknollsociety.org.

Copyright © 2014 by Miguel A. De La Torre

Published by Orbis Books, Maryknoll, New York 10545-0302

Manufactured in the United States of America

Queries regarding rights and permissions should be addressed to
Orbis Books, P.O. Box 302, Maryknoll, New York 10545-0302.

Library of Congress Cataloging-in-Publication Data

De La Torre, Miguel A.
    Doing Christian ethics from the margins / by Miguel A. De La Torre.—
2nd Edition Revised and Expanded.
        pages   cm
    Includes bibliographical references and index.
    ISBN 978-1-62698-075-4 (pbk.)
    1. Christian ethics—Textbooks. 2. Marginality, Social—Moral and
ethical aspects—Textbooks   I. Title.
    BJ125   1.D38 2014
    241—dc23   2013031886

To my brother Ricky

Contents

PART I
ETHICAL THEORY

PART II
CASE STUDIES OF GLOBAL RELATIONSHIPS

PART III
CASE STUDIES OF NATIONAL RELATIONSHIPS

PART IV
CASE STUDIES OF BUSINESS RELATIONSHIPS

Preface

Preface to the 2004 Edition

The classroom is appropriately named, for it is indeed a room of class—a room where students learn the class they belong to and the power and privilege that come with that class.[1] The fact that some students are able to pay sufficient money to attend particular rooms of class located on prestigious campuses indicates that they will have certain opportunities that are denied to those of lower economic classes, those who are more often than not students of color residing on the margins of society.

Our educational system is far from being objective or neutral, and students who attend classrooms, from community colleges to highly selective universities, can be conditioned either to accept the present system of social structures or to seek liberation from said structures. All too often, the educational system serves to normalize these power structures as legitimate. The task of educators, specifically those who call themselves ethicists, is to cultivate students' ability to find their own voices by creating an environment in which individual and collective consciousness-raising can occur.

As an ethicist unapologetically grounded in a Latino/a social context, I create an environment within the classroom that attempts to perceive the will of the Divine from within the social location of marginalized people— that is, those who are not usually able to participate in the classroom where I teach. Such a process analyzes their reality, a reality tied to an ethical perspective that demands a sociopolitical response to oppression. In this way a relationship can develop between intellectuals aware of the structural crises faced by people of color and the disenfranchised in the United States.

Nevertheless, the danger facing liberative scholars is that they can become an intellectual elite disconnected from the everyday struggles of the marginalized and have little or no impact upon the churches in disenfranchised communities. Ethicists from the margins attempting to overcome this disconnect advocate connecting the work done by Christian ministers serving disenfranchised communities with the academic work done by faculty and students in our colleges and universities. These ministers and scholars attempt to learn from the disenfranchised while serving them as organic intellectuals (to borrow a term from Antonio Gramsci)—that is, intellectuals grounded in the social reality of the marginalized and acting in the consciousness-raising process of the faith community.

---

1. I am indebted to one of my mentors, John Raines, who constantly reminded me of this fact during my doctoral studies.

The pedagogy that I employ in my classroom, and will attempt to unfold in this book, seeks to open Christian ethics to the rich diversity found among those who are usually excluded—those who are part of a multiracial and multicultural people. In my "room of class" I attempt to construct a collaborative ethics through studying and reflecting on the lives and circumstances of marginalized people. This is not to make students aware of some quaint or exotic perspective of those who are disenfranchised; rather, it is to help them realize that because the gospel message was first proclaimed in the colonized spaces of Judea, those who reside in these marginalized spaces, then and now, hold the key to interpreting this message properly. In this way the salvation of the usually Eurocentric dominant culture depends on hearing what is proclaimed by those from the margins.

This approach entails a response to injustice and oppression. By forcing my students to occupy an uncomfortable space, I feel that I can provide them with a unique outlook, a view that I believe enhances more traditional learning. I try to bring their lifetime of experiences and knowledge into conversation with people whose lives and experiences may be quite different from theirs, people who may often be thought of as having little to contribute to the educational process.

This pedagogy, however, is useless if it is restricted solely to the classroom. The liberating ethical praxis that I advocate is pertinent to the larger community as well. For example, the community in which my school is located, Holland, was settled by the Dutch in the early 1800s. Located on Lake Michigan, Holland has wooden-shoe factories, a windmill imported from the Netherlands, and an annual May festival called Tulip Time, which attracts over a hundred thousand visitors to celebrate Holland's Dutch heritage.

But Holland is also a town where all are not Dutch. On the underside of Holland we discover Hispanics, who comprise approximately 22.2 percent of the overall population. (If those who are undocumented were counted, the numbers would hover at 30 percent.) In addition, 3.5 percent of the population is Asian, and 2.3 percent black. In spite of these demographics, those who live on the margins of Holland are seldom seen walking or shopping on 8th Street, the main business center of the city, even if they live a few blocks away.

Holland is a town where many from the dominant culture may wish to live in a more just and equitable society, but they also find themselves trapped within social structures created long ago (and some more recently) to protect their privilege by masking racism and classism. Consequently, those who are oppressed by these structures, along with those who benefit, are in need of liberation, another word for salvation.

To bring about liberation as salvation, Christianity must become a way of life rather than just a doctrinal belief. If simple belief is all that is required for salvation, then complicity with structures that perpetuate oppression is inconsequential to the Christian life. Besides, do not the demons themselves believe that God is one? The perspectives of Christian liberative ethicists are crucial to help establish a more just society. Faculty and students alike can contribute to the struggle against oppression that has often become institutionalized. For this reason, my role as an ethicist must include participation in a faith community and the overall society. What I *do*—my praxis—is more crucial than any book that I might write. Most Christian ethicists working from a liberation framework write, or teach, to give voice to the voiceless, to shout from the mountaintop that which is commonly heard among disenfranchised people, to put into words what the marginalized are feeling and doing. No doubt, such writing may anger or alienate those who view their power and privilege as a birthright; nonetheless, these things must be said to bring about repentance for those who participate in injustice through their privilege, and to bring about salvation for those who suffer from injustices.

As can be imagined, this type of pedagogy does not come easily in a conservative religious and political environment such as Holland, Michigan. It might be wiser to simply conform to the dominant culture and remain silent in the face of racism, classism, sexism, and heterosexism. There is a tremendous temptation to turn my back on the oppression that surrounds me. But it seems that my scholarship has been influenced by Don Quixote, and, like him, I feel the need to charge the windmills of Holland. But in a world that normalizes oppression—our world today—maybe some Don Quixotes can bring hope when there is none as they set out on a path of a justice-based ethics to take on the foes of power and privilege.

Preface to the 2014 Edition

My students and I were sitting on a dirt-floor hut in a squatter village on the outskirts of Cuernavaca, Mexico. Joining me were mostly white, economically privileged students who sought to learn about God from the poor. Our "teacher" that day was an illiterate *mestiza* who was patiently answering our questions (with me serving as translator). We asked who is God to her; who is Jesus Christ; who is the Virgin Mary? Her answers, theologically speaking, were frightful. They were a mixture of superstition and popular Catholicism. It soon became clear that she lacked orthodoxy—correct doctrine. Then her barefooted boy (about eleven years old) entered the one-room hut with a few pesos earned from selling Chiclets to tourists. As she collected the money, she placed one peso aside. I asked her what that was for. She replied that it was for the poor. At that moment, the orthopraxis—correct action—of this poor woman taught my students (and me) more about the essence of the Divine than all of the academic books that we have read. Seeing the giving of the "widow's mite" was more effective than any lecture that I could have given.

When those who have so little *do* their faith by providing for those who have even less, those of us privileged by class should be profoundly humbled. It is the privileged who see the oppressed and do nothing that are the ones who do not know God. I may have the educational training to tease out the inconsistencies in this woman's beliefs, but she knew far more about God than I did. This is not a romanticization of the poor, for surely there is nothing romantic about poverty; rather, it is a theological truth that I learned directly from this poor woman's actions.

When we get to heaven, we will discover how wrong we were. No group has a monopoly on truth. So in a sense, orthodoxy—correct belief—is not that important. What should take precedence is orthopraxis—correct action. For this reason, academics who do ethics from the margins are scholar-activists. Perceiving great theoretical thoughts about the Divine is less important than doing the works of love as called for by the Divine.

The poor of Cuernavaca, and elsewhere throughout the world, bring our privileged suppositions into conversation with those whom many may consider to have nothing to offer the intellectual dialogue. Only by being scholar-activists can my students and I contribute to the struggle against oppression that has become institutionalized. The praxis of dealing with oppressive structures within dispossessed communities is more crucial than books published by the "experts," including the book you hold in your hands. No doubt, such a methodology usually will anger those accustomed to their power and privilege; still, doing ethics from the margins of society is imperative if we want to be faithful to what we, as Christians, claim to believe.

Since the publishing of this book a decade ago, my resolve that a closer understanding of the Divine can be attained only by listening carefully to those on the margins has been strengthened. In all the books I have written, in all the classes I have taught, in all the lectures I have given, the wisdom expressed has never been something that I produced while sitting in my ivory tower. Whether visiting the squatter villages of Cuernavaca, walking the migrant trails taken by the undocumented entering the United States, or working beside poor rural rice farmers in Indonesia, everything that I hold true I learned from them. This book is a product of the margins.

Acknowledgments

Acknowledgments for the 2004 Edition

Even Don Quixote had his Sancho. Likewise, this book is a reality because of the many who labored with me to bring it to fruition. It would be a travesty to take full credit for what appears on these pages. Many of the ideas and insights for this book took shape in a senior-level class that I taught at Hope College by the same name, "Doing Christian Ethics from the Margins." Although the class was composed of approximately twenty students (Anglo students, save one), with most sharing in middle- and upper-class privilege, these students were committed to seeking justice. They seriously undertook the quite difficult task of reflecting upon ethical case studies by seeking the voices of those who usually are disenfranchised by the prevailing social structures. I give my heartfelt thanks to these students. Specifically, I wish to highlight three of them: Dustin Janes, Lauren Hinkle, and Phil Johnson, who worked with me for an additional semester as research assistants, spending countless hours gathering and organizing data.

Thanks to a McGregor Fund grant offered through Hope College, Phil Johnson was able to continue assisting me with this project through the summer months. I am also indebted to librarian Anthony Guardado at Hope College, who worked with us in locating hard-to-find sources. I also greatly appreciated the Religion Department at Hope College, whose faculty set up a colloquium to read early versions of this manuscript and provided valuable feedback. In addition, I am grateful to John Raines and Allan Verhey, who carefully read sections of the manuscript and provided much constructive criticism. Any success that this book has is due to their wise counsel. I continue to be indebted to Jonathan Schakel for his faithfulness in proofreading my text, and to my editor, Susan Perry, who was always ready to prod me toward excellence. As always, I owe eternal gratitude to my children, Vincent and Victoria, and my soul mate, Deborah, my moral compass, who continues to be the source of my strength.

Acknowledgments for the 2014 Edition

During an academic lecture, a colleague approached me and asked when I was planning to update *Doing Christian Ethics from the Margins*. Frankly, I had not given it much thought until then. The book was being used in many ethics classes and was selling well, but it was outdated. Since it was written, the wars in Afghanistan and Iraq began winding down. The Supreme Court made decisions in campaign financing and affirmative action. The country elected its first biracial president. The Great Recession of 2008 hit, devastating the middle class. Much has changed, except for the formula that the many are sinking in greater want so that the few can continue to enjoy their excess. Yes, it was time to update the book.

Since the first edition a decade ago, I left (or better yet, was forced out of) Holland, Michigan, when I began to advocate for LGBT civil rights. Standing with the oppressed can at times be costly. The children whom I acknowledge in the first edition, Victoria and Vincent, are now college graduates starting out in a world with fewer opportunities available than in the past. For their sake, and the sake of this new generation, this books attempts to ask why.

Finding the latest statistics and updated facts was not an easy task. It never would have been accomplished without the help of a small cadre of research assistants, specifically Patrick Bowen, Rebecca Chabot, and Sarah Neeley. A special thanks to Samuel (Slam) Trujillo, who was my assistant on this project for over a year. And yes, my wife, Deb, continues to be my moral compass as we discuss (debate?) a multitude of ethical issues.

Part I

Ethical Theory

Chapter 1

Doing Christian Ethics

Even the wicked are virtuous. The Ku Klux Klan, probably the oldest hate group in the United States, bases its beliefs and actions upon what it perceives to be Christian values and virtues. According to its official website,

> The fiery cross is a Klan symbol representing the ideals of Christian of civilization. . . . [The cross] is a constant reminder that Christ is our criterion of character and his teachings are our rule of life. . . . By the fire of Calvary's cross we mean to cleanse and purify our virtues by burning out our vices from the fire of his word.[1]

Likewise, the Creativity Movement (formally the Church of the Creator) one of the newest and fastest-growing hate groups, operates according to its own code of ethics. But unlike the Ku Klux Klan, it is constructed as a non-Christian organization. According to its official website,

> Christianity teaches love your enemies and hate your own kind, while we teach exactly the opposite, namely hate and destroy your enemies and love your own kind. Whereas Christianity's teachings are suicidal, our creed brings out the best creative and constructive forces inherent to the White Race. Whereas Christians are destroyers, we are builders. . . . Our Golden Rule briefly can be summarized as follows: That which is good for the White Race is the highest virtue; that which is bad for the White Race is the ultimate sin.[2]

In all fairness, hate groups such as these advocate motherhood, patriotism, and the welfare of children. They exhort their members to live by a code of ethics that celebrates and defends values and virtues that some of the world's great faith traditions also advocate. It would be somewhat reductionist simply to write off these groups as purely evil with no comprehension of good. In fact, as these two websites indicate, they do have a set of ethics, a sense of proper behavior, and a self-imposed mandate to live an honorable life, hence proving Augustine of Hippo's dictum, "There is a kind of honor even among thieves."

---

1. www.kkk.net/America.html (2013).
2. www.creativitymovement.net/site/faq.html (2013).

3

The problem with the value systems of the KKK and the Creativity Movement is that others, among them people of color, disagree with their understanding of morality. The issue, then, is not so much whether humans should follow some set of ethical precepts, but rather, *whose* ethical precepts. Moral relativism recognizes the variety of ethical beliefs existing between different racial and ethnic groups, economic classes, and gender preferences. But if ethics is simply relative, whereby no one group's ethics is necessarily superior or inferior to another group's, then adhering to the ethics spouted by the Ku Klux Klan, or the Creativity Movement, should be as valid as any ethics coming from the marginalized spaces of society, or any other spaces for that matter. It appears as though a preferential option needs to be made for some set of ethical precepts. The question is: Whose?

The Ku Klux Klan and the Creativity Movement are extreme examples, but other ethical perspectives expounded by many Christians within the U.S. Eurocentric culture also raise questions and concerns about the incongruence existing with what they conceive to be moral and day-to-day experiences of marginalized people. Regardless of the virtues expounded by the dominant culture, there still exist self-perpetuating mechanisms of oppression that continue to normalize and legitimize how subjugation manifests itself in the overall customs, language, traditions, values, and laws of the United States. Our political systems, our policing authorities, our judicial institutions, and our military forces conspire to maintain a status quo designed to secure and protect the power and wealth of the privileged few. In some cases, the ethics advanced by the dominant culture appears to rationalize these present power structures, hence protecting and masking the political and economic interests of those whom the structures privilege—in effect, an ethics driven by the self-interest of Euroamericans.

As long as the religious leaders and scholars of the dominant culture continue to construct ethical perspectives from within their cultural space of wealth and power, the marginalized will need an alternate format by which to deliberate and, more importantly, do ethics. Through critical social analysis, it is possible to uncover the connection existing between the prevailing ideologies (namely, the ethics of the dominant culture) that support the present power arrangement and the political, economic, and cultural components of the mechanisms of oppression that protect their power and wealth. Anchoring ethics on the everyday experience of the marginalized challenges the validity, or lack thereof, of prevailing ideologies that inform Eurocentric ethics.

For example, the fact that once upon a time in U.S. history the "peculiar" institution of slavery was biblically supported, religiously justified, spiritually legitimized, and ethically normalized raises serious questions concerning the objectivity of any particular code of ethics originating from that dominant white culture. At the very least, the marginalized are suspicious of the ethics of those who benefit from what society deems to be Christian or moral— then, as well as today. Although hindsight facilitates our understanding of how unchristian and unethical previous generations may have been, we are left wondering whether perspectives considered by some to be morally sound today might be defined as unchristian and unethical by future generations. Regardless, extreme groups like the Ku Klux Klan or the Creativity Movement are not, nor should they be, our focus. Instead, our concentration rests with ethics advocated by traditionally based Christian congregations found throughout the United States.

I aim to describe how the disenfranchised struggle against societal mechanisms responsible for much of the misery that they face, preventing them from living out the mission of Christ as recorded in the Gospel of John: "I came that they may have life, and have it abundantly" (John 10:10).[3] Christian liberative ethics becomes the process by which the mechanisms that dehumanize life, as well as cause death, are dismantled. All too often, ethics, as presented by the dominant culture, explores Christian virtues without seriously considering the existence of the oppressed majority of people. The hope of God, like the hope of the marginalized, is the re-creation of proper relationships whereby all people can live full, abundant lives, able to become all that God has called them to be, free from the societal forces (racism, classism, sexism, and heterosexism) that foster dehumanizing conditions. Within such relationships exist healing, wholeness, and liberation.

Why Christian?

One may ask why this book unapologetically centers ethical reflection upon the Christian perspective, relying mainly on Christian sacred texts (specifically the Hebrew Bible and the New Testament) and Christian theological concepts (specifically the liberationist motif advocated by many marginalized groups). Should not ethical perspectives incorporate a wide variety of responses, including those that are not necessarily Christian-based? Given the absence of a homogeneous cultural and religious center upon which to deduct moral reasoning, does it not make sense to reflect the world's religious diversity when determining proper ethical responses? Surely there is much to learn about ethical deliberation from major world religions such as Islam,

---

3. All scriptural quotations are my translations from the original Hebrew or Greek. Additionally, it will be assumed that the stories and traditions appearing in the biblical text have been accurately preserved by the early faith communities. Usually, biblical scholars discuss the authenticity of authorship, as well as the accuracy of particular events, stories, or statements appearing in the text; however, such an analytical endeavor is beyond the scope of this book. Instead, my use of Scripture attempts to read the text from the perspective of the faith community. Such a reading is conducted from the marginalized spaces of society, attempting to understand and apply the biblical message to the reality of disenfranchisement.

Judaism, Hinduism, and Buddhism, as well as overlooked earth-based religions from Africa, Australia, and the pre-European Americas. As worthy as such an exploration of comparative religious traditions may be, it is beyond the scope of this book.[4]

Ethics remains a reflection of the social location and theological beliefs (or disbeliefs) of a given people. We focus on the Christian perspective because this book is written by and for those who claim to be followers of Jesus Christ. Although ethics can be done devoid of Jesus Christ (as well as devoid of the influence of a supreme god-type deity), such ethics, although valid for those constructing it, is not necessarily Christian-based, even though agreement may be found in several areas of deliberation.

That being said, it is crucial to realize that the Christianity upon which the ethical perspectives of this book are based is not necessarily Christianity as defined and understood by those privileged by the dominant culture. Rather, it is Christianity as forged from the underside, by those who exist on the margins of society. For those who struggle within oppressive structures, the personhood of Jesus Christ as a source of strength becomes crucial. The life and sayings of Christ, as recognized by the faith community that searches the biblical text for guidance to life's ethical dilemmas, serve as the ultimate standard of morality. While Eurocentric theology, and the ethics that flow from it, have a tendency to abstract the Christ event, those on the margins recognize that Christ remains at work in the United States today.

Theologian James H. Cone reminds us that it is from within the oppressed black community (and I would add any oppressed community) that Christ continues to bring about liberation from oppressive structures (1990, 5). For this reason, Jesus Christ, as understood by the disenfranchised faith community, becomes authoritative in how ethics develops within marginalized groups. For them, the incarnation—the Word taking flesh and dwelling among us—becomes the lens through which God's character is understood. Although Christ remains the ultimate revelation of God's character to humanity, the biblical text becomes the primary witness of this revelation and, as such, forms Christian identity while informing moral actions. The ultimate values advocated by the revelation of God through Christ as witnessed in the biblical text become the standards by which individuals and, more importantly, social structures are judged. Regardless of how many different ways the biblical text can be interpreted, certain recurring themes, specifically a call to justice and a call to love, can be recognized by all who call themselves Christians.

---

4. Those interested in exploring liberative ethical perspectives from the matrix of world religions can see Miguel A. De La Torre, ed., *The Hope of Liberation in World Religions* (Waco, TX: Baylor University Press, 2008).

Why Ethics?

Neither the overall biblical text nor the pronouncements of Jesus are silent or abstruse concerning the type of actions or praxis expected of those who claim to be disciples of Christ. The prophets of old would answer the ethical question of what God wants of God's people in a very straightforward matter. God was not interested in church services devoid of praxis toward the marginalized. As the prophet Isaiah reminds us, "Do not bring me [your God] your worthless offerings, the incense is an abomination to me. I cannot endure new moon and Sabbath, the call to meetings and the evil assembly" (Isa. 1:13). Instead, the prophets proclaimed justice for society's most vulnerable members as true worship, a testimony of one's love for God and neighbor.

Jesus sounds an eschatological admonishment on what is expected from his followers. In the Gospel of Matthew he warns, "Because lawlessness shall have been multiplied, and the love of many will grow cold, the one enduring to the end, this one will be saved" (Matt. 24:12–13). In short, there can be no faith, in fact no salvation, without ethical praxis, not because such actions are the cause of salvation, but rather are their manifestation. To participate in ethical praxis is to seek justice. For those on the margins of society, the ultimate goal of any ethical praxis is to establish a more just society. Yet "justice" has become a worn-out, hollow expression, an abstract and detached battle cry. Every political action initiated by the dominant culture, no matter how self-serving, is construed as just. The maintenance of an economic system that produces poverty is heralded as being based on the just principle of *suum cuique tribuere* (to each what is due). Sending military personnel into battle to protect "our" natural overseas resources is understood as securing our freedoms and way of life. The most unjust acts are portrayed as just by those with the power and privilege to impose their worldview on the rest of society.

This is what sociologist Emile Durkheim meant when he insisted that the beliefs and sentiments held in common by the inhabitants of the dominant culture become the moral norms codified in laws, customs, and traditions. Consequently, the primary function of society becomes the reaffirmation, protection, and perpetuation of this "collective or common conscience" (Durkheim 1933, 79–82). If this is true, then those on the margins of society must ask if it is possible to formulate a universal principle of justice apart from the definitions imposed by the collective conscience of the dominant culture.

Two of the most important components of ethics are the concepts of justice and love, both rooted in the biblical narrative. Although these are two separate concepts, for the liberationist they are forever connected. The importance of justice to ethical living is expounded by biblical scholar Gerhard von Rad, who wrote,

> There is absolutely no concept in the Old Testament with so
> central a significance for all the relationships of human life as
> that of [tsedaqah]. It is the standard not only for man's relation-
> ship to God, but also for his relationship to his fellows, reaching
> right down to the most petty wrangling—indeed, it is even the
> standard for man's relationship to the animals and to his natural
> environment. (1962, 370)

"Justice," the English equivalent of tsedaqah, can never be reduced simply
to some ideal to be achieved or a code of precepts to be followed. Rather, "justice" denotes how a real relationship between two parties (God and human,
human and human, nature and human, and/or human and society) is conducted. The emphasis is not on some abstract concept of how society is to
organize itself, but rather on loyalty within relationships, specifically those
dealing with humans (von Rad 1962, 371). Right relationship with God is
possible only if people act justly toward each other.

Right relationships are prevented from securing an abundant life (here
understood as intellectual, physical, and material development) when one
party, in order to secure greater wealth and power, does so at the expense of
the Other. Injustice thus becomes a perverted relationship that ignores coor-
dinating the proper good or end of individuals with that of their community.
Such perverted relationships insist that individuals should pursue their own
self-interest, for only then will they be capable of contributing to the overall
common good.[5] Such thinking asserts that everyone has a moral obligation
to follow self-interest so as to establish justice. Still, such an approach to
relationships is fundamentally incongruent with how justice is defined in the
biblical text, specifically the apostle Paul's admonition to put the needs of
others before one's own (Eph. 5:21; Phil. 2:4).

The danger of failing to incorporate the relational aspects of the term
"justice" is that it can lead to the rejection of God, even while one professes to belong to God and to live a pious life. Liberation theologian Gustavo Gutiérrez reminds us, "To know Yahweh, which in biblical language is
equivalent to saying to love Yahweh, is to establish just relationships among
persons, it is to recognize the rights of the poor. The God of biblical revelation is known through interhuman justice. When justice does not exist, God
is not known; God is absent" (1988, 110–11).

If justice is what Christians are called to do, it is done in obedience
to love. Love can never be understood or defined as an emotional experience (although such feelings could and usually do become a symptom of the
love praxis). Nor is justice a response born out of pity or a duty based on

---

5. For example, Adam Smith makes such an argument within the economic sphere in his book
The Wealth of Nations (1776).

paternalism. Brazilian theologians Leonardo Boff and Clodovis Boff remind us that "love is praxis, not theory" (1984, 4). "Love" is an action verb that describes something that is done by one person to another, an action taken regardless of how one feels. As the author of 1 John stated, "Let us not love in words, nor in mere talk, but in deed and in truth" (1 John 3:18). Love is the deed of justice, or, as the Medellín documents eloquently stated, "Love is the soul of justice. [The Christian who] works for social justice should always cultivate peace and love in one's heart" (CELAM 1968, 71). For the Christian, this deed is done in spite of the Other deserving to be loved. Paul reminds us, "But God loved us by commanding Christ to die for us, even while we were still sinners" (Rom. 5:8). It is this same type of love that binds the believer to the abundant life of the Other. Hence, to love in this fashion is to question, analyze, challenge, and dismantle the social structures responsible for preventing people from reaching the fullest potential of the abundant life promised by Christ.

Love becomes the unifying theme of the biblical text, specifically when expressed as a relational love for God and for one's neighbor. The false dichotomy between faith (love the Lord your God) and ethics (love your neighbor as yourself) is collapsed by Jesus, who demands manifestations of both by those who want to be his disciples. The doing of love becomes the new commandment that Christians are called to observe (John 13:34–35). The apostle Paul understood how paramount Christ's command was for all ethical actions committed by those who identify themselves as Jesus' followers. Hence he wrote to the Corinthians, "If I can speak in the tongues of humans, even of angels, but I do not have love, I become like a sounding brass or clanging cymbal. And if I have prophecies, and know all mysteries, and all knowledge, and if I have all faith so as to move mountains, but I do not have love, I am nothing" (1 Cor. 13:1–2).

The love that liberates can be known and experienced only from within relationships established upon acts of justice. Relationships with each other, and with God, become a source for moral guidance, capable of debunking the social structures erected and subsequently normalized by the dominant culture. By first learning to love humans through just relationships, the ability to love God also becomes possible. For as 1 John 4:20 reminds us, how can we love God, whom we cannot see, unless we first learn to love humans whom we do see? It is love toward the least among us, demonstrated through a relationship founded on justice, that manifests love for God. Only by loving the disenfranchised, by seeing Jesus among the poor and weak, can one learn to love Jesus, who claims to be the marginalized. To love the marginalized is to love Jesus, making fellowship with God possible as one enters into just fellowship with the disenfranchised.

In conclusion, the basis for all ethical acts can be reduced to one verse from Galatians: "The whole law is fulfilled in one word, 'Love your neighbor as yourself'" (Gal. 5:14). How do we love our neighbor? We can look to the biblical narrative, seeking concrete examples of love manifested as an act of God's work to create justice-based relationships. The very identity of those claiming to be Christian becomes defined by their relationship to their God and to their neighbor. The attempt to construct justice apart from a love relationship with others becomes a perversion designed to protect the privilege of the ones doing the construction. If Jesus came to "proclaim liberation to the captives . . . [and] set free the oppressed" (Luke 4:18), how can the bondage of many be preferred simply because it protects the power and privilege of the few? For this reason, an option for the poor characterizes a sincere commitment to justice, not because the poor are inherently more holy than the elite, but because they lack the elite's power and privilege. Consequently, we must now ask, why from the margins?

Why from the Margins?

If the dominant culture continues to be the sole interpreter of moral reality, its perspectives will continue to be the norm by which the rest of society is morally judged. The danger is that, to some extent, the dominant culture's ethics has historically been and, some would argue, continues to be a moral theorizing geared to protect the self-interest of those who are privileged. Consequently, which ethical perspectives are chosen or discarded becomes a decision that establishes power relationships. To choose one ethical precept over another justifies those who will eventually benefit from what is chosen. Once members of the dominant culture recognize the ethical precepts that support their lifestyle, claims of moral absolutism can be made. When members of the dominant culture legitimize the values that advance their power within the social structures as moral "truths," they fail to realize that at times the Christian ethics that they advocate in fact legitimize power, specifically, who has it, and how it is to be used. This form of Eurocentric moral imperialism forces serious consideration of the question asked by Argentinean theologian José Míguez Bonino: "In this world of power, of economic relations and structures, a world that maintains its autonomy and will not yield to voluntaristic moral ideals imposed from the outside, a world in which power and freedom seem to pull in opposite directions— what can Christians say and do?" (1983, 21). For those who do ethics from the margins, the issue of power becomes paramount in the development of any ethical discourse. Foremost for those who are marginalized is the ethical response to the use, misuse, and abuse of power rather than issues of character, values, virtues, or moral principles.

Any ethics arising from Christianity that seeks to remain faithful to the gospel message must remain rooted in the praxis of liberation. Christian ethics should first struggle with the question of power and how to crucify power and the privilege that comes with it so that justice and love instead can reign. Yet if those who are privileged by the present political, economic, and social structures refuse to acknowledge that being wealthy and white provides specific advantages over against the disenfranchised, how can they participate with integrity in any discourse that addresses injustices? For Christian ethics to be relevant, the faith community's struggles with oppressive living conditions must be engaged, always with the goal of dismantling the mechanism responsible for creating the inhumanity faced within marginalized spaces.

Jesus can never belong to the oppressors of this world, for he is one of the oppressed. The radicalness of the gospel message is that Jesus is in solidarity with the very least of humanity. The last shall be first; the center shall be the periphery. In Matthew 25:31–46 Christ returns to earth to judge between those destined for the reign of heaven and those who are not. The blessed and the cursed are separated according to what they did or did not do to the least among us. Specifically, did they or did they not feed the hungry, welcome the alien, clothe the naked, and visit the infirm or the incarcerated? Is the ethical lifestyle of individuals in solidarity with the marginalized demonstrated in liberative acts that led others toward an abundant life? So that there would be no confusion about God's preferential option, Jesus clearly states, "Truly I say to you, inasmuch as you did it to one of these, the least of my people, you did it to me" (Matt. 25:40).

The church of Jesus Christ is called to identify and stand in solidarity with the oppressed. The act of solidarity becomes the litmus test of biblical fidelity and the paradigm used to analyze and judge how social structures either contribute to or eradicate the exploitation of the marginalized. To be apart from the marginalized community of faith is to exile oneself from the possibility of hearing and discerning the gospel message of salvation—a salvation from the ideologies that mask power and privilege and from the social structures responsible for their maintenance.

Ideologies and social structures are shaped and formed by individuals who are in turn shaped and formed by these same ideologies and social structures. Like everyone else, Christians are born into a society where the dialectical relation between the person and the community informs their beliefs and their character—in short, their identity. For this reason, the sociohistorical context of any people profoundly contributes to the construction of their ethical system. When Christians, in accordance with their faith, attempt to develop ethical responses to the conflicts of human life, they participate in a dialogue between Christianity and what their community defines as Christian.[6]

Unfortunately, those who control the instruments of social power claim a monopoly on truth to the detriment of the disenfranchised. Black ethicist Katie Cannon succinctly captures the confusing of the dominant culture's self-interest with the interest of the public when she writes,

> The welfare of the state is now fully identified with the interests of the wealthy class. Everything else is subordinate to the prosperity of the wealthiest business people and to the welfare of the commercial class as a whole. . . . Their control of taxation, judiciary, and the armed forces gives them free access to all political processes. . . . The interest of the ruling class becomes de facto the interest of the public. (1995, 150)

The common good becomes restricted to those who benefit from the privilege obtained within these same social structures. Yet seldom do those in power admit that they are disproportionately rewarded by society. Concealing this truth makes any ethics emanating from that same dominant culture incomplete and heretical. Appeals to Christianity or reason will fail to affect the existing power structures, for the dominant culture uses both to defend their interest. Thus, the disenfranchised can bring liberative change only through empowerment.[7]

The immoral hoarding of power and privilege by the dominant culture makes it difficult for those benefiting by the status quo to be able to propose, with any integrity, liberative ethical precepts. For this reason, James Cone,

---

6. H. Richard Niebuhr was correct in observing that Christian ethics are fused and confused with what the civil social order determines is best for the common good. However, Darryl Trimiew calls Niebuhr to task for the underlining principle of his Christian social action. According to Niebuhr, "Responsibility affirms: 'God is acting in all actions upon you. So respond to all actions upon you as to respond to his action'" (1963, 126). Niebuhr continues by claiming, "The will of God is what God does in all that nature and men do. . . . Will of God is present for Jesus in every event from the death of sparrows, the shining of sun and descent of rain, through the exercise of authority by ecclesiastical and political powers that abuse their authority, through treachery and desertion by disciples" (1963, 164–65). Trimiew finds Niebuhr's admonition troubling for marginalized communities because it encourages believers to interpret all actions, regardless as to how repressive such actions may be to the disenfranchised, as God's providence. Oppression becomes conformity to the will of God, who is chastising the marginalized for their sins. But how can any "responsible self," Trimiew wonders, claim that the misery and the death faced by those marginalized at the expense of the privileged are God's providence (1993, xi, 8)?

7. Reinhold Niebuhr makes a similar point. He writes, "Dominant classes are always slowest to yield power because it is the source of privilege. As long as they hold it, they may dispense and share privilege, enjoying the moral pleasure of giving what does not belong to them and the practical advantage of withholding enough to preserve their eminence and superiority in society. . . . It must be taken for granted therefore that the injustices in society, which arise from class privileges, will not be abolished purely by moral persuasion. That is a conviction at which the proletarian class, which suffers most from social injustice, has finally arrived after centuries of disappointed hopes" (1960, 121, 141).

as well as many other theologians of color, concludes that there can exist no theology (and I would add ethics) based on the gospel message that does not arise from marginalized communities (1990, 5). Francisco Moreno Rejón, a Latin American ethicist, maintains that for ethics to be liberative, it must be formulated as follows:

1. *From the underside of history and the world*: from among the losers of history, from within the invaded cultures, from dependent countries without genuine autonomy and suffering the manifold limitations that all this implies.

2. *From the outskirts of society*, where the victims of all manner of oppression live, the ones who "don't count"—the ones whose faces reflect "the suffering features of Christ the Lord" (Puebla Final Document, no. 31).

3. *From among the masses of an oppressed, believing people*: it cannot be a matter of indifference to moral theology that the majority of Christians and humanity live in conditions of inhuman poverty. (1993, 215)

Only from the margins of power and privilege can a fuller and more comprehensive understanding of the prevailing social structures be ascertained, not because those on the margins are more astute, but because they know what it means to be a marginalized person attempting to survive within a social context designed to benefit the privileged few at their expense. Cone says it best when he writes, "Only those who do not know bondage existentially can speak of liberation 'objectively.' Only those who have not been in the 'valley of death' can sing the songs of Zion as if they are uninvolved" (1999, 22).

Is there any hope, then, for those who benefit from the present oppressive structures? Before answering this question, we must realize that those who benefit from the current sociopolitical and economic structures are themselves oppressed. Though not to the extent of intellectual, physical, and material deprivation felt in economically deprived areas, still, the oppressor lacks the full humanity offered by Christ. To oppress another is to oppress oneself. German philosopher G. W. F. Hegel's (1770–1831) concept of "lordship and bondage," as found in his *Phenomenology of Mind*, avers that the master (the oppressor) is also subjugated to the structures that the master creates to enslave the laborer (1967, 238–40). Because oppressive structures also prevent the master from obtaining an abundant life (specifically in the spiritual sense), those supposedly privileged by said structures are also in need of the gospel message of salvation and liberation.

Participation in ethical praxis designed to establish justice bestows dignity on the marginalized "nonpersons" by accentuating their worth as receptacles of the *imago Dei*, the very image of God, but it also restores the humanity of the privileged who falsely construct their identity through the negation of the Other. Using the work of psychoanalyst Jacques Lacan, we can conclude that those from the dominant culture look into the mirror and recognize themselves as superior through the distancing process of negative self-definition: "I am what I am not." The subject "I" is defined by contrasting it with the Objects residing on the margins. In the formation of the "I" out of the difference from the "them" there exist established power relations that give meaning to those differences (1977, 1–7). By projecting the "I" upon the marginalized, those of the dominant culture are able to define themselves as worthier of the benefits that society has to offer, because they either are more industrious (the Protestant work ethic) or are simply wiser.

The ethical task before both those who are oppressed and those who are privileged by the present institutionalized structures is not to reverse roles or to share the role of privileged at the expense of some other group, but rather to dismantle the very structures responsible for causing injustices along race, class, gender, and orientation lines, regardless of the attitudes bound to those structures. Only then can all within society, the marginalized as well as the privileged, achieve their full humanity and become able to live the abundant life offered by Christ.

How, then, can those who are privileged by the present social structures find their own liberation from those structures, a liberation that can lead to their salvation? By nailing and crucifying one's power and privilege to the cross so as to become nothing. According to the apostle Paul, "[Jesus Christ], who subsisting in the form of God thought it not robbery to be equal with God, but emptied himself, taking the form of a slave, in the likeness of humans, and being found in the fashion of a human, he humbled himself, becoming obedient until death, even the death of the cross" (Phil. 2:6–8). At the cross Jesus becomes nothing so as to redeem the world.

Ethics begins with our own surrender, with our self-negation. Those who benefit from the power and privilege of social structures can encounter the Absolute only through their own self-negation by crucifying their power and privilege. The Spanish mystic Juan de la Cruz (John of the Cross) (1542–1591) captures this concept of self-negation in his *Ascent of Mount Carmel*: "To reach satisfaction in all, desire its possession in nothing. To come to the knowledge of all, desire the knowledge of nothing. To come to possess all, desire the possession of nothing. To arrive at being all, desire to be nothing" (1987, 45).

Jesus was fond of saying, "For whoever desires to save their life shall lose it, but whoever loses their life for my sake and the sake of the gospel, that one shall save it" (Mark 8:35). True liberation takes place when the individual sees into her or his own nature and thus becomes Christlike. This praxis liberates those trapped by their race, class, gender, and heterosexual privilege, so that they, in solidarity with the marginalized, can bring about a just society based on the gospel definition of justice.

Still, with which marginalized group will those from the dominant culture stand in solidarity? Does each group create its own ethical reflection, or do they work together to overturn oppressive structures that affect all marginalized people? Darryl Trimiew, a black ethicist, has asked similar questions. He warns,

> The refusal of various liberation movements to concern themselves with the fates of others is the self-issued death warrant of these moral movements. This new universalism is daunting, as it will require the cooperation of strangers, even strangers who may be competing for the very same scarce resources. . . . Yet the tendency of liberationists to concern themselves with parochial interests cannot be underestimated. In this country alone, liberation ethicists show little interest in working together on projects of solidarity in order to overthrow common oppressions. (2004, 108–9)

Unlike biblical interpretation, theology, or other religious disciplines, ethics should not be conducted from only one marginalized perspective. Although black theology, Latino/a hermeneutics, Native American worldview, and/or Asian American Christian history provide unique and distinctive perspectives to different religious disciplines, ethics from only one marginalized perspective may prove counterproductive. Nuances between the different races and ethnicities exist and must be articulated in the overall conversation. Still, if the ultimate goal of ethics is to create a Christian response that brings change to existing oppressive structures, then no one group contains the critical mass required to bring about the desired just society. In fact, keeping marginalized groups separated ensures and protects the power and privilege of the dominant culture.

When a front-page article in the *New York Times* (January 22, 2003) proclaimed, "Hispanics Now Largest Minority, Census Shows," some Latino/as felt that they had finally come into their own, receiving long overdue recognition. Yet an unspoken underlying message was being communicated to other marginalized groups, specifically African Americans: "Hispanics are now the top dog, so you are going to have to compete against them for resources." But as Justo González perceptively observed, justice can never be served by having marginalized groups compete with each other for the meager resources doled out. For example, within churches, seminaries, church agencies, and church colleges, a small portion of the budget, a few positions, and a couple of courses are reserved for minorities, who are encouraged to fight among themselves for their small slice of the pie (1990b, 36). These Christian institutions can now point at programs run, in spite of such limited resources, to herald their political correctness, all the while continuing institutionalized oppressive structures that secure the dominant culture's privilege. In effect, marginalized groups often are prevented from working together to bring changes to these institutions.

This is not the first time the dominant culture has fostered division between marginalized groups to secure its power. In fact, this strategy is older than the nation. Thandeka, a professor of theology and culture, shows how Virginians in colonial America learned to better secure their power by forcing what could have been natural allies against their rule to compete against each other. The dominant culture succeeded in preventing alliances from developing between two oppressed groups, slaves (blacks) and ex–indentured servants (poor whites), by endowing the latter with white privilege. Prior to 1670, little difference existed between poor white indentured servants, considered "the scruff and scum of England," and black slaves, considered possessions.[8]

As more slaves flooded the colonies, an economic shift developed from a white indentured servitude–based economy, where the poor whites worked for a limited number of years, to a black slave–based economy, where Africans, although costing twice as much to acquire as poor white indentured servants, worked, along with their progeny, for life. Fear of future rebellions and a changing economic base led the Virginia elite to pass legislation to create social divisions between blacks and poor whites in order to secure its privileged place in the emerging nation (Thandeka 1999, 42–47). These laws effectively caused a division based on race between natural allies, a strategy that has continued to serve the privileged class well throughout this country's history.[9]

Then, as now, the dominant culture's privilege is maintained because different marginalized groups fight with limited resources for black justice, Latino/a justice, Native American justice, gender justice, Asian American justice, LGBT justice, and so on. Any intellectual resistance against injustice

---

8. Both the indentured servant and the slave lived an underfed and ill-clad existence in separate inadequate quarters, supervised by overseers who would whip them as a form of correction. Both groups would run away from the oppression, while others, specifically freemen (former indentured servants who were without property) formed alliances to rebel. The most intense challenge to the status quo came in the form of Bacon's Rebellion of 1676, which ended with Jamestown being burned to the ground. The last rebels to surrender were eighty slaves and twenty indentured servants.

9. In 1670 the Virginia Assembly forbade Africans and Native People from owning Christians (hereby understood as white), and non-Christians from Africa were to be slaves for life; in 1680 any white Christian was permitted to whip any black or slave who dared lift a hand in opposition to a Christian; in 1682 conversion to Christianity would not alter lifelong slavery for Africans; in 1705 white indentured servants could not be whipped naked, only blacks, who could also be dismembered for being unruly; also in 1705 all property (horses, cattle, hogs) was confiscated from slaves and sold by the church so that the proceeds could be distributed among poor whites (Morgan 1975, 329–33).

must include a concerted effort to eliminate the abuses of all oppressed groups. Although it is obvious that differences, particularly in cultural expressions, exist among numerous marginalized groups within the United States, a shared common history of disenfranchisement and the common problems of such a history create an opportunity to work together to dismantle oppressive structures that affect all who live on the periphery of power and privilege.

Ethics must be conducted from the overall margins of society more so than from any one particular marginalized perspective in order to avoid what Cornel West fears would be equating liberation with the white American middle-class man (1982, 112). Although equal access to the socioeconomic resources of our society is desirable, the marginalized must stand vigilant against the danger of simply surmounting the present existing structures that cause oppression. Ethics is, and must remain, the dismantling of social mechanisms that benefit one group at the expense of another, regardless of whether the group privileged is white, black, brown, yellow, red, or any combination thereof. Not until separate marginalized groups begin to accompany each other toward justice, understood here as the dismantling of oppressive structures, can the hold of the dominant culture upon resources be effectively challenged.

Chapter 2

The (De)Liberation of Ethics

My mother (may she rest in peace) was illiterate. She never had the opportunity to go to school and obtain an education. Growing up in Cuba, she spoke one language—Spanish. Upon arriving in the United States, she had difficulty communicating in English. But what my mother lacked in formal education she made up for with street smarts. Needing employment, she, like so many other refugees, did whatever had to be done to procure a job. Failure meant that her child would go hungry. "Do you know how to waitress tables?" she would be asked. "But of course. Back in the old country I was the head waitress in one of the most famous and busiest restaurants in the city," she would respond, even though she had never carried a tray of dishes in her life. "But can you read English well?" the potential employer would ask. "But of course," she would reply, "I have a high school diploma from the old country." In reality, she simply memorized some important phrases found on most menus. She did get the job, and I, her son, got fed.

Had I been an ethicist back then and approached my mother questioning her character, her virtues, or her values, she simply would have laughed at me for my naiveté. If she demonstrated the virtue of honesty and confessed that she had no work experience, no education, and could barely speak the language, she never would have been hired. Yet the moral reasoning that she employed enabled her to surmount societal structures fundamentally averse to her very existence. "Which is more ethical," I imagine her asking me, "doing what needs to be done to get the job, or letting the sins of others force us to live on the streets?" For her, living on the streets was not hyperbole or a hypothetical case study; it was a reality she faced. She sought to meet the basic needs of her family—in other words, to survive—while retaining her dignity. Because she was a woman and had been impoverished as a child (through sexism and classism), she had no opportunity to obtain a formal education. Because she was a Latina in the United States living within a social structure hostile to her presence, few employment opportunities were available (racism). She simply did not have the luxury to wait for the "art of the possible" to feed her family.

Although my mother never read the theological works of historically marginalized women, such as Delores Williams's *Sisters in the Wilderness*, I have no doubt that Williams's alternative ethical paradigm would have resonated with my Latina mother's experience. Just as heroes of the faith

Abraham and Sarah exploited and abused their slave girl Hagar, so too was my mother exploited and abused by self-professing Christians who capitalized on her inability to resist structures designed to benefit them at her expense due to her marginalized status as a woman, specifically a poor Latina woman. Although God did not liberate Hagar from her oppression (surely a concern for those of us engaged in liberative ethics), God did empower her to survive and endure the institutionalized forces responsible for her marginalization. In her book, Williams balanced resistance to oppression (by whatever means possible, even escaping to the desert) and survival with a liberation that may be far in the future, if at all. A spring found in the desert, where none had existed before, enabled Hagar to survive, at least momentarily.

Likewise, God enabled my mother, who lacked language skills and work experience, to "make a way out of no way" by waitressing. My mother never read Williams's book, but in the depth of her soul she understood its message, for she too was a sister in the wilderness. Although illiterate, she understood what black ethicist Katie Cannon claims is the essence of Howard Thurman's theological ethics: "the religion of Jesus is a 'technique of survival for the oppressed'" (Cannon 1988, 21). The hope of my mother was to rely on a God who always provides the means and resources to meet the harsh realities of life. She did not write a thesis on this subject, but in her often-stated aphorism, "Dios aprieta pero no ahoga" ("God squeezes but does not choke"), she communicated to me the message of a survival ethics that relies on a God who at times does not see.

How easy it is for the intellectual elite to dismiss my mother, along with the others who are disenfranchised, as unschooled and untrained in understanding the proper implementation of sound ethical principles. In their minds, her "opinions" are biased perceptions based on her circumstances, unfortunate though they may have been. Nevertheless, although she might have lacked the means to articulate her ethics properly to a learned audience, it is my mother, along with others who are marginalized, who is constantly in the back of my mind as I wrestle with the ethical paradigms constructed in the prestigious halls of academia. Their moral reasoning is not the product of neatly categorized concepts found in theological textbooks; rather, it is the product of the messiness of struggling to meet basic needs within a social structure that successfully facilitates the failure of the marginalized. What, then, does Eurocentric ethical theory, formulated from the secure space of privilege where employment is taken as a given, have to say to my mother? And more important, what can my illiterate mother teach those at the center of society about their own "biased opinions" of ethics as it relates to the everyday?

The Dilemma

In the name of Jesus Christ, crusades were launched to exterminate the so-called Muslim infidels; women seeking autonomy were burned as witches; indigenous people who refused to bow their knees to God and king were decimated; Africans were kidnapped, raped, and enslaved; and today the pauperization of two-thirds of the world's population is legitimized so that a small minority of the planet can consider itself blessed by God. Yet the ethical pronouncements articulated within traditional Christian institutions such as churches, seminaries, Christian colleges, and Bible institutes tend to reinforce the ideologies of the dominant culture—ideologies that have brought untold death and misery to humanity. If those in power wish to remain in power, then the moral precepts they create, the political states they fashion, and the religious orders they support must either explicitly or implicitly maintain, if not justify, the status quo.

Even when ethical pronouncements are made that are critical of the power or privilege amassed by few at the expense of many, little if any praxis is put forward to dismantle the mechanisms responsible for maintaining the status quo. Usually, cosmetic reforms are offered, with no serious consideration of the structural forms of injustices or social sin. As long as oppressive social structures persist, actions by individuals, no matter how well intended, are incapable of liberating those existing on the margins of society. Liberation can occur only through radical structural change. Reform simply avoids questioning the basics of the dominant culture's lifestyle, a lifestyle that many ethicists share.

White male (and increasingly female) ethicists with the economic privilege that comes with endowed chairs or full professorships at prestigious academic institutions do not theorize in a vacuum. Like the rest of the privileged dominant culture, they live in a certain location—an environment or context—that influences, affects, and shapes their ethical deliberations, deliberations that tend to justify their social location while consciously or unconsciously disenfranchising those on the margins of society. If we are to deal with issues of ethics, grounded in the reality of today's world, then we are forced to deal with the structural forces that form the *habitus* of those who benefit from the present social structures. If Christian ethics, constructed at the center of society, is rooted in a cultural discernment of the Bible as understood from a position of power and privilege, then to do ethics from the margins becomes an attempt to transform how ethics itself is done. Some ethicists from the periphery or margins of the dominant culture believe that their voices, usually silent or ignored, are capable of radically changing the theology, doctrine, practices, mission, and teachings of Christian institutions, starting at the grassroots level. To participate in an ethical discourse from the margins is to engage the proactive practices that precede the liberation and salvation of the least among us.

(De)Liberating Liberation

Since the start of the twentieth century, ethicists of the dominant culture gradually moved away from discussing which praxis should be employed when facing an ethical dilemma and instead devoted more of their energies to issues that dealt with the nature of ethics, specifically questions concerning virtues and the good. The proclivity of the dominant culture to deliberate ethics by pursuing the abstract good usually concludes with ethics being (de)liberated. Praxis leading toward a more just social order was a first casualty of abstract ethical thought. Even though such abstract deliberations may be sympathetic to the plight of the oppressed, they still fall short by failing to alleviate the root causes of disenfranchisement and dispossession.

To some degree, Eurocentric ethics has become a matter of explaining what is ethical. For those doing ethics from the margins, the issue is not to determine some abstract understanding of what is ethical, but rather, in the face of dehumanizing oppressive structures, to determine how people of faith adapt their actions to serve the least among us. Ethics becomes the process by which the marginalized enter a more human condition by overcoming oppressive or controlling societal mechanisms. For them, the starting point is not some ethical truth based on church doctrine or rational deliberation; instead, the starting point is analyzing the situation faced by the disenfranchised of our world, our nation, and our workplace and then reflecting with them theoretically, theologically, and hermeneutically in order to draw pastoral conclusions for actions to be taken.

Still, when ethical perspectives are voiced from the margins of society, all too often they are easily dismissed, especially if their spokespersons have not developed their methodology along the lines of acceptable Eurocentric thought, usually viewed as the only appropriate form to participate in academic discourse. For some Euroamerican ethicists, the praxis of liberation is reduced to a "theological symbol" designed to garner support from Christians for a particular social movement. But liberation is not just a symbol; it should mean a radical break with the status quo designed to maintain oppressive structures. Nonetheless, several ethicists of the dominant culture have responded by accusing those doing ethics from a liberative perspective of "moving from theology to politics without passing through ethics." Such arguments dismiss the formation of ethics from the margins as a very limited understanding of ethics.[1]

---

1. See, for example, Gustafson 1974; 1975. See also McCann and Strain 1985, 146–52.

While proficiency with the Eurocentric ethical canon is the admission ticket to academic discussions of ethics, those doing ethics at the margins of power and privilege concentrate on practical praxis—behavior and actions. It is not what is said that bears witness to the good news of the resurrection, but rather what is done to those still trapped in the forces of death. When abstract deliberations are applied to reality, the attempts to create a more just society, though admirable in their aspirations, most often fail to assist those who are marginalized. Such deliberations continue to reinforce the very social structures responsible for much of the oppression felt by the disenfranchised. In large part, this is due to the present social structures being viewed and accepted as necessary to maintain a well-ordered society.

In *The City of God*, Augustine explains that the ultimate good is eternal life, while the ultimate evil is eternal death. The ultimate moral response for those living in the earthly city is a life lived in faith, awaiting the heavenly city to come (*City of God* 19.4). Augustine goes so far as to suggest that if we remain loyal to the heavenly city through faith, all other aspects of living a moral life will ensue. Nonetheless, shaken by Rome's political vulnerability and eventual sack in 410 CE by the Goths, Augustine looked to the civil structure to provide peace and order.[2] Although salvation could be achieved only through the church, the state, though usually corrupt, was a necessary evil that maintained law and order. "Every use of temporal things is related to the enjoyment of earthly peace in the earthly city, while in the heavenly city it is related to the enjoyment of everlasting peace" (*City of God* 19.14). Acknowledging injustices and advocating their redress, Augustine insisted nevertheless that correcting injustice should never involve endangering the social order and peace. This social order was arranged according to a hierarchy whereby husbands ruled over wives (sexism) and masters ruled over slaves (classism) so that peace could be maintained (*City of God* 19.14).

Martin Luther (1483–1546) was greatly influenced by Augustinian thought. Luther maintained that the gospel is to be placed in heaven and the law on earth, erecting a barrier between the two. Humans are to obey the laws on earth, even when those laws dehumanize others. When peasants fought for the abolition of serfdom, Luther reminded them that earthly kingdoms can exist only if there is inequality, where some are free and others subservient. Repudiating the oppressed peasants' demand for their full humanity, Luther wrote to them:

---

2. Non-Christian writers such as Celsus and Porphyry blamed the deterioration of the Roman Empire on the rise of Christianity, which embraced such "weak" virtues as love. They claimed that Christianity was a seditious movement that undermined the traditional brute militarism that originally forged the empire. One of the reasons why Augustine wrote *The City of God* was to refute such accusations.

You assert that no one is to be the serf of anyone else, because Christ has made us all free. . . . Did not Abraham and other patriarchs and prophets have slaves? . . . A slave can be a Christian, and have Christian freedom, in the same way that a prisoner or a sick man is a Christian, and yet be free. [Your claim] would make all men equal, and turn the spiritual kingdom of Christ into a worldly, external kingdom; and that is impossible. A worldly kingdom cannot exist without an inequality of persons, some being free, some imprisoned, some lords, some subjects. (1967, 39)

Luther went so far as to advise those in authority to "smite, slay, and stab, secretly or openly" the rebelling peasants, who like "mad dogs," must be killed (1967, 50). According to Luther, political stability, even if maintained through the oppression of the marginalized, takes precedence over the humanity of the marginalized.

The influence of these patriarchs of Western Christianity continues to be felt today. Some ethicists of the dominant culture, such as James Gustafson, warn of the danger of "[upsetting] a necessary equilibrium in society" (1975, 119–20). Liberative praxis is fine, as long as society's equilibrium is maintained. Ethicist John Rawls insisted that the pursuit of justice be constrained within the limits of ensuring a well-ordered society, for only through such a society can a sense of justice be acquired (1971, 453–57). Yet according to Reinhold Niebuhr, the quest for justice, by its very nature, will disrupt the peace of society. Niebuhr wrote,

Since every society has an instinctive desire for harmony and avoidance of strife, this is a very potent instrument of maintaining the unjust status quo. . . . Those who would eliminate the injustice are therefore always placed at the moral disadvantage of imperiling its peace. The privileged groups will place them under that moral disadvantage even if the efforts toward justice are made in the most pacific terms. They will claim that it is dangerous to disturb a precarious equilibrium and will feign to fear anarchy as the consequence of the effort. (1960, 129)

Although those from the dominant culture strive to maintain society's equilibrium—an equilibrium that secures their place within the overall social order—those who remain marginalized hope to disrupt that same equilibrium. They see clearly that their needs are subordinated to those of the "well-ordered" society (understood here as a society that continues to privilege one group). They also recognize that those who benefit from the status quo will never voluntarily forfeit their privilege.

While we may all agree on the need for a well-ordered society, the question under dispute is who determines how and what form of a well-ordered society is to be maintained. For example, in his 1961 book concerning the sit-ins being conducted by African Americans protesting segregation at lunch counters, ethicist Paul Ramsey heaped praise upon these protestors and their calls for more equitable race legislation. Yet he found the sit-ins to be contradictory to proper Christian social action because they disrupted a well-ordered society. For him, the sit-ins promoted "lawlessness" and violated the rights of others, specifically the orderly stewardship of private property (1961, xiv). While desiring to end the racist segregation of his time, he first insisted on the preservation of the existing well-ordered society. According to Ramsey,

> But in the Christian view, simple and not so simple injustice alone has never been a sufficient justification for revolutionary change. There is always also the question of order to be considered, and a need for restraints placed upon all and upon the injustice infecting even our claims for greater justice. The Christian stands, then, for the rule of law against every utopian liberalism, however highminded. (1961, 48–49)

Raising the consciousness of the marginalized always endangers the secure space of those calling for "law and order" who envision their privilege as being threatened. All too often, in the name of "law and order," structures oppressive to marginalized groups are legitimized. For those on the underside of society's equilibrium, upsetting the dominant culture's serenity is the primary goal. As Martin Luther King Jr., reminds us, "We know through painful experience that freedom is never voluntarily given by the oppressor; it must be demanded by the oppressed" (1964, 80). It can be expected that such demands will create disharmony within "well-ordered" societies.

Nevertheless, there have been (and occasionally still are) great religious scholars of the dominant culture who tolerate a social order regardless of how unethical it may appear to be, where the marginalized are to respect and honor those who are at the center not just for the good of society, but because this is how God ordained the social structure. With suspicion, those on the margins approach scholars like John Calvin (1509–1564), who insisted that those who are marginalized, specifically the poor, should respect and honor those who are economically their superiors because God in God's wisdom bestowed the "elect" with special material gifts. In the political realm, Calvin called citizens to submit to governments regardless of how tyrannical their rulers may have been, because it is up to the Lord to avenge such despots, while it is up to the citizens to simply "obey and suffer" (*Institutes* 4.20.31). Furthermore, Calvin stated that the "poor must yield to the rich; the common folk, to the nobles; the servants, to their masters; the unlearned, to the educated" (*Institutes* 3.7.1–5). Clearly, Calvin ignored the connection between the amassing of power and privilege and the marginalization of the poor, the common folk, the servants, and the unlearned. Thus, for ethicist Sharon Welch, the danger of our present society is the assumption that those in the center of society, understood to be God's elect, possess "the prerequisites for moral judgment and that other groups [the poor, the common folk, the servants, and the unlearned] are devoid of those same prerequisites" (1990, 126).

The Social Power of Ethics

Since the rise of modernity, specifically manifested in the eighteenth century as the age of the Enlightenment, ethicists have moved away from religious ethical systems founded on revelation, biblical hermeneutics, or church tradition. For the "modern" mind, there existed unambiguous universal truths about the very nature of reality, and reliable methodologies for arriving at the answers to all the dilemmas that humanity faces. All that was required was their discovery. The process of discovering these truths made God, to some extent, irrelevant. God was, in effect, replaced with a scientific process of secularization that found the answers to ethical dilemmas in humanistic or naturalistic moral deliberations. The Enlightenment asserted that the individual was capable, via his or her own reasoning ability, of discovering absolute and universal moral laws. An instinctive moral compass found within human nature could guide the individual in determining to do good and in refraining from doing evil.[3] Other ethicists, employing a utilitarian approach, defined what is ethical by the principle that all actions can be numerically scaled; hence, the action whose net benefits are greatest is the correct moral choice.[4] Yet more often than not, such appeals to self-evident propositions become a justification for those in power to protect their self-interest.

As previously mentioned, ethical precepts do not develop in a social or cultural vacuum. Yet, ironically, the social context for the construction of ethics usually is ignored. What is termed moral is more often a product of the power residing within a person's social location than of a person's understanding of natural law or, for that matter, an "objective" reading of the Scriptures, or of enlightened moral reasoning or logic. Nonetheless, the reasoning or logic of the center is often inappropriate for the margins. As Malcolm X (1925–1965) reminds us,

---

3. Ethicists such as John Rawls suggest that an intuitive sense of justice will guide humans in making correct moral decisions (1971, 114–15).

4. Most ethicists today, including utilitarians, would agree that if a society is unjust to a minority portion of its population, even though greater utilitarian benefits are enjoyed by the majority of the population, then that society as a whole is acting unjustly.

What is logical to the oppressor isn't logical to the oppressed. And what is reason to the oppressor isn't reason to the oppressed. The black people [and I would add all who are from the margins] in this country are beginning to realize that what sounds reasonable to those who exploit us doesn't sound reasonable to us. There just has to be a new system of reason and logic devised by us who are at the bottom. (1968, 133)

The reality from the margins of society is that those with power impose their constructs of morality upon the rest of the culture. Even though the privileged are quite adept at convincing themselves that their acts are altruistic, those who are disenfranchised are seldom convinced of this. Virtues, no matter how desirable, can be imposed to ensure the subservience of the marginalized.[5]

Ethics from the margins insists that racism, sexism, heterosexism, and classism are the end products of the exercise of power. The power of the dominant culture that creates Christian ethics can no longer be explained simply as a group of institutions that ensures obedience, or as a mode of subjugation, or as a form of domination exerted by one group over another. Rather, power is used to normalize what the dominant culture determines to be ethical; it does so by harnessing the existing forces to which it has access (Foucault 1988, 18). For this reason, power's hold upon people is based on its ability to produce. Power creates pleasure, constructs knowledge, and generates discourse. In this sense, power can be understood as something positive, producing reality and creating the subject's opinion of what is "truth" (Foucault 1984, 60–61). Whether consciously or unconsciously, Christians of the dominant culture, while truly wishing to remain faithful to their religious convictions, at times construct ethical perspectives to preserve their power, defining their self-serving ethical response as Christian. In their minds, their perspectives are viewed as "truth," answering the question concerning what Jesus himself would do.

These perspectives are then taught as truth to those who suffer at times from how these very same ethical perspectives are employed within society. The illegitimate power to subjugate the race, gender, orientation, or class of

---

5. Martin Luther King Jr. made a similar point when discussing the difference between just and unjust laws. In his letter from a Birmingham jail he wrote,

> Sometimes a law is just on its face and unjust in its application. For instance, I have been arrested on a charge of parading without a permit. Now, there is nothing wrong in having an ordinance which requires a permit for a parade. But such an ordinance becomes unjust when it is used to maintain segregation and to deny citizens the First-Amendment privilege of peaceful assembly. (1964, 83)

This is not to say that the law that King refers to, or certain virtues, are unimportant; it is to insist that whatever becomes law, or is defined as virtue, is more often a product of power relationships than we are willing to admit.

others is legitimized and normalized by the dominant culture. French philosopher Michel Foucault, through his analogy of an insane asylum, explains how this process of normalization takes place. Individuals committed were freed from their chains if they promised to restore themselves; in other words, if they imposed upon themselves their own "domestication." Those deemed mentally insane were treated as children who needed to learn how to respect the authority of their superiors. The asylum became a religious domain without religion, where the mad were taught ethical uniformity. Although free, their chains could always be reinstated (1965, 246–59).[6]

Like the patients in the asylum, the marginalized suffer from their own "madness"—their refusal to conform to the ethical standards of the "civilized" dominant culture. In the minds of those with power and privilege, marginalization is self-imposed, a refusal on the part of the disenfranchised to assimilate to what is perceived as the common good. When they behave, when they submit to the law and order of the dominant culture, they are "free." Those who reject the dominant view are eyed with suspicion. Their rejection of the superiority of the dominant culture, and the morality that it advocates, proves that they have not yet been cured of their "madness."

The danger of doing ethical reflection from the center of power and privilege is that any moral truth may be distorted or perverted when the perspectives of the marginalized are ignored. Yet for these ignored voices to question the validity of how the dominant culture arrives at ethical precepts becomes an act of madness, or even sacrilege. As in Foucault's asylums, those who benefit from the present power structures get to legitimize their version of ethical truth for all, including the disenfranchised. The dominant culture operates within a framework constructed from the social location of privilege, and the resulting system of ethics functions to justify the norm. Even when such ethical deliberations assail poverty, the economic structures responsible for causing poverty, which are also responsible for assuring the privilege of the dominant culture, are seldom analyzed.

This process of normalizing the ethical views of the dominant culture can best be understood as a product of its *habitus*, a product of the social location of its members. *Habitus* can be defined as a system of internalized dispositions that mediates between social structures and practical activities, shaped by the former and regulating the latter (Brubaker 1985, 758). Those born into positions of privilege possess a socially constructed lifestyle that

---

6. One cure employed for madness was tea parties. Because civilized people knew how to act during tea parties, patients, in order to prove that they were no longer mad, had to behave with the proper decorum befitting civilized persons, learning, in effect, to become an anonymous "normal" person. Because the patients were always observed, they learned how to watch themselves. In short, they learned how to police their own actions. With time, the patient internalized the behavior that was acceptable through self-discipline (Foucault 1965, 246–59).

facilitates their ability to justify their privilege. This lifestyle, in a sense, unconsciously teaches them how to understand their economic and social success. Their identity is indebted to the community from which they come, which is primarily responsible for their "personal" opinions. Their position within society, justified through customs, language, attitudes, dispositions, beliefs, traditions, values, and so on, existed prior to their birth and will continue to shape future generations after they are dead. As the "memory of the body," they bear the culture within them, assimilating from childhood the community's knowledge and experiences. From the moment of birth, these constructs were imposed on them, molding their childhood and guiding them through adulthood by decoding and adjusting to new situations. When their position within the privileged class is threatened, they protect their self-interest without realizing that they are doing so. To protect their self-interest, they merely have to assert what they were born into in order to become what they are, an effort done with the lack of self-consciousness that marks their so-called nature (Bourdieu 1977, 72–73, 78–87).

One's *habitus* so imprisons the mind that it becomes difficult to move beyond a particular social location without making a major shift in how reality is conceived and understood. Consequently, few members of the dominant culture question the construction of their conscience. Accordingly, those who approach ethics from positions of power and privilege must remain vigilant during their moral deliberations, lest they confuse what is ethical with what is their *habitus*. Their only hope is to move beyond their social location by forming relationships of solidarity with the marginalized. According to José Míguez Bonino, a Latin American theologian, ethical reflection done from the margins becomes a resource by which the overall society can be transformed, so that human possibility can be maximized at a minimum human cost (1983, 107).

We are left questioning the role that social factors play in influencing how ethical reflection is constructed and conducted. Those of the dominant culture often find it difficult to accept the thought that much of their moral understanding may in fact be a product of their privileged position rather than a gift handed down to them by a Supreme Being. The morality that protects the status quo often is supported through religious symbols and taboos to ensure that ethical precepts are regulated and enforced. By defining Christian ethics as commands proceeding from the Divine or as interpretations of Scripture, rather than as formulations from the center of privilege, any arguments that question privilege can be dismissed as a distortion of morality.

It is not that the marginalized lack the academic rigor to do ethical reflection or that they simply bypass ethical reflection altogether; rather, their approach to their oppressive situation produces a different way of doing ethics. The schism existing between privileged academic centers and the ghettos or barrios that surround them is so wide that many Christian "principles" become abstract concepts that lack any application to the lives of the marginalized.

Incarnation: Experiencing in the Flesh

All that is known is filtered through the lens of our social location. What is perceived to be morally true is determined by experience. The danger of creating an ethical structure based on experience is that the experiences of those who write books, preach at influential churches, or teach at prestigious academic centers usually become the norm for making ethical determinations. By contrast, this book argues for an ethics rooted in the experiences of the marginalized, an experience that was, and continues to be, shared by God.

"In the beginning was the Word, and the Word was with God, and the Word was God. . . . And the Word took on flesh and resided among us" (John 1:1, 14). God does not stand aloof from human experiences but rather enfleshes Godself in the concrete events of human history. Not only do we learn from the gospel how to be Christlike, but also God, through the Christ event, "learns" how to be humanlike. God understands the plight of today's crucified people, who hang on crosses dedicated to the idols of race, class, gender, and heterosexual superiority. The crucifixion of Christ is God's solidarity with the countless multitudes who continue to be crucified today. Jesus' death on the cross should never be reduced to a sacrifice called for to pacify some angry God offended by human sin. Christian theology ignored for centuries the fact that Jesus, as fully human, was put to death, like so many today, by the civil and religious leaders who saw him as a threat to their power. There is nothing redemptive in the suffering of the just. The importance of the cross for the marginalized is that they have a God who understands their trials and tribulations because God in the flesh also suffered trials and tribulations. The good news is not so much that Jesus was crucified, but that Jesus rose from the dead, not to demonstrate God's power, but to assure the marginalized that crucifixion is not how the story ends.

This God who became human continues to enflesh Godself in the everyday lives and experiences of today's crucified people. An important element in ethical reflection is what Hispanic theologians have called *lo cotidiano*, Spanish for "the everyday."[7] Ethics from the margins is contextual, where the everyday experience of the disenfranchised becomes the subject and source

---

7. Latina theologian María Pilar Aquino, among others, avers the importance of the "everyday" (*lo cotidiano*) in the doing of theology. For Aquino, the salvific experience of God in the here and now is experienced by the marginalized in their "daily struggles for humanization, for a better quality of life and for greater social justice" (1999, 39). As such, I insist that *lo cotidiano* is the necessary source of all liberative ethical reflection.

of ethical reflection. To do ethics from the margins is to reflect on autobiographical elements in order to avoid creating a lifeless ethical understanding.

"Story theology," a major theme within Asian American theological reflection, attempts to challenge the West's hyperemphasis on grounding all theological thought on the rational. Similarly, the "third eye," according to Japanese Zen master Daisetz Suzuki, is an Asian attempt to become open to that which is unheeded due to one's own ignorance. To perceive reality with a "third eye" allows Christianity to turn to the abundant indigenous stories, legends, and folklore of the people, as well as the experiences of the marginalized. An autobiographically based ethic resonates among the disenfranchised, who find that the inclusion of their stories provides a needed "heart" to the Western emphasis on the rational (Yang 2004, 178).

Additionally, the methodological inclusion of one's story into an ethical dilemma powerfully connects reality with theory. Such an inclusion challenges the predominant assumption that all ethical deliberations must occur apart from and independent of the interpreter's social location or identity. Rather than verifying what is truth as explicated by those who are traditionally viewed as authorities (such as clergy or ethicists), or through sacred texts as historically interpreted by experts, the source of ethical deliberation begins with *lo cotidiano*, as experienced and understood by those existing on the margins. The perspective of those who are considered nonpersons because of their race, class, orientation, or gender becomes the starting point for any Christian ethical action. And this shatters the grip of those at the top of theological hierarchies on being the sole legitimate interpreters or arbiters of what is ethical.

Christian Ethics from the Center

We live in a world where social, political, and economic offenses are common. Only a privileged few can use institutionalized racism, classism, sexism, and heterosexism to insulate themselves from the ravages of maltreatment. If doing ethics from the margins provides liberation for both the oppressed and the oppressor, then to insist on doing ethics only from the center of power and privilege frustrates the hopes not only of the disenfranchised, but also of the privileged. Before we can begin to participate in a liberative ethics, we must explore how the ethics of the dominant culture can mask the oppression of those who are disenfranchised. How is ethics constructed so as to encourage the dominant culture to remain complicit with institutionalized racism, classism, sexism, and heterosexism?

A Wretch Like Me

Are humans innately good or innately evil? If human nature is good, is society then responsible for human corruption? If so, ethics is reduced to education in order to reveal the error that is responsible for present injustices, given the assumption that good people will not knowingly participate in evil actions.[8] If, however, human nature is evil, then legal sanctions are needed to force humans to live morally.[9] Regardless of how one answers questions concerning the inherent nature of humans, the fact remains that depravity does exist. The depravity found in humans often is caused by the sins of those who have power over other humans. Because all are created in the image of God, all are good and all have the potential to walk in justice, even those who are non-Christians. We are not evil vassals devoid of all good, as some would have us believe.[10]

When aligned with colonial and imperialist thinking, the sin that exists among humans can contribute to relegating people of color to the level of nonpersons. As nonpersons, their land can be stolen, their bodies raped, their labor exploited, and their humanity disregarded. Some from the dominant culture repent and attempt to live a more humble life. For them, there is an emphasis upon repentance for their depraved nature or acknowledgment, as the slave captain who penned the words to "Amazing Grace" wrote in self-deprecation, that grace exists for such "a wretch like me." For those who live a life of privilege due to advantages paid for by those who were made to believe in their nonpersonhood, such emotions of self-derogation may prove to be a healthy step toward a spiritual path of healing. The danger occurs when those with power impose upon the wretched of the earth the require-ment that they be "saved" in similar fashion.

One size does not fit all. It was, and often continues to be, assumed that the salvation needed by those on the margins is the same yearned for by those from the dominant culture. An assumption usually is made that the sins of the dominant culture (as Reinhold Niebuhr did with the sin of pride) are also the sins of those on the margins of power. While those who formulated the theological concepts and ethical precepts, usually from locations of power and privilege, may have wrestled with the prideful sin of self-centeredness, the marginalized have instead suffered from a lack of self-identity. It is the images and thoughts of the dominant culture that usually are at the center. Thus,

---

8. Eighteenth-century French philosopher Jean-Jacques Rousseau, according to his *Second Dis-course*, would then be correct in viewing the original human as living in a state of innocent harmony with nature. Even though today humans are wicked, originally they were naturally good in the state of nature. They were, in effect, a type of noble savage.

9. Thomas Hobbes, the seventeenth-century English philosopher who formulated the doctrine of psychological egoism, would then be correct in his assertion that the state of nature is one "where every man is enemy to every man," so that human life in this state of nature is one that is "solitary, poor, nasty, brutish, and short" (1909, 96–97).

10. Protestant theologian Karl Barth (1886–1968) understood that the depravity of humanity for-bade any goodness from residing within individuals, making it impossible for them to be ethical—that is, determining the good. Only Christ can do this, and only by faith can the Christian rely on God's grace and participate in an authentic ethical dimension. Apart from grace, humans lack the capacity to distinguish good from evil. For those lacking Christ in their lives, anything proposed as the good is simply a distortion (1928, 136–82).

the marginalized often interpret reality through the eyes of their oppressors rather than through their own, disenfranchised eyes. This is why many from the centers of society preach self-denial, submission, and unworthiness to the marginalized, when the disenfranchised should instead be hearing about pride in self, liberation, human dignity, and worth.

There is no need to preach humility to those who are already humble. Humbled by the sins of the dominant culture, they do not need to be exhorted to become still more lowly—quite the contrary. Salvation for the marginalized is the transformation from nonperson to personhood. The liberating message of the gospel that they need to hear is that they are worthy, precious, and due dignity because they are created in the very image of God. Jesus understood that part of his salvific message was to humble the proud and lift up the lowly. As Mary the mother of Jesus says in the Magnificat, "[God] pulled down the powerful from their thrones, and exalted the humble ones. God filled the hungry with good things, and the rich God sent away empty" (Luke 1:52–53). It is the privileged who need to come to terms with their spiritual wretchedness; it is the wretched who need to come to terms with their infinite worth.

Grace, Not Works

Martin Luther, like Augustine before him, believed that good works would flow from any individual who has been freed from the bondage of sin through the justifying love of God. For Augustine, grace did not free the moral agent from his or her obligations to perform good works; in fact, conversion generated a new creature in Christ now capable of doing good because his or her life was dominated by God's grace. Still, experiencing the forgiveness of Christ took precedence over any need to know the good. And although Luther fought against a misinterpretation of his doctrine of justification by faith that advocated a release from ethical obligations, nonetheless the Reformation formula *sola fide* ("by faith alone") undermined the need to consider ethics crucial to Christian identity. Contrary to what Augustine or Luther may have said or meant about the duty of Christians to do good works, the way some Christians from the dominant culture have put *sola fide* into practice has proven detrimental to the marginalized. It is wrong to reduce Christianity to an issue of grace where one can profess Christ as Lord without seriously implementing Christ's demands that justice affect and impact the believer's life.

Sola fide as practiced by those who are privileged is harmful for those existing on the margins of privilege. Used in this manner, the doctrine of justification, which encompasses the forgiveness of sin, freedom from guilt, and reconciliation with God, fosters among the powerful and privileged a sense of impunity. It gives the impression that those who benefit from the present power structures can receive pardon for their sins from Christ without any need to convert from the practices and actions that contribute to oppressive social structures. Relationships are thus limited to the vertical, without seriously considering the neighbor who continues to be marginalized.

At the other extreme is the danger, pointed out by Jesus Christ, of solely relying on works for justification. During Jesus' time the Pharisees created a set of rules that excused them from fulfilling their obligations to their faith. Although maintaining strict adherence to tithing, they ignored issues of justice. Jesus condemned them by stating, "Woe to you scribes and Pharisees, hypocrites! Because you tithe of the mint, the dill, and the cumin, yet you have ignored the weightier matters of the law, like justice, mercy, and faith" (Matt. 23:23). On another occasion Jesus condemned the hypocrisies of the religious scholars who "dedicated" their property to God so as to avoid the just praxis of caring for their aging parents (Mark 7:11–13). Rather than being legalistic, as were the Pharisees and religious teachers of the time of Jesus, some of today's ethicists and theologians from the dominant culture have gone to the other extreme. Unquestioning obedience to the law undermines the establishment of a justice-based relationship with the marginalized, but so too does an unquestioning acceptance of grace contribute effectively to ignoring the needs and concerns of the disenfranchised.

Heaven-Bound

Ethical praxis that can lead to a more just society is at times ignored because of an overemphasis on the hereafter rather than the here and now. If belief in Christ is all that is required for a blessed hereafter, those with the power to form theological discourse can present heaven to the wretched of the earth as a future place where they will be rewarded for their patient suffering. The present state of misery endured by the disenfranchised is justified as a consequence of some original sin. Their doleful existence on earth will be compensated by heavenly mansions and ruby-crusted crowns of gold. Such escapist illusions only help to pacify the disenfranchised by encouraging them to shrug off their misery as God's will. But, as Charles Kammer reminds us, concepts such as the reign of God are not spiritual escape hatches; they are evidence of the eruption of God's activity into history to transform personal, social, and political relationships (1988, 44).

If the hereafter becomes a narcotic (similar to Karl Marx's reference to opium), it negates what is of value in the here and now. Christian ethics, as formulated within the margins of society, rejects the notion that God somehow wills God's children to live under oppressive structures so that eventually they can live in everlasting riches. In fact, such a view of the afterlife is satanic. "The reign of God is at hand," Jesus was fond of saying. God's reign is not in some far-off place disconnected from the trials and tribulations here on earth. No. God's reign is a present-day social, political, public, and personal reality evident among God's people. While not negating some form of final reward in the hereafter, the gospel message is primarily for the here and now. Salvation, understood as liberation in its fullness, has as much to do with the now as with a final resting place. And even though praxis (or what Luther called "works") is insufficient for obtaining salvation, which remains a gift of God's grace, praxis still becomes an act of obedience, an outward expression of an inward conversion.

Juan Luis Segundo, a Latin American liberation theologian, insists that this genuine conversion makes true reconciliation with God and with one another possible. Conversion requires a confession of the causes of estrangement (specifically those dealing with power and privilege) and an attempt to take action to eradicate these causes. If not, premature reconciliation will develop, masking unresolved structures of oppression. Although "conversion" is gospel language, Segundo uses it to indicate a change of attitude (1993, 37, 51). If conversion does not establish justice-based relationships with God and with fellow human beings, then salvation has not taken place. Any conversion devoid of actions for human liberation from structures of oppression is a façade that only normalizes present oppressions along gender, orientation, race, and class lines and masks forms of repression. Any salvation based on Jesus Christ should free the believer from the bondage, whether socially, culturally, or legally imposed, that reduces humans to disposable objects. In short, conversion, as a spiritual dimension, heals. If not, old enmities and unresolved hatreds from present systems continue in any supposedly reconciled future.

If conversion is understood as a break with and turning away from sin (sin caused by individual actions and sin caused by social institutions), then salvation can occur only through the raising of consciousness to a level that can recognize the personal and communal sins preventing the start of a new life in Jesus. Conversion is a witness, a testimony to an unsaved world, whose rejection of God, through the worship of the idol of self-interest, is manifested in oppressive relations according to orientation, race, class, and gender. Conversion to Christ does not correspond to some abstract concept of Jesus sitting on a throne in heaven, nor is it an ethereal emotional experience; rather, conversion to Christ serves the oppressed flesh-and-blood neighbor, who, as "the least of my people," is in reality Jesus in the here and now (Matt. 25:40). Salvation through Christ is at its essence a relationship with God and with one another, a justice-based relationship whose very nature transforms all aspects of humanity so that the abundant life can be lived by all to its fullest.

Unfortunately, in too many cases the pursuit of salvation has been privatized. Peruvian theologian Gustavo Gutiérrez reminds us,

> Faith cannot be lived on the private plane of the "interior life." Faith is the very negation of retreat into oneself, of folding back upon oneself. Faith comes alive in the dynamism of the good news that reveals us as children of the Father and sisters and brothers of one another, and creates a community, a church, the visible sign to others of liberation in Christ. (1984, 67)

Too often personal salvation has become spiritual escapism rather than a justice-based transformation. Some conservative evangelicals are consumed with a passion to witness for life after death. Although the message of life after death is important, the real message that the vast majority of those living in oppression hunger for is life *prior to* death. Such a message must be communicated through action rather than through words alone. Christian evangelism is thus understood as any action that leads toward the transformation of the individual, as well as the community, to the basic principles of justice lived and taught by Jesus Christ. The conversion resulting from such an evangelical venture leads not toward a "once saved, always saved" understanding, but rather toward a lifelong process of working out the liberation made possible by Christ, or, as the apostle Paul would suggest, "[the working out of] your salvation in fear and trembling" (Phil. 2:12).

Sometimes attempts are made to Christianize the social order in order to remedy social ills, believing that society's "peccadilloes" are caused by the decisions made by "non-Christians" within positions of power. Yet "saving" the powerful individual so that a "Christian" will make decisions in the public arena will not necessarily reform the social structure. As previously mentioned, most moral precepts reflect the cultural and philosophical milieu of a people, not of an individual. While the conversion of decision-makers within the social structures may be propitious, it often has little or no impact on how these social structures operate. Concentrating solely on personal piety, morality, or virtues without engaging the actual structures responsible for producing injustices will only lead to discouraging results. A change of heart of individuals usually is insufficient to produce a more just social order. The social structures themselves require transformation and conversion. Without such transformation, reform may occur, but more often than not, the marginalized will still find themselves disenfranchised due to race, orientation, class, and/or gender.

Salvation, in its truest sense, becomes liberation from sin—sins committed by the individual and, just as important, those committed through social institutions. Reducing salvation to personal choice, disconnected from the community, is foreign to the biblical text. Take the example of Moses in the Hebrew Bible or Paul in the New Testament. Both were willing to be cut off from God and face damnation for the sake of the community's liberation. Moses pleaded with God to blot him from the book of life if it would save God's people (Exod. 32:32), while Paul was willing to be condemned and cut off from Christ if it would help his Jewish compatriots find salvation (Rom. 9:3). Both Moses and Paul refused to exchange their quest to transform society as an expression of their love for their neighbor for some privatized faith that assured them of individual immortality. They serve as models of a self-sacrificing faith that places the needs of the community before personal reward. They understood the depths of the words of Jesus when he said, "A person can have no greater love than to lay down one's life for one's friends" (John 15:13).

While belief in Christ is important, if not crucial, it remains insufficient. Jesus states, "If then you offer your gift on the altar, and there remember that your companion has something against you, leave your gift there before the altar and go. First be reconciled to your companion, and then come offer your gift" (Matt. 5:23–24). The implication is that God is more concerned with loving and reconciling with those who have a grievance than with the would-be worshiper's personal relationship with God or his or her attempt to gain moral perfection through obedience to religious law, tradition, or custom.

Although conversion is a gift from God, the individual still must choose to accept such a gift. How? Conversion for those of the dominant culture must move beyond simple belief. Conversion moves toward a consciousness-raising experience that is linked to a specific praxis, a praxis that breaks with personal and social sin and leads the new believer to turn away from the old life of privilege and begin a new life in Christ manifested as solidarity with the same people whom Jesus sought to identify himself with, the outcasts. Consciousness-raising becomes the process by which persons become cognizant of their existential being, leading toward a self-reflective, critical awareness of how a person benefits or is oppressed by the prevailing social structures. For both the privileged and disenfranchised, conversion as a consciousness-raising praxis leads to the transformation of the person and society so that the convert can encounter the "neighbor" in the fullness of the other's humanity. Regardless of the neighbor's belief or confession in Christ, that neighbor still has worth before God.

Still, salvation can never be equated with a social system or agenda created by humans (such as socialism, capitalism, neoliberalism); liberation is a theological enterprise with a social ethical agenda of establishing justice so that all human beings can live in what Martin Luther King Jr. called "the beloved community," where justice rolls down like living water. In order for

Christian ethics to take hold, radical concrete changes are required in the public arena (as well as in the life of the believer) so as to bring salvation, understood as liberation, both to the marginalized and to those who benefit from their disenfranchisement. Such radical actions move the church from teaching ethics as a collection of moral precepts for private living to teaching ethics as political and social actions that reflect one's Christian testimony. The basic criterion for doing ethics from the margins becomes the salvation and liberation of all, both the privileged and the disenfranchised, who are oppressed by political, social, and cultural structures that overtly or covertly foster racism, classism, sexism, and heterosexism. This evangelistic action for liberation is the ultimate love praxis.

A Personal Relationship

The pervasiveness of individualism, specifically the rugged individualism celebrated in the United States, relegates moral decisions to the private sphere, in a sense essentially relegating views on morality to the individual. This tends to weaken social bonds and hamper the development of a communal apparatus authorized to foster and implement ethical actions that can lead to a social order grounded on relationships. When morality is privatized, individual members of the dominant culture can shop for a set of values or virtues, like any other consumer good, which is appropriate to the particular individual at a given place and time. This is not to minimize the importance of the individual, but because the self should never be considered apart from the communal, ethics must be fashioned to acknowledge the relationships established by the interrelatedness of the individual and the community of faith, where actions committed by one profoundly affect the other.

Psychologist Carol Gilligan, well known for her work in gender studies, has proposed that psychology has ignored and misunderstood women's moral commitments because the discipline has historically focused on observing the lives of men. She maintains that men usually approach morality from an individualistic perspective that deliberates on issues of rights in a way that is interconnected with the celebration of personal autonomy. On the other hand, she observes, women approach moral dilemmas from the context of relationships grounded in the ability to care (1982, 17). I contend that the approach to moral reasoning of women, as described by Gilligan, is more similar to how ethics is conducted by both men and women in disenfranchised communities.

Lacking privilege and power, members of marginalized communities find themselves clinging to each other in order to survive oppressive structures. They are supported by these relationships of caring, which become crucial in understanding ethics from the margins. Ethical praxis from the margins arises from the relational links of communal morality and the injustices caused by social structures, whether manifested as traditions, customs, or laws. To divorce ethics from critical social analysis is to reduce ethics to an individualistic morality that often is of little use to those struggling to survive. Those doing ethics on the margins of society realize that unequal alignments of power within social structures (male over female, heterosexual over non-heterosexual, white over nonwhite, wealthy over poor) usually are the root causes of injustice and are the antithesis of the gospel message.

To counter this trend, Christian ethics as done from the margins becomes a *koinonia* ethics, a political calling for radical structural changes in how society is ordered. *Koinonia*, the New Testament Greek term used to describe the faith community, connotes relationships and fellowship, where all things are held in common. Not only are material possessions held in common (Acts 2:44–45; 4:32), but also experiences. Paul writes, "If one member [of the *koinonia*] suffers, with it suffer all members; or if one member is glorified, with it all members rejoice" (1 Cor. 12:26). *Koinonia* occurs when the faith community gathers to stand in solidarity, sharing the trials and joys of the human condition. Any ethic labeled as Christian must reflect the response of *koinonia* to the dilemmas that prevent Christians from fulfilling Christ's mission that all experience "life abundantly."

Because ethics from the margins emphasizes praxis, it interacts with the political and social structures that normalize injustices. Consequently, ethics that is done from the margins influences the political realm. One cannot read the story of liberation found in Exodus, the call for justice found in Amos, the stories of Jesus, or the account of Paul's dealing with the imperial powers of Rome without coming to the conclusion that these are not simply religious documents, but also calls to political action. Although Christian ethics from the margins is not a political ethics, it does influence change in the political sphere when it remains faithful to its Christian foundations. Consequently, the *koinonia* ethics[11] sought by those on the margins often conflicts with the individualistic ethics of the dominant culture; the former recognizes the unity Jesus expressed between God and neighbor, while the latter emphasizes a personal relationship between Jesus and the individual.

To some extent, ethical responsibilities often are compartmentalized into two spheres: either two cities, as in Augustine, or two swords, as in Martin Luther. These theological perspectives allow Christians to formulate two types of ethics, one for the private life (the heavenly city) and a different, if not contradictory, ethics for the public life (the earthly city). Why an ethical dualism?

---

11. Still, *koinonia* ethics is understood as being "of the political" rather than simply a *koinonia* political ethics. Following Clodovis Boff's lead, I use the preposition "of" to maintain a distance between the (political or social) object and its (theological or scientific) theory, "[keeping] what it unites at an appropriate distance" (1987, xxv).

A major error made by ethicists of the dominant culture is to depend excessively upon the great reformers of the faith and to fail to recognize their limitations in bringing about justice in light of the oppression faced by the marginalized of their time. James Cone reminds us that great reformers such as Calvin and Wesley did little to make Christianity a religion of the marginalized. Cone writes, "Though no one can be responsible for everything that is done in their name, one may be suspicious of the easy affinity among Calvinism, capitalism, and slave trading. John Wesley also said little about slaveholding and did even less" (1990, 34).[12] Some philosophers, such as Immanuel Kant (1724–1804), insist that ethics belongs to the private and inner realm of human existence. Any public ethic that exists is simply the spillover of the individual conscience.[13]

Within this compartmentalized tradition, a dichotomy emerges between the Christian as individual and the Christian as public servant. For example, while a Christian might be inclined to follow God's commandment prohibiting killing and, in fact, may desire to offer the enemy the other cheek in obedience to Christ, still the Christian would have to remain responsible to the duty of the office placed upon his or her shoulder. For example, a soldier would have a duty to kill in order to preserve the overall social structure. Individual feelings must be put aside for the administration of this duty. The duty of obedience by the individual is so binding that the citizen should be willing to suffer death rather than rebel. Duty ensures that the government can continue to keep a check on the wickedness brought forth by humans. What reformers such as Luther and Calvin ignored was that for the disenfranchised, it is the government, working to preserve the rights of the privileged, that usually perpetuates wickedness. In such cases, the duty of the citizen may well be to reject the duality of responsibility established to maintain the status quo and actually rebel against it.[14]

---

12. In Calvin's case, this may partially be due to his following Luther's thinking in separating the private ethical sphere from the public. Calvin writes,

> We may call the one the spiritual, the other the civil kingdom. Now, these two, as we have divided them, are always viewed apart from each other. When the one is considered, we should call off our minds, and not allow them to think of the other. For there exists in man a kind of two worlds, over which different kings and different laws can preside. (*Institutes* 3.19.15)

13. It is important to note that during the Reformation the Anabaptists rejected the distinction between the Christian as individual and the Christian as public servant. This refusal to create a dichotomy between a private and public ethics led their spiritual descendants (the Amish, the Mennonites, the Quakers) to become pacifists. Their refusal to justify war as a moral option for Christians can be accomplished only through their rejection of compartmentalization.

14. It should be noted that Calvin, unlike Luther, did not see the magistrate as a substitute for divine rule and thus made allowance for the overthrow of tyranny if obedience to the ruler led one to disobey God (*Institutes* 4.20.29–32). Luther, on the other hand, exhorted Christians to obediently follow tyrants, for in so doing, they deprive the tyrant of power, for obedience is then freely given, not coerced.

Compartmentalizing Christian ethics into two cities or two swords, one spiritual and the other civil, places the former under the authority of the gospel message while it unbinds the latter from following the same set of precepts. The result is an ethical understanding, particularly prevalent within the United States, that is highly privatized with little commitment to transforming the social injustices. To do ethics from the margins is to insist that while the two realms may be distinct, they are in fact related. The ethics advocated for the private life is the same as that advocated for the public life. The maintenance of a false dichotomy has facilitated the justification of some of the worst atrocities within Christian history, from the Crusades, to the Inquisition, to our very own "peculiar" institution of slavery.[15]

A dichotomy in Eurocentric thought develops between the private and public life when moral purity is sought for the private life but not for the public life. This may stem from the conviction that the public life is incapable of obtaining the purity that only the private life can obtain. Justice, while desirable for earth, is reserved for heaven, so the only hope offered the oppressed is a spiritual liberation from their individual sins. Christians on the margins of power and privilege reject this interpretation of the dominant culture, which suggests that the intent of the biblical text is to liberate the soul, but not necessarily the body.

Influential ethicist Reinhold Niebuhr illustrated the fallacy of Martin Luther's severance between the experience of grace and the possibility for justice, which has the overall effect of reducing liberation to nothing more than liberation from God's everlasting wrath toward human sin (1943, 192–93). However, Niebuhr continued the spiritual compartmentalization of Augustine, Luther, Calvin, and Kant by relegating love to the private sphere and social justice to the public realm. His commitment to Christian realism led him to conclude that the ideal of love as the basis for public action is simply impractical and unable to deal with the complexity of modern life. Nations, multinational corporations, and other collective entities, unlike humans, are simply incapable of moral behavior.[16] In fact, he main-

---

15. Even the neoorthodox theologian Karl Barth blames Luther's form of compartmentalization for the rise of Nazism. According to Barth, "Martin Luther's error on the relations between law and gospel, between the temporal and the spiritual order and power . . . established, confirmed, and idealized the natural paganism of the German people of limiting and restraining it" (1941, 7).

16. Christian realism, rooted in the tradition of the Italian philosopher Niccolò Machiavelli (1502–1527), usually is associated with the neoorthodox movement of the 1930s and 1940s, which challenged the prevailing view that society was continuously evolving toward universal justice. The social optimism of the turn of the twentieth century held that the upward-moving enlightenment of humanity was about to break through into an era of worldwide peace and prosperity. Even the ethical movement known as the social gospel, as articulated by American theologian Walter Rauschenbusch (1861–1918), saw the social ills of the time as soon being cured and eliminated through education and spirituality. Instead, a great worldwide depression and two world wars (the first optimistically called "the war to end all wars") culminated with death camps and the first use of the atomic bomb. Consequently, any remaining optimism from earlier in the century was dashed.

tained that certain inequalities are necessary in order for society to function properly.[17]

The impracticality that Niebuhr feared is specifically the type of radical commitment to Christ that those from the margins demand from themselves and from those who benefit from the present social structures. Can Christians obligated to turning the other cheek go off to war and kill Muslims to ensure the flow of oil to the United States? Can Christians commanded to give away both cloak and tunic to those in need be entitled to bring a lawsuit against anyone? Can Christians told to walk the extra mile for those who ask be content simply to leave the "colored" urban centers after five o'clock in the afternoon for the secluded white suburbs, where their children can receive a superior education and they can rest easy at night due to beefed-up security? Compartmentalizing love and justice into two separate spheres of human existence allows a person to claim to be a Christian (hence full of love) while supporting public policies that perpetuate mechanisms of death for marginalized persons.

But how, then, can a judge mete out punishment during a court procedure? If no ethical dichotomy exists between the public and private sphere, can a judge who is committed to unconditional love punish a wrongdoer? Can a soldier ever fight in a war? Such questions, while valid, miss how the status quo is detrimental to the most marginalized. Take the example of the judge. When we consider that a majority of those in prison are people of color from mainly economically deprived areas, we can conclude (1) that people of color are engaged in crime as a negative consequence of their marginalization, where the lack of economic opportunities coupled with an inadequate education system contributes to wrong (legal and moral) decisions on their part, and/or (2) that the judicial and legal system is skewed to convict people of color at a greater rate than whites. While the question concerning how a judge should deliberate may appear to be an issue of retributive justice, in reality, at its very core, it is an issue of distributive justice.[18] Hence, the dominant culture, often refusing to deal with the causes responsible for crime and the procedures by which those accused of crimes are convicted, instead deliberates about how a judge can hand down punishment while remaining a faithful Christian.

While the dominant culture asks, "How does one remain ethical in a corrupt society like this?" those who are marginalized ask, "How does one make a corrupt society like this just?" Because different questions are being

---

17. According to Reinhold Niebuhr, "No complex society will be able to dispense with certain inequalities of privilege. Some of them are necessary for the proper performance of certain social functions; and others (though this is not so certain) may be needed to prompt energy and diligence in the performance of important functions. . . . No society has ever achieved peace without incorporating injustice into its harmony" (1960, 128–29).

18. Retributive justice is concerned with determining a just punishment or penalty for those who commit illegal or immoral acts; distributive justice concerns itself with the fair and equitable distribution of the benefits and burdens of society.

asked, different answers are being formulated. And while the question of how a Christian judge can reconcile love with meting out punishment may be crucial for the powerful and privileged, it remains irrelevant for the marginalized because it refuses to deal with the causes of injustice. Questioning how a judicial system metes out justice becomes an important discourse for the marginalized only after they have some sense that justice exists for them. The barrios and ghettos of this nation testify to the prevalence of systemic injustice in our society. Such injustice is maintained, in large part, by an ethical compartmentalization that allows those with power to continue benefiting from unjust social structures in the public sphere while claiming to be Christian in the private sphere.

Subjective versus Objective

Any system of ethics reflects the activity of a given space. All of us bring our location to how we fashion our ethical perspectives. We also bring our subjective understanding of God based on our experience and our location. However, systems of ethics often tend to mirror more information about who we are than information about what God wants. And, in reality, ethics derives from theologies, which themselves are rooted in prior political commitments and thoughts. Even an "impartial" reading of a biblical text is understood by the reader within a particular socioeconomic setting. All ideas are fastened to the social situation from which they arise, and it would be naive to believe that we could develop objective ethical propositions in a vacuum. Still, some Eurocentric Christian moral agents assume that they are able to arrive at an objective response to whatever dilemmas arise.[19] In the end, the question remains: Whose understanding of Christianity?

Those doing ethics from privileged communities assume that "pure" reason or "proper" biblical hermeneutics are employed. These moral agents from the dominant culture assume that their conclusions are objective; similarly, these same agents assume that those coming from the periphery of society have to be subjective because they are influenced by their marginality. In reality, what moral agents from the dominant culture call "objective" is highly subjective, as it is a product of the social location of the one engaged in moral reasoning. What the moral agent concludes is a universal morality is, in fact, a morality that resonates among those from the same background, those who possess so-called economic and racial superiority. The ethical conclusions of marginalized groups often are considered viable depending on how close they come to the Eurocentric ideal.

---

19. Ethicists such as Emil Brunner conclude that non-Christian ethical systems are unable to provide the whole answer to any ethical problem. Indeed, he says, only a Protestant understanding of Christianity can do so (1947, 41–43, 57). John Rawls, on the other hand, accepts the possibility of developing a neutral framework of basic rights, believing that society can objectively develop principles conforming to a concept of right (1971, 130–36).

Nevertheless, the work of theologians such as James Cone helps define the meaning of ethical terms such as "right" and "wrong" while showing why those of the dominant culture—or any culture for that matter—are incapable of fashioning an objective ethical code of behavior. Cone writes,

> All acts which impede the struggle of black self-determination—black power—are anti-Christian, the work of Satan. The revolutionary context forces black theology to shun all abstract principles dealing with what is the "right" and "wrong" course of action. There is only one principle which guides the thinking and action of black theology: an unqualified commitment to the black community as that community seeks to define its existence in light of God's liberating work in the world. . . . The logic of liberation is always incomprehensible to slave masters. (1990, 10)

What is true for the black community is not limited to the black community; Cone's words ring true for all marginalized groups. Here lies a major difference between systems of ethics advocated by the dominant culture and systems of ethics constructed from the margins of society.

In choosing a preferential option for the marginalized, ethicists of the dominant culture discover that the "objectivity" for which they strive is only the subjectivity of those who possess the power to make their view normative. A harmonious narrative based on some value-neutral analysis concerning the definition of justice simply does not exist. Injustice, oppression, and abuse are part of the human condition. A preferential option for the marginalized prevents the creation of neat ideologies that, theoretically, might help improve the situation of the marginalized yet fail to provide any holistic form of liberation. No ethics, and no theology for that matter, can be socially uncommitted. All ethics and all theologies are and will forever remain subjective; they are incapable of fully comprehending the infinity of the Divine.

Pie in the Sky

Unfortunately, the dominant culture often dismisses the hope of the marginalized for a just social order as utopian. The idea of a just society is as utopian as Isaiah's messianic dream, in which "the wolf shall stay with the lamb, and the leopard shall lie with the kid" (Isa. 11:6). Yet even though ethics from the margins stands in open rebellion against the "opium" of otherworldliness, the "utopias" of Isaiah and of the marginalized are still affirmed with an open-eyed awareness of the present power structures, all the while moving toward a future reality. The hope of the marginalized is not a utopian dream based on the fantasy world of imagination; it usually is a feet-on-the-ground utopianism anchored in the realism of the disenfranchised. Gustavo Gutiérrez insists that pessimism comes from reality because reality is tragic, while optimism comes from action because action can change reality (1984, 80–81). Commenting on an ethic of solidarity, Gutiérrez claims,

> Today, more than ever, is the time to remember that God has given to all humanity what is necessary for its sustenance. The goods of this earth do not belong exclusively to certain persons or to certain social groups, whatever their knowledge or place in society may be. The goods belong to all. . . . We can call this a utopian perspective, but in a realistic sense of the word, which rejects an inhuman situation and pursues relationships of justice and cooperation between persons. (1998, 121)

Hence, the desire for a utopia is not a flight from present reality to an illusionary world; it is a struggle to perfect our reality and prevent the status quo from absolutizing itself. The utopianism called for by those doing ethics on the margins of society is not some naive idealism whereby a future perfect social order is established. Utopianism, as understood here, is a rejection of the present social order grounded in structures designed to perpetrate heterosexism, racism, sexism, and classism. It protests the way things presently are, and it imagines, based on the reality of the oppressed, how society can be restructured to create a more just social order. The function of utopian thought is to guide praxis.

Latin American theologian José Míguez Bonino succinctly captures this so-called utopian vision. He writes, "The true question is not 'What degree of justice (liberation of the poor) is compatible with the maintenance of the existing order?' but 'what kind of order, which order is compatible with the exercise of justice (the right of the poor)?'" (1983, 86). Míguez Bonino correctly points out the ineffectiveness of an ethics that refuses to challenge or change the status quo in the name of realism. The radical love ethic propounded by the gospel message of Christ is not served by compromising with the ambiguities of reality.

As Paulo Freire reminds us, "The radical, committed to human liberation, does not become the prisoner of a 'circle of certainty' within which reality is also imprisoned. On the contrary, the more radical the person is, the more fully he or she enters reality so that, knowing it better, he or she can better transform it" (1994, 21). Because they fail to address the need to reform unjust social structures, realist or rationalist approaches are unresponsive to the social realities of the disenfranchised. What is needed is a feet-on-the-ground ethics, an ethics tied to the experiences of the marginalized in the midst of their reality in facing a particular dilemma or situation.

The system of ethics constructed from the margins is an ethics that pro-claims a God who exists in the midst of the people's suffering, and that seeks to be faithful to the praxis of the gospel message in spite of existing social structures that thwart the faith community's struggle for justice. In the next chapter I will provide a fluid paradigm to elucidate how the disenfranchised, and those of the dominant cultures wishing to stand in solidarity with them, can operate as moral agents.

Chapter 3

The Liberation of Ethics

Womanist ethicist Katie Cannon provides us with a rich definition of liberation ethics:

> Liberation ethics is debunking, unmasking, and disentangling the ideologies, theologies and systems of value operative in a particular society. "How" is it done? By analyzing the cultural, political and economic presuppositions and by evaluating the legitimate myths that sanction the enforcement of such values. "Why" is it worth doing? So that we may become responsible decision makers who envision structural and systemic alternatives that embrace the well-being of us all. (2001, 14)

Choosing to do a liberative ethics from the margins is a proactive option made with, by, and for those who are disenfranchised. Christians make an option for the poor, for those on the margins, not so much because it is the "ethical" thing to do, but because of the need on the part of believers to imitate God as revealed in the life of Jesus Christ. Two Latin American liberation theologians, Clodovis Boff and George Pixley, remind us,

> Before being a duty . . . the option for the poor is a reality of faith, or theological truth. . . . Before being something that concerns the church, the option for the poor is something that concerns God. God is the first to opt for the poor, and it is only as a consequence of this that the church too has to opt for the poor. (1989, 109)

For Christians, no real dichotomy or separation can exist between ethics and social action if social action is understood as the praxis of ethics, the process by which privileged Christians are transformed into the image of Christ. Solidarity that comes from making an option for the poor is crucial not because Christ is with the marginalized, but because Christ *is* the marginalized. In the words of the apostle Paul, "Remember the grace of our Lord Jesus Christ, who for [our] sake, although rich became poor, so that [we] might become rich through the poverty of that One" (2 Cor. 8:9). Who Christ is, is directly linked to what Christ does. Likewise, Christian ethics is directly linked to Christian praxis.

46

The Hermeneutical Circle for Ethics

God wills that all come into salvation—that is, liberation from sin. "Sin" includes individual sins as well as social sins, those that result from social structures. Ethics is the action by which liberation, or salvation, can be manifested. Any model or paradigm used to assist the faith community in developing ethical precepts must start with the experience of those most affected by the sin of oppression, those suffering most from the political and economic structures of society. Christian ethics should result in the transformation of such structures into a more just social order.

Liberation theologians generally have relied on a process called the "hermeneutical circle" as a guide for their reflection. Several ethicists from the margins have also adopted the hermeneutical circle as a paradigm by which to do ethics. Such a paradigm, motivated by a passion to establish justice-based relationships from which love can flow, begins with the lived experience of oppressive social situations and proceeds by working out a theory and then a course of action that will dismantle the mechanisms that cause oppression. It usually proceeds through different but closely related stages that are described below.[1] The purpose of the hermeneutical circle is to formulate a praxis—a system of Christian ethics—to change the reality faced by those living on the margins of society.

Step 1. Observing—An Analysis

To gaze upon an object is not an entirely innocent phenomenon involving the simple transmission of light waves. To "see" also encompasses a mode of thought that transforms the object being seen into a concept for intellectual assimilation and possession. Think of the process of looking at a photograph of a loved one. Observing can be a very rich and emotional experience. We observe inanimate objects and persons, and we also observe their interactions as they exist together to form a society.

Within a society people can be viewed as both subjects and objects. Those whom society defines as "subjects" normally have far more power, including the power to legitimize and normalize what they see. In "first world" countries the dominant Euroamerican culture, which tends to be white, defines reality for those on the periphery or margins (De La Torre and Aponte 2001, 11–12). This is because seeing is political—a social construction that endows the person doing the observing with the power to provide meaning to an object. Probably the worst consequence to befall persons who are viewed as "objects"

---

1. The framework provided here is based on the model of (1) seeing, (2) judging, and (3) acting employed by liberation theologians in Latin America who have been influenced by the Catholic Church's documents *Gaudium et Spes* (1965) and *Octogesima Adveniens* (1971). It is essential to keep in mind that this paradigm, like so many others, is a working model, not an absolute.

is that they see themselves through the eyes of their oppressors, as inferior and lacking power. This is antithetical to the gospel message and an affront to the social dignity of all human beings. When persons viewed as objects accept their oppressors' worldview as their own, they often feel compelled to behave and act according to the way in which they have been constructed by others.

It would be naive to view power as centralized in the hands of the elite of the dominant culture. Power is everywhere as it forms in and passes through a multitude of institutions. It is most effective when it is exercised through coercion that appears natural and neutral—a coercion based simply on the ability to observe.

The starting point for doing ethics, then, becomes the observing, which is done in most first-world countries by members of a white, male, Eurocentric culture. Their understanding of morality and virtues has great importance for those who are disenfranchised. What can those who unjustly benefit from white, male privilege say about morality to those who suffer unjustly because of this privilege?

Distrust of and experience with the ethics constructed by the dominant culture lead those on the margins to observe and discern the reality faced by marginalized people for themselves. Using the eyes of the marginalized, or observing from below, becomes the first step in arriving at any ethical response; it informs how God is understood, how Scripture is read, and how society is constructed. As the causes for oppression are unmasked through this analysis, consciousness of what is happening is raised, and the object, which has now become the subject, gains a deeper understanding of reality.

During the process of observing, it is also essential to consider seriously the historical situation that gave rise to the present situation. If we define history as the memory of a people, how do those on the margins recall their history apart from the imagery imposed upon them by those with power? And most often the "official" history is devoid of the voices of the disenfranchised. In the words of Frantz Fanon, a radical political thinker and writer from Martinique, "The history which [the colonizer] writes is not the history of the country which he plunders but the history of his own nation in regard to all that she skims off, all that she violates and starves" (1963, 51). The history of marginalized people in the United States is written primarily by those who have the power to determine the official story. It is, in short, the history of the dominant power. Nation-building normally requires an epic tale of triumphant wars, heroic figures, and awe-inspiring achievements that elevate the dominant culture while disenfranchising the history of the defeated, or their "other." Homi K. Bhabha, a postcolonial theorist, has termed this the "syntax of forgetting" (1994, 160–61). In the United States the common narrative of nation-building not only disguises the complex political forces responsible for bringing forth that history, but also, more important, it suppresses sexual differences, racial divisions, and class conflicts.

Any thorough understanding of an ethical dilemma must include the historical causes of the dilemma and a study of the ways in which the society maintains structures that caused the dilemma. Michel Foucault has pointed out that the domination of certain people by others creates values. Historical writings, in their turn, justify the values and social positions of those who write the history. This relationship of domination becomes fixed throughout history by means of procedures that confer and impose rights on one group and obligations on another. In this way, the dominant culture normalizes its power by engraving its memories on both people and institutions (1984, 83–85).

The victors of U.S. history inscribe their genealogies upon the national epic, emphasizing military victories, technological advances, and political achievements. These deeds become the official history. Yet the truth of the subject is not necessarily found in the history written by the subject. Psychoanalyst Jacques Lacan insists that truth is found in the "locus of the Other" (1977, 286). Precisely for this reason, the dominant culture attempts constantly to obliterate the Other's locus. Or, as Frantz Fanon eloquently stated,

> Perhaps we have not sufficiently demonstrated that colonialism is not simply content to impose its rule upon the present and the future of a dominated country. Colonialism is not satisfied merely with holding a people in its grip and emptying the native's brain of all form and content. By a kind of perverted logic, it turns to the past of the oppressed people, and distorts, disfigures, and destroys it. (1963, 210)

To seek the voices of those who do not inhabit history is to critique those with power and privilege for substituting their memory for forgotten history. On the other hand, ignoring the voices of those neglected by history can be used to justify yesterday's sexual, racial, and economic domination while normalizing today's continuation of that oppression; it also prevents hope for tomorrow's liberation.

The approach to ethics from the margins seeks to understand what justice is by exploring and understanding how justice was historically denied. If the mechanisms that produce death, such as hunger, nakedness, and homelessness, can be recognized historically as part of the lives of the marginalized, then the reverse—praxis or actions leading to life, and this means abundant life—should inform any system of ethics. For this reason, ethics done on the margins is and must remain a contextual ethics that seeks to see the liberating work of God through the eyes of those made poor, those victimized, and those made to suffer because they belong to the "wrong" gender, race, orientation, or economic class. We exchange the history constructed by the academy, the affluent, and the power-holders for one created from history's underside, whose ongoing struggle is to overcome oppression. We not only search for the God of history, but also claim that God orients history to establish justice and takes sides with the faceless multitude suffering from oppression.

Step 2: Reflecting—Social Analysis

Social analysis is required before social structures can be transformed. Instead of turning to philosophical concepts or abstractions, an attempt is made, using the tools of sociology, anthropology, economics, and political theory, to ground ethics in analysis in order to best discern reality. By providing raw data, the social sciences provide a productive methodology to discern the structures of social phenomena and thus illuminate the reality faced by those marginalized by these structures.

It should be noted that Christian ethicists can legitimately borrow analytical methods from other academic disciplines. Whatever tools of human thought are available should be used to illuminate the social location of the marginalized and to identify oppressive structures. To engage in the self-liberating praxis of naming one's own reality and to point out how political mechanisms maintain institutionalized oppressive structures is to point out sin—sin being understood as the product of existing social, political, and economic systems designed to secure the power and privilege of one group through domination of others.

Analysis of social systems is an integral component of ethical deliberation because it provides a necessary critique of how the present social structures justify racist, heterosexist, sexist, and classist norms. Ethics can never adequately respond to oppressive structures if it fails to understand fully how these structures are created and preserved through economic, social, and political forces. Ignoring social analysis prevents ethics from providing an informed and intelligent practical response to oppression.

In the same way that biblical interpretation is never totally objective, social analysis is incapable of being fully neutral. Both biblical interpretation and social analysis—or any similar thought process—include the biases of the group undertaking the reading or analysis. For this reason, more weight, termed the "epistemological privilege," is given to the marginalized. This privilege accorded the disenfranchised is based on their ability to know how to live and survive in both the center and periphery of society, unlike the dominant cultures, which generally fail to understand the marginalized experience. Consequently, the primary source for doing ethics is the lived, everyday experience of marginalized people.

As important as social analysis may be, it cannot become the totality of an ethicist's reflection. Christian ethical reflection must also be based on the life of Jesus and on his mission, as illustrated in his pronouncement in John 10:10: "I came that they may have life, and have it abundantly." Simply put, if the implementation of an ethical action prevents life from being lived abundantly by a segment of the population or, worse, brings death, then it is anti-gospel. When Christian ethics ignores how minority groups are denied access to opportunities, or reinforces the power and privilege amassed by one segment of the population, or when ethics is relegated to abstract discussions that seldom question how our social structures are constructed, then such ethics ceases to be Christian. Only ethical reflections that empower all elements of humanity, offering abundant life in the here and now instead of the hereafter, can be determined to be Christian. Jesus Christ and his life-giving mission became the lens through which Christian ethical reflection is conducted. Such reflection leads to the praxis of liberation, a process of using reflection to develop actions that bring about the transformation—understood as both liberation and salvation—of all individuals and social structures.

Step 3: Praying—A Theological and Biblical Analysis

If we move directly from observing and reflecting to actions for liberation, ethics from the margins can be accused of being some sort of radical reaction to a given situation. For this reason, praying becomes a crucial step in the ethical paradigm as it ties theory based on observation with the faith community most affected by the ethical dilemma. As Francisco Moreno Rejón, a moral theologian working in Latin America, reminds us, "A salient note in liberation theology and ethics is rooted in their effort to reconcile the requirements of a theoretical, academic order with a pastoral projection. Thus, we are dealing with a moral theology that, far from repeating timeless, ahistorical principles, presents itself as a reflection vigorously involved with the people's daily experience" (1993, 217).

As used here, prayer is not limited to an individual closed in a room to have a private conversation with God in hopes of gaining wisdom and guidance. While personal prayer is important and not to be neglected, prayer is also understood to be communal, bringing together the different members of the spiritual body to pray together. Prayer can be a communal process by which a disenfranchised faith community accompanies its members and stands in solidarity during its trials and tribulations. Ethics is also a communal activity. As such, it is within the faith community (often called by the Greek word *koinonia*), particularly those established on the margins of power and privileged by the Christ event that happened in their midst, that God's ongoing activity within humanity finds its locus. God continues to move in history within the faith community. Ethics, then, can never be reduced to a personal choice or an individual morality; it must instead remain a communal action guided by the relationships established in *koinonia*.

Koinonia is based more on the relationships within the faith community than on precepts or principles. Solidarity and constant communication with the people of faith situated in marginalized communities afford a perspective that is lost on ethicists who confine their deliberations to theories found in academic books. Because morality is communal, ethics from the margins means listening critically to the stories of the marginalized and committing to work in solidarity with them in their struggle for full liberation, both spiritually and physically. Failure to incorporate the voices of the voiceless makes ethics useless for the vast majority of the world's people, who struggle each day for the basic necessities of life—food, clothing, shelter.

Praying also includes a critical application of the biblical text to the ethical situation faced by the marginalized. For Christians, the concept of justice is rooted in the life and acts of Jesus Christ as articulated in the biblical text. The biblical text should influence how moral decisions are arrived at and implemented. The Bible is read as a book of life, one that should shape all of existence, providing keys to an abundant life now and an eternal life later. As such, the Bible becomes a source of inspiration by which both Christian individuals and communities can undergo radical changes, otherwise known as conversion, from a life dominated by sin to a life lived in solidarity with Christ and with "the least among us," those whom Christ chose to be in solidarity with.

For black biblical scholar Brian Blount, fusing the biblical narrative with the life situation of the marginalized produces a biblical witness uniquely capable of addressing their tragic circumstances. "In other words, they contextually construct their biblical story" (2001, 24). Doing ethics through prayer and biblical reflection becomes a process of interconnecting the reality faced on the margins of society with the Scriptures, fully aware of the contradictions existing between the biblical mandate for the fullness of the abundant life in Christ and how those from the center of society interpret sacred texts. All too often, the dominant culture views the Bible as God's "owner's manual," a book of moral precepts from which a "thou shalt not" list can be derived. Codifying the biblical text as a scriptural law book to be obeyed was an error made by the Pharisees of Jesus' time as well as an error that can be made today. Following specific precepts tends to excuse a person from living a life faithful to the call of Christ. Jesus did not provide a legalistic moral code for his disciples to follow. Even if he had done so, the world in which we live, with all of its global complexities and technological advances, is vastly different from the social context in which Jesus found himself. Jesus had no need to speak of issues concerning affirmative action or the ethical dimensions of driving an SUV.

For the Bible to be taken seriously as a source of ethical guidance, we must examine the relationships that Jesus established. By examining the actions taken by Jesus toward others, a pattern emerges that can inform present-day praxes. Jesus articulated moral values that he contextualized within his social location, that of a Jew living in a basically agrarian economy in first-century Palestine, a colonized land that formed part of the Roman Empire.

For liberation theologian Jon Sobrino, applying the values proclaimed by Jesus to present situations is informed by the recognition that Jesus' message of justice and love was brought to all people through his identification and solidarity with one particular group, the marginalized. In Palestine, as today, the marginalized lived in conflict with the privileged and powerful. In addition, Jesus battled against sin manifested as specific social injustices, a conflict that found its conclusion in the execution of Jesus. The Bible's authoritative role in the formation of Christian ethics is established if and when the principles lived and spoken by Jesus are contextualized for the present day. In this way, ethics can move away from abstract notions toward concrete praxes that, when arising from marginalized communities, become universally valid (1978, 124–25, 138).

Nevertheless, there is not always a clear biblical mandate as to what action is moral. At times the biblical text even contradicts itself. For example, although the sixth commandment clearly states, "Thou shalt not commit adultery" (Exod. 20:14), the Leviticus code suggests that men can have multiple sex partners, even to the point of maintaining a harem (Lev. 18:18). Other laws simply cease to be applicable, as in the case of dietary regulations throughout the book of Leviticus. Still other pronouncements offend modern Christian sensitivities, specifically sections that reduce women and slaves to objects, as in the case of the tenth commandment, which prohibits the coveting of another man's possessions, specifically his ox, donkey, house, wife, and slave.

Even though those on the margins look toward the Scriptures for the basis of ethical reflection, it is important to remember that a certain amount of self-criticism should also be employed. How do one's race, class, gender, and orientation influence how the text is interpreted? Even though the Bible remains, apart from Christ, the highest authority for most Christians, turning to the biblical text for guidance requires a critical analysis of the social context that gave rise to the text, a social context whose own milieu (such as patriarchy, for example) affected how the text was written. For example, a social order that advanced patriarchal structures would likely not criticize the creation of harems or the sanction of bigamy. This kind of examination of a biblical text employs what is called the "hermeneutic of suspicion." A second type of danger exists when those in power use a biblical text to advance or justify their own ideologies; this is called "prooftexting." For these reasons, the Bible is not read literally to determine how one group interprets a certain passage, but rather to learn God's character and how that character manifests itself throughout history.

Step 4: Acting—Implementing Praxis

Even the most liberal-minded member of the dominant culture must recognize that in spite of sympathetic statements concerning the plight of those of other races, genders, and classes, the privilege of the dominant culture remains protected through social structures that normalize and legitimize the status quo, even if it is oppressive. Theorizing about justice, regardless of a person's best intentions, changes nothing. In Matthew 7:12 Jesus states what has come to be known as the Golden Rule: "In all things, whatsoever you desire that others should do to you, you should do to them." Simply stated, ethics from the margins is about doing rather than theorizing. Theory is not totally dispensed with, but ethicists on the margins commit to grounding their praxis in the experience of the disenfranchised; ethical theory, then, is a reflection of that action, and theory is subordinated to the praxis.

While all may agree, for example, that poverty should be eliminated, specific acts need to be taken to move this "utopian" concept toward a reality. All too often, concepts remain simply concepts and never become praxis. Because the basic needs of the marginalized are most often impeded by social structures established by the dominant culture, most praxis will concentrate on transforming the social institutions from being disabling to being enabling. This action can attempt to meet basic human needs such as feeding the hungry, clothing the naked, and visiting the imprisoned; or, on the other hand, such action can attempt to change the actual social structures responsible for causing hunger, nakedness, and imprisonment. In the end, both forms of action are needed; however, although those of the dominant culture often are willing to participate in the former through undertaking "charity work," seldom does the desire exist to participate in the latter, since it threatens their privileged space.

As a result, Eurocentric ethics, usually beginning with a "truth" discovered based on some teachings, revelation, sacred text, or rational analysis, lacks the ability to transform the overall power structures. When conducted from the margins, ethics attempts to work out truth and theory through reflection and action in solidarity with the oppressed. In this sense, praxis is not guided by theory. Ethics done from the margins is not deductive; that is, it does not begin with some universal truth and determine the appropriate response based on that truth. Those on the margins tend to be suspicious of such universal claims, which in the past have been used to justify their oppression. The function of theory is an intellectual way of comprehending the reality experienced by the marginalized. It is not, nor should it be, construed as a truth by which a course of action is deduced.

Praxis becomes the Christian's pastoral response toward the structures responsible for heterosexism, racism, classism, and sexism. Although pastoral, the Christian response can also be highly political because, by its very nature, it challenges the overall political structure designed to benefit one group over others. Ethics can thus be understood as orthopraxis, which is the "doing" within a reality informed by theory and doctrine. Orthopraxis is opposed to orthodoxy, which involves arriving at the correct theory or doctrine. This doing of ethics attempts to bring the social order into harmony with the just society advocated by Christ's example, a community devoid of race, class, and gender oppression.

Still, given the multiplicity of possibilities, how do Christians decide what praxis should be used for the liberation of God's people? José Míguez Bonino provides us with an ethical thesis to inform the decision-making process: "In carrying out needed structural changes we encounter an inevitable tension between the human cost of their realization and the human cost of their postponement. The basic ethical criterion is the maximizing of universal human possibilities and the minimizing of human costs" (1983, 107).

Bonino's thesis, when coupled with the foregoing four steps of the hermeneutical circle for ethics, provides sufficient information for a moral agent to decide on an ethical process. Will it be the correct action? This is unknown until the final step, which reassesses the action taken. For now, the moral agent must take a "leap of faith" that his or her action is congruent with the liberative message of the gospel.

Step 5: Reassessing—New Ethical Perspectives

The praxis of liberation, at its core, can be understood as the process by which consciousness is raised. But praxis, in and of itself, is insufficient. At most, it informs ethicists about the validity of their interpretations of the oppression faced by a faith community. Further reflection is needed. Has the implementation of praxis brought a greater share of abundant life to the disenfranchised? If so, what additional praxis is required? If not, what should be done to replace the previous praxis with new and more effective action? The implementation of any additional praxis or a totally new praxis will depend on a reassessment of the situation.

Besides analyzing the effectiveness of the course of actions being taken, the process of reassessing also creates systems of ethics. As we have seen, Eurocentric ethics is deductive, beginning with a "truth" and moving toward the application of that "truth," subordinating ethics to dogma. Doing ethics from the margins reverses this model. After praxis, as part of the reassessment, the individual returns to the biblical text with the ability to more clearly understand its stories and mandates. Through actions, the moral agent experiences the fullness of the dilemma, allowing him or her to ascertain better the proper moral response. As this response is formed, it is again tested by the hermeneutical circle. And the process continues through additional reassessment and further corrections, if necessary. In the end, it is praxis that forms doctrine, informs the interpretation of Scripture, and shapes the system of ethics.

THE HERMENEUTICAL CIRCLE FOR ETHICS

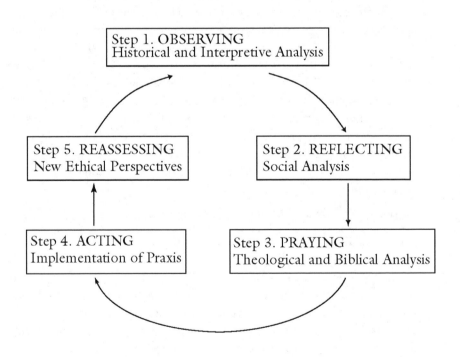

Step 1. OBSERVING
Historical and Interpretive Analysis

Step 5. REASSESSING
New Ethical Perspectives

Step 2. REFLECTING
Social Analysis

Step 4. ACTING
Implementation of Praxis

Step 3. PRAYING
Theological and Biblical Analysis

Part II

Case Studies of Global Relationships

Chapter 4

Introducing Global Relationships

Every person remembers the horror of 9/11. More disturbing than the memory of the World Trade Center towers collapsing is the fact that close to three thousand individuals created in the image of God perished. Some died because they were at work on time, and others because they were heroes who rushed into collapsing buildings in an attempt to save lives. In their honor the *New York Times* published short biographies of those who perished that fateful day.

All of us know about the three thousand who died during the 9/11 terrorist attacks, but how many of us are aware that according to the United Nations Development Programme (UNDP), ten times that number of children—thirty thousand—died of hunger and preventable diseases that same day, or that thirty thousand children have died of hunger and preventable diseases every single day since (Fukuda-Parr 2003, 8)?[1] While these children perish, impoverished countries are spending three to five times as much to pay off foreign debt as they spend on basic services to alleviate the silent genocide of children. Whereas many of those targeted by terrorists die quickly, these children die slowly over time. Their pictures rarely appear in newspapers, and their deaths may not even be noted in any special way. Nonetheless, they too are created in God's image. They have worth and dignity. If we can agree that their deaths are an affront to God, then their deaths should also be an affront to our humanity.

The death of the wretched of the earth can be understood as the byproduct of institutional violence. The normative everyday experience of violence found throughout the global south, affecting their world's most vulnerable members, is closely linked to the reality of socioeconomic injustice, ecological destruction, societal militarization, inequitable distribution of wealth, and inadequate education and healthcare, as well as poverty, unemployment, racism, ethnic discrimination, gender inequality, and global economic policies that benefit a small portion of the world's population at the expense of the many. Violence moves beyond the personal dimension when

---

1. In addition, the United Nations estimates that about 300,000 children that year were involved as soldiers fighting in wars. Between 1990 and 2005, more than 1.5 million children have been killed in armed conflicts (Rutkow and Lozman 2006, 161). Sadly, according to the United Nations website, the United States is the only country in the world that has signed but not ratified the United Nations' 1989 landmark treaty (Convention on the Rights of the Child) that attempts to deal with this atrocity (see http://treaties.un.org/).

the socioeconomic and political dimensions are considered. True, the act of flying a plane into a skyscraper is one of immediate and bloody violence, but the death of a child due to lack of food or sanitary conditions over a period of years, though not immediate or bloody, is no less violent.

The institutional violence that these children experience can be understood as a violence created, supported, and rooted in institutions and powerful groups whose purpose is to maintain an unequal, unjust, and repressive sociopolitical order that blocks the human development of its citizens, especially those considered as inferior, abnormal, or threatening to the given global order. Institutional violence is more than the inadequate distribution of a country's or community's resources; it presupposes an organization, justification, and normalization of unjust socioeconomic relationships through legal and cultural frameworks that supports the mechanisms of justice and establishes a coercive force to maintain an unjust established order. This form of violence is maintained through a repressive social structure that justifies its existence and incorporates its premises into the cultural, educational, and daily experiences of a given society. In this way, the system justifies the cycle of violence protecting the structures and the social groups that benefit most from it.

The targeting of the World Trade Center in New York and the Pentagon in Washington, DC, was no coincidence. These structures served as symbolic headquarters of the world empire and the institutional violence that it unconsciously (or consciously) supports. We still live in a world where during the 2010–2012 period 850 million people (12.5 percent of the global population) are malnourished (UNFAO 2012, 8). Meanwhile, people in the United States spend millions of dollars annually trying to lose weight. By 2010, of the 7 billion people inhabiting the earth, about 1.75 billion people in 104 countries (about a third of their population) were living in multidimensional poverty, reflecting acute deprivation in health, education, and standard of living. This block of the population exceeds the 1.44 billion people in those countries who live on $1.25 a day or less, but not the 2.6 billion living on $2 or less a day. The 2008 Great Recession only exasperated the situation, pushing 64 million more people under the $1.25-a-day poverty threshold. In Africa alone it is estimated that an additional 30,000 to 50,000 children will die as a direct result of the 2008 financial crisis (UNDP 2010, 78, 80, 96).

The global policies that make an economically disproportionate world possible are also responsible for much of the world's poverty, hunger, destitution, and death. The gluttonous consumption of many first-world countries not only is morally indefensible, but also is the root cause of much of the present instability in the world. This instability is a breeding ground for violence, fertilizing the mindset that birthed the 9/11 tragedy. Massive poverty is, without a doubt, the greatest threat to world peace and security. According to former U.N. Secretary-General Kofi Annan, "No one in this world can feel comfortable or safe while so many are suffering and deprived."[2]

We have passed the era when the Marines were used to secure the interests of U.S. corporations (such as the United Fruit Company) throughout Latin America. Today the greatest military force ever known to humanity, simply by its presence, creates a global hegemony that secures the expansion of the global market. If we can come to understand the depth of the misery of the world's marginalized as a byproduct of U.S. affluence created in part by its global economic policies of exclusion, we might begin to appreciate why "they" hate "us" and why our symbols of power became terrorist targets.

The Economic Might of the United States

The cultural influences of the Greek Empire, the imperial might of the Roman Empire, the religious supremacy of the Holy Roman Empire, and the global reach of the British Empire pale in comparison with the cultural dominance, the military might, the capitalist zeal, and the global influence of the U.S. empire. The term "empire" can no longer be narrowly defined as the physical possession of foreign lands that must pay tribute. Today "empire" is understood as a globalized economy that provides economic benefits to multinational corporations whose influences are secured through the military might of one superpower.

Indeed, the sun never sets today on the dominating influence of the United States. At no other time in human history has one nation enjoyed such supremacy of power. Whereas empires of old relied on brute force, the U.S. empire relies mainly on economic force (though it also possesses the most potent fighting force known to humanity). Through its economic might the United States dictates terms of trade with other nations, guaranteeing that benefits flow to the United States and the elite of countries that agree to the trade agreements.

Take corn, for example, a staple of life in many parts of the world. During the first decade of the new millennium many poor nations experienced sharp spikes in food costs, especially corn. For example, Mexico experienced a 60 percent hike in the price of tortillas in 2007, sending tens of thousands into the streets to protest. The importance of corn to the Meso-American diet cannot be overestimated. Along with beans and squash, it has been the main source of nutrition and sustenance for centuries. To a great extent, the entire culture of the Americas revolved around its cultivation and consumption.

---

2. Tim Weiner, "More Entreaties in Monterrey for More Aid to the Poor," *New York Times*, March 22, 2002.

Until recently, Mexican farmers for centuries cultivated corn the way their ancestors did, using a burro on a small plot of land and relying on the rain to irrigate the fields. A third of the crop was reserved to feed the family; the rest was sold at local markets. This simple formula kept the people fed during both good and bad economic times.

However, since the passage of the North American Free Trade Agreement (NAFTA), at least 1.7 million Mexican farmers have lost their small plots of land, unable to compete with cheaper, U.S.-subsidized corn. Many Mexican farmers were forced to migrate to large border cities with high unemployment rates or risk the dangerous border crossing to the United States. Ironically, NAFTA was also not a windfall for U.S. farmers who do not grow corn. More than thirty-eight thousand U.S. farms went out of business since NAFTA's passage, unable to compete with Mexican farmers who rely on large numbers of cheap farm workers to harvest crops other than corn. In order to survive, U.S. farmers were forced to mechanize their farms and employ fewer people. It seems like the only winners from NAFTA were a handful of multinational corporations, especially those who had a hand in drafting NAFTA (De La Torre 2009, 39).

Originally, NAFTA set a fifteen-year period for gradually raising the amount of U.S. corn that could enter Mexico without tariffs; however, Mexico willingly lifted the quotas in less than three years in order to assist its chicken and pork industries. According to Mexican NAFTA negotiators, the suspension of quotas directly benefited fellow negotiator Eduardo Bours, whose family owns Mexico's largest chicken producer. Although the lifting of quotas rewarded his family business, Mexico lost some $2 billion in tariffs, while half a million farmers who grew corn abandoned their lands and moved to the cities in hope of finding a new livelihood.[3]

Because the United States provides subsidies to U.S. farmers, underwriting the cost of their crops (especially corn), U.S. farmers were able to sell their crops below international market price. According to the Environmental Working Group, of the $277.3 billion spent between 1995 (start of NAFTA) and 2011 in subsidies to U.S. farmers, over $81.7 billion went specifically to corn producers.[4] Meanwhile, the World Bank imposed structural adjustments on Mexico in 1991, eliminating all government price supports and subsidies for corn production. When U.S.-subsidized corn is exported to developing countries, like Mexico, local farmers who receive no subsidies from their government are unable to compete with the cheaper, U.S.-subsidized corn (De La Torre 2009, 39).

---

3. See Tina Rosenberg, "The Free-Trade Fix," *New York Times Magazine*, August 18, 2002; "Why Mexico's Small Corn Farmers Go Hungry," *New York Times*, March 3, 2003; see also Celia Dugger, "Report Finds Few Benefits for Mexico in NAFTA," *New York Times*, November 19, 2003.

4. A summary of the U.S. farm subsidy figures is available at http://farm.ewg.org/.

But the availability of cheaper corn was not a windfall for the Mexican people. The suspension of price control on tortillas and tortilla flour caused their prices to triple. During the first decade of NAFTA, corn-growing rural Mexican farmers witnessed corn prices plunge by as much as 70 percent, while the cost of food, housing, and other essential services skyrocketed by as much as 247 percent since the start of NAFTA. Some products, such as tortillas, increased in price by more than 483 percent from January 1994 to January 1999 (López 2007, 7–9, 41). Studying the impact of NAFTA, the Carnegie Endowment for International Peace concluded that ten years of NAFTA has brought hardship to hundreds of thousands of subsistence farmers.[5] Not surprisingly, many of these farmers who have abandoned their lands have since made the journey north, following their resources.

For centuries corn has mainly been used to feed humans and animals. It has also been converted to sugar and alcohol (the cause of the 1791 U.S. Whiskey Rebellion). But today, with the record-breaking increases in the price of gasoline, it is becoming more profitable to convert corn to ethanol to run engines. This new, versatile use of corn is rapidly changing the role that corn has historically played in the Americas. For the ethanol industry to operate at full efficiency, larger shares of corn production must be acquired, diverting corn from human and animal consumption, thus causing steep rises in corn prices, which in turn negatively affect the poor of the world (De La Torre 2009, 40).

The rising price of corn is further exacerbated by transnational traders such as Cargill and Maseca, which are able to speculate on trade trends. With Mexican farmers squeezed out because of their inability to compete with U.S.-subsidized corn, U.S.-owned transnational traders are able to step in and monopolize the corn sector. They can use their power within the market to manipulate movements on biofuel demand and thus artificially inflate the price of corn many times over.[6]

There is no hurry for the United States to change the present system of subsidies to U.S. farmers. Agriculture is one of the few sectors of the economy where the United States runs a trade surplus. But what profits American businesses causes economic devastation for the rest of the world. Former World Bank president James D. Wolfensohn makes the connection between the $1 billion a day that wealthy nations "squander" on farm subsidies and their devastating impact on poor nations. To make matters worse, many wealthy nations place tariffs (at times exceeding 100 percent) on agricultural imports from two-thirds-world nations, making any attempt at market accessibility a

---

5. Walden Bello, "The World Bank, the IMF, and the Multinationals: Manufacturing the World Food Crisis," *The Nation*, June 8, 2008; Celia Dugger, "Report Finds Few Benefits for Mexico in NAFTA," *New York Times*, November 19, 2003.

6. Bello, "The World Bank, the IMF, and the Multinationals."

"sham" (Wolfensohn 2001). This led former World Bank vice president Ian Goldin to conclude that "reducing these subsidies and removing agricultural trade barriers is one of the most important things rich countries can do for millions of people to escape poverty all over the world."[7] C. Fred Bergsten, director of the Institute for International Economics in Washington, was blunter: "Our American subsidy system is a crime, it's a sin, but we'll talk a good game and get away with doing almost nothing until after the presidential election."[8] Every rural peasant forced to leave the land means that another producer who is forced to migrate to the city becomes, along with her or his family, one more consumer. This migration greatly contributes to the perpetual need for future food aid (S. George 1987, 8).

American Exceptionalism

"U.S. exceptionalism" has become the justification used to rationalize foreign policies that would be condemned if other nation-states were to implement similar policies. Imagine another nation using drone strikes to kill "terrorists" on American soil, or another nation maintaining military bases within U.S. territories. The rhetoric of the United States being "the greatest country on earth" permits it to suspend ethical and moral imperatives used to keep other countries in check. Furthermore, the exceptionalism rhetoric prevents constructive dialogue on how to create a more just and liberative global order. The modern-day jingoistic proclamation of American exceptionalism, so often voiced in chants like "We're number one!" is but the latest manifestation of the previous generation's white supremacy. Now, however, this white supremacy is also being adopted by people of color attempting assimilation.

A previous generation of Americans considered it a birthright, due to their whiteness, to have those who fell short of the white ideal labor and sacrifice for the benefits of all whites. Jim and Jane Crow, and slavery before it, maintained that whiteness provided certain benefits and privileges unavailable to nonwhites. Likewise, our present discourse concerning exceptionalism maintains the operation of American supremacy, benefiting and privileging "real" (i.e., mostly white) Americans. The world, with all of its inhabitants, is at the service of the United States because of our exceptionalism. Hence, no one blinks at the fact that the bulk of the world's resources flow in the direction of the United States to support about 6 percent of the world's population.

The usage of the term "American exceptionalism" by politicians is the stuff of empires. Claiming exceptionalism by any nation-state means that normative global ethical rule of order and conduct do not apply because

---

7. Edmund L. Andrews, "Rich Nations Criticized for Barriers to Trade," *New York Times*, September 30, 2002.

8. Elizabeth Becker, "Western Farmers Fear Third-World Challenge to Subsidies," *New York Times*, September 9, 2003.

exceptionalism implies a moving beyond good and evil; this explains the aversions of neoconservatives to be a part of international organizations such as the World Court and the United Nations. We do not have to play by anyone else's rules because, the logic goes, "we are the shining city upon the hill" that is the light to and for the rest of the darkened world.

U.S. exceptionalism does not occur by being number one. Ironically, the United States is ranked as occupying last place when it comes to Americans' quality of life. Among the thirty-three countries with "advanced economies" as defined by the International Monetary Fund, the United States in 2010 ranked thirty-third in infant-mortality rates. Americans are also among those with the shortest life expectancy, ranking twenty-eighth, at 78.24 years. Additionally, we are among the nations with the largest income inequality, ranking thirty-first, with only Hong Kong and Singapore having greater income inequalities among its citizens. When it comes to education, eighty thousand of the hundred thousand public schools fail under our own qualitative measures known as No Child Left Behind. And yet, to point out that there exist incongruences between our claims of exceptionalism and the economic realities faced by most Americans is to be accused of waging "class warfare." However we wish to examine quality of life in 2010, there was nothing exceptional about the United States, except how poor Americans' quality of life is in comparison to that in other industrial nations.

Maintaining the concept that America is number one accomplishes two important tasks. First, it masks growing inequality as the elite few continue to enrich themselves at the expense of middle-class America through tax breaks, deregulation, and the elimination of social services (themes and issues to be discussed in greater detail in the next section of this book). Second, it allows the elite few to expand their wealth by imposing their "supply-side" economics on a global scale (again, something to be discussed in greater detail below). "Exceptionalism" may provide the moral, ideological, and philosophical justification for neoliberalism; nevertheless, the globalization of capital still requires strength to impose the will of the few upon the vast majority of the world's population. We need to be number one in at least one area: our military—a necessity if we wish to continue the flow of resources to our shores to benefit an elite few.

The Rise of Neoliberalism

The rise of the U.S. empire was neither an accident nor the result of luck. Near the close of World War II, the Bretton Woods Conference (1944) attempted to create an economic order that would rebuild Europe so as to prevent any further world wars. Free trade was perceived as the means by which to bring stability to the global order. Although the original intentions may have been noble, in the end the new economic order promoted the development of first-world banks and institutions (both the World Bank and the International Monetary Fund [IMF] were created at Bretton Woods) and transnational corporations. This new global economic order helped the United States and its Western European allies to develop their economic wealth at the expense of the peripheral nations, which provided raw materials and cheap labor.

Underdevelopment of the periphery became a byproduct of development of the center. What was once accepted as colonialism, whereby world powers directly occupied the lands of others to extract their national resources and human labor, was replaced with a more modern form of global exploitation, often termed "neoliberalism." Underdevelopment will continue to persist so long as neoliberalism continues to privilege the nations that have placed themselves at the world's center. This is why any Christian ethical response to global injustices must start with a comprehension of neoliberalism.

"Neoliberalism" is a relatively new economic term. It was coined in the late 1990s to describe the social and moral implications of the free-trade policies of global capitalism since the collapse of the Eastern Bloc. Critics maintain that neoliberalism is responsible for the increasing disparity in global wealth, and that it has created a parasitic relationship whereby the poor of the world sacrifice their humanity to serve the needs, wants, and desires of a privileged few. It provides the few with the right to determine what will be produced, who (nation-state or group of individuals) will produce it, under what conditions production takes place, what will be paid for the finished product, what the profits will amount to, and who will benefit from the profits. In spite of foreign aid programs designed by rich nations to assist so-called underdeveloped nations, more of the world's wealth, in the form of raw materials, natural resources, and cheap labor, is extracted through unfair trade agreements than is returned under the guise of humanitarianism or charity. The first world continues to appropriate the resources of weaker nations through the open market, causing internal scarcities in basic living needs required to maintain any type of humane living standard.

Ensuring stable political systems, regardless of how repressive they may be, is a prerequisite for the economic marketplace to function. Political stability, which is needed to ensure the steady and profitable flow of goods, supersedes the need for freedom and liberty. Thus, a history exists of U.S. pressure to topple democratically elected governments and install tyrants who secured stability (as has happened with the governments of Árbenz in Guatemala, Allende in Chile, and Mossadegh in Iran). Ironically, supporters of the continuing expansion of neoliberalism often confuse this economic structure with democratic virtues such as liberty. Raising questions about ethics of the present economic structure can be construed as an attack on democracy itself (S. George 1999).

To some degree, neoliberalism can be understood as a religion, with the World Bank akin to its ecclesial institution. According to economic development experts Susan George and Fabrizio Sabelli, the World Bank is a "supernational, non-democratic institution [that] functions very much like the Church, in fact the medieval Church. It has a doctrine, a rigidly structured hierarchy preaching and imposing this doctrine [of neoliberalism] and a quasi-religious mode of self-justification" (1994, 5).

For Latin American theologians Clodovis Boff and George Pixley, "The theological status of [neoliberalism] today is precisely that of a vast idolatrous cult of the great god Capital, creator and father of so many lesser gods: money, the free market, and so on" (1989, 144). Like most religious beliefs, the economic pronouncements expounded by the World Bank or the IMF can be neither validated nor invalidated, but usually are accepted on faith. The ethics employed by these institutions is based not on concepts of morality, but rather on interpreted principles of economics and the power amassed by the institution. This point is best illustrated by a statement of Brian Griffiths, vice-chairman of Goldman Sachs International and member of the British House of Lords: "What should be the Christian response to poverty? First, to support global capitalism by encouraging the governments of developing countries to privatize state-owned industries, open up their economies to trade and investment and allow competitive markets to grow" (2003, 171).

For neoliberalism, market forces are more important than ethics, even when the market causes widespread hunger and poverty. Economist Milton Friedman once said, "Indeed, a major aim of the liberal [market] is to leave the ethical problem for individuals to wrestle with. The 'really' important ethical problems are those that face an individual in a free society—what he should do with his freedom" (1962, 12).

Any focus on individual and personal issues of faith and redemption poses problems for Christian ethicists, especially those working on the margins. Daniel Bell best captures this new neoliberal attitude toward ethics: "Capitalism has put a new twist on Augustine's famous dictum, 'Love and do as you please.' Now it is, 'Produce for the market and do as you please'" (2001, 18). The pursuit of gain for the few most often creates scarcity for the many. Liberation theologians such as Peruvian Gustavo Gutiérrez insist, "In the Bible, material poverty is a subhuman situation, the fruit of injustice and sin" (1984, 54). Here, then, is the crux of the conflict between neoliberalism and the gospel message of liberation: neoliberalism lacks a global ethical perspective because it reduces ethics to the sphere of individualism.

The dichotomy between communal and personal ethics—or between market forces and human development—allows Christians to accept the market as a "good." The market, then, determines the fate of humanity and humans exist for the market. Maximization of wealth becomes a virtue in and of itself, as well as a reason for being, and competition separates the sheep from the goats. Economic "losers" are such because they lack the personal ethics to manage their own lives properly. Failure to be employable indicates a collapse of moral duty to maximize one's potential in the labor marketplace. Transnational corporations also compete by eliminating competitors through mergers and acquisitions, which usually result in job losses. As technological advances reduce the need for manual labor, humans become dispensable, nonessential units that are rendered superfluous. Although raw materials remain in high demand, the populations of the two-thirds world are no longer needed (Hinkelammert 1995, 29–30).[9]

Neoliberalism tends to encompass and dictate every aspect of human existence. Nothing can exist outside the market. Even nations are reduced to "companies" with which the transnationals form alliances. Every thing and body is reduced to a consumer good. If a nation is unable to compete in the global marketplace, then a process of financial prioritizing, called "structural adjustments" or "austerity programs," takes place so that the nation can become a stronger player, usually at the expense of their populations, whose living conditions worsen.

The Structures of Neoliberalism

The World Bank and the IMF are key institutions (churches?) of neoliberalism. They impose "conditions" and "structural adjustments" (normally severe cuts in health, education, and social services) on member states starving for credit. A key component of "structural adjustments" is turning national enterprises over to private investors. The privatization of national economies shifts the emphasis from achieving social goals to profit-making. Workers most often face massive wage cuts and layoffs as private owners seek to improve their bottom line by cutting labor costs. The result of privatization in many underdeveloped countries entails a disappearance of social benefits and a direct reduction of the standard of living for workers.

---

9. The term *tiers monde* was coined by Alfred Sauvy in 1952 by analogy with the "third estate," a reference to the commoners of France prior to the French Revolution. The third estate stood in contrast to nobles and priests of the first and second estates, respectively. The term implies the exploitation of the third world, similar to the way the third estate was exploited. Although better terminology to describe the relationship between the first- and third-world nations might be "dominated" and "nondominated" nations, or sometimes "developed" and "undeveloped," I choose to refer to these countries as the "two-thirds world," a term used by others who come from these areas. "Two-thirds" refers to approximately two-thirds of the landmasses, resources, and humanity contained within these countries.

It is now the market that dictates how a society is to be ruled. Global financial institutions set political policies that impact millions of lives. The power of the World Bank and the IMF to impose structural adjustments facilitates their ability to force nations to participate in the world economic order even if the terms of participation are unfavorable, especially to those who are disenfranchised (Hinkelammert 2001, 29). These structural adjustments invariably include devaluing the currency, correlating price structures to global markets, terminating import restrictions and exchange controls, imposing user fees on services (such as water, healthcare, and education), and reducing national sovereignty. The result is usually that the world's marginalized witness the weakening if not the outright dismantling of their economic safety net (protection for women and children in the workplace, social security benefits, labor unions), coupled with increased unemployment and pending ecological collapse. In a twisted form of logic, the increase of unemployment, which leads to increasing poverty and misery among the world's poor, is hailed as a plus. For the World Bank, unemployment means that "bloated" enterprises become lean units capable of competing in the open world market.

In the end, the state can become the servant of the capitalist structures responsible for maintaining "law and order" by squelching any resistance to the status quo. Human freedom and liberty are redefined to mean freedom for the flow of capital and goods, access to a ready and flexible labor pool, and the dissolution of state's rights to determine a separate and contrary destiny. Those who question neoliberalism are not necessarily opposed to globalization, which has become a reality of modern life; rather, they are against how globalization has come to be defined. This new political, social, and economic order called "neoliberalism" negatively impacts all humanity, especially the marginalized.

Moving beyond Production

Capitalism has historically been based on making things (manufacturing) and growing things (agriculture) with the end goal of selling what is produced. In order to accomplish this goal, laborers were needed to toil in factories or harvest fields. In order to build factory buildings or buy heavy farming equipment, proprietors engaged in financial transactions as a means to the end of bringing their product to market. Neoliberalism, however, has moved beyond these traditional ways of making money. Instead, financial transactions, specifically international financial transactions, have become the means, in and of themselves, by which wealth is built without the need of producing anything tangible, which in turn creates employment.

Compare the global transactions for actual goods and services in 2002 ($32.5 trillion) and 2010 ($62.5 trillion) with the activities in the world of exotic global financial transactions in 2002 ($1,122.7 trillion)[10] and 2010 ($3,456.5 trillion).[11] The ratio between the nontangible economy, where money makes money on only money, and the real economy that produces goods and services (and jobs) was 1:34.5 in 2002, increasing to 1:55.3 in 2010 (Raines 2012). Even Nicolas Sarkozy, pro-laissez-faire conservative and former French president, explains why these ratios are problematic:

> This crisis is not just a global crisis. This crisis is not a crisis in globalization. This crisis is a crisis of globalization. . . . Globalization took a wrong turning the moment we accepted unconditionally, unreservedly and without any limit the idea that the market was always right and that there could be no argument against it. Let us go back to the root of the problem: it was the imbalances in the world economy which fed the growth of global finance. Financial deregulation was introduced in order to be able to service more easily the deficits of those who were consuming too much with the surplus of those who were not consuming enough. The perpetuation and accrual of these imbalances was both the driving force and consequence of financial globalization. . . . Globalization of savings has given rise to a world where everything was given to financial capital, everything, and almost nothing to labor, one where the entrepreneur gave way to the speculator, where those who lived on unearned income took precedence over workers, where the use of leverage . . . was becoming unreasonably disproportionate, and all this created a form of capitalism in which it had become normal to play with money, preferably other people's money, to make easily and extremely rapidly, effortlessly and often without creating either prosperity or jobs, absolutely enormous sums of money. . . . The crisis we are experiencing is not a crisis of capitalism. It is a crisis of the distortion of capitalism. . . . Purely financial capitalism is a perversion which flouts the values of capitalism. (Sarkozy 2010)

Huge transfers of wealth from the global middle class toward an elite global minority have radically changed the foundations of capitalism. Ironically, it appears that the continuous demise of entrepreneurship capitalism is caused by the rise of global neoliberal financial markets.

---

10. $1,122.7 trillion represents $699 trillion in derivative product transactions, $384.4 trillion in currency exchange transactions, and $39.3 trillion in the purchase of financial titles (i.e., stocks and bonds).

11. $3,456.5 trillion represents $2.703.5 trillion in derivative product transactions, $675 trillion in currency exchange transactions, and $78 trillion in the purchase of financial titles (i.e., stocks and bonds).

Using Case Studies in Ethics from the Margins

In closing, let us consider these words of former Brazilian archbishop Dom Hélder Câmara: "When I feed the hungry, they call me a saint; when I ask why they are hungry, they call me a communist." Any ethical praxis geared to dismantling global injustices must begin there—asking why people are hungry. We cannot begin to deal with the liberation of the world's marginalized unless we first deal with the root cause of all their misery and suffering: economic injustice. The next three chapters will briefly explore some of the consequences of neoliberalism: global poverty, warfare, and abuse of the environment.

Traditionally, the usual approach to teaching ethics is to emphasize theory: the student learns an ethical theory and then applies it to a hypothetical case study. The purpose of the case study is to determine objectively which ethical response is proper, based on a multitude of possibilities. The focus is not on the dilemma outlined in the case study, but rather on the methodology employed to arrive at the ethical response. Such a case study might involve a car that is out of control and crashes into a brick wall, catching fire. You come upon the scene in hopes of providing assistance to the driver, alone in the vehicle, who is alive and pinned inside the wreckage. You try to pry open the doors, but to no avail. The fire is rapidly spreading. Within minutes, if not seconds, the driver will be engulfed in flames. There is absolutely no means by which you would be able to open the doors so as to free the driver. It so happens that you are carrying a loaded pistol. Do you pull out the pistol and administer a "mercy killing," or do you take no action and watch the injured but conscious driver burn to death?

Such case studies form a false dichotomy between ethical theory and practice. The purpose is not to determine what moral action should be taken when approaching persons trapped in burning cars, but rather to answer the abstract question, "Is there ever a situation in which killing is justified?" Regardless of how clever or creative such case studies may appear to be, they are useless to those residing on the margins of society because they fail to foster a concrete act to bring about change. While the question concerning a trapped person in a burning car may prove intriguing, the fact remains that very few people will ever come across such a situation. Such case studies reinforce a spectator-type ethics in which debating theory, rather than transforming society, becomes the goal.

For those doing Christian ethics from the margins, relevant case studies must be contextualized in *lo cotidiano*, the everyday experience of marginalized people, the subject and source for all ethical reflection. Unfortunately, many ethicists of the dominant culture maintain that considering the interpreter's identity or social location interferes with the job of ascertaining a so-called objective rendering. The approach employed in this book, and particularly in the following case studies, challenges the assumption that ethical deliberation can be understood apart from what the interpreter brings to the analysis. The case studies and analysis in this book are unapologetically anchored in the experience of society's disenfranchised communities. The theologian Karl Barth once said that theology should be done with the Bible in one hand and a newspaper in the other. In reality, it is ethics that needs to be done with an open newspaper. By grounding case studies in the everyday, the margins are brought to the center.

The remaining chapters will deal with ethical dilemmas from the perspective of the disenfranchised. They will apply the hermeneutical circle for ethics described in chapter 3 to a particular social issue through the eyes of the marginalized. The reader is invited to analyze and reflect on the situation in order to determine what praxis may be appropriate. After the third step of praying (theological and biblical analysis), each chapter will present several short case studies. The fourth (taking action) and fifth steps (reassessment) are missing so that the reader can ponder the case studies through the worldview of the marginalized.

Chapter 5

Global Poverty

Step 1. Observing

Since the collapse of the Soviet Union, the United States has emerged as the undisputed world power, both economically and militarily. The might of the U.S. military facilitates the ever-expanding influence of transnational corporations whose single goal is to satisfy their stockholders by increased profits. One way to keep profit margins high is to pay low wages. Wages paid to workers, especially workers who are part of the global poor, are not determined by textbook economic theories of supply and demand, or by the laborer's need to survive, but rather by the needs of the transnational corporation to increase profits. Many theologians, such as Enrique Dussel of Mexico, remind us that God's reign in community is an affirmation that people are created to live in a positive relation with the Divine and with each other. This cannot happen when individuals are reduced to their economic value, when they become objects or resources to be exploited (1988, 17).

This happens today throughout the world whenever humans are reduced to being production tools, the means by which corporations profit at their expense. The disenfranchised become a commodity, an object, within an integrated global market; their sole purpose is to provide the world's powers with a reservoir of cheap labor. As theologian John Cobb observes, "Now that Marxism has been discredited, however, the capitalist countries no longer find it necessary to check the concentration of wealth in fewer hands. By moving from national economies to a single global economy, they can pit the workers of one country against the workers of all others" (1998, 36). The ever-present corporate goal of increasing profits creates a race to the bottom among transnational corporations as they seek the lowest possible wage to be paid. There was a time when business innovation (the automobile, the camera, the plane, the television, the computer) provided long-term economic growth and millions of local jobs. However, today there is nothing anchoring an American business to the United States. A quick look at one company illustrates this point.

Steve Jobs and Steve Wozniak, tinkering with electronic components in Jobs's parents' garage, built the first Apple computer in 1976. It did not take long for Apple to start manufacturing its new product, first at a building in San Francisco, then at a plant in Fremont, California. Bill Stamp was among the first employees at the Fremont plant, joining Apple in 1984. Soon, other assembly plants were opened, one of which opened in 1992 at Fountain, Colorado, near Colorado Springs. Stamp was offered an opportunity to transfer to the new plant; he accepted. There he met his future wife, Christy, who also was an Apple employee. The Fountain plant was well run and profitable, becoming the company's largest manufacturing facility, producing about one million laptop and desktop computers a year. Rather than opening more plants within the United States, Apple instead moved its operations overseas, mainly to China. Apple closed the Fountain plant four years later in 1996, creating a 40 percent regional loss of fifteen thousand manufacturing and information technology jobs that paid $55,000 to $80,000 per year plus benefits. The local economy lost an estimated $500 million (Barlett and Steele 2012, 84–86).

Stamp stayed working at the plant under new owners, SCI Systems Inc., which had a three-year contract to continue producing Apple computers. But when the agreement was not renewed, SCI shifted its manufacturing offshore. Stamp tried his hand doing other work in lesser-paying jobs, but to no avail. He finally left Fountain in 2001. In 2008, when his newest job was shipped to Singapore, Stamp, then fifty years old with a lengthy résumé, was unable to get a job interview. The Stamps went through their saving accounts and retirement accounts, and at the end, they lost their home. By 2011, after three years of unemployment, the Stamps found themselves renting a two-bedroom apartment and working at temporary jobs with no benefits. Meanwhile, almost all of Apple products—Macs, iPods, iPhones, iPads—are made in China (Barlett and Steele 2012, 88).

The problems that Bill and Christy Stamp face are being repeated in towns and cities throughout the United States. The high-paying Apple jobs that the Stamps lost are being replaced with low-paying Apple retail jobs. Take the example of Jordan Golson, who in a three-month stretch sold $750,000 worth of Apple products at $11.25 an hour. Golson is not alone. Apple retail workers make the least when compared to the amount they sell. An average hourly wage of $11.91 represents .21 percent of sales. Compare this to Costco employees, who at $13.87 an hour represent 1.51 percent of sales.[1]

Once upon a time, a high school graduate was able to obtain a factory job and live a comfortable lifestyle. Unfortunately, the factory job that used to be the backbone of America's prosperity has been disappearing. Today, many with college degrees are employed in retail jobs that require only a high school diploma; unable to sustain themselves, many are forced to live with their parents or in group housing, trying to get by, unable to save enough to establish

---

1. David Segal, "Apple's Retail Army, Long on Loyalty but Short on Pay," *New York Times*, June 24, 2012.

themselves. Older Americans are losing their security for their golden age, and the concept of retirement is becoming an unattainable illusion.

But the loss of the so-called American Dream for U.S. workers like the Stamps is not a gain for the new Chinese Apple employees working in high-tech sweatshops. The heart of Apple production in China is near Shenzhen, a megalopolis of some ten million inhabitants. Outside the city is Longhua, a walled-off, fortress-like, high-security compound containing numerous factories and dormitories. Owned by the Taiwan-based company Foxconn Technology Group, the largest manufacturer of electronics and computer components in the world,[2] Longhua is home to some three hundred thousand laborers. Apple is able to skirt fair labor standards, workplace safety regulations, and environmental standards by subcontracting all its manufacturing to companies like Foxconn, one of China's largest employers, with 1.2 million workers assembling about 40 percent of the world's smartphones, computers, and other electronic gadgets.[3]

In 2010 Apple employed 43,000 people in the United States (of which 30,000 work in retail averaging $11.91 an hour)[4] and some 20,000 overseas. However, through their subcontractors Apple has an additional seven hundred thousand people who engineer, build, and assemble their products.[5] Subcontractors like Foxconn are infamous for subjecting workers to widespread beatings. The company is willing to do whatever it takes to meet the high quotas set by Apple.[6] For example, when Apple at the last minute redesigned the iPhone's screen, the foreman at the factory was able to rouse eight thousand workers at the company's dormitories, guide them to a workstation to begin a twelve-hour shift fitting the new glass screens unto the frame, producing over ten thousand iPhones a day in a mere ninety-six hours after the new screen design was introduced.[7]

In 2010 Apple earned $400,000 in profit per employee, while workers at Foxconn earned less than $17 a day, working twelve-hour shifts, six days a week (at times all seven days). Over a quarter of the workforce lives in crowded company barracks.[8] Workers sleep in tiny dorms, six or eight to a room for $17 a month.[9] It is common for three-room apartments to house

2. It should be noted that Apple is not the only company for which Foxconn is a subcontractor. Other companies include Asus, Dell, Hewlett-Packard, IBM, Intel, Lenovo, Microsoft, Motorola, Nintendo, Nokia, Samsung, Sharp, Sony, and Panasonic. Foxconn plants are also responsible for making the Kindle, PlayStation, and Xbox.

3. David Barboza and Charles Duhigg, "Pressure, Chinese and Foreign, Drives Changes at Foxconn," *New York Times*, February 20, 2012.

4. Segal, "Apple's Retail Army."

5. Charles Duhigg and Keith Bradsher, "How the U.S. Lost Out on iPhone Work," *New York Times*, January 21, 2012.

6. Mike Daisey, "Against Nostalgia," *New York Times*, October 6, 2011.

7. Duhigg and Bradsher, "How the U.S. Lost Out on iPhone Work."

8. Ibid.

9. David Pogue, "What Cameras Inside Foxconn Found," *New York Times*, February 23, 2012.

twenty people. Some of these employees are forced to stand for so long that their legs swell, making walking difficult.[10] Workers are not allowed to speak to each other while working, nor are they able to leave their workstation. If they want to use the bathroom, they must first obtain permission from guards (Barlett and Steele 2012, 92). Underage workers with falsified records are common. Hazardous conditions within the plant caused by lack of proper ventilation were ignored, leading to two explosions within seven months of each other in 2010, killing four people and injuring seventy-seven. The working conditions are so bad that employees at times believe that their only means of escape is suicide. At least two dozen workers were so desperate that they jumped to their deaths from their dormitories.[11] The situation has become so dire that large safety nets were attached to buildings to catch possible jumpers.[12]

Those building Apple products are perceived and treated as cattle. The CEO of Foxconn, Terry Gou, said it best: "As human beings are also animals, to manage one million animals gives me a headache."[13] And yet in spite of these horrendous working conditions, former CEO Steve Jobs boasted that Apple "does one of the best jobs of any company . . . of understanding the working conditions in [their] supply chain."[14] Although Apple is playing the role of the socially conscious employer, past actions leave much to be desired. When 137 workers were harmed at another one of Apple's subcontractors, Wintek, suffering nerve damage and paralysis from a toxic chemical (n-hexane) used in the making of the iPhone's slick glass screen, the company declared the incident a "core violation" of worker safety, ordering that the chemical no longer be used until safety conditions are improved, and made a commitment to monitor the medical conditions of the affected employees. Nevertheless, those who were injured said that they were forced to accept a cash settlement that absolved the factory of any future liability and then resign. Others claim that Apple was slow to address the cause of the health injuries.[15] One Apple executive, speaking on the condition of anonymity, revealed, "We've known about labor abuse in some factories for four years, and they're still going on. Why? Because the system works for us. Suppliers would change everything tomorrow if Apple told them they didn't have another choice. If half of iPhones were malfunctioning, do you think Apple would let it go on for four years?"[16]

10. Charles Duhigg and David Barboza, "In China, Human Costs Are Built into an iPad," *New York Times*, January 25, 2012.

11. Ibid.

12. Miguel Helft, "Apple Says Chinese Supplier Made Changes after Suicides," *New York Times*, February 15, 2011.

13. John Markoff, "Skilled Work, without the Worker," *New York Times*, August 19, 2012.

14. Duhigg and Barboza, "In China, Human Costs Are Built into an iPad."

15. David Barboza, "Workers Sickened at Apple Supplier in China," *New York Times*, February 22, 2011.

16. Duhigg and Barboza, "In China, Human Costs Are Built into an iPad."

Apple has become the most valuable company in the world; its stock value in January 2012 was $422 billion. At times the company has more cash in its bank accounts than the U.S. Treasury (Barlett and Steele 2012, 97). When Tim Cook became CEO after Steve Jobs retired, his cash salary was $900,000, plus an award of Apple stock worth a staggering $376.2 million. Cook was earning about $1 million a day, or about $42,000 an hour, or roughly an amount equal to the pay of more than five thousand U.S. factory workers who still had Apple jobs, or about 60,919 years of employment at Foxconn. Further benefiting Cook was that within a year the value of the stock increased to about $634 million.[17]

When President Barack Obama asked then–Apple CEO Steve Jobs what would it take to make iPhones in the United States, Jobs bluntly responded, "Those jobs aren't coming back." Contrary to popular opinion, the reason is not always because workers are paid substantially less overseas. Academic and manufacturing analysts estimate that if American wages were paid, iPhone prices would only increase by about $65 per phone.[18] Why, then, are U.S. jobs vanishing? Why will those that went overseas not return? What happened that led us to this economic predicament?

In June 1979 the United States reached its zenith of manufacturing jobs. But years of low tariffs, unrestricted imports, and refusal to insist on reciprocal trade agreements with partnering countries—advocated and supported by Democrats and Republicans alike—eroded the economic backbone of the United States. The number of manufacturing jobs fell from the all-time high of 19.5 million in 1979 to 11.6 million in 2011. The United States went from 18.2 percent of the work force employed in good-paying jobs in 1979 to only 9 percent in 2011. Even though manufacturing wages are lower in the United States than in about a dozen developed nations, 7.9 million manufacturing jobs disappeared between 1979 and 2011. In the first decade of the millennium 14 percent of the nation's factories (56,190 establishments) closed their doors, most moving their operations overseas. These closures resulted in 5.7 million factory workers losing their jobs, representing a 33 percent decline, exceeding the manufacturing jobs lost during the Great Depression of the 1930s (Barlett and Steele 2012, 40, 45, 47).

The last year the United States posted a trade surplus was 1973. Since that anemic $911 million surplus, the United States has posted, every year since, a trade deficit. By 2011 the trade deficit stood at $560 billion. When trade is in balance—when imports and exports are about the same—good-paying jobs exist. But when there are more imports than exports, as has been

---

17. Natasha Singer, "C.E.O. Pay Gains May Have Slowed, but the Numbers Are Still Numbing," *New York Times*, April 8, 2012.

18. Duhigg and Bradsher, "How the U.S. Lost Out on iPhone Work."

the case for over forty years, then the industries that provide good-paying jobs are undercut, resulting in vanishing jobs. Why, then, should we be surprised when major industries, such as the once vigorous furniture industry of central North Carolina, have been decimated? North Carolina furniture companies were unable to compete with waves of imported Chinese furniture that were subsidized by that government. During the first ten years of the new millennium, over three hundred North Carolina furniture plants employing thousands of workers closed, reducing the industry's production capacity by 70 percent (Barlett and Steele 2012, 46, 48, 123).

Many of these manufacturing jobs, according to the U.S. Department of Labor and the Bureau of Labor Statistics, have been mainly replaced by governmental jobs (increasing the size of the bureaucracy) and service jobs (including retail). Exporting manufacturing jobs overseas has led to an economic shift from high-paying to low-paying wages within the United States. In the 1950s most jobs were in the high-paying manufacturing sector. After peaking at 19.5 million jobs in June 1979, manufacturing jobs by January 2013 dropped to 11.9 million, or just 8.8 percent of all U.S. nonfarm jobs. Meanwhile, retail and service jobs have skyrocketed to represent a majority of all U.S. jobs (U.S. Department of Labor 2013b).

When we consider that an average manufacturing job in 2012 earned $23.93 an hour for a 40.8-hour workweek (U.S. Department of Labor 2013c), while the mean retail wage was $12.17 an hour for a 30.9-hour workweek (U.S. Department of Labor 2013a; 2013d)—a difference of $600.29 a week or $31,215 yearly—we can begin to appreciate the extent to which transnational corporations and the neoliberalism that they practice in their quest for the cheapest labor are dismantling the U.S. middle class.

The loss of jobs is not limited manufacturing positions. Take the example of IBM, which has shifted service jobs, including software design jobs, to other countries. In 2003 IBM had 9,000 workers in India; by 2010 that number had skyrocketed to 75,000. Since 2003 IBM has been eliminating about 8,000 U.S. employees each and every year.[19] Why pay $60,000 a year for a skilled Java programmer in the United States when you can get one in India for less than $5,000 a year? The total savings to a U.S. company that shifts its job overseas can be as high as 50 percent, even when allowances are made for the extra cost of transportation, communication, and other expenses not needed if the work was done in the United States.[20]

According to a study conducted by the U.S. Bureau of Economic Analysis, large U.S. firms in 2010 added workers within the U.S. at about .01 percent,

---

19. Steve Lohr, "IBM Rides Global Focus on Services to Deliver a 12 percent Increase in Profits," *New York Times*, October 19, 2012.

20. Louis Uchitelle, "A Missing Statistic: U.S. Jobs That Have Moved Overseas," *New York Times*, October 5, 2003.

TABLE 1
Manufacturing jobs, 1939 through 2013
(all figures represent millions of jobs)

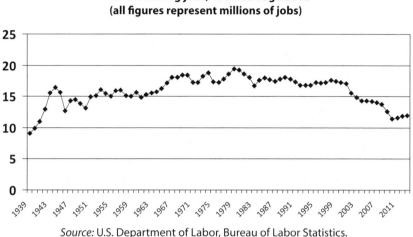

Source: U.S. Department of Labor, Bureau of Labor Statistics.

while increasing their foreign workforce by about 1.5 percent. Between 2004 and 2010, foreign affiliates of U.S. companies hired some 2 million workers while adding only 600,000 jobs at home.[21] Of the 3.3 million service-sector jobs that Forrester Research estimates will be conducted overseas by 2015, 70 percent of these positions will migrate to India, which has a large pool of English-speaking inhabitants, 2 million of whom have a college education.[22] Ironically, even the U.S. government participates in the exportation of its bureaucratic labor force. Today's operators in Bombay, Bangalore, or Gurgaon are likely to handle calls from welfare and food stamp recipients. U.S. state governments alone were forecasted to spend up to $11.4 billion by 2012 in outsourcing activities (Mutiangpili 2010, 2). There is great irony in the fact that taxpayer dollars, including those from the federal stimulus package created to deal with the 2008 Great Recession, go to create jobs overseas that handle food stamps, unemployment insurance, and other public benefits needed by Americans whose jobs went overseas.

Not only do these overseas workers assist U.S. citizens with questions about their welfare benefits, but also they prepare U.S. tax returns, evaluate health insurance claims, handle airline reservations, transcribe doctors' medical notes, analyze financial data, and read CAT scans. These skilled workers in India can earn about $3,000 to $5,000 a year (in a country where

21. Tom Hamburger, Carol D. Leonnig, and Zachary A. Goldfarb, "Obama's Record on Outsourcing Draws Criticism from the Left," *Washington Post*, July 9, 2010.

22. Jennifer Bjorhus, "U.S. Economic Slowdown Sends Technology Jobs Overseas," *San Jose Mercury News*, October 21, 2002; Amy Waldman, "More 'Can I Help You?' Jobs Migrate from U.S. to India," *New York Times*, May 11, 2003.

the per capita income is $500),[23] which is less than what is received by the welfare recipients whom they are helping or what they could earn in the United States, where an entry-level position at a call center would pay at least $20,000 a year. Ironically, India's jobs (which formerly were American jobs) themselves are being outsourced. In 2011 the Philippines, with a population one-tenth that of India, surpassed India's call center operations. Now, an American is more likely to speak with a Filipino than an Indian when calling a service center, mainly because India, colonized by the British, speaks British-style English, whereas the Philippines, colonized by the United States, speaks a more American-style English.[24]

Besides participating in the quest for the lowest possible wage, the U.S. government encourages U.S. industry to outsource jobs to countries such as India based on the theory that it benefits the market. In an interview with the *Cincinnati Enquirer* on March 30, 2004, John W. Snow, then secretary of the U.S. Treasury, explained the government's position. The practice of moving American jobs to low-cost countries "is part of trade . . . There can't be any doubt about the fact that trade makes the economy stronger." His comments are reminiscent of the remarks made by N. Gregory Mankiw a month earlier. Mankiw, then chairman of the White House Council of Economic Advisers, defended outsourcing as merely another form of international trade that ultimately would be a "plus" for the United States. William Poole, the president of the Federal Reserve Bank of St. Louis, agreed. He sees outsourcing as benefiting the United States by reducing prices domestically while expanding export markets.[25] Not much has changed under the Obama administration. In 2010 the U.S. Agency for International Development (USAID) used $10 million of American tax money to assist Sri Lanka in developing its own outsourcing industry (Barlett and Steele 2012, 109).

However, it would be erroneous to believe that countries such as India and Mexico have achieved a financial windfall from the importation of manufacturing jobs. For example, Mexicans have sunk deeper into poverty, in spite of the opening of *maquiladoras* (assembly plants) along the border. Many Mexican peasants, many of whom used to live off the corn that they grew, have surrendered to the fact that they can no longer compete with agricultural goods imported from the United States. Because the land could no longer support them, they abandoned their homesteads and moved to *colonias* (poor, sprawling slums of shacks patched together from pieces of metal, wood, and plastic) surrounding the *maquiladoras*.

The 1994 North American Free Trade Agreement (NAFTA) scheme of moving goods freely across borders—free from tariffs or taxes—was supposed

---

23. Bjorhus, "U.S. Economic Slowdown Sends Technology Jobs Overseas."
24. Vikas Bajaj, "A New Capital of Call Centers," *New York Times*, November 25, 2011.
25. Rebecca Leung, "Out of India," CBS *News*, February 11, 2009.

to be a bonanza for U.S. exporters and provide high-paying jobs to U.S. workers. Of course, workers looking for better jobs were never intended to also freely cross borders, only their cheap labor as part of the goods being exported. Moving factories rather than people across borders kept high profit margins by paying the lowest possible wages. The quest for the lowest possible wages meant that industries needed to relocate south of the border. It is estimated that in the first ten years since the implementation of NAFTA, approximately 780,000 jobs in textile and apparel manufacturing were lost (Labor Council for Latin American Advancement and Public Citizen 2004, 5). Five years prior to NAFTA the United States maintained a $168 million trade surplus with Mexico; five years after NAFTA the surplus plunged to a $12.5 billion deficit. The trade surplus with Mexico that was supposed to be the result of NAFTA ballooned into a $698 billion deficit by the end of 2011. By 2016 this trade deficit should reach $1 trillion! According to the Economic Policy Institute calculations, an estimated 1.5 million jobs were eliminated from the United States by 2011 due to Mexican imports (Barlett and Steele 2012, 55–56).

Still, as already stated in the preceding chapter, there was no windfall for Mexico. Many Mexican farmers were forced to abandon their lands, unable to compete against U.S. subsidized imported agricultural goods. Dumping U.S. surplus of subsidized corn (at about $4 billion a year from 1995 to 2004)[26] on Mexico meant a 70 percent drop in Mexican corn prices and a 247 percent increase in housing, food, and other living essentials, with millions of farmers losing their land (López 2007, 7–9, 41). Our trade policy pushed migrants out of Mexico and other Central American countries, while our hunger for cheap labor that native-born Americans do not want to do pulled them toward the United States (De La Torre 2009, 13–14).

While numerous *maquiladoras* opened along the border since the implementation of NAFTA, Mexicans sank deeper into poverty. At first, the poor of Mexico found salvation in the *maquiladoras*. But salvation proved illusionary. Towns straddling the border offered few other opportunities. Mexican wage earners have lost 20 percent of their purchasing power since NAFTA spurred the growth of the *maquiladoras*, even though wages and benefits for *maquiladora* employees rose by 86 percent from 1997 to 2002 to an average of $6,490 a year. This increase in wages is deceptive. In 1975 Mexican production workers earned 23 percent of U.S. wages. Since the relocation of U.S. jobs to Mexico, that number has continued to drop, which is one reason why more dissatisfied workers attempt the hazardous U.S. border crossing.[27]

---

26. Alexei Barrionuevo, "Mountains of Corn and a Sea of Farm Subsidies," *New York Times*, November 9, 2005.

27. The difference in the standards of living between the United States and Mexico, which was about 3:1 in the 1950s, is 8:1 since the new millennium. The Mexican government estimates that

The move from the United States to Mexico is only the first step. As the worsening conditions of Mexican workers raised questions about plant safety, living wages, and the environment, factories began to look elsewhere. Although first attracted to Mexico by low wages, low taxes, and few if any environmental regulations, some of these multinational corporations are again seeking to relocate. In the competition for the lowest wages and labor standards, China is emerging as the new leader. A benefit to relocating was that Asian women and children, who earn less than men, usually were employed in these low- or semi-skilled jobs.

In the first half of 2002, direct foreign investment in Mexico dropped by 15 percent ($6.1 billion), while investment in China rose by 19 percent ($24.6 billion). According to the U.S. Census Bureau, U.S. imports from China have been steadily rising, from $4 billion in 1986 to $114 billion in 2002.[28] At the same time, Mexico's exports to the United States have begun to decline. During the first two years of the new millennium, more than five hundred plants along the border have either shut down or moved their operations to China, reducing the number of jobs in Mexico by 256,000 (Mireles 2002, 26, 28). For example, in 2000 the *maquila* city of Chihuahua, which specializes in automotive parts and electronics, led Mexico in employment. By the close of 2002 Chihuahua led in unemployment. Companies like General Electric, which over the years moved many jobs from the United States to Mexico, are now relocating those same jobs to China.

Yet China's entry into the global market has not translated into an economic boom for China's working class, as demonstrated by our exploration of Foxconn. China, like Russia, had an economy completely controlled by the state. Such a system guaranteed jobs for life and then retirement. But guaranteed jobs and retirement were the first casualties of privatization. Entire cities were built around huge mills, mines, and factories that provided a multitude of social benefits, from subsidized housing to hospitals and childcare. Privatization has brought an end to these guarantees and social benefits as plants closed, leaving retirees to go hungry and workers to face a bleak future (Jiang 2002).

In the race to be competitive, other companies have followed Apple's lead. The movement of jobs to China triggered a currency crisis leading to

---

40 million of its citizens live in poverty, with an additional 25 million living in extreme poverty, most of whom reside in the rural areas. Mexico's independent union federation, the National Union of Workers (UNT), places unemployment at over 9 million people, a quarter of the work force. Half of those who have jobs are employed by companies that, despite the law, pay less than the minimum wage and offer no health insurance or retirement benefits. While the economic situation differs from country to country, the situation faced by Mexican workers indicates what is occurring globally. In many cases, it is even worse (Bacon 2000).

28. Elisabeth Malkin, "Manufacturing Jobs Are Exiting Mexico," *New York Times*, November 5, 2002.

greater migration of Mexican undocumented workers moving northward (Greider 2001; Landau 2002). In the end, China may not long remain the capitalist's paradise. The Philippines, Vietnam, and Thailand are beginning to offer cheaper labor than China. Ironically, while the average Mexican wage in 2003 was 188 percent higher than in China, by 2013 Mexican hourly wages dropped to 19.6 percent lower. Lower Mexican wages are starting to bring manufacturing jobs back. This massive drop in Mexican wages has led to an increase in its U.S. market share, growing at a faster pace than China over the previous six years. And even though China still maintained the larger share (17.5 percent) of U.S. imports at the close of 2012, Mexico accounted for 12.4 percent over the same period.[29]

Step 2. Reflecting

Who are the poor? The continuously growing income gap has led J. C. Speth, then general secretary of the United Nations Development Programme, to conclude, "If present trends continue, the economic disparity between industrial nations and developing nations will assume proportions which are no longer merely unjust, but inhuman" (Moltmann 1998, 77). And a text from the biblical book of Proverbs reminds us, "Those who oppress the poor curse their Maker, but those honoring God, favor [make a preferential option for] the needy" (Prov. 14:31).

The world today faces no greater global ethical dilemma than the question of poverty. The poor are understood as those deprived of the basic necessities needed to live a life of dignity. According to Clodovis Boff and George Pixley, the poor represent three distinct groups: (1) the socioeconomic poor, comprising those outside the prevailing economic order (the unemployed, beggars, abandoned children, outcasts, prostitutes) and the exploited (industrial workers paid substandard wages, rural workers, seasonal wage-earners, tenant farmers); (2) the sociocultural poor, consisting of blacks, indigenous people, and women; (3) the new poor of industrial societies, encompassing the physically and mentally handicapped abandoned to the streets of huge cities, along with the unemployed, the homeless, the suicidal depressed, the elderly dependent on insufficient state pensions, and the young addicted to drugs (1989, 3–10).

The poor of the world are not necessarily lazy, backward, or underdeveloped, as so many people believe. If that were the case, then their only hope would rest with the generosity of the wealthy who might attempt to help them by providing food, education, or loans. Rather, the poor are made so by economic forces that cause the prosperity of one nation to be rooted in the poverty of other nations. These forces constitute a social phenomenon that enriches the few through the impoverishment of the many.

29. "Mexico Hourly Wages Now Lower Than China's—Study," *Reuters*, April 4, 2013.

Treating workers as objects means that they are defined only by what they contribute to the profitability of the corporation. Seldom are they defined by their humanity. Human rights are first and foremost about removing obstacles so as to engage in trade and commerce rather than achieving human flourishing or self-fulfillment. For reasons like this, neoliberalism is incapable of incorporating the basics of Christianity. How does one reconcile the biblical mandate to forgive debts with the insistence that foreign debts be paid off at the expense of people obtaining basic human needs? Ironically, toward the end of the 1970s in Latin America, as growing foreign debt was negatively impacting the lives of most people, some Catholic and Protestant clergy changed words of the Lord's Prayer from "forgive us our debts" to "forgive us our offenses." Fears existed that Christians, pauperized by the policies of the World Bank and the IMF, might take the Lord Prayer's literally and actually demand that debts be forgiven so that they could have their daily bread. Churches succumbed to economic pressures by neutering the potency of the biblical message (Hinkelammert 1995, 333–34).

Step 3. Praying

The most prominent feature of the Christian worship tradition is the concept of sacrifice, which is rooted within the Jewish faith. Among the many reasons mentioned by the Hebrew Bible for offering a sacrifice (such as tribute, cleansing, thanksgiving, supplication, ordination, and peace), most crucial for Christians were the sin and guilt offerings. Spilling the blood of an unblemished animal for the atonement of sin became the basis for understanding the crucifixion of Christ.[30] For many Euroamerican Christians, the death on the cross of Jesus, "the lamb of God who takes away the sins of the world" (John 1:29), becomes the ultimate sacrifice that serves to reconcile God with sinners. The death of a sinless Jesus, as a substitute for a sinful humanity that deserves God's punishment, restores fellowship between God and humans. Suffering and death become salvific.

Jesus paid by his death so that others might live. But this concept is not limited to the Christ event. For some to live in abundance, others must die. Theologian Mark Lewis Taylor explains, "Nascent capitalism of modernity is a sacrificial economy worshiping money as its fetish, and sacrificing the subjective corporeality of the [marginalized]. So necessary is the sacrifice that it is rationalized as legitimate" (2001, 52).

The center of power can participate in all the riches that life has to offer because those on the periphery die producing those riches. The death of those perceived to be inferior can be viewed as a sacrifice offered to neoliberalism

---

30. For Jews, sin offerings were not given for the atonement of sin. Sins committed against others were handled with an appropriate punishment or restitution formula, while deliberate sins against God were beyond redemption (Num. 15:30–31).

so that a few can enjoy their abundance. Like Christ, the marginalized of the earth die so that those with power and privilege can have life abundantly.

Those suffering on the margins of society epitomize what liberation theologians call God's "crucified people," for they bear in a very real way the brunt of the sins of today's oppressive social and economic structures. As a crucified people, they provide an essential perspective on salvation. Theologians coming from the margins of power insist that God intentionally and regularly chooses the oppressed of history and makes them the principal means of salvation. They maintain that this is done in the same fashion as God chose the "suffering servant," the crucified Christ, to bring salvation to the world (Sobrino 1993, 259–60). God has always chosen the disenfranchised as agents of God's new creation. It was not to the court of Pharaoh that God's will was made known; instead, God chose their Hebrew slaves, the Jews, to reveal God's movement in history. It was not Rome, the most powerful city of the known world, where God chose to perform the miracle of the incarnation, nor was it Jerusalem, the center of Yahweh worship; it was in impoverished Galilee that God chose to proclaim first the message of the Gospels. Nazareth, Jesus' hometown, was so insignificant to the religious life of Judaism that the Hebrew Bible never mentions it (De La Torre and Aponte 2001, 78). This theme of solidarity between the crucified Christ and the victims of oppression permeates Scripture.

Still, liberative ethicists insist that there is nothing salvific about suffering itself, for it tends to reinforce domination. Ethicists such as Delores Williams find the image of Christ as surrogate victim too painful to incorporate into the experience of black women, who during and after slavery were forced and coerced into a similar role (1991, 8–13). Stephanie Mitchem, like other black feminist theologians and womanist thinkers, reminds us, "Suffering in itself is not salvific. It is redemptive only in that it may lead to critical rethinking of meaning or purpose, as might any life crisis. Such reexamination is part of the process of human maturation. However, suffering is a distinctive starting place for thinking about salvation as it brings into sharp focus human experience in relation to God" (2002, 109).

Forgetting that the cross is a symbol of evil allows for the easy romanticization of those who are marginalized as some sort of hyper-Christians for the "cross" that they are forced to bear. Such views tend to offer honor to those suffering, encouraging a form of quietism whereby suffering is stoically borne instead of encouraging praxis that can lead toward the end of suffering. Take, for example, an argument by ethicist Stanley Hauerwas that proves detrimental to disenfranchised communities. He reminds the marginalized that salvation is in fact "a life that freely suffers, that freely serves, because such suffering and service is the hallmark of the Kingdom established by Jesus" (1986, 69–70). All who know disenfranchisement should be concerned when

Euroamericans tell them why their suffering, usually caused by Euroamericans in the first place, makes them better saved Christians!

If salvation exists in the life and resurrection of Jesus Christ as well as in his death, then his crucifixion can be seen for what it was: the unjust repression of a just man by the dominant culture of his time. The crucifixion becomes an act of solidarity with those relegated to exist on the underside of our present economic structure. Ethicists from the margins maintain that the importance of the crucifixion lies in Christ's solidarity with the oppressed, Christ's understanding of how those who are oppressed suffer, reassurance for the disenfranchised that Christ understands their sufferings, and the hope that because of the resurrection, final victory exists.

All too often the romanticization of the crucified people leads to disturbing biblical interpretations that reinforce oppressive structures rather than seek liberation from said structures. This occurs especially when the Bible is read from a position of power and privilege, even to the point of making the condition of those oppressed models for the victims of racism, classism, heterosexism, and sexism. In Mark 12:41–44 and Luke 21:1–4 we are told the story of a poor widow who gives all that she has to the temple. The story of the widow's mite is generally idealized by the dominant culture as an example of Christian behavior for those who are poor. Those who are poor are expected, if they wish to be considered faithful, to give to the church, even if it means that they go without. But missing from the interpretation is how the widow's self-sacrifice is related to the self-indulgence of the religious leaders who profit from her religious commitment.

When we read this story from a place of economic privilege, we ignore how the normative interpretation maintains societal power relationships detrimental to the poor. Yet if we were to read the story of the widow's mite from the perspective of the poor, we would discover that in Mark's account the story of the widow's offering is immediately preceded by Jesus' outrage toward the religious leaders who devour the possessions of widows. Mark writes, "And Jesus said, . . . they [the religious leaders] are devouring the houses of the widows under the pretense of praying at length" (Mark 12:38–40). We discover that Jesus is not praising the widow's offering as a paragon to be emulated by the poor. Instead, Jesus is denouncing a religious social structure that cons the widow out of what little she has. It is bad enough that the biblical text is misinterpreted to mask the sin of the religious leaders who fleece the poor; what is worse is when the poor begin to interpret the text in such a way that they maintain the structures designed to oppress them.

Step 4. Case Studies

1. Rukkibai and her husband, Lakshman Ratohre, are among the wretched of the earth. They live in Omla Naik, India, where he toils in someone else's fields for $1.00 to $1.50 a day. Rukkibai, who works by his side doing the same work, earns 60 cents a day. When she gave birth to their fifth daughter, she sold the baby for 1,100 rupees, roughly $20. Chances are the child was eventually sold into the sex trade or to an orphanage that would offer the child for adoption, most likely to Westerners. Rukkibai is pregnant again. If she has a son, they will keep him, since he will be able to work the fields with his father; if she has a daughter, more likely than not they will again sell the child.[31]

   — What are the ethical implications in selling one's children so that the whole family can survive? If adopted by Westerners, the child will have a more secure financial future. What importance does this have? Is being adopted by the West a good thing? It is possible that the daughter might be raised to be a prostitute. Is it still worth taking a chance that she might be adopted by Westerners?

   — Some argue that poor women should be sterilized to prevent such dilemmas. How ethically valid is this solution? Why? Would it be better if the poor women of the world had access to contraceptives or abortions? If so, what about the religious sensitivities of her communities that might oppose any form of family planning? If the West helps establish family planning programs, does this mean that it is imposing its values on the world?

   — Do first-world nations have any obligations toward Rukkibai's family? Is her poverty linked to the abundance in the West? If so, how? If not, why not?

2. On February 7, 2012, ABC broadcasted an investigative report on Foxconn on its popular news program *Nightline*. The show explored the working conditions at Foxconn, looking for underage workers, hazardous work environment, overcrowded living conditions, suicides, long hours, and little pay. What they discovered was that during Monday morning's recruiting sessions, some three thousand young Chinese workers lined up each week at the Foxconn's gates hoping to obtain one of these supposedly horrid jobs. If working at Foxconn is so terrible, why is there such a demand to work there? A young Chinese man studying in the United States provides a possible explanation:

---

31. Raymond Bonner, "Poor Families Selling Baby Girls Was Economic Boon," *New York Times*, June 17, 2001.

My aunt worked several years in what Americans call "sweat shops." It was hard work. . . . Do you know what my aunt did before she worked in one of these factories? She was a prostitute. Circumstances of birth are unfortunately random, and she was born in a very rural region. Most jobs . . . were held by men. Women and young girls, because of lack of education and economic opportunities, had to find other "employment." The idea of working in a "sweat shop" compared to that old lifestyle is an improvement, in my opinion. I know that my aunt would rather be "exploited" by an evil capitalist boss for a couple of dollars than have her body be exploited by several men for pennies. . . . Anyway, now my aunt has been living in New York for one year after saving up money for a plane ticket and visa, and she is wonderfully happy to have escaped Asia and reunited with our family. None of this would be possible if it wasn't for that "sweat shop."[32]

— Are companies such as Foxconn the salvation of the ultrapoor? Would closing these factories create greater misery among workers who come from rural areas? Would demanding higher wages mean the hiring of fewer workers?

— Do we consider the workers' conditions at Foxconn to be horrible because we are comparing them with U.S. work standards? Are the conditions at Foxconn better than the alternatives? Are the working conditions at Foxconn any better or worse than those at other subcontractors? In the messiness of life, is one form of exploitation better than another?

— How should we respond to the young Chinese man studying in the United States? To his aunt? Do they represent the views of all Foxconn workers? How do we proceed in seeking justice? Should the focus be on shutting down sweatshops? Reforming them? Is this more an issue of sexism and how women's bodies are globally commoditized? If so, how should we proceed?

— Shortly after numerous exposés in early 2012 on the poor working conditions at Foxconn, wages were raised, work hours were shortened, and chairs with backs were provided at workstations. Are these changes cosmetic or structural? What else should be done? Is shaming corporations the best strategy to bring about justice-based change?

32. Pogue, "What Cameras Inside Foxconn Found."

Are these reforms a commitment to justice, to the workers, or is it simply fixing an image problem?

— *Nightline* is produced by ABC News, which is owned by the Walt Disney Company, whose chief executive sits on Apple's board of directors. Also, the Steve Jobs Trust is Disney's largest shareholder. In like fashion, Apple pays six figures to the Fair Labor Association to conduct independent audits on Foxconn's working conditions. Fair Labor Associates notified Foxconn well in advance as to when inspectors were going to tour the factories. Are there too many conflicts of interests for these investigations and audits to be objective?

3. Lisa Rahman is a nineteen-year-old who used to work at the Shah Makhdum garment factory in Dhaka, Bangladesh, assembling "Winnie the Pooh" shirts. She was paid the equivalent of 5 cents per shirt to assemble shirts that the Walt Disney Company retails at $17.99 each. In 2002, when workers united to publicly complain of poor working conditions, Disney canceled all future work orders, leaving workers like Lisa Rahman with few options.[33] This wage theft resulted in different protest demonstrations, more recently in August 2012, when garment workers took to the streets protesting wage cuts on already pitifully low wages, considered to be the lowest in the world. They were brutally suppressed by the police and paramilitary officers. Labor leaders disappeared or turned up tortured and dead. And yet ironically, this poor nation of Bangladesh, once irrelevant in the global economy, is now a major exporter of clothes, accounting for 80 percent of manufacturing exports and some three million jobs. This $19-billion-a-year industry is expected to triple by 2020.[34] Not surprisingly, Disney, the world's largest licensor, with sales close to $40 billion, did not leave Dhaka, nor did the company address workers' grievances. In April 2013 one of the factories making Disney garments[35] in Rana Plaza collapsed, killing over 1,100 Bangladesh workers, mostly women and girls (80 percent of garment workers are female, about 2.5 million), and injuring approximately 2,500 more. Even though large cracks appeared in the building beforehand, the lure of profit kept the factories operating. Rather than dealing with the consequences of the factory collapse, Disney chose to cut Bangladesh from its supply chain.

---

33. Gary Gentile, "Group Slams Disney for Sweatshop Conditions in Bangladesh," *Associated Press State & Local Wire*, October 7, 2002.

34. Jim Yardley, "Export Powerhouse Feels Pangs of Labor Strife," *New York Times*, August 24, 2012.

35. Other labels and documents have connected this particular factory with Benetton, Children's Place, Calvin Klein, Tommy Hilfiger, and Cato Fashions.

After all, less than 1 percent of the factories in Bangladesh were used by Disney's contractors.[36]

— The collapse of the factory was due mainly to the negligence of the building engineers and the factory owner. Do companies such as Disney share in the responsibility? Why or why not? Does Disney have any responsibility toward these workers? Should Disney abide by worker demands? Which is more important: the basic rights of the workers or the profit margin of Disney? Is Disney ultimately responsible for its refusal to pay more for the garments and to demand that seamstresses receive a more just wage?

— Is it ethical for a Christian to own stock in a company such as Disney or mutual funds (even in the form of a retirement fund) when the profits earned by that Christian stem from the impoverishment of the world's most vulnerable members? Given that most garment factory owners serve in a parliament and/or operate news sources, how effective would any action taken by global corporations be?

— Should a Christian profit from stock dividends paid out by companies, such as Apple, whose race to the bottom is responsible for creating dangerous working conditions in China and unemployed workers in the United States? Why or why not? Do multinational corporations have any obligations toward any particular nation-state? If so, what type of obligations? What ethical responsibilities, if any, do dividend earners have in how transnational corporations operate? Does a moral connection exist between the person forced into poverty by the drive to increase dividend earnings on stocks and the person receiving those dividends?

— What responsibility, if any, do companies whose garments are cheaply made in substandard and dangerous factories have to the women and girls killed when the factories catch fire or collapse? Do consumers have any responsibility when they purchase garments or merchandise made at the cost of blood? If a boycott against such garments and merchandise were implemented, would the workers suffer more if they lost their jobs due to the resulting lack of consumer demand? These factory jobs have been a source of liberation for many poor rural women who are not even given a surname at birth. Some of these women have found a level of agency never before experienced, making the garment

36. Susan Berfield, "For Retailers, Getting Out of Bangladesh Isn't So Easy," *Businessweek*, May 2, 2013.

industry a source of empowerment. Can companies such as Disney, along with local factory owners, actually be seen as liberators?

— Since the 2013 collapse of the Rana Plaza factory, mounting global pressure led several of the world's largest apparel companies to improve working conditions by paying for fire safety and building improvements. Additionally, the Bangladesh government has pledged to raise wages (which are the lowest in the world) and allow trade unions to form with fewer difficulties.[37] Must blood (usually that of the oppressed) flow in order for justice to be considered? Walmart, whose labels and purchase orders were found among the debris, has refused to join other global apparel companies in their broad safety plan.[38] Does Walmart have a right not to join its competitors and implement its own safety standards? If so, how effective can they be expected to be?

4. Nelly Kwamboka of Kenya wailed, cursed, and collapsed in anguish at the foot of the bed where her young son had just died of malaria. Next to her, three other children were battling for their lives.[39] If malaria does not kill a child, it often marks the beginning of a lifetime of illness and poverty. As malaria breeds poverty, poverty breeds malaria. If a child has a malaria episode five to ten times throughout the year, and the anti-malarial drug (Coartem, Riamet) to treat it costs $8 to $10, the price of treatment comes to about $100 a year, about a third of one's yearly income if based on $1 a day. Now multiply the cost of medicine by four or five children, and there is no money left for anything else—housing, food, clothing.[40] Bill Gates, former CEO of Microsoft, was listed by *Forbes* in 2011 as the richest individual living in the United States, with an estimated worth of $59 billion, greater than the gross national product of several countries. His net worth is equivalent to the combined net worth of the bottom 40 percent of U.S. households. In 1999 he started the Bill and Melinda Gates Foundation with $32.8 billion in assets. In its first four years the Gates Foundation distributed $6.2 billion, of which more than half ($3.2 billion) was earmarked for improving health in two-thirds world nations.[41] In 2003 the foundation pledged $168 million for malaria research. By 2012 the foundation was providing $750 million to fight global AIDS, tuberculosis, and malaria. Thanks in part to the Gates

---

37. Steve Greenhouse and Jim Yardley, "Global Retailers Join Safety Plan for Bangladesh," *New York Times*, May 13, 2013.

38. Steve Greenhouse, "As Firms Line Up on Factories, Wal-Mart Plans Solo Effort," *New York Times*, May 14, 2013.

39. John Oywa, "Kenya: A Predictable and Preventable Killer," *Africa News*, August 11, 2002.

40. Alex Perry, "Malaria: Epidemic on the Run," *Time*, September 24, 2011.

41. Stephanie Strom, "Gates Billions Reshape Health of World's Poor," *New York Times*, July 13, 2003.

Foundation, malaria deaths sharply decreased from a peak of 1.8 million in 2004 to 1.2 million in 2010.[42] Some people have criticized Gates for participating in a public relations campaign to polish the image of a ruthless monopolist, and others are quick to point out that the IRS rewards philanthropy by allowing tax deductions for donated funds. Yet the generosity of the Gates Foundation has contributed to rising vaccination rates in some of the poorest countries of the world.

— Are the criticisms of Gates justified? For the Kwambokas of the world, does it matter why he is donating money if its outcome is saving lives?

— Fourteenth-century Dominican nun Catherine of Siena prayed, "How can these wretched evil people share their possessions with the poor when they are already stealing from them?" (1980, 33). Is Gates being generous with money obtained through Microsoft's monopoly of a computer operating system? In other words, is he simply being generous with other people's monies?

---

42. Jason Koebler, "Worldwide Malaria Deaths Double WHO Estimates," *U.S. News & World Report*, February 2, 2012.

Chapter 6

War

STEP 1. Observing

Major General Smedley D. Butler, USMC, was the most decorated Marine in U.S. history at the time of his death in 1940. He fought for the United States in the Philippines, China, Central America, the Caribbean, and in France during World War I. He was also a critic of U.S. military adventurism, what today we would call "empire building." He said, "War is a racket," a statement that served as the title of his antiwar classic (Butler 1935). In a 1933 speech Butler said,

> A racket is best described, I believe, as something that is not what it seems to the majority of people. Only a small inside group knows what it is about. It is conducted for the benefit of the very few at the expense of the masses. . . . [Basically] the flag follows the dollar and the soldiers follow the flag. . . . I spent most of my time being a high class muscle-man for Big Business, for Wall Street and for the Bankers. In short, I was a racketeer, a gangster for capitalism. . . . I helped make Mexico, especially Tampico, safe for American oil interests in 1914. I helped make Haiti and Cuba a decent place for the National City Bank boys to collect revenues in. I helped in the raping of half a dozen Central American republics for the benefits of Wall Street. The record of racketeering is long. I helped purify Nicaragua for the international banking house of Brown Brothers in 1909–1912. . . . I brought light to the Dominican Republic for American sugar interests in 1916. In China I helped to see to it that Standard Oil went its way unmolested. . . . Looking back on it, I feel that I could have given Al Capone a few hints.[1]

According to Butler, the most powerful military force the world has ever known exists for one reason: to make sure that the majority of the world's resources flow to our shores. If the United States were to be invaded, then yes, we should defend ourselves. But if we look at all the military conflicts before and since World War II, we see that we were the ones doing the invading. We entered other countries to protect and secure neoliberalism.

---

1. http://www.fas.org/man/smedley.htm.

War, in most cases, remains an attempt by one nation to dominate another by superior military power, usually to procure or protect property rights, which can include both resources and labor. To this end, the United States, the prime expansionist power since 1945, ensures its peace and security through the freedom of the open market. Peace is crucial to achieving and maintaining prosperity for the dominant culture. To protect this *Pax Americana*, a superior military force must be maintained to ensure that a nation with only 6 percent of the world's population can continue to benefit from 50 percent of the world's resources. When President George W. Bush announced his National Security Strategy in September 2002, he committed the United States to lead other nations toward "the single sustainable model for national success," meaning the model of the open market through free trade, or, we might say, the preservation of neoliberalism through economic or military force.

The expansion and preservation of a new economic world order will at times require a regime change in nations that refuse to succumb to neoliberalism. The wake of the 9/11 terrorist attack ushered in a new doctrine for engaging nations hostile to U.S. supremacy, granting the United States the right to start a war through a preemptive attack on any nation that might pose a possible future danger. In effect, American exceptionalism reserves for itself the right to engage in military action against any hypothetical threat before any and all other avenues for conflict resolution (such as the United Nations) have been exhausted. "First strike" to bring about "regime change" replaces the "containment"[2] and "deterrent"[3] strategies of the latter part of the last century. In reality, this new doctrine is but a repackaging of the U.S. foreign policy toward Latin America during the early twentieth century—a policy that reserved the right to determine what constituted a threat to U.S. interests and security in "our" hemisphere and then to act unilaterally.

Under President Theodore Roosevelt (1858–1919), the nexus of the "first strike" and "regime change" doctrines took place. At that time, "gunboat diplomacy," as it was known, went by the slogan "Speak softly but carry a big stick." During the last century every country bordering the Caribbean and several countries in South America were invaded by U.S. forces (or covertly subverted by the CIA) to bring about regime change when those countries chose to follow their own destinies in ways not seen favorable to the United

---

2. The policy of coexisting with the threat of the Soviet Union while preventing the expansion of communism.

3. The policy of building U.S. defenses to assure a devastating response if attacked, thus keeping the Soviet Union from aggressively acting.

States.[4] In some cases, brutal dictatorships and military juntas were installed after the United States deposed democratically elected presidents, as in Guatemala in 1954. Millions of peasants, students, church leaders, and intellectuals were abducted, tortured, or killed while opposing the U.S.-backed installed governments. It can be argued, given this background, that the 2003 attack on Iraq is better understood as a preventive measure than as a preemptive strategy.

Any discussion of the issues of war among people at the margins takes on a quite different tone. The argument moves from a just-war debate to a discussion of racism and classism, as military violence usually stimulates and is stimulated by race and class oppressions. The margins of society raise issues of the re-creation of the other's history (racism) and of the spoils of war (classism). These concerns played themselves out during the 2003 war on Iraq, which we will now explore in greater detail.

For violence to occur, history must be re-created, usually to the disadvantage of those who will become the victims of war. The nation initiating the military conflict must reconstruct itself as the defender of virtue and appear to have no ulterior motive for gaining from the military conflict. Actions undertaken that may have made the war inevitable are conveniently forgotten.

Take, for example, comments made by Colin Powell, then U.S. secretary of state, in a 2002 interview with the *New York Times*. Powell made a case for the moral right to attack Iraq: "Our record and our history is not one of going out looking for conflict, it is not one of undertaking pre-emptive acts for the purpose of seizing another person's territory, or to impose our will on someone else. Our history and our tradition is always one of defending our interest."[5]

But history is usually the meganarrative of the dominant culture. Conveniently forgotten by Powell was the history concerning the U.S. invasion of Mexico. The justification for this massive land acquisition was based on a theology that saw the dominant Euroamerican culture as having been chosen by God. This concept, known as Manifest Destiny, taught that God had intended Euroamericans to acquire the entire continent. The expansionist war against Mexico was then masked by the re-creation of the nation's historical meganarrative. Absent from the rhetoric is the true motive for the

---

4. During the twentieth century, either U.S. military incursions (*italicized*) or covert/indirect operations (**boldfaced**) occurred in the following countries so as to bring about regime change or protect the status quo: Cuba, *1906, 1912, 1917, 1933,* **1960, 1961**; Costa Rica, **1948**; Dominican Republic, **1904**, *1916–1924,* **1930, 1963,** *1965*; El Salvador, **1932, 1944, 1960, 1980, 1984**; Granada, *1983*; Guatemala, **1921, 1954,** *1960,* **1963, 1966**; Haiti, *1915,* **1994**; Honduras, *1905, 1907,* **1911, 1943, 1980**; Mexico, *1905, 1914, 1917*; Nicaragua, **1909,** *1910, 1912, 1926,* **1934, 1981, 1983, 1984**; Panama, *1908, 1918, 1925,* **1941, 1981, 1989.**

5. James Dao, "Threats and Responses: Perspectives; Powell Defends a First Strike as Iraq Option," *New York Times,* September 8, 2002.

Mexican invasion: acquisition of land and its resources, specifically the gold of California, the silver of Nevada, the oil of Texas, and all the natural harbors needed for commerce along the western coast.

In the case of Iraq, the CIA in 1963 conducted a "regime change" by collaborating with the relatively small but anticommunist Baath Party to overthrow Abel Karim Kassem. Once in power, the Baath Party unleashed a bloodbath, murdering leftist sympathizers named on lists of suspected communists provided by the CIA. This "housecleaning" allowed Western corporations such as Mobil, Bechtel, and British Petroleum to conduct business with Baghdad for the first time. By 1968, infighting among Baath leaders threatened business interests, so with CIA backing Saddam Hussein seized power.

Even though the United States knew that Saddam Hussein supported terrorists, killed his own people, and was attempting to build nuclear weapons, Donald Rumsfeld (as President Reagan's special envoy to the Middle East) traveled in 1983 to meet Hussein in hopes of establishing warmer relations. Later, as President George W. Bush's secretary of defense, Rumsfeld executed the war against Hussein. But in 1983 Iraq was seen as strategic to U.S. attempts to thwart Iran's growing influence in the crucial oil-producing states along the Persian Gulf. During the Iran-Iraq war (1980–1988) the United States provided Hussein with satellite photography of the battleground. The U.S. Commerce Department reports that during the early 1980s the United States provided Iraq with numerous shipments of "bacteria/fungi/protozoa" that could be used to create biological weapons (such as anthrax), along with 1.5 million atropine injections to be used against the effects of chemical weapons. When Hussein used chemical weapons against the Kurdish rebels in 1988, the Reagan administration responded by blaming Iran, only later relenting when mounting evidence pointed to Iraq.[6]

Until the eve of the 1991 Gulf War, the United States had been providing Iraq with billions of dollars in financing and millions of dollars in equipment to build Iraq's missiles, conventional bombs, and nuclear, chemical, and biological weapons—all to stem the influence of Iran.[7] Most damning was the proposed mid-1990 sale, approved by the U.S. Department of Commerce, of

---

6. See Christopher Dickey and Evan Thomas, "How Saddam Happened," *Newsweek*, September 23, 2002; Patrick E. Tyler, "Officers Say U.S. Aided Iraq in War Despite Use of Gas," *New York Times*, August 18, 2002.

7. Iraq, after being removed in 1983 from the list of terrorist-supporting nations, became the largest recipient of the U.S. Department of Agriculture's Commodity Credit Corporation (CCC) credits, acquiring 20 percent of all guarantees granted between 1984 and 1989. By 1989, the senior President Bush signed National Security Directive 26, calling for "improved economic and political ties with Iraq." This improved relationship meant an approval of $1 billion in CCC credits. When the Gulf War broke out shortly afterward, Hussein reneged on a total of $2 billion in CCC loans, leaving U.S. taxpayers to foot the bill (Hartung 1994, 238, 241).

"skull furnaces," used to produce the components of nuclear weapons (Hartung 1994, 222, 232).[8]

Before military conflict began in Iraq, a narrative had to be created, and then re-created when it became obvious that the first narrative was faulty. According to Douglas J. Feith, undersecretary of defense for policy from 2001 until 2005, President Bush gave his first major speech on Iraq on September 12, 2002 (a year after 9/11). For the next year, Bush gave nine major talks on Iraq. Each speech, on average, contained fourteen paragraphs stressing Saddam Hussein as an enemy, aggressor, tyrant, and danger. The danger to the United States, of course, was weapons of mass destructions (WMD). But by the fall of 2003, a few months after Hussein's overthrow, no stockpiles of WMD were found. A radical shift in the narrative was needed. Starting in September 2003 and until September 2004, Bush gave fifteen major talks on Iraq. On average, the numbers of paragraphs devoted to Hussein's threat was one, while the number devoted to promoting democracy was eleven (Feith 2008, 475–77). The failure to find WMD meant that the original narrative to go to war was at best wrong, at worst a lie, hence the need to re-create the past by developing a new narrative that focused on fostering democracy.

In addition to the need to re-create the past there is the desire to profit from the present—"To the victors of war go the spoils." In the case of Iraq, the spoils included a proven reserve of 112 billion barrels of crude oil, the largest in the world outside Saudi Arabia. The first major contract for the reconstruction of Iraq, worth $680 million, was awarded to Bechtel, with only token competition. Bechtel's chief executive served on the U.S. Commander in Chief's Export Council, and a Bechtel director, George Shultz, served as the first secretary of state in the first Bush administration, raising serious issues of impropriety. More questionable are contracts estimated to have reached $60 billion that were initially awarded with no public bids or discussion, and sometimes secretly, to politically connected firms such as Halliburton, directed by former vice president Dick Cheney from 1995 until 2000. While Cheney was defense secretary (1989–1993) under George H. W. Bush, he asked then Halliburton subsidiary Brown & Root to conduct a study of the cost effectiveness of outsourcing military operations to private contractors. Based on the study produced, the Pentagon hired Brown & Root to implement the outsourcing plan, only for Cheney to then go to Halliburton, the parent company, as its new CEO in 1995.

Kellogg Brown & Root (KBR)[9] was among the first contractors to prosper from the Iraq war and occupation, awarded $33 billion to support military

---

8. The sale was called off after Stephen Bryen of the *Philadelphia Inquirer* wrote about the transaction, bringing pressure upon the first Bush administration to cancel the agreement two weeks before Iraq invaded Kuwait.

9. Brown & Root, through mergers, was renamed "Kellogg Brown & Root." Although Halliburton continued to own KBR during the height of the Iraq war, it sold the company in 2007.

bases.[10] The work conducted by KBR was so shoddy that it brought harm to U.S. soldiers. For example, the family of Ryan Maseth, a Green Beret staff sergeant, was informed by an army criminal investigator that their son's death on January 2, 2008, was a case of negligent homicide by KBR. Maseth was electrocuted while taking a shower at his base in Baghdad. As Maseth showered, an underground water pump short-circuited, and electricity traveled through to the water. Maseth was found on the shower floor after suffering a heart attack. His parents believed that his death could have been prevented if KBR contracted qualified electricians and plumbers to work at the barracks rather than pursue profits by employing unqualified personnel.[11] KBR did not challenge the merits of the couple's claims, but instead argued that although it had the maintenance contract for the building, the U.S. Army decided not to make the building electrically safe. U.S. District judge Nora Barry Fischer ruled in July 2012 that KBR could not be held liable because military commanders, and not the contractor, made the decisions on where to house soldiers and whether buildings with substandard electrical systems were suitable or not.[12] Shortly after the ruling, Robert Matthews, attorney for KBR, filed a motion that a federal judge should dismiss fifty-five pending lawsuits by military personnel and veterans, arguing that KBR should be exempt from litigation because it deserves the same immunity given government entities and personnel. This is KBR's second attempt to toss out the lawsuits, which involve more than two hundred plaintiffs in forty-two states.[13] The message becomes clear: Corporate profits trump the lives of military personnel.

Attempting to obtain immunity from persecution for wrongdoings for companies like KBR contributes to a continuous slide toward privatizing future wars. Even during 2007, when the U.S. military presence in Iraq surged to 160,000 soldiers, U.S.-paid private contractors exceeded American combat troops, with more than 180,000 on the ground. The largest employer of contractors was KBR. These contractors are supposed to support the combat troops, but they remain employees, employees who can jeopardize the mission, as in 2004, when drivers refused to take food rations to forces in a combat zone. Just as troubling are those contractors working for heavily armed private security companies, such as Blackwater, Triple Canopy, and Erinys, which at times found themselves engaged in firefights with insurgents (twenty-one security firms were responsible for deploying 10,800 armed personnel). As Peter Singer, a Brookings Institution scholar, quipped, "This is

---

10. Rod Nordland, "Iraq, Rebuilding Its Economy, Shuns U.S. Firms," *New York Times*, November 13, 2009.

11. Peter Spiegel, "Army Investigator Cited 'Negligent Homicide' by KBR," *Los Angeles Times*, January 23, 2009.

12. Joe Mandak, "Judge Nixes Suit in Soldier's Iraq Electrocution," *Associated Press*, July 16, 2012.

13. Patricia Kime, "KBR Seeks Dismissal of Lawsuits over Burn Pits," *Air Force Times*, July 16, 2012.

not the coalition of the willing. It's the coalition of the billing."[14] The Iraq war became the first outsourced war that relied heavily on corporations (specifically the company previously run by then–vice president Dick Cheney) at a substantial profit, paid for with U.S. tax dollars.

Besides building and maintaining military bases, KBR was given control of the entire Iraqi oil operation, including distribution. Such acts violate international law. The World Trade Organization forbids discrimination against companies of its member nations in the awarding of contracts. Ironically, Halliburton conducted business with Iraq (as well as with two other members of the so-called axis of evil, Iran and North Korea) during Cheney's term as the head of the corporation. In addition to being fined $3.8 million in 1995 for reexporting U.S. goods through a foreign subsidiary to Libya in clear violation of U.S. sanctions, Halliburton has been accused of overcharging the U.S. government for work conducted during the 1990s, resulting in a $2 million settlement to ward off criminal prosecution for price gouging.[15]

In 2009 the U.S. government agreed to pay nearly $1 million to Bunnatine Greenhouse, a former top Army Corps of Engineers contracting official, who charged that she was demoted when she objected to a $7 billion no-bid contract granted to Halliburton to repair Iraq oil fields, thus bringing to a close a six-year legal battle.[16] She charged that Halliburton was awarded contracts without following rules designed to ensure competition and fair prices to the government. In one case that she witnessed, Halliburton representatives were allowed to sit in as army officials discussed the terms of the contract that the company was to receive.[17]

To make matters worse, KBR has been accused of defrauding the U.S. government by billing everything from meals that it did not serve, to inflated gas prices, to bill duplication, to excessive administrative costs. Even though the Pentagon's own auditors identified more than $250 million in unjustified or excessive charges, the army decided to reimburse KBR for nearly all of the distributed items on its $2.41 billion no-bid contract. Henry A. Waxman

14. T. Christian Miller, "Contractors Outnumber Troops in Iraq," *Los Angeles Times*, July 4, 2007.

15. Bob Herbert, "Dancing with the Devil," *New York Times*, May 22, 2003; Michael Kinsley, "To the Victors Go the Spoils," *New York Times*, April 20, 2003; Neela Banerjee, "2 in House Question Halliburton's Iraq Fuel Prices," *New York Times*, October 16, 2003; Don Van Natta Jr., "High Payments to Halliburton for Fuel in Iraq," *New York Times*, December 10, 2003; Douglas Jehl, "Evidence Is Cited of Overcharging in Iraq Contract," *New York Times*, December 12, 2003; Joel Brinkley and Eric Schmitt, "Halliburton Will Repay U.S. Excess Charges for Troops' Meals," *New York Times*, February 3, 2004.

16. Erik Eckholm, "Army Corps Agrees to Pay Whistle-Blower in Iraq Case," *New York Times*, July 29, 2011.

17. Erik Eckholm, "A Top U.S. Contracting Official for the Army Calls for an Inquiry in the Halliburton Case," *New York Times*, October 25, 2004. The awarding of no-bid contracts is not limited to times of war. KBR received a questionable $500 million contract from the Defense Department after Hurricane Katrina to do major repairs at Navy facilities along the Gulf Coast. See Philip Shenon, "Official Vows Investigation of No-Bid Relief Contracts." *New York Times*, September 14, 2005.

(D-CA), then the ranking minority member of the House Committee on Government Reform, probably said it best: "Halliburton gouged the taxpayer, government auditors caught the company red-handed, yet the Pentagon ignored the auditors and paid Halliburton hundreds of millions of dollars and a huge bonus."[18] More recently, in 2009, Halliburton agreed to repay the Pentagon $6.3 million in subcontractor overcharges when it discovered that two workers were receiving kickbacks from vendors.[19] Yet this amount pales in comparison to a Pentagon criminal inquiry that accuses KBR of overcharging $61 million for gasoline deliveries and $67 million in overcharged cafeteria services.[20]

Both Bechtel and Halliburton also received big loan guarantees ($178.1 million for Bechtel, $481.4 million for Halliburton, also $675 million for Enron) from the Export-Import Bank, a federal agency, thanks to legislation signed by President George W. Bush, to provide up to $100 billion in international trade assistance, with taxpayers' monies, in effect subsidizing these foreign capitalist ventures.[21] Other transnational corporations have also benefited from the war in Iraq. In return, the executives and/or political action committees of the seventy companies to receive lucrative government contracts for billions of dollars in reconstruction work in either Iraq or Afghanistan contributed at least $500,000 to the 2000 Bush-Cheney election campaign. Nine of the ten biggest contract recipients (Bechtel and Halliburton were at the top of the list) employed senior governmental officials or had close ties to government agencies and the U.S. Congress.[22] And, as already mentioned, most of the contracts awarded were conducted secretively, without competitive bidding, and without a single agency supervising the contracting process for the government.

Since the American-led invasion of Iraq, almost all of Iraq's largest reconstruction projects have been under U.S. control. Nevertheless, as the war began to wind down and attempts to rival Saudi Arabia as the world's top oil producer picked up steam, many more rebuilding contracts became available for drilling hundreds of new oil wells, repairing thousands of miles of pipelines, and constructing giant floating oil terminals in the Persian Gulf.

---

18. James Glanz, "Army to Pay Halliburton Unit Most Costs Disputed by Audit," *New York Times*, February 27, 2006.

19. James Glanz, "Officials at Saudi Company and Ex-Employee at Halliburton Unit Accused in Kickback Inquiry," *New York Times*, March 14, 2006; "Halliburton to Pay Pentagon $6.3M," *Associated Press*, February 11, 2009.

20. James Glanz, "Cost of Taking Fuel to Iraq Is Questioned in New Audit," *New York Times*, November 7, 2006; "Halliburton: $61M Overcharge?" *CBS News*, December 5, 2007.

21. Leslie Wayne, "A Guardian of Jobs or a 'Reverse Robin Hood'?" *New York Times*, September 1, 2002.

22. Edmund L. Andrews and Elizabeth Becker, "Bush Got $500,000 from Companies That Got Contracts, Study Finds," *New York Times*, October 31, 2003; Douglas Jehl, "Insiders' New Firm Consults on Iraq," *New York Times*, September 30, 2003.

It is estimated that between 2010 and 2015 these contracts could amount to $10 billion.[23] A wave of U.S. companies has swept into Iraq to pursue these contracts, expecting most of them to go to them.[24] War, commoditized within the neoliberal paradigm, has indeed become a profitable venture.

But even as military contractors face federal budget cuts as the United States withdraws from two wars, billions can still be made in the name of security. Half a dozen military contractors, including General Dynamics, Lockheed Martin, Northrop Grumman, and Raytheon, hope to secure Homeland Security Department contracts for the continuous militarization of the border between the United States and Mexico. The need for drones mounted with tracking devices surveying the 1,969-mile border can mean an economic boon for these military contractors. In 1961 President Dwight D. Eisenhower warned the American public of the "military-industrial complex," which exists in our own times. Eisenhower raised the concern that the defense industry quest for profit, coupled with a close working relationship with politicians, would pervert American foreign policy while causing stagnation in the domestic economy. Not only was the economic well-being of the nation threatened, but so too was its spiritual health. Between 1998 and 2011 military spending doubled. By 2012, U.S. military spending surpassed the $711 billion mark, representing about 41 percent of the world's total military spending (SIPRI 2012, 9), equal to the next fourteen countries combined,[25] a figure that more than likely would gravely disturb Eisenhower were he alive today.

Additionally, most of the weapons used throughout the world are made in the United States. According to a study conducted by the Congressional Research Service, an arm of the Library of Congress, weapon sales by the United States tripled in 2011, driven by major arms sales to Persian Gulf allies. Overseas U.S. weapon sales totaled $66.3 billion, more than three-fourths of the entire global arms market. Russia, a distant second, sold only $4.8 billion (Grimmett and Kerr 2012, ii). The United States is the major exporter of lethal weapons, selling the mechanisms by which so many of the world's marginalized die.

What may be profitable for corporations was extremely costly to the average person caught in the grinding of war. In Iraq, the strongman in

---

23. Timothy Williams, "U.S. Companies Race to Take Advantage of Iraqi Oil Bonanza," *New York Times*, January 14, 2010.

24. Among the U.S. companies seeking these lucrative contracts are Halliburton, KBR, Bechtel, Baker Hughes, Weatherford International, Schlumberger, Parsons, Foster Wheeler, and Fluor, even though companies such as Halliburton, KBR, Bechtel, and Parsons have been singled out by the Special Inspector General for Iraq for criticism during their previous work during earlier no-bid reconstruction work.

25. China ($143B), Russia ($71.9B), United Kingdom ($62.7B), France ($62.5B), Japan ($59.3B), Saudi Arabia ($48.2B), India ($46.8B), Germany ($46.7B), Brazil ($35.4B), Italy ($34.5B), South Korea ($30.8B), Australia ($26.7B), Canada ($24.7B), and Turkey ($17.9B) total to $711.1 billion.

charge before the war was replaced with a newer strongman cloaked in a quasi-democratic veneer, overseeing a country rife with sectarian abuses and violence. Al Qaeda, almost nonexistent in Iraq before the war, has a presence now, making the country more dangerous to American interests. With the enactment of the 2011 fiscal budget, a total of $1.283 trillion was spent for military operations, base security, foreign aid, embassy costs, and veterans' healthcare ($806 billion, or 63 percent, went for Iraq operations; $444 billion, or 35 percent, went for Afghan operations; $29 billion, or 2 percent, went to enhance base security). According to government projections, the cost of war, through the 2021 fiscal budget, is expected to total between about $1.56 trillion and $1.88 trillion (Belasco 2012, 1, 31). Not included in these figures are the incurred obligations for veterans' medical and disability through 2051. If these numbers are added in, the total cost of American wars (not including interest) would instead be between $3.7 and $4.4 trillion (Eisenhower Research Project 2011, 6).

Just as costly is the measure in human lives. An extremely conservative estimate of those killed or wounded due to these military conflicts through 2011 stands at 225,000 dead and about 365,000 wounded (Eisenhower Research Project 2011, 2). Of those fatalities, 6,658 (as of March 2013) were Americans. Even those who survive war are left with psychological scars. In 2012 more active-duty soldiers committed suicide than those who died during battle.[26] This tragedy is not limited to American soldiers. More British soldiers and veterans took their own lives in 2012 than died fighting in Afghanistan over the same period.[27]

One way to deal with this phenomenon is to medicate combat personnel. Between 2005 and 2011 there has been a 682 percent increase in the number of psychoactive drugs (antipsychotics, mood stabilizers, sedatives, stimulants) prescribed to active U.S. troops. Compare this with a 22 percent increase among the civilian population. These prescriptions are dispensed in ways not approved by the Food and Drug Administration, nor do they meet the usual psychiatric standards of practice.[28] We are literally drugging our soldiers so that they can conduct war.

As bloody as war can be, new technology is leading the United States into a new phase of eliminating potential threats to the nation without the apparent need of committing boots on the ground. War can now be delivered to the enemy from the sky via the semi-secretive drone program. However, as cost effective such a program may appear to be, it raises some disturbing questions. Take the example of Anwar al-Awlaki and Samir Khan, two American

26. Richard A. Friedman, "Wars on Drugs," *New York Times*, April 6, 2013.
27. "UK Soldiers and Veterans Suicides' Outstrip Afghan Deaths," *BBC News*, July 14, 2013.
28. Friedman, "Wars on Drugs."

citizens. On the morning of September 30, 2011, the two Americans were headed toward their trucks at a remote desert patch, the Jawf Province, in Yemen. From a secret CIA airstrip in Saudi Arabia, a group of U.S. drones, operated from thousands of miles away, took off and headed toward their targets. Shortly afterward, for the first time since the American Civil War, the U.S. government deliberately killed American citizens as wartime enemies without a trial. One month after the September 2011 attack another drone mistakenly killed al-Awlaki's sixteen-year-old American-born son, Abdulrahman, who ventured into the desert in search of his father.[29]

The use of drones is efficient and cost-effective, allowing the United States to continue its far-flung global wars. But should we equate the ethical with efficiency or cost-effectiveness? It is true that Anwar al-Awlaki was suspected of being an operative for Al Qaeda, although his father, Nasser al-Awlaki, argues to the contrary, pointing out that no U.S. court ever reviewed the U.S. government's claims or examined any evidence of criminal wrongdoing.[30] Still, Samir Khan, according to U.S. officials, was not a significant threat to warrant targeted assassination[31] and Abdulrahman's only crime was being Anwar's son. American citizens' constitutional rights are being denied; they are being sentenced to death without any charges being lodged, trials conducted, or judicial process followed. U.S. technology has advanced to such a degree that enemies can now be surgically eliminated. Such strikes routinely rain fire from the skies over places like Pakistan and Yemen. White House counterterrorism adviser John Brennan (confirmed in 2013 as CIA director)[32] has defended drone strikes as "legal, ethical and wise."[33]

Although targeting "terrorists" is theoretically the goal, the fact remains that the distinction between a terrorist whose intent is to do bodily harm and a sympathizer who visited a training camp is an important one. According to the New America Foundation (an independent Washington think tank that closely tracks the drone program and relies on local media and reports from observers in Pakistan), during President Obama's first term in office some 250 strikes occurred in Pakistan, killing about 2,345 individuals. With so many deaths, one can expect some "collateral damage," a euphemism for the killing of innocent civilians. Although Brennan states that such deaths are

---

29. At least one more American, Jude Kenan Mohammad, was killed by a drone strike on a compound in South Waziristan, Pakistan, on November 16, 2011. See Scott Shane and Eric Schmitt, "One Drone Victim's Trail from Raleigh to Pakistan," *New York Times*, May 22, 2013.

30. Nasser al-Awlaki, "The Drone That Killed My Grandson," *New York Times*, July 18, 2013.

31. Shane and Schmitt, "One Drone Victim's Trail."

32. In March 2013 Senator Rand Paul (R-KY) conducted a thirteen-hour filibuster to block a vote on the nomination of John Brennan as CIA director to bring attention to the concern of killing Americans without due process.

33. Charlie Savage, "Top U.S. Security Official Says 'Rigorous Standards' Are Used for Drone Strikes," *New York Times*, April 30, 2012; Mark Mazzetti, Charlie Savage, and Scott Shane, "How a U.S. Citizen Came to Be in America's Cross Hairs," *New York Times*, March 10, 2013.

"exceedingly rare," it is estimated that more than 471 civilians have been killed since the program began in 2004, of which 309 occurred during President Obama's watch.[34]

Permission to fly drones over Pakistan was the product of a secret deal between the CIA and Pakistan. The CIA received permission to carry out "targeted killing" if it first assassinated an enemy of the state of Pakistan. Hence in June 2004 a Pashtun tribesman, Nek Muhammad, who was neither a top operative of Al Qaeda nor a major threat to U.S. security, was the first victim, along with his two boys, ages ten and sixteen, of a drone attack in Pakistan.[35]

The CIA's Counterterrorism Center has managed the deadly campaign of drone strikes since 2006. Since 9/11 the CIA has evolved into a paramilitary agency, focused on hunting terrorists and killing them. A 2013 *New York Times/CBS News* poll revealed that while 72 percent of the U.S. population supports the use of drones against suspected terrorists, 66 percent are concerned that the program lacks "enough oversight."[36] In May 2013 President Obama signaled that the agency was to return to its traditional spying and strategic analysis, and the drone operations be placed under the jurisdiction of the State Department.

But what happens when other countries start developing similar technology? For example, on December 4, 2011, about 140 miles inside Iran from its border with Afghanistan, a drone, supposedly off course (or simply doing covert surveillance), fell into Iranian hands. On April 22, 2012, BBC News reported General Amir Ali Hajizadeh boasting that the Iranians have broken its encryption codes and reverse-engineered the aircraft to make their own copy. True, it is questionable that the Iranians will soon be flying their own drones. But what if they share the drone's schematics with the Chinese? Will the Chinese eventually develop their own drones? What happens when China has drones and decides to also target their terrorists—"terrorists" such as the Dalai Lama? After all, the Chinese foreign ministry has accused the Dalai Lama of "terrorism in disguise" for supporting Tibetans who have set themselves on fire in protest against Beijing's rule. Our unilateral killing of those whom we call "terrorists" anywhere in the world without some type of global consensus has created a precedent for other nations to follow suit.

Two wars lasting over a decade plus an amorphous, never-ending war on terror have transformed the United States. The wealth of the nation has been ransomed on the altar of Mars, or in President Eisenhower's own words,

34. See Savage, "Top U.S. Security Official"; Tania Branigan, "Dalai Lama's Prayers for Tibetans 'Terrorism in Disguise,' China Says," *The Guardian*, October 19, 2011.

35. Mark Mazzetti, "A Secret Deal on Drones, Sealed in Blood," *New York Times*, April 6, 2013.

36. Sheryl Gay Stolberg and Dalia Sussman, "Same-Sex Marriage Is Seen in Poll as an Issue for the States," *New York Times*, June 6, 2013.

Every gun that is made, every warship launched, every rocket fired signifies, in the final sense, a theft from those who hunger and are not fed, those who are cold and are not clothed. This world in arms is not spending money alone. It is spending the sweat of its laborers, the genius of its scientists, the hopes of its children. The cost of one modern heavy bomber is this: a modern brick school in more than 30 cities. It is two electric power plants, each serving a town of 60,000 population. It is two fine, fully equipped hospitals. It is some 50 miles of concrete highway. We pay for a single fighter plane with a half million bushels of wheat. We pay for a single destroyer with new homes that could have housed more than 8,000 people. This is, I repeat, the best way of life to be found on the road the world has been taking. This is not a way of life at all, in any true sense. Under the cloud of threatening war, it is humanity hanging from a cross of iron. (1953)

Step 2. Reflecting

Most societies create systems designed to define what is good and what is evil. Such binary systems also define what is legal and illegal, acceptable and unacceptable, criminal and noncriminal, and so on. What one society determines to be proper may be viewed with horror by another. Political assassinations, restriction of free expression, and brute intimidation could be construed as necessary evils for the advancement of a sacred cause. While all persons within that society might agree on the ultimate end, not all would necessarily subscribe or acquiesce to such tactics to achieve the goal.

The question then, is how do such violent tactics become an acceptable procedure within the eyes of the society at large? French philosopher Michel Foucault maintains that it can be done only by reducing what is good to "normal" and what is evil to "abnormal" or pathological (1965, 73). By extension, when a just war is being waged, warlike activities such as killing, bombing, and censorship must be employed to ensure the final victory of good. Terror, then, is understood as the legitimate use of violence to enforce justice. Terror, the spilling of blood, and other acts of war become "normal," regardless of how distasteful they might be. In fact, they become an inevitable moral imperative. The "enemies of freedom and democracy" (i.e., those opposed to the neoliberalism of today's Western capitalism) are a threat to "truth," and, as such, they must be silenced at all cost. Many unjust attempts at power can be concealed in a "holy war" that rallies the people around the concepts of freedom, democracy, and justice.

War is inevitable because we choose to maintain international structures that make war possible and profitable. Still, can any war be considered "just"?

Just-war theory, a medieval concept embedded in international law, was first formulated by Augustine in the early fifth century (and expanded by Thomas Aquinas in the thirteenth century) to provide guidelines for "Christian" rulers of empire to determine when the presence of evil and injustice justified the use of violence to stamp it out.[37] Under certain circumstances, it was believed, God condoned wars (i.e., crusades) conducted to destroy evil and rectify injustices.[38]

Can just-war guidelines impartially help people decide if the use of military force within a given conflict is just? Or is the determination to conduct a war simply the subjective views of those applying the just-war theory? Take, for example, the early debate in 2003 over the possible U.S. entry into a war with Iraq. The majority of religious leaders and denominations, using the principles of just-war theory, conclusively determined prior to hostilities that the U.S. preventive attack on Iraq did not meet the criteria for a just war.[39] One hundred Christian scholars of ethical theory issued the following statement: "As Christian ethicists, we share a common moral presumption against a preemptive war on Iraq by the United States."[40] Likewise, the United States Conference of Catholic Bishops issued a statement on November 13, 2002, urging President George W. Bush not to engage in a preventive attack on Iraq.

Nonetheless, a few ethicists believed that the conflict in Iraq met the demands of Christianity's just-war doctrine, most notably, Jean Bethke Elshtain and Michael Novak.[41] While it would not be appropriate to question the sincerity of these ethicists in arriving at their conclusions, it is reasonable to explore whether just-war theory can conclusively indicate the correct ethical path. Why were two different conclusions reached after following the

---

37. Traditional just-war theory is based on six *jus ad bellum* principles that are concerned with establishing the moral justification for engaging in violence: (1) just cause; (2) legitimate authority to declare hostilities; (3) just intention; (4) reasonable chance of success; (5) proper announcement of beginning hostilities; (6) the means used being proportional to the desired objective. In addition, two *jus in bello* principles apply for how violence is to be morally conducted: (1) determining legitimate targets and (2) how much force is morally appropriate.

38. Pope Gregory VII (1073–1085) assured combatants engaged in "holy" war that they would be forgiven from the consequences of their sins.

39. The notable exception was Richard Land, then president of the Ethics and Religious Liberty Commission of the Southern Baptist Convention (SBC). The SBC, as a whole, supported the war in Iraq. Its decision was greatly influenced by its unwavering support for Israel.

40. Shaun Casey, a just-war ethicist, and Stanley Hauerwas, a pacifist, prepared the statement and circulated it among ethicists of different theological and political leanings. I was one of the signatories.

41. Novak, a Roman Catholic philosopher, argued that the conflict with Iraq was not a "preventative war," but rather the "lawful conclusion" of the 1991 Gulf War that attempted to enforce the disarmament terms that Iraq accepted at the close of that conflict. Elshtain, a Protestant social ethics professor, argued that Christians have a moral duty to defend the innocent. Those brutalized by Saddam's regime and the neighboring countries threatened by the regime constituted the innocent, which requires U.S. military involvement. See Richard N. Ostling, "Against Widespread Clergy Protest, Some Lay Christians Justify War against Iraq," *Associated Press*, February 26, 2003.

same precepts of just-war theory? One significant observation that can be made is that even though ethicists employed the same just-war theory, they arrived at different conclusions, partly because they approached the dilemma from diverse social locations. All had a certain prior bias that prevented them from being completely objective.

Even if some sort of objectivity could have been achieved by those employing the just-war theory, history has demonstrated that clerics are often used by politicians or governments to manipulate believers to support war. This is evident when reviewing "war sermons" given mainly by white evangelicals prior to hostilities. Charles Marsh, religion professor at the University of Virginia, shows how supporters of the Iraq war, such as Pat Robertson of *The 700 Club*, referred to the upcoming military conflict as "a righteous cause out of the Bible." Pastor Charles Stanley of the First Baptist Church of Atlanta and former president of the Southern Baptist Convention counseled his followers, "We should offer to serve the war effort in any way possible." Jerry Falwell, founder of the Moral Majority political organization, wrote an essay titled "God Is Pro-war." Tim LaHaye, co-author of the popular *Left Behind* book series, saw Iraq as "a focal point of end-time events." A missionary writing to the Southern Baptist press wrote, "American foreign policy and military might have opened an opportunity for the Gospel in the land of Abraham, Isaac, and Jacob," a sentiment shared by Franklin Graham (evangelist Billy Graham's son), who saw the war as creating opportunities for proselytizing Muslims. Not surprisingly, 87 percent of all white U.S. evangelicals supported President Bush's decision to invade Iraq.[42] Why, when it came to Iraq, was white evangelical Christianity standing on the wrong side of history? We are left wondering if white evangelical Christianity has become so interconnected with empire that it is now more likely to advocate violence required to maintain empire rather than peace as preached by the Prince of Peace.

Nor should the discussion of violence be limited to war. Torture is also a form of violence. President Bush in 2005 strongly defended U.S. interrogation practices for detainees, insisting, "We do not torture,"[43] and President Obama declared shortly after assuming the presidency that "America doesn't torture,"[44] but the fact remains that the United States does so.[45] A

---

42. Charles Marsh, "Wayward Christian Soldiers," *New York Times*, January 20, 2006.

43. Richard Benedetto, "Bush Defends Interrogation Practices: 'We Do Not Torture,'" *USA Today*, November 7, 2005.

44. Barack Obama interview, "Obama on Economic Crises, Transition," *60 Minutes*, CBS, aired February 8, 2009 (transcript of interview available at http://www.cbsnews.com/).

45. In January 2002 then–attorney general Alberto Gonzales sided with the Justice Department assessment that the Geneva Convention's stipulations regarding prisoners of war did not bind the United States in its treatment of prisoners captured while fighting in a war zone. By August of that year, a classified memo from the Justice Department concluded that "physical pain amounting to torture must be equivalent in intensity to the pain accompanying serious physical injury, such as

2013 independent, nonpartisan, 577-page review of interrogation and detention programs since 9/11 by the Constitution Project concluded that "it is indisputable that the United States engaged in the practice of torture," with ultimate responsibility resting with the nation's highest officials.[46]

A popular torture technique employed by the United States is waterboarding, a forced suffocation caused by the inhalation of water, or as the CIA euphemistically prefers to call it, a "professional interrogation technique." Waterboarding has been used by the United States for over a century to obtain information from prisoners. Ironically, after World War II, Yukio Asano, a military officer with the Japanese Imperial Army, was sentenced to fifteen years of hard labor for administrating a form of waterboarding on U.S. civilians. And yet it was determined by the Attorney General in 2012 that CIA agents were not to be persecuted when "enhanced interrogation techniques" (euphemism for torture) such as waterboarding led to the death of prisoners.[47] Ironically, waterboarding is a punishable offense when the technique is used against Americans, but is an acceptable interrogation procedure when used by Americans.

And yet contrary to popular mythology, the use of torture has failed to provide useful information. The Constitution Project's nonpartisan, independent review concluded that while "a person subjected to torture might well divulge useful information," much of the information obtained via enhanced interrogation techniques was unreliable.[48] Additionally, according to an unreleased six-thousand-page report (containing over thirty-five thousand footnotes) produced by the U.S. Senate Intelligence Committee on CIA methods of interrogation, which itself was based on some six million pages of agency documents, found that the use of so-called enhanced interrogation techniques was not a central component in finding Osama bin Laden. The Senate Committee report documents one of the CIA's worst-kept secrets: following the 9/11 terrorist attacks, the agency began and maintained overseas prisons (called "black sites") where coercive methods of interrogation are employed. Contrary to pronouncements made by Presidents Bush and Obama, the report showed that "coercive and abusive treatment of detainees was far more widespread and systematic than we thought." And even though coercive interrogation methods have been banned since 2009, when Obama

---

organ failure, impairment of bodily function, or even death." By December 2004, a second Justice Department memo was produced broadening the definition of torture to include "severe physical suffering" as well as "severe physical pain." See Richard W. Stevenson and Joel Brinkley, "More Questions as Rice Asserts Detainee Policy," *New York Times*, December 8, 2005.

46. Scott Shane, "U.S. Engaged in Torture after 9/11, Review Concludes," *New York Times*, April 16, 2013.

47. Scott Shane, "No Charges Filed in Two Deaths Involving C.I.A.," *New York Times*, August 31, 2012.

48. Shane, "U.S. Engaged in Torture after 9/11."

took office, the facts remain that anything detainees might say concerning their CIA interrogations is treated as classified.[49]

Commenting on the committee's report, Senator John McCain, himself a victim of torture while a prisoner of war in North Vietnam, said, "What I have learned [from the report] confirms for me what I have always believed and insisted to be true—that the cruel, inhuman and degrading treatment of prisoners is not only wrong in principle and a stain on our country's conscience, but also an ineffective and unreliable means of gathering intelligence."[50]

Torture's ineffectiveness in providing reliable intelligence is best demonstrated by the case of Ibn al-Sheikh al-Libi, a Libyan national arrested in Pakistan several months after 9/11. The CIA took custody of him in 2002 and transferred him, via the navy ship USS *Bataan*, to Egypt, where he was tortured. In order to avoid torture and receive better treatment, he fabricated information—specifically, that Iraq provided chemical and biological weapons training to Al Qaeda. This information was used by then–secretary of state Colin Powell during his 2003 U.N. speech to justify starting a war against Iraq. By 2004, after the invasion of Iraq, when it became obvious that there were no weapons of mass destruction, al-Libi recanted. He eventually was transferred to Abu Salim prison in Tripoli, Libya, to serve a life sentence, but in 2009 he was found dead in his cell (Singh 2013, 41).

The European Court of Human Rights condemned the CIA's extraordinary rendition programs, understood as the transfer of a detainee without legal process to the custody of a foreign government for detention and interrogation. The court's condemnation was due to the case of a German car salesman, Khaled El-Masri, who, mistaken for a terrorist suspect, was kidnapped from Macedonia in 2003 and held for four months, brutally interrogated at the CIA Afghan-run prison known as the Salt Pit. El-Masri, an innocent man, was severely beaten, sodomized, shackled, and hooded at the hands of the CIA and in the presence of Macedonian authorities.[51] In December 2012 the court ruled against Macedonia, finding that El-Masri's treatment at the hands of the CIA amounted to torture. The court could not rule against the United States because it lacks jurisdiction to do so.

Shortly after 9/11, then–vice president Dick Cheney set the tone for handling potential enemies of the United States:

> We also have to work, through, sort of, the dark side, if you will.
> We've got to spend time in the shadows in the intelligence

---

49. Scott Shane, "Portrayal of C.I.A. Torture in Bin Laden Film Reopens a Debate," *New York Times*, December 13, 2012; idem, "Senate Panel Approves Findings on Prisoners," *New York Times*, December 14, 2012.

50. Shane, "Senate Approves Findings on Prisoners."

51. Angela Charlton, "European Court Condemns CIA in Landmark Ruling," *Associated Press*, December 14, 2012.

world. A lot of what needs to be done here will have to be done quietly, without any discussion, using sources and methods that are available to our intelligence agencies, if we're going to be successful. That's the world these folks operate in, and so it's going to be vital for us to use any means at our disposal, basically, to achieve our objective.[52]

Although President Obama ordered the end of President Bush's torture policies, even closing CIA detention facilities, he has failed to repudiate the CIA rendition policies; has suggested that some secret CIA prisons may still be operable, specifically in Somalia; and has adopted the Bush administration's presumed "right" to target the killing of suspected terrorists, including Americans. According to an extensive report conducted by the Open Society Justice Initiative, the number of detainees who experienced extraordinary rendition and enhanced interrogation techniques and the locations of the CIA prisons where these tortures occurred remain unknown. Nevertheless, 136 cases of tortured individuals were documented, although many more cases are expected to exist. Additionally, at least fifty-four foreign governments participated in this CIA operation, several of which are notorious for violating basic human rights of its citizens (Singh, 5–8). The participation of the United States in these nefarious activities diminished its moral standing in the world, undermining global human rights advances.

Rather than noting moral complexities of employing torture, Christian leaders such as James Dobson, founder of Focus on the Family; Albert Mohler, president of Southern Baptist Theological Seminary; and Daniel R. Heimback, ethics professor at Southeastern Baptist Seminary, support the use of torture (Towery 2008, 19). Modernity is not the first time that the use of torture been justified by Christian scholars. For example, Augustine, the original author of just-war theory, condones torturing the innocent in order to obtain information (*City of God* 6.19.6).

In 2004 the American Red Cross charged the U.S. military with intentionally using psychological and physical coercion tantamount to torture at the U.S. naval base in Guantánamo (aka "Gitmo").[53] Prisoners were chained in uncomfortable positions for up to twenty-four hours and left to urinate or defecate on themselves; men were sexually abused by female interrogators (e.g., the squeezing of the prisoners' genitals), were given forced enemas, and subjected to sleep deprivation and sensory overload.[54] An FBI inquiry found that prison-

---

52. Dick Cheney, interview with Tim Russert, *Meet the Press*, September 16, 2001.

53. Neil A. Lewis, "Red Cross Finds Detainee Abuse in Guantánamo," *New York Times*, November 30, 2004.

54. Neil A. Lewis and David Johnston, "New F.B.I. Files Describe Abuses of Iraq Inmates," *New York Times*, December 21, 2004; "Ex-G.I. Writes about Use of Sex in Guantánamo Interrogations,"

ers at Gitmo had lit cigarettes placed in their ears, and also were subjected occasionally to beating or choking.[55] By 2006, Amnesty International accused the United States of committing widespread abuses, including torture and the continued detention of thousands of individuals without a trial, even calling Gitmo "the gulag of our times" (Amnesty International 2006, 1–8).[56]

Generally, there are two types of torture. The first encompasses psychological techniques meant to disorient and wear down the prisoner, such as sleep deprivation, exposure to extreme temperatures, lack of medical treatment, and being forced to sit in painful and uncomfortable positions for long periods of time ("soft" torture). The second type of torture includes physical violence ("hard" torture). Although soft torture admittedly was used on prisoners held at Gitmo, military and government officials denied the use of hard torture until the infamous photographs from Abu Ghraib prison became public. Members of the U.S. Army's elite 82nd Airborne Division confessed that fellow soldiers routinely beat and abused prisoners at Abu Ghraib to gather intelligence on the insurgency, and also just to amuse themselves. Limbs, according to one sergeant, often were broken; in at least one case, a prisoner's leg was broken with a metal baseball bat.[57]

When the Abu Ghraib atrocities became public, our government reassured the public that these abuses were an aberration conducted by a few rogue soldiers who have sullied the name of all Americans. In reality, Abu Ghraib was part of a systemic process of abuse. Take the example of Task Force 6–26, the shadowy American military unit that operates another prison, Camp Nama. This camp, complete with a torture chamber known as the Black Room, was secretly housed at Baghdad International Airport. Prisoners were repeatedly beaten with rifle butts and used for target practice in a game played by guards called "jailer paintball." Game players dubbed themselves the "High Five Paintball Club." Under the mantra "no blood, no foul" (i.e., if the victim does not bleed, the jailer cannot be prosecuted), prisoners were routinely tortured to obtain information about insurgents. Stories of prisoners punched in the spine until they fell unconscious, or kicked in the stomach until they vomited, or stripped naked and doused with ice water in refrigerated rooms, or deprived of sleep via rap music played at deafening decibel levels were all too common. Camp Nama was usually the first stop

New York Times, January 29, 2005; Neil A. Lewis and Eric Schmitt, "Inquiry Finds Abuses at Guantánamo Bay," *New York Times*, May 1, 2005; Neil A. Lewis, "Fresh Details Emerge on Harsh Methods at Guantánamo," *New York Times*, January 1, 2005.

55. Neil A. Lewis and David Johnston, "New F.B.I. Memos Describe Abuses of Iraq Inmates," *New York Times*, December 21, 2004.

56. Alan Cowell, "U.S. 'Thumbs Its Nose' at Rights, Amnesty Says," *New York Times*, May 26, 2005.

57. Eric Smith, "3 in 82nd Airborne Say Beating Iraqi Prisoners Was Routine," *New York Times*, September 24, 2005.

before prisoners were transferred to Abu Ghraib. Torture routinely continued even after Abu Ghraib's abuses came to light.[58]

Detainees, according to allegations made by Lieutenant Colonel Steven L. Jordan, were kept off official rosters so that they could be speedily transferred from prisons like Abu Ghraib to Gitmo or off-site torture prisons, where they could not be protected by the Geneva Conventions.[59] Still, Kenneth Roth, executive director of Human Rights Watch, noted that the United States has been handing over some suspects to countries such as Egypt, Saudi Arabia, and Jordan that were not averse to employing physical torture to gain information that could be passed along to the United States (Nelson-Pallmeyer 2001, 2–5).[60] Ironically, although Syria in 2012 was condemned by the international community for torturing its people and prolonging a brutal and bloody civil war, the United States had no qualms about handing over its prisoners to Syrian torturers to gather information. These transfers were a clear violation of American laws and the 1984 international convention that bans such transfers.

But can violence ever be harnessed for good and/or declared just? Violence is not a political tool that can be picked up and used, and then put down later, never to be used again. The use of violence forever changes a person and a society. Generally, those engaged in violence and the hate that it unleashes become unfit for the process of creating a new, just, social order. According to the biblical text, King David was forbidden to build a temple for God in Jerusalem because of his use of violence, for he had "waged great wars" and "shed much blood" (1 Chron. 22:8).

At times, is violence the only option? Thomas Schubeck provides the example of a homeowner who confronts a burglar in the very act of robbing the homeowner's prized possessions. The homeowner has two options: either recognize the humanity of the burglar as a troubled person and begin a dialogue based on a genuine interest in the burglar's well-being, or see the burglar as a thief who needs to be physically expelled from the premises by whatever means necessary. While the former may be closer to the gospel call to turn the other cheek or forgo the spare cloak, the latter takes into account other considerations—specifically, protecting one's family or one's self from the possible violence that the burglar may inflict (1993, 70).

Nevertheless, while those of the dominant culture continue to struggle with the issue of whether violence can be ethically employed, for the

58. Eric Schmitt and Carolyn Marshall, "In Secret Unit 'Black Room,' a Grim Portrait of U.S. Abuse," *New York Times*, March 19, 2006.

59. Douglas Jehl, "Inmates Were Reported Kept Off Books to Speed Transfer," *New York Times*, October 9, 2004.

60. Peter Maass, "Torture, Tough or Lite: If a Terror Suspect Won't Talk, Should He Be Made To?" *New York Times*, March 9, 2003.

marginalized, violence is already a reality. Internationally, violence continues to be used to secure financial markets and financial gain, and the United States has engaged in violence for this purpose. For example, ethicist Charles Kammer reminds us that when the former Soviet Union invaded Afghanistan, it was viewed as a savage act depriving Afghans of their right to self-determination. However, when the United States has overthrown governments, some of which were democratically elected, it has been labeled an act of liberation, even when the end result was the installation of a brutal, undemocratic, unpopular regime (1988, 27, 143). It seems that the primary difference between the actions of the former Soviet Union and those of the United States is that the aggressive international acts of the latter were cloaked in moral rhetoric, sometimes justified by the use of just-war theory.

Aggressive violent acts can also entail lopsided trade agreements in which, as purchaser of the world's resources and labor, the United States sets deflated prices or engages in war when what is considered the U.S. birthright to those resources is jeopardized by other nation-states. If "our" oil supplies are threatened, we have no qualms about sending military forces to protect the continuous flow of oil, all the while claiming to engage in a crusade to uproot Islamic terrorism. Whoever happens to be sitting in the Oval Office has the job of protecting the interests of corporate America abroad. Therefore, in terms of U.S. global economic policies, it really does not matter if the people elect a black man or a woman, or conclude that all the change really needed is another white man. Our democratic system has reduced our electoral choice to one between two pro-empire individuals who will show no significant difference in their commitments to protecting the rights of multinational companies to expand globally. When push comes to shove in the global arena, the president, whether a conservative or a liberal, will protect the interests of Exxon, Microsoft, and Walmart, even at the expense of establishing justice and even at the cost of committing U.S. troops.

Can any war, then, be just, especially if war represents Satan's triumph over the love called for by Christ? Are all wars morally reprehensible, but sometimes pardonable? Can the conditions for a just war ever be obtained? Regardless of moral discussions that take place within the dominant culture, one fact remains constant: those on the periphery of power are seldom consulted, even though they are disproportionately on the receiving end of the violence of war. It also seems today that while pacifism is an ethical option, absolute pacifism may be unattainable. There are differences between killing someone as an offensive strategy, defending oneself from violence inflicted by an oppressor, and protecting the most vulnerable from certain death at the hands of an oppressor. If we are forced to engage in violence, is it better to recognize it for the evil that it is and rely on God's grace for forgiveness than to try to reason through the gospel message in order to justify warlike actions by using just-war type theory?

Can nonviolence ever succeed as a strategy in the international arena? At the close of World War I, the Treaty of Versailles sought revenge on Germany, creating an atmosphere that eventually led to World War II. But by the close of World War II, the lesson had been learned. Rather than punish Germany and Japan for the violence that they unleashed, the United States embraced their enemies by rebuilding their nations. The result was strong alliances with those countries that continue to stand the test of time. Yet at the close of the first Gulf War, the United States imposed an embargo on Iraq that brought the death of thousands of Iraqis, mostly children. How, then, can we convince an Iraqi mother and her starving child of the moral superiority of a supposedly Christian nation? How can we convince her not to hate us? The *imago Dei* of the enemy must be recognized at all levels of conflict, for the enemy is also created in the image of God and thus has dignity and worth. This is as true for the Afghan or Iraqi populations as it is for people in the United States.

Generally, less value is given to those who are marginalized within an empire. As noted above, those who live on the margins of society are never consulted in the process of deciding to go to war. To go or not is determined in the halls of power, with an eye toward the geopolitical gains of such an encounter. It is not the Native American living on a reservation, the African American relegated to the urban ghetto, or the Latino/a of this country's borderlands who is calling for more missiles, aircraft carriers, or the latest fighter jet. Ethical debates concerning what makes a war just may have validity among ethicists of the dominant culture, but for the masses that live under the strain of racism and classism, such debates are irrelevant.

Although some, like multinational corporations such as Bechtel and Halliburton, stand to benefit financially from the war, others, specifically those who are economically disenfranchised, suffer during the preparation for war. Increases in military spending are directly related to increases in the poverty rate. Increased military spending during peacetime has a direct relationship to increased unemployment, which is clearly linked to increased poverty.[61] High military spending in advanced industrial economies diverts capital to non-growth-producing sectors, crowding out investments, reducing productivity, and increasing unemployment (Abell 1990; 1994; Henderson 1998). Complicating the economic impact of the war in Iraq (and Afghanistan) is that for the first time in U.S. history the United States engaged in a war without committing to pay for it through up-front taxes. The increase in defense

---

61. Yet it is important to note that increased military spending during wartime has the reverse effect, decreasing poverty.

spending, financed through deficit spending, creates an inflationary impact on the economy that disproportionately harms the poor, contributing to an increase in income inequality. In short, while war financially benefits the nation's elite class, the preparation for war further devastates the poor. Perhaps a move away from the traditional understanding of security is needed, one that does not rely on the mechanisms of war. The 1994 U.N. Human Development Report probably provides us with a better understanding of what security should be:

> In the final analysis, human security is a child who did not die, a disease that did not spread, a job that was not cut, an ethnic tension that did not explode in violence, a dissident who was not silenced. Human security is not a concern with weapons—it is a concern with human life and dignity. (UNDP 1994, 22)

Step 3. Praying

Among Christians, one of the most powerful biblical stories is the exodus, where God enters history and guides God's chosen people toward the promised land. The trek of former slaves toward liberation resonates with many who today are dispossessed. Unfortunately, what we usually ignore is that this promised land was already occupied by the Canaanites, who first had to be slaughtered before God's chosen could take possession. The Hebrews, according to the book of Joshua, "enforced the ban on everything in [Jericho]: men and women; young and old; ox, sheep, and donkey, massacring all of them" (Josh. 6:21). While most marginalized Christians read themselves into the story of the oppressed slaves marching forward, many first-nations people see themselves as the modern-day Canaanites.

When God's chosen people entered the land of Canaan, they found other people living there. How do you claim a land when it is already occupied? According to the biblical text, God commanded that everything be put to death. The spears of God's people were thrust through babies. The swords of God's people lopped off the heads of children. Pregnant women were disemboweled. Families were decimated before each other's eyes. A gory bloodbath took place.

Today we call God's command a war crime. Today we call God's command genocide. Today we call God's command crimes against humanity. The Christian is left with disturbing questions. Does the book of Joshua depict a nonbiblical God? Some might argue that the Canaanites worshiped false gods and did despicable things. Do we then have a right to kill everything that does not recognize the true God, with the true God being as Christians define God? Should we then invade and decimate all nonbelievers who in our eyes do despicable things?

The Hebrew's (European) dream of religious freedom and liberation became the Canaanite's (Native American) nightmare of subjugation and genocide. Like the Canaanites before them, Native Americans were viewed as a people who could not be trusted, a snare to the righteous, and a culture that required decimation. Robert Allen Warrior provides a rereading of the exodus story from the Canaanite perspective, questioning if it is an appropriate biblical model for understanding his people's struggle for dignity. He calls for a Christian reflection that places the Canaanites at the center of theological thought and that considers the violence and injustice rarely mentioned in critical works concerning the exodus (1989).

Scholars such as Vine Deloria Jr. are quick to remind us that the conquest of Native American land by "God's chosen people" ended their liberation, understood as communal and personal harmony and balance. Hence, any discussion of liberation and freedom among indigenous people must be understood as liberation and freedom from European Christian invasion and its consequences. These consequences are witnessed today when we consider that Native Americans are the poorest of the poor in a "Christianized" North America, a poverty maintained by structures that politically, socially, psychologically, and economically oppress them. True liberation among Native American people, according to scholars like Deloria, begins with a firm "no" to Jesus Christ and Christianity, the source of their bondage. "There is no way," according to Deloria, "to combine white values and Indian behavior into a workable program or intelligible subject of discussion" (1969, 10). Can any student of history blame them for saying no?

Christians who take the biblical text seriously, and what that text says about war, must recognize that in some cases God commands blood-soaked war, even against Israel, while at other times God forbids war, even to protect Israel. In the Hebrew Bible the violence caused by war is condoned some of the time and condemned at other times. Within the New Testament Jesus abhors violence, yet he warns of the violence that will be committed against those who follow him to the cross. All too often the commitment of the believer to follow Jesus' example leads to violence. However, violence should never be accepted as a necessary evil, nor should it be rejected as antithetical to Jesus (he clearly used violence to cleanse the temple and prophesied the violence of the day of judgment).

Violence is a reality today, and often it arises from challenges to the dominant culture's grip on power. Such violence can be immediate or drawn out, as in the case of institutional violence, such as the economic forces that foster ghettos and barrios. Governments act violently when they maintain social structures that inflict prolonged harm or injury upon a segment of the population and that segment is usually disenfranchised due to race or economic standing. The choice facing the believer is whether to participate in the use of violence or to advocate nonviolent resistance to oppressive structures. As Gustavo Gutiérrez reminds us, it is important to distinguish between "the unjust violence of the oppressors (who maintain this despicable system) with the just violence of the oppressed (who feel obligated to use it to achieve their liberation)" (1988, 64). Not only does Gutiérrez distinguish between the two types of violence, but also he questions the prevailing double standards that exist: "We cannot say that the violence is all right when the oppressor uses it to maintain or preserve 'order,' but wrong when the oppressed use it to overthrow this same 'order'" (1984, 28).

To remain silent or to do nothing in the face of violence is to participate in it through complicity. At times, in the face of the violence being committed upon the marginalized, some purposely remain silent or speak their disapproval in muted voices, lest they jeopardize their privileged space. How, then, should disenfranchised Christians react to the constant institutional violence that they face?

When asked if counterviolence is ever an option for Christians, Gutiérrez, along with other liberation theologians, reminds us that violence already exists in the hands of the oppressor. Thus, the question is not "Should Christians utilize violence?" but rather, "Do Christians have a right to defend themselves from the already existing violence?" For example, biblical scholar George Pixley maintains that the massacre of Egypt's firstborn can be understood as a terrorist act, an act inspired by God (1987, 80). He goes on to note Moses' violent act of killing an Egyptian, a member of the dominant culture, for striking a Hebrew slave, a member of a marginalized group (Exod. 2:11–22). This act appeared justified even though a future commandment received by Moses would state, "Thou shall not kill." Pixley suggests that certain exceptions to the fifth commandment exist, such as capital punishment or the killing of enemies in times of war. Pixley also implies that the preferential option for the oppressed may lead to the act of taking life. Moses' killing of the Egyptian could be seen as a defensive act to protect the life of the marginalized. And it appears that God (the ultimate defender of the oppressed) accepts Moses in later years, justifying Moses' earlier use of violence for the sake of defending the oppressed (1987, 8–9).

During the period of slavery in the United States many slave rebellions were violent and bloody, most notably the 1831 revolt in Southampton, Virginia, led by Nat Turner. As a preacher, Turner believed that God directed him to live out his faith through actions that could lead to the liberation of the slaves. Biblical authority for such action was seen in the exodus story of slave liberation from the tyranny of Pharaoh. Slaves had a moral obligation to find liberation by whatever means possible.

Interpreting Scripture in this way has led ethicists such as José Míguez Bonino to support violence (even revolution) when employed to protect the humanity of the marginalized (1975, 116–18). If the oppression of the marginalized is maintained through institutionalized violence—that is, through social structures designed to privilege the few at the expense of the many—then any hope of finding salvation or liberation from the status quo will inevitably confront those same social structures. History has demonstrated that denouncing unjust social structures is simply not enough, for those accustomed to power and privilege will never willingly abdicate what they consider to be a birthright. Some ethicists from the margins maintain that violence, when employed by the marginalized to overcome their own oppression, is in reality self-defense and can never be confused with the continuing violence employed by those in power.

Accordingly, some advocate a quest for liberation "by any means possible." They argue that to wash one's hands of violence is to allow violence to be done to the marginalized. Latin American theologian Juan Luís Segundo recognizes that while all violence is evil, not all decisions to use violence are unethical. *Agape* (unconditional love) for the very least among us might lead a person, in an unselfish act, to stand in solidarity with the oppressed in their battle for self-preservation. Protecting a "nonperson" might invite a violent confrontation as the oppressor, feeling backed into a corner, may fight tooth and nail to maintain the status quo. Persons making a preferential option to love the oppressed may very well find themselves harming the oppressor.

Unfortunately, the call for nonviolence may come from those who wish to maintain the unjust status quo. Writing in 1969, during the height of racial unrest and the Vietnam War, James Cone astutely observed,

> It is interesting that so many advocates of nonviolence as the only possible Christian response of black people to white domination are also the most ardent defenders of the right of the police to put down black rebellion through violence. Another interesting corollary is their defense of America's right to defend violently the government of South Vietnam against the North. Somehow, I am unable to follow the reasoning. (1969, 138–39)

For Cone, African Americans, along with other "unwanted minorities," were placed in a situation in which only one option was made available to them, "deciding whose violence [will be] supported—that of the oppressors or the oppressed . . . Either we side with the oppressed . . . in a dehumanized society, or we stand with the President or whoever is defending the white establishment for General Motors and U.S. Steel" (1975, 219). No middle ground, Cone insisted, was available.

The early Christian community (pre-Constantine) maintained an absolute prohibition on violence, even to the point of refusing to fight the Romans when Jerusalem was burned and sacked in 70 CE. Warfare was understood to be a denial of Jesus' message to love one's enemies and a rejection of the life that he asked his disciples to follow. For the early church, though Jesus Christ may not have been a zealot, he was a revolutionary leading a rebellion to be won through his crucifixion. Not until 313 CE, when Christianity became the state religion and took on political power under Constantine, was it necessary to develop concepts for just war to maintain the empire.

For Martin Luther King Jr., the aim of nonviolence was the creation of a relationship with the oppressors in the hopes that they too could be redeemed by God's grace. He rejected Niebuhr's understanding of pacifism as an unrealistic submission to evil power, insisting instead that it is better to be the recipient of violence than the inflictor of it (1958, 98).[62] King did not advocate passivity; rather, he called for an active confrontation with injustice. Nonviolence was the embodiment of the Christian ideal of *agape*, an unconditional love that confronts the aggressor so that he or she can also learn the gospel demand for *agape*.

Pragmatically, Martin Luther King Jr. insisted that the use of violence by the marginalized only encourages the oppressor (who controls the tools of torture) to unleash even greater violence, leading to a never-ending spiral of hatred. He maintained that violence only provokes greater retribution, and those who are unarmed will find themselves at a greater disadvantage. Rather than continuing the cycle of violence, King looked toward the radical love advocated by Christ as the solution to oppression. He wrote, "Returning hate for hate multiplies hate, adding deeper darkness to a night already devoid of stars. Darkness cannot drive out darkness; only light can do that. Hate cannot drive out hate; only love can do that. Hate multiplies hate, violence multiples violence, and toughness multiplies toughness in a descending spiral of destruction" (1963, 37).

1980 Nobel Peace Prize recipient Adolfo Pérez Esquivel pointed to the Plaza de Mayo mothers as a paragon that best illustrated the responsibilities of Christians.[63] For Pérez Esquivel, Christians, using Jesus as a model, must refuse to carry out violence, even though seeking to transform humanity probably will lead to violent upheaval. He was adamant that terrorism,

---

62. There are basically two types of pacifists. The "absolute" pacifist renounces violence under every circumstance, and the "contextual" pacifist looks for acts of nonviolent resistance, reserving the option that under exceptional circumstances violence may be a necessary alternative.

63. Argentinian mothers of those who "disappeared" during that country's "dirty war" would gather regularly in the early 1980s at the Plaza de Mayo across from the federal complex in Buenos Aires in a silent demonstration. They silently held a family picture with the caption "Where is my child?" Many of them also ended up disappearing; however, they are credited with turning the tide and ushering in a new Argentina.

despite its source, is an attack on a human being, thus on humanity and thus on God. He questioned armed liberation movements, fearing that today's oppressed would become tomorrow's oppressors. For him, revolutions that programmatically embraced violence risk their own undoing (1983, 71–72).

For social activist César Chávez, those involved in something constructive tend to refrain from violence, while those not committed to the rebuilding of a more just order tend to advocate the more destructive path of violence. Chávez insisted that nonviolence requires greater courage and militancy. He once said, "I am not a nonviolent man. I am a violent man who is trying to be nonviolent" (Dalton 2003, 120). In short, those who are familiar with the violence of the oppressor must seriously consider this admonition by ethicist Major J. Jones: "Every Christian who accepts Jesus Christ as his example will have to deal with the ultimate question as to whether he takes the principle of the sanctity of life so seriously that he would rather give his own life than take the life of another, even when the other is the aggressor" (1974, 171).

But is this principle concerning the sanctity of life limited just to issues concerning war and peace? Most who identify themselves as pro-life or believe in the sanctity of life are neither. To truly be pro-life is to believe that all life, created by God, has worth, dignity, and purpose; therefore, no human, under any circumstance, has the right to play God and terminate any life. To truly be pro-life is to consistently maintain this view in all issues. Because all life has an opportunity to reconcile with the Creator, all life must be preserved at all cost. For those who believe in Christian dogma, to terminate life early robs the person of coming into a saving knowledge of God and the hope of relying on God's grace. As it stands today, most conservatives and liberals are pro-life on certain political issues and not others. Conservatives usually are pro-life when it comes to abortion and euthanasia, while liberals usually advocate a pro-life stance when it comes to war and capital punishment. Conservatives' pro-life views are trumped by national security concerns, while the liberals' pro-life stance is trumped by personal freedoms.

Does this mean that to truly advocate for the sanctity of all life, an individual must stand against abortion, euthanasia, war, and capital punishment? To support or participate in any of these four things forfeits any claims to a pro-life advocacy. Hence, most conservatives and liberals are not pro-life, regardless of what they profess. Each group allows either the government or personal freedom to take precedence over and against the sanctity of life.

Step 4. Case Studies

1. Camilo Mejia is a permanent U.S. resident who joined the armed forces when he was nineteen. With the rank of staff sergeant, Mejia served for five months in Iraq in 2003. During his tour of duty he was assigned to

guard prisoners at a detention facility where he witnessed the employ-ment of psychological torture in violation of the Geneva Conventions. Also, he was assigned to instigate gun battles with insurgents in order to win battle medals. He and others were ambushed, and innocent civilians were hit in the ensuing firefight. He admits, "Being an occupier changes you. You become an agent for brutalizing a country." After a leave of absence, he refused to report for duty, becoming among the first to desert. "This is an oil-driven war, and I don't think any soldier signs up to fight for oil," said Mejia.[64] Mejia was court-martialed and spent nine months in prison for refusing to return to duty.

Some fifty years ago, Martin Luther King Jr. proclaimed that the United States was the "greatest purveyor of violence in the world today" (1986b, 636). According to the Congressional Research Service, the United States has been engaged in 163 military deployments since World War II, 144 of them over a forty-year span between 1973 and 2013.[65]

— Does Camilo Mejia have the right to renounce his military oath? Does he have an obligation to complete his military duty? Can soldiers choose which wars they will participate in? Why or why not?

— Non-U.S. residents who serve in the military have been deported fol-lowing honorable discharge from the military. Their deportation is at times due to crimes committed, such as domestic violence, bar brawling, or resisting arrest.[66] Should they be deported? Should they have been made U.S. citizens while serving? If they had been killed in action, what about their undocumented, immediate family? Is Mejia's decision not to fight, even at the cost of possible deportation, morally correct for him?

— Was Martin Luther King Jr. correct in his characterization of the United States? Why or why not? Of the 163 military deployments since World War II, which ones can be considered a "just war?"[67] Who

64. Erik Schelzig, "Soldier: 'I Have Not Committed a Crime,'" *Grand Rapids Press*, March 16, 2004; Margaret Fosmoe, "Anti-War Veteran Talks at IUSB," *South Bend Tribune*, March 17, 2009.

65. Karl W. Eikenberry and David M. Kennedy, "Americans and Their Military, Drifting Apart," *New York Times*, May 26, 2013.

66. Nancy Lofholm, "Veterans to Protest Deportations at President Obama's Buckley Air Base Visit in Colorado," *Denver Post*, January 26, 2012.

67. Some of the major conflicts since 1980: (1) Libya conflict, 1981; (2) war in Lebanon, 1982–1983; (3) Nicaragua: the covert Contra wars, 1982–1990; (4) invasion of Grenada: Operation Urgent Fury, 1983; (5) Libya conflict, 1986; (6) Iran: Operation Earnest Will or the Tanker War, 1987–1988; (7) invasion of Panama: Operation Just Cause, 1989; (8) Iraq: the Gulf War or Operation Desert Storm, 1991; (9) Iraq: the No-Fly Zone War, 1991–2003; (10) intervention in Somalia, 1992–1994; (11) Yugoslav Wars: Operation Deliberate Force, 1992–1999; (12) Haiti: Operation Uphold Democracy, 1994; (13) Afghanistan and Sudan bombings: the bin Laden War, 1998; (14) Iraq: Desert Fox Campaign, 1998; (15) Serbia: Kosovo War, 1999; (16) Afghanistan: Operation Enduring Free-dom, 2001; (17) Iraq: Operation Iraqi Freedom, 2003; (18) intervention in Haiti civil conflict, 2004; (19) intervention in Somalia Civil War, 2006–2009; (20) intervention in Libyan Civil War, 2011.

was the aggressor? Do the recent wars in Iraq and Afghanistan meet the principles of just-war theory?

2. Rufina Amaya was a poor, middle-aged woman who lived in El Mozote, a small village in El Salvador. On December 11, 1981, government soldiers entered the village and ordered all inhabitants into the streets. Roughly nine hundred civilians, mostly women and children, were shot point-blank. Amaya, who witnessed the event, survived because she was able to hide among some bushes. Recounting her experience, she says, "I heard the screams of the children, and I knew which ones were mine, they were crying, 'Mommy, they're killing us!' "[68] Ten of the twelve officers responsible for the massacre of El Mozote were trained by the U.S. military. Located in Fort Benning, Georgia, the Western Hemisphere Institute for Security Cooperation (WHINSEC, formerly known as the School of the Americas) has trained over sixty thousand Latin American soldiers in commando operations, psychological warfare, and counterinsurgency techniques. In the past, training manuals produced by the Pentagon for WHINSEC (made public through the Freedom of Information Act) advocated executions, torture, false arrest, blackmail, censorship, payment of bounty for murders, and other forms of physical abuse against enemies.[69] Among the graduates of the school were two of the three officers cited for the assassination of Archbishop Óscar Romero; three of the four officers cited in the rape and murder of the four U.S. church women; the founder of El Salvador's death squads and the future president of the country (Roberto D'Aubuisson); nineteen of the twenty-six officers cited in the murder of six Jesuit priests, their housekeeper, and her teenage daughter; and the brutal military dictators who formerly ruled Bolivia, Argentina, Guatemala, Panama, El Salvador, and Honduras, to name a few. Rufina Amaya, the lone survivor of the massacre of El Mozote, concludes, "The only thing the School of the Americas has accomplished is the destruction of our countries in Latin America."What responsibility, if any, does the United States have toward Rufina Amaya? Can the U.S. government be held responsible for the actions of Latin American soldiers, trained by the U.S. military, who commit atrocities against humanity? Why or why not?

---

68. *School of Assassins*, documentary produced by Maryknoll World Productions, 1995.

69. A U.S. Congressional Task Force, headed by former representative Joseph Moakley (D-MA), concluded that those responsible for many of the government-led massacres in Latin America had been trained by the U.S. Army at Fort Benning, Georgia. According to former representative Joseph Kennedy (D-MA), "The Pentagon revealed [through these training manuals] what activists opposed to the school have been alleging for years—that foreign military officers were taught to torture and murder, [in order] to achieve their political objective" (Nelson-Pallmeyer 2001, 2–5).

— What, if any, are the ethical ramifications of supporting this institution through U.S. tax dollars?

— Is it ethical for the United States to maintain a school with a history of conducting terrorist acts in Latin America even though leaders at the school insist that they are no longer engaged in such activities? Why or why not?

3. MaherArar, a naturalized Canadian citizen, changed planes at Kennedy International Airport on September 26, 2002, during his return trip home. He was seized by U.S. authorities, held in solitary confinement for two weeks, deprived of sleep and food, denied contact with a lawyer and with his family, then handed over to Syrian authorities to be interrogated under torture (beaten with a metal cable) and held for ten months because he was suspected of being a member of Al Qaeda. The Syrian authorities cleared Arar of having any terrorist connections. Arar was just one of the estimated 100 to 150 people seized by intelligence officials and transferred to other countries that practice torture by 2005. His ordeal seems to be based on nothing more than eating shawarma at a restaurant with a man who may or may not have known another man who may have had an Al Qaeda connection. In 2004 Arar filed a civil suit against the United States, which a federal judge dismissed in 2006. Arar appealed, but in 2009 the Court of Appeals for the Second Circuit upheld the ruling against him based on national security claims made by the Bush administration and extended by the Obama administration. In 2010 the Supreme Court refused to consider Arar's case based on solicitor general Elena Kagan's (now on the Supreme Court bench) usage of overwrought secrecy claims. Nevertheless, in 2007 the Canadian government formally apologized to Arar and announced that he would receive C$10.5 million in compensation.[70]

— Is it ethical to participate in physical torture to safeguard national security? What about psychological torture?

— Is it ethical for the United States to obtain vital information through physical torture conducted by other countries? Why or why not?

— Is outsourcing torture a betrayal of American values? Is the violation of human rights justified in order to bring human rights to former oppressive regimes such as Iraq and Afghanistan?

---

70. Scott Shane, "The Costs of Outsourcing Interrogation: A Canadian Muslim's Long Ordeal in Syria," *New York Times*, May 29, 2005; Nina Bernstein, "U.S. Defends Detentions at Airport," *New York Times*, October 10, 2005.

— Are acts of torture justifiable if they lead to valuable information? Is torture used to obtain information that can lead to fewer U.S. casualties a necessary evil of war? Is the punishment being meted out to those who participated in the acts of torture necessary or sufficient?

4.   An email on how to make a flour-based explosive sent by an Al Qaeda facilitator to Najibullah Zazi, a coffee vendor who at the time lived in Aurora, Colorado, led to foiling a plot to bomb the New York City subway in the fall of 2009. The email apparently was intercepted by the National Security Agency (NSA). President Obama used this incident to defend the NSA's Internet surveillance, stockpiling of telephone call logs, and collecting other data about Americans from companies such as Microsoft, Google, and Yahoo. The president argued that "modest encroachments on privacy" are worth making in order to protect the country against terrorist attacks. According to Obama, "You can't have 100 percent security and then also then have 100 percent privacy and zero inconvenience."[71]

— Senator Dianne Feinstein (D-CA), chair of the Senate Intelligence Committee, linked NSA's Internet surveillance system, called Prism, with foiling eight terrorism-related cases. Is stopping just one terrorist attack worth the "modest encroachments on privacy"? Should emails and phone records be examined without a warrant if that could save American lives? Prevent another 9/11? Is the cost to democracy worth the sense of greater security? And yet the New York City police department claims that it was they, due to a tip from Scotland Yard, who uncovered the Zazi plot.[72] If this is true, does it change the justification for Prism? Is surveillance versus security a false dichotomy?

— Prism is supposed to target only foreigners, even if they happen to be on American soil. Is this sufficient assurance? Can the government be trusted to follow these directives? Should people be concerned about the ability of the government to create extensive, secret digital dossiers on individuals? Are Americans in danger of repeating the abuses that occurred during J. Edger Hoover's tenure as director of the FBI, when he collected dossiers on political leaders and activists in order to enhance his own power? The government has long possessed the ability to submit cases to a secret intelligence court and obtain warrants to monitor emails and phone calls. So far the courts have rejected

71. Eric Schmitt, David E. Sanger, and Charlie Savage, "Administration Says Mining of Data Is Crucial to Fight Terror," *New York Times*, June 7, 2013.

72. Michael Powell, "Using a Would-Be Subway Bomber to Justify Sweeping Surveillance," *New York Times*, June 11, 2013.

eleven of the thirty-four thousand requests. Why forgo this legal procedure and instead violate the privacy of law-abiding Americans? Can less intrusive tactics achieve the goals of security? Are the present procedures a violation of the Fourth Amendment's protection against "unreasonable searches and seizures"? Supporters of the NSA's surveillance argue that the Patriot Act, ratified shortly after 9/11, provides them with the necessary authorization; yet according to Representative F. James Sensenbrenner (R-WI), "I authored the Patriot Act, and this is an abuse of that law."[73]

— Prism was leaked by a low-level NSA contractor, Edward J. Snowden. As of this writing, Snowden is a fugitive who, if caught and tried, could serve a lengthy prison term. Is Snowden a traitor, as is claimed by Representative John Boehner (R-OH) and Senator Dianne Feinstein (D-CA), or is he a hero? What about the news reporters at *The Guardian* and *Washington Post* who reported Snowden's information? Did their actions give aid and comfort to Al Qaeda and their associates? What punishment, if any, should Snowden receive? Should others leak secret information to the public if they believe that the government is acting immorally?

— A 2013 Washington Post–Pew Research Center poll revealed that 62 percent of Americans believe that it is important for the government to investigate terrorist threats even if the investigations intrude on personal privacy, while only 34 percent say that privacy should be the focus.[74] Are the NSA's activities a problem if the majority of the public and government approves of the surveillance? If a person has nothing to hide, why should he or she be concerned? Does a danger exist that racial and ethnic group profiling will come into play in decisions about whose phone calls or emails to monitor? The American Civil Liberties Union filed a lawsuit against the Obama administration on June 11, 2013, asking that the actions of the NSA be declared illegal and stopped. Are they making much ado about nothing, given that most Americans want the surveillance to continue?

---

73. Charlie Savage, "A.C.L.U. Files Lawsuit Seeking to Stop the Collection of Domestic Phone Logs," *New York Times*, June 12, 2013.

74. Jon Cohen, "Most Americans Back NSA Tracking Phone Records, Prioritize Probes over Privacy," *Washington Post*, June 10, 2013.

Chapter 7

Environment

Step 1. Observing

"Earth itself has become the nigger of the world," writes award-winning poet Alice Walker. She goes on to elaborate:

> It is perceived, ironically, as other, alien, evil, and threatening by those who are finding they cannot draw a healthful breath without its cooperation. While the Earth is poisoned, everything it supports is poisoned. While the Earth is enslaved, none of us is free. While the Earth is a "nigger," it has no choice but to think of us as all as Wasichus. While it is "treated like dirt," so are we. (1981, 147)

While the earth is poisoned, we ignore our complicity with said poisoning. Although a small conservative Christian segment of the American population dismisses global warming as a hoax, the fact remains that a 2007 U.N. report concluded that evidence for global warming is unequivocal, and that the actions of humans are primarily responsible (UNDP 2007, 1).

The first six months of 2012 were the hottest in the United States since record keeping began in 1895, as the country experienced the worst drought in fifty-six years (Glenn, Gordon, and Florescu 2012, 3). The United Nations has estimated that by 2050, the adverse impact of climate change on grain yields will double the price of wheat, leaving twenty-five million additional children malnourished (UNDP 2010, 102). An eighteen-month 2012 study commissioned by the CIA concluded that climate-driven crises could lead to domestic instability or international crises in food markets, water supplies, energy supplies, and public health systems. More frequent climate extremes, such as Hurricane Sandy's destructive path through the Northeast in 2012, are but a foretaste of what might become the new norm, causing strains on U.S. intelligence and military agencies, thus aggravating national security concerns.[1]

In response to the overwhelming evidence concerning global warming, upon which climate scientists are in agreement, the world's richest nations are spending billions to limit their own risks from global warming's consequences,

---

1. John M. Broder, "Report Outlines Climate Change Perils," *New York Times*, November 10, 2012.

specifically rising sea levels and drought. And yet those located farthest from the equator, specifically the industrial North, which is responsible for most of the global warming, will be affected least. Continents such as Africa, which accounts for less than 3 percent of the global emissions of carbon dioxide from fuel burning since 1900, face the greatest risks caused by drought and the disruption of water supplies.[2] The poorest 40 percent of the world's population, some 2.6 billion people, will experience "a future of diminished opportunity" as they bear the brunt of climate change (UNDP 2007, 2).

Limiting the risk of the industrialized North is directly linked to increasing the risk of the global South. Lawrence H. Summers was the World Bank's chief economist and vice president for development economics from 1990 until 1993. He left the World Bank to serve as undersecretary of the U.S. Treasury Department during the Clinton administration, eventually serving as Clinton's secretary of the treasury from 1999 until 2001. Afterward, from 2001 to 2006, he served as the president of Harvard University, ending his tenure amidst controversy. President Obama tapped him in 2009 to serve as the director of the White House National Economic Council.

While working at the World Bank in the early 90s, Summers made a name for himself as the bank's "high priest," responsible for supervising all economic publications, including the pacesetting *World Development Report*. Commenting on the topic of "dirty industries," the theme discussed in one of the publications that he oversaw, he wrote a memo to six highly placed colleagues. This private memo eventually was leaked to the press. In it, he wrote,

> Just between you and me, shouldn't the World Bank be encouraging more migration of the dirty industries to LDCs [less developed countries]? . . . The measurements of the costs of health impairing pollution depends on the foregone earnings from increased morbidity and mortality. From this point of view a given amount of health impairing pollution should be done in the country with the lowest cost, which will be the country with the lowest wages. I think the economic logic behind dumping a load of toxic waste in the lowest wage country is impeccable and we should face up to that. . . . I've always thought that under-populated countries in Africa are vastly under-polluted, their air quality is probably vastly inefficiently low compared to Los Angeles or Mexico City. (George and Sabelli 1994, 98–100)

In other words, if "a load of toxic waste" were dumped in a rich country, it would cause the infirmity and death of high-wage earners with normally

---

2. Andrew C. Revkin, "Poorest Nations Will Bear Brunt as World Warms," *New York Times*, April 1, 2007.

long life expectancies. According to Summers's own publication, $20,000 per year of potential earnings for a forty-year-old with an estimated twenty-five more years of productivity can contribute $500,000 to the global economy. By contrast, if the "load of toxic waste" is dumped in a poor country where the average worker earns $360 a year and has a life expectancy of fifty-five years, the contribution of a worker to the global economy could be figured at a measly $5,400 (George and Sabelli 1994, 98–100). Such an approach reduces humans to their economic value; people of Eurocentric origins nearly always possess economic privilege worth more than the disenfranchised. The sacredness of profits replaces the sacredness of life. Lethal pollutants, therefore, should be "dumped" in poor countries, perpetuating the old patterns of colonialism and imperialism. This link between the domination of the earth and the domination of the disenfranchised has been termed "environmental racism."[3]

The implementation of Summers's worldview has materialized in Savar, Bangladesh, where a toxic stench rises off a polluted canal into which garment factories dump their wastewater. These factories, which provide clothes for Western department stores such as Walmart, J. C. Penney, and H&M, have contributed to the ecological devastation of the area. Many rice paddies are inundated with toxic wastewater, fish stocks are decimated, coconut trees no longer produce coconuts, and smaller waterways are filled with sand and garbage to sell off as land for further housing or factory development. The situation is so bad that the children of garment workers who attend Genda Government Primary School are often dizzy and lightheaded, with some vomiting during class; all are unable to concentrate on their studies. These students know what colors are in fashion every time they look at the canal that runs by their school because the flowing water is at times red, turning to purple, gray, or blue, depending on the dyes used by the factories upstream. To make matters worse, Bangladesh is acutely vulnerable to global climate change. Millions could be displaced, and crop yields can significantly drop with the onslaught of changing weather patterns and rising sea levels.[4]

The dumping of pollutants upon certain people groups is not limited to poor countries. Within the United States, environmental hazards likewise are not randomly distributed. According to a 2012 study published in the *American Journal of Public Health*, a correlation exists between the race, ethnicity, and socioeconomic status of a community with the greater concentration and higher magnitude of environmental hazards containing significant health

---

3. The term "environmental racism" was first coined in the 1980s by Benjamin Chavis, a minister and chair of the Committee on Racial Justice for the United Church of Christ (Baker-Fletcher 1998, 4).

4. Jim Yardley, "Bangladesh Pollution, Told in Colors and Smells," *New York Times*, July 15, 2013.

risks. These communities tend to have fewer political, economic, or social resources to advocate on their behalf or to mitigate the health risks faced, thus creating what has come to be known as a "double jeopardy" (Huang and London 2012).

Concerns for the environment include groundwater pollution, acid rain, deforestation, global warming, ozone depletion, toxic and chemical spills, strip mining, and a host of other calamities. Most affected by environmental blight are people living on the margins of privilege. As transnational corporations race for the lowest wage, they also compete to identify locations with few or no regulations governing pollution or safe working environments. Energy production is one striking example. Within the United States, energy companies face intense pressure to produce power safely with a minimum of negative effects on the environment. But across the Mexican border few environmental regulations or oversight exist. On the edge of the city of Mexicali, three miles from the California border, two huge power plants were constructed, commencing operations in 2003. Owned by InterGen and Sempra Energy, the two plants generate billions of watts of electricity for millions of Californians. By constructing the plants south of the border, these corporations avoided the more stringent U.S. federal and state air pollution regulations.

Ironically, as its need for energy increased and electricity bills doubled, Mexico witnessed three-quarters of the power produced at its expense being exported to California. In return, Mexico received few jobs (paying about $2 an hour on a monthly contract).[5] According to a 2011 report by Resources for the Future, a nonprofit organization that conducts independent research on environmental issues, the health impact from these plants has "nontrivial health effects." While the health effects from nitrogen dioxide (NO_2) pollutants caused by the plants were negligible due to sparse populations downwind of the plants, fine particles found in the air at 2.5 micrometers or less in size ($PM_{2.5}$) posed a relatively serious problem, resulting in either hospital visits or mortality, mainly because $PM_{2.5}$ is responsible for producing respiratory and cardiovascular illnesses. The health concerns caused by $PM_{2.5}$ plumes do not stay in Mexico; they are transported northwest into the neighboring Imperial Valley in California, which lies just across the border (Blackman et al. 2011, 22). Not surprisingly, California's Imperial Valley is a heavily Latino/a region. Nevertheless, a federal judge in 2006 ruled in favor of the two plants, satisfied that they met their obligations under the U.S. Clean Air Act and several other federal regulations, thus creating a legal precedent for future power plants to be built in Mexico to serve the U.S. market while contributing

---

5. Tim Weiner, "U.S. Will Get Power, and Pollution, from Mexico," *New York Times*, September 17, 2002.

to environmental racism.[6] These energy *maquiladoras* represent a new form of environmental imperialism whereby energy is generated for the United States by capitalizing on lax environmental regulations on the other side of the border, with those negatively impacted by the pollutants generated being primarily populations of color.

The United States not only creates energy to the detriment of Mexico, but also uses Mexico as the dumping ground for its hazardous-waste material. For example, according to a study conducted by the Commission for Environmental Cooperation (an agency created under the auspices of the North American Free Trade Agreement), U.S. companies export lead batteries to Mexican recycling plants that fail to meet U.S. environmental standards for workers and public health safety. Mexico's less stringent limits for lead pollution, coupled with less vigorous enforcement, makes it an ideal locale to dispose of lead batteries. By 2012, 30 to 60 percent of all batteries recycled in Mexico came from U.S. firms, an increase of 449 to 525 percent since 2004 (Secretariat of the Commission for Environmental Cooperation 2012, v, x). According to the report, the United States does not follow common procedures among developed nations that treat lead batteries as hazardous waste. Yet lead poisoning, a byproduct of the battery recycling process when no attention is given to worker and public safety, is linked to kidney damage and high blood pressure. Among children, lead poisoning leads to stunted growth development and behavioral problems.

A Mexican battery recycling plant owned by Johnson Controls International puts out more than thirty times as much lead emission than its newest plant in the United States. The Milwaukee-based company acquired the recycling plant in 2005 to reduce its environmental footprint. Nevertheless, soil samples collected in a school playground close to the recycling plant outside Mexico City found lead levels to be five times that of the United States.[7] The United States has successfully learned how to export its environmental pollution to the detriment of inhabitants of other countries. But obviously, the United States is not alone in abusing the environment in order to make a profit.

An increase in environmental pollution is also seen in the growing energy needs and rapid industrialization of countries like China. For example, from 1980 to 2010 global coal usage has almost doubled, driven by Asia, specifically China, whose demand increased almost fivefold during that same period, accounting for 73 percent of Asia's coal consumption and almost half of the 2010 global coal consumption (U.S. Energy Information Administration

6. Diane Lindquist, "Permits on 2 Power Plants in Mexico OK—Environmental Issues Satisfied, Judge Rules" *San Diego Union-Tribune*, December 1, 2006.

7. Elisabeth Rosenthal, "Report Faults U.S. Use of Mexican Battery Recyclers," *New York Times*, February 9, 2013.

2011, 1–2). According to a U.S. Energy Information Administration 2010 analysis brief, coal use has climbed faster in China (the world's largest coal producer and consumer) than anywhere else in the world. Originally a major net exporter, China, since 2009, also became a net importer. Additionally, China is the second-largest oil consumer (after the United States), representing about a third of the consumption growth of 2009 (U.S. Energy Information Administration 2010, 1, 16). Coupled with soaring car sales,[8] Chinese emissions, in 2007, surpassed the United States, making China the world's largest annual emitter of carbon dioxide (CO_2),[9] threatening international efforts to curb global warming (International Energy Agency 2011, 24).

A significant part of China's growth in energy consumption is due to that country's emergence as a leading exporter of manufacturing goods to the United States. A desire to minimize labor costs, along with the cost of adhering to basic environmental regulations, makes China attractive to multinational corporations. Take, for example, Chen Xilong, a twenty-three-year-old employee at a leather ware factory in Guangzhou, who now lies in a hospital bed wearing adult diapers, unable to move his head because he is too weak, unable to feed himself, and unable to calculate simple mathematical equations, such as multiplying two by two. Chen suffers from acute dichloroethane poisoning caused by inhaling the glues used at the factory. According to the Chinese Ministry of Health, 27,240 new cases of occupational diseases were reported in 2010.[10] Occupational diseases, such as the one suffered by Chen, overtook workplace accidents as the biggest danger to Chinese workers. About 90 percent of occupational disease cases come from of pneumoconiosis, or black lung disease, caused by inhaling dust, especially mineral or metallic.[11]

The majority of China's 230 million migrant workers lack stable employment. A surplus labor force led many to settle for work paid at less than a dollar an hour for twelve to eighteen hours a day, with no healthcare benefits, employment contracts, or union representatives. Being grateful for any job regardless of the hazardous conditions, workers are exposed to conditions under which many end up experiencing fatal respiratory, circulatory,

---

8. China has the world's largest auto market. In 2011 the Chinese purchased almost 16.5 million automobiles, a jump from 7.56 million in 2009. During the first decade of the millennium China's vehicle sales increased by more than fivefold. Among first-time auto buyers, the increase between 2000 and 2008 was more than eightfold. See Bruce Einhorn, "The Surge in China's Auto Sales May Soon Slow," *Bloomberg Businessweek*, April 5, 2012; Keith Bradsher, "With First Car, a New Life in China," *New York Times*, April 24, 2008.

9. Although CO_2 is measured in cumulative and per capita terms, the United States remains the largest contributor to greenhouse gasses.

10. Sally Wang, "Safety Down the Tube," *South China Morning Post* (Hong Kong), March 28, 2012.

11. Chen Xin, "200m Chinese in Danger of Contracting Workplace Disease," *China Daily* (People's Republic of China), April 12, 2011.

neurological, and digestive illnesses. The producers of today's neoliberalism are beginning to create horrors equal to those suffered by workers during the dawn of the industrial age.

But workers are not the only ones impacted by runaway pollution. As Beijing's smog rises to record levels, the most vulnerable—children—pay a hefty price. Consider Zhang Zixuan's son. Since the age of three, this child has struggled with a chronic cough and stuffy nose. Every night he requires a sinus cleaning with saltwater piped through machine tubes. With deadly pollutants up to forty times the recommended exposure limit in Beijing, most children seldom go outdoors, as schools cancel outdoor activities. A new generation, imprisoned in their homes, is nevertheless being choked to death. The smog is at such extreme levels that during one exceptionally bad week in January 2013 the Beijing Children's Hospital admitted up to nine thousand patients a day for emergency treatment, of which half were for respiratory problems.[12]

Not all of what is wrong with the environment can be blamed on industrialization. World poverty also has a negative effect. Take Africa as an example. During the 1990s Africa had the world's highest rate of deforestation as the poor cut down trees for firewood, their only source of fuel. As poor Africans burned firewood and coal to keep warm and cook, the amount of air pollutants rose to three times the health-standard level. In Zimbabwe children who were diagnosed with recurrent pneumonia were found to be more likely to live in homes that used indoor wood fuel. This dilemma is not limited to Africa; half of the world's population cooks with solid fuels (Schluger 2010, 56). The situation is aggravated as migration to urban shantytowns from rural villages increases. A direct link exists between poverty and the environment. Nations that suffer from massive poverty are simply unable to safeguard their natural resources.

Deforestation and its negative environmental consequences are not due solely to global poverty and the actions taken by the world's poor to cook their meals and keep warm. Deforestation and global warming are also the result of the meat-based eating habits within industrial nations, specifically the United States. Over nine billion livestock must be maintained in order to supply the animal protein consumed each year by Americans (Pimentel and Pimentel 2003, 661). Furthermore, an increasing global desire for a U.S.-type diet is leading experts from the Food and Agriculture Organization of the United Nations to envision a doubling of meat production during the first half of the present century (Steinfield et al. 2006, xx). Drastic increases in livestock create greater competition for scarce resources, specifically

---

12. Edward Wong, "In China, Breathing Becomes a Childhood Risk," *New York Times*, April 22, 2013.

sufficient land for grazing. Ironically, the land used by animal grazing could feed more of the world's population if it were diverted for crops grown for human consumption.

According to a U.N. study, grazing takes up 26 percent of the land on earth that is not covered by ice. An additional 33 percent of the planet's arable land is required for feed-crop production. Production of livestock accounts for 70 percent of all agricultural land use and almost one-third of the entire land surface of the planet. The need for grazing land is so acute that it is the main cause of global deforestation, especially in Latin America. In South America 70 percent of what was the Amazon forest is now used for animal grazing and feed crops (Steinfield et al. 2006, xxi). In Central America forest area has been reduced by almost 40 percent between 1960 and 2000 (Rosales 2011, 2).

In addition to this increasing land shortage caused by the needs created by livestock production are the repercussions of freshwater shortages and depletion. Although the earth is largely covered in water, occupying 70 percent of the globe, less than 1 percent of it is freshwater. Every year five million people, mostly children from the global South, die from water-borne diseases. About one billion out of the six billion who inhabit the earth cannot turn on a tap and obtain clean water, and two billon lack basic sanitation. And yet livestock production is considered to be responsible for most of water pollution, due mainly from animal waste runoffs, chemical contaminations from tanneries, pesticides and fertilizer runoff from feed crops, and the emergence of antibiotic resistance (Steinfield et al. 2006, xxi). Besides contaminating water, livestock production is a main user of freshwater. Half of the world's available freshwater is consumed by humans, of which 70 percent is diverted to agriculture (Picone and Van Tassel 2002, 102). The production of 1 kilogram of grain-fed beef requires 100,000 liters of water, due mainly to feed crops. By contrast, the production of 1 kilogram of soybeans requires 2,000 liters of water; of rice, 1,912 liters; of wheat, 900 liters; and of potatoes, 500 liters (Pimentel and Pimentel 2003, 662). Sustaining the U.S. meat-based diet is causing global ecological damage, specifically in the global South.

The ecological global damage caused by the United States is not limited to those living beyond our borders. Environmental racism, defined as the link between the degradation of the environment and the racial composition of the areas where degradation takes place, is faced by communities of color within the U.S. borders. According to a 2011 study conducted by the U.S. Department of Health and Human Services, a correlation exists between ethnicity and the counties with the most unhealthy air quality. Asians (26.2 percent) and Latino/as (26.6 percent) have the greatest percentage of residency in counties with "24 hours fine particulate matter ($PM_{2.5}$) nonattainment." A similar pattern appeared when the study considered the proportion of Asian (50.2 percent) and Hispanic (48.4 percent) persons living in eight-hour ozone nonattainment counties. Even short-term exposure to ozone (caused by industrial and vehicular emissions) and $PM_{2.5}$ (solid or liquid particles suspended in the air) has been associated with mortality, cardiovascular- and respiratory-related hospitalization, and exacerbation of asthma, emphysema, and bronchitis (Yip et al. 2011).

Race, according to a growing body of empirical evidence, continues to be the most significant variable in determining the location of commercial, industrial, and military hazardous-waste sites. Race is the most significant predicator in forecasting where the nation's commercial hazardous-waste facilities are located. According to 2000 U.S. Census data, people of color represent 56 percent of the population that lives less than 1.8 miles from one of the 413 commercial hazardous-waste facilities (Acevedo-Garcia et al. 2008, 27–28). This means that of the 9 million Americans living in neighborhoods hosting one of these commercial hazardous-waste facilities, more than 5.1 million of them are of color, comprising 2.5 million Hispanics, 1.8 million African Americans, 616,000 Asians, and 62,000 Native Americans (Bullard et al. 2007, 46). The poorer the community, the greater the risk of environmental abuse, because the economically privileged are able to move away from such sites, an option unavailable to the poor, who mostly are people of color. Forty of the 44 states (90 percent) with hazardous-waste facilities have disproportionately high percentages of people of color living in the host neighborhoods. Out of the 149 metropolitan areas with hazardous-waste sites, 105 (70 percent) have host neighborhoods predominantly composed of people of color. Out of the 44 states, African American neighborhoods within 38 states, Hispanic neighborhoods within 35 states, and Asian neighborhoods within 27 states are more likely to host a hazardous-waste facility (Bullard, Johnson, and Torres 2011, 23). Between 1999 and 2009 the National Academy of Science produced five environmental justice reports showing that "low-income and people of color communities are exposed to higher levels of pollution than the rest of the nation and that these same populations experience certain diseases in greater number than more affluent White communities" (Bullard, Johnson, and Torres 2011, 53). Black ethicist Emilie Townes has said that the effects of toxic waste on the lives of people of color who are relegated by their poverty to live on ecologically hazardous lands are akin to a contemporary version of lynching a whole people (1995, 55).

Environmental racism is not limited to hazardous-waste sites. Violators of pollution laws received less stringent punishments when violations occurred in nonwhite neighborhoods than when they occurred in white neighborhoods; fines often were 500 percent higher in white communities than in communities of color. When violations occurred in minority communities, the government was slower to act, taking as much as 20 percent more time than when violations occurred in white communities (Acevedo-Garcia 2008, 27–28). And even when a lawsuit was brought before the Eastern District Federal Court of Virginia about the placement of landfills in predominantly black King and Queen County (*R.I.S.E. v. Kay*), the U.S. judge, while acknowledging the historical trend of disproportionately placing landfills in African American areas, still ruled that the case failed to prove discrimination (Bullard 1993, 28).

Environmental racism also takes a heavy toll on children of color. For example, in a U.S. Department of Health and Human Services study released in 2011, of the 7.8 percent of the population who suffer from asthma, a disproportionate number of them are people of color. Asthma prevalence among poor children was highest among Puerto Ricans at 23.3 percent, multiracial children at 21.1 percent, and African Americans at 15.8 percent, while among whites it was at 10.1 percent (Moorman et al. 2011). It is no coincidence that the predominantly black neighborhood of central Harlem in New York City has the highest percentage of documented cases of asthma in the United States. In 2008 African Americans had a 35 percent higher rate of asthma than whites, suffering from inflammation and constriction of the airways that makes breathing difficult. The worst triggers of asthma are found in abundance in central Harlem (and the South Bronx), specifically insect (cockroach) droppings, mold, mildew, diesel exhaust, and cigarette smoke. African American children living outside of Harlem are still vulnerable to asthma because 68 percent of blacks live within thirty miles of a coal-fired power plant. Nationwide, African American children have a 500 percent higher death rate from asthma compared to white children. Additionally, they have a 260 percent higher emergency rate, and a 250 percent higher hospitalization rate. And yet Senator Jeff Sessions (R-AL), during a Senate hearing on the EPA budget in 2012, claimed that air pollution victims are "unidentified and imaginary."[13]

The military is also a major threat to the environment where people of color reside. Of the 651 nuclear weapons or devices exploded on the U.S. mainland by the military, all test sites occurred on Native American territories (Seager 1993, 63). The vast majority of these detonations occurred on the lands of the Shoshone nation (LaDuke 1993, 99). Uranium, used for atomic weapons, is mined mostly in Navajo territory. Worldwide, 70 percent of all uranium resources are located on indigenous lands. Even though most U.S. uranium mines are presently abandoned, they can still emit high levels of radioactive gases. One of the ingredients of the solid waste from uranium

---

13. Dominique Browning, "The Racial Politics of Asthma," *Time*, March 29, 2012.

mining is radium-226, which remains radioactive for some sixteen thousand years (LaDuke 1993, 99, 102). It is reported that Navajo teenagers have a rate of organ cancer seventeen times the national average (Hamilton 1993, 71).

People of color also suffer from environmental hazards in the workplace. Because of discrimination, they often are relegated to the most perilous of jobs. The myth that people with darker skin have a greater ability to withstand heat was used to justify assigning African Americans to work at the extremely dangerous coke ovens in the iron and steel industry. Similarly, within the electronic industries, "darker" workers have been regularly assigned jobs dealing with caustic chemicals. The rationale used is that skin irritations caused by chemical exposure are less pronounced on dark skin than on white skin (Wright and Bullard 1993, 155, 157).

Finally, since stress is known to be a major cause of illnesses, the environment and work assignments delegated to people of color contribute to shorter life expectancies. Social factors such as poverty and the environmental hazards that attracts are beyond the control of individuals. They certainly contribute to hypertension (elevated blood pressure), a major cause of organ damage and heart disease, within the African American community, resulting in hypertension rates in the black community being twice as high as within the white community. It should be noted that hypertension is not a genetic trait among African Americans; in some other countries hypertension rates are lower among blacks than among whites (Wright and Bullard 1993, 156–57).

In the final analysis, Summers enunciated the neoliberal position when he said, "Promoting development is the best way to protect the environment" (George and Sabelli 1994, 170). Those from the margins of society who experience "a load of toxic waste" dumped upon them in the name of development might have a different opinion.

Step 2. Reflecting

Generally speaking, Eurocentric theology has concerned itself with the relationship between the Deity and humans, as well as with relationships among humans. The prominent Eurocentric thread within Christianity, as practiced by the powerful and privileged, has created a faith with little connection to or understanding of a collective or communal spirituality linked to the land. The emphasis remains, among many Protestants, on a "personal" relationship with Jesus. Nor has much attention been given to the relationship between humans and creaturekind.[14] Instead, the industrialization of agriculture has

---

14. I am influenced by Carter Heyward, who uses the term "creaturekind" to refer to all that God has created that is other than human, meaning animals, plants, and minerals. While the term encompasses humans, Heyward struggles for language that avoids defining all that God created that is not human as "other-than-human" (2004, 18, 20).

led to a disregard of animal welfare, which comprises a major proportion of creaturekind. Few are concerned with how food arrives at their supermarkets. Industrialization has replaced husbandry, leading to the breaking of the human-animal social contract as concerns for animal well-being make way for cost-effectiveness. At one time a farmer would have spent more time or money than an ill animal was worth; today, however, attention to corporate profit discourages spending more in caring for animals than their book value. Yet we know that ignoring the conditions that food animals must endure leads to ecological concerns.

Today, the most effective way for an individual to reduce the size of his or her carbon footprint probably is to eat less meat. Nevertheless, a Western meat-based diet, mainly affordable to a global minority living in industrial nations, is accepted as some type of human right, regardless of how this diet in negatively impacting the global ecology (as well as our individual health). According to the Food and Agriculture Organization of the United Nations, the U.S. livestock sector is one of the top two or three significant contributors to the most serious environmental problems faced at every level of society, from local to global, impacting climate change and degradation, air pollution, water pollution, water shortage, and loss of biodiversity. Food production and distribution account for one-third of all human-caused global warming. The fuel required by the U.S. agricultural sector greatly contributes to greenhouse gas emissions. Roughly 123 million barrels of oil are consumed during the production of synthetic fertilizers and pesticides (Giani and Ahrensfeld 2002). If we add to this figure the transportation cost of getting the average American meal, which travels some fifteen hundred miles from point of origin to our plates, a total of 450 billion gallons of oil is required each and every year to sustain the U.S. food system (Cool Foods Campaign 2009, 120).

Also contributing to the greenhouse gas problem are the animals themselves, along with their waste. The methane released by cows and pigs, while less prevalent in the air than carbon dioxide, is twenty-three times more potent as a heat-trapping gas, making livestock responsible for 18 percent percent of the world's greenhouse gas problem, compared to transportation, which is responsible for 13 percent (Steinfield et al. 2006, xxi). Of the gases emitted in 2006 due to human activity, livestock (or more specifically, the manure of our livestock) are responsible for 37 percent of the methane, 65 percent of nitrous oxide, and 64 percent of ammonia (Bonney and Dawkins 2008, 2–3). The sheer number of livestock in crowded facilities makes it impossible to process properly the manure generated. A dairy farm with 2,500 cows produces as much waste as a city of 411,000 individuals; but unlike the city, no sewage treatment plant exists (Haines and Staley 2004, 7). Properly processing animal waste becomes a logistical impossibility. Animal waste is sprayed onto the land, creating cesspools that pollute groundwater, streams, and rivers, leading to health problems among workers and nearby neighbors. When we consider that two-thirds of all human infectious diseases are zoonotic, we should not be surprised that respiratory illnesses, cardio-vascular problems, and prenatal and neonatal health concerns are on the rise wherever livestock-based environmental contamination occurs (Rollin 2008, 15).

And yet we ignore the ecological damage caused by the eating habits of industrialized nations because, for the most part, the environment has been seen as a means of satisfying the wants and desires of human beings. Human beings, viewing themselves as the center of the created order, have histori-cally perceived the environment as an unlimited storehouse of raw materials provided by God for human convenience. Thus, the resources of the earth often have been sacrificed in the quest for economic growth and meeting our personal desires. Yet all that has life is sacred before the Creator of life, making it difficult to limit spiritual worthiness and well-being only to human beings.

Native Americans remind us that within the circle of creation all are equal in value to the Creator. George "Tink" Tinker expresses this view: "A chief is not valued above the people; nor are two-legged valued above the animal nations, the birds, or even trees and rocks" (1994, 126). Human beings' relationships to creation become a matter of life and death, balancing one's needs and place within the world with preserving the world for one's descendants who will live "seven generations from now." While one takes from the plenty of creation, something must always be returned to main-tain balance (Kidwell, Noley, and Tinker 2001, 33). Others, such as Indian scholar Aruna Gnanadason, totally reject the dualism intrinsic in Western theological thought, which sees an opposition between spirit and flesh, men and women, mind and body. She instead avers a cosmology that affirms the interdependence and harmony of all life forms (1996, 77). Instead of a binary opposition, many Asian theologians, such as Kwok Pui-lan, emphasize the balance of "heaven and earth, yang and yin, sun and moon, and father and mother," where they are "complementally, mutually reinforcing and inter-playing with one other" (2000, 90).

The earth's resources, as we are slowly learning, are not everlasting. Proper stewardship requires creating a harmonious relationship with nature, as with other human beings. Poor care of the environment creates pollution, lowers life expectancy, and is a major source of many illnesses and diseases for those living close by, who are predominantly poor and of color. The exploitation of the earth's resources and the exploitation of the earth's marginalized are interconnected, making it difficult, if not impossible, to speak of one without mentioning the other. Brazilian theologian Leonardo Boff has given voice to the cry of the oppressed, connecting it with the very cry of the earth. He insists that the logic and justification that lead the powerful and privileged to exploit and subjugate the world's marginalized are the same logic and justification that plunder the earth's wealth and lead to its devastation (1997, xi).

Some women ethicists such as Karen Warren advocate ecofeminism, an environmental theology that seeks to overcome the hierarchy and dualism imposed upon nature. She states that ecofeminism is based on four central claims: (1) there are important connections between the oppression of women and the oppression of nature; (2) there is a need to understand the nature of these connections in order to understand the oppression of women and oppression of nature; (3) feminist theory and practice must include an ecological perspective; (4) solutions to ecological problems must include a feminist perspective (1987, 4–5). The interconnectedness between women and nature has always existed. Wilderness or virgin land awaits insemination with man's seed of progress and civilization, for nature as feminine (Mother Nature) has always required its domination and domestication (De La Torre 2003b, 96) or, in the words of Vandana Shiva, "a woman to be raped" (1996, 69).

For Lois Daly, the ethical goal is to reconceptualize the links between oppressors and oppressed in nonhierarchical and nonpatriarchal ways. Stress is placed on living in the world as co-members of the ecological community (1994, 300). While ecofeminism unmasks the interconnectedness between the oppression of women and the oppression of nature, white feminists, unfortunately, often fail to develop fully the need to expand the paradigm to encompass marginalized groups of color. Eurocentric women, with the privilege of not living in toxic, infested neighborhoods, at times fail to consider how race and ethnicity, more so than gender, remain the main indicators of who lives in ecologically hazardous areas and who does not. Karen Baker-Fletcher makes a similar observation:

> There is a tendency among middle-class eco-feminist and mainstream eco-theologians to enjoy the privilege of extensive international travel which informs their spirituality. Such a privilege enables them to have the luxury of providing a global analysis. In contrast, there are many within the U.S. environmental justice movement who would find it a luxury to leave their own neighborhoods. This is the cause of a credibility gap between theologians in the academy and the grassroots from which liberation spirituality emerges. (2004, 125–26)

While environmentalists from the dominant culture concern themselves mainly with issues of clean air and water and the protection of habitats of endangered species, Robert Bullard observes,

The environmental-equity movement is an extension of the social justice movement. Environmentalists may be concerned about clean air, but may have opposing views on the construction of low-income housing in white, middle-class, suburban neighborhoods. . . . It is not surprising that mainstream environmental organizations have not been active on issues that disproportionately impact minority communities. . . . Yet minorities are the ones accused of being ill-informed, unconcerned, and inactive on environmental issues. (1994, 128–29)

When those who are racially and ethnically marginalized compare the environmental quality of life of where they live with that of the larger white society, it becomes all too obvious that a link exists between polluted sites and disenfranchisement. Few white environmentalists seriously consider this link, and consequently they fail to understand a major reason why pollution occurs disproportionately in certain areas. The failure of the environmental justice movement to come to terms with the inherent racism that relegates those on the margins to the greatest ecological health risks prevents fostering a truly global, holistic approach to the environment. Environmentalists benefiting from white privilege cannot continue to isolate ecological concerns from environmental racism. Continuing to mask environmental racism limits, if not frustrates, any attempt or hope for the liberation of humans and creaturekind alike.[15]

Step 3. Praying

If the creation story describes humanity's appointment as stewards of the earth's resources, then as caretakers, human beings are called to protect, preserve, and safeguard those resources so that all can benefit and enjoy its fruits. Creation as gift means that all living creatures have a basic right to its products, and that no group has the right to hoard its resources. Hoarding the earth's resources upsets the delicate balance between life and the resources needed to sustain life.

Ironically, Christianity, to some degree, has encouraged the destruction of God's creation. The first creation story ends with God saying, "And God said to [human beings], be fruitful and multiply, and fill the earth, and subdue it, and have dominion over the fish of the sea, over the birds of the heavens, and over the beasts creeping on the land" (Gen. 1:28). Biblical passages such as these have led to and been used to justify human domination of nature. Historically, we have come to read this verse as permission to use and abuse

---

15. Few white ethicists are attempting to learn from the margins. However, an excellent example of an effort to understand environmental problems at the margins is *Women Healing Earth* (Ruether 1996).

creation, similar to how the ancient rulers used and abused their subjects. Man, like the ancient king, is ordained to rule over all. This understanding of humans (specifically the male) occupying the pinnacle of creation has been echoed throughout Christian history, most recently by Pope John Paul II, who stated, "Everything in creation is ordered to man and everything is made subject to him" (1995, 61).

Western Christianity's understanding of stewardship and domination as subjugating nature has contributed to the present ecological challenges facing humanity. The belief that the destiny of human beings is to reside with God in heaven and that the earth is but a place of sojourn until we reach that destiny has encouraged, at the very least, neglect of our environment. The greatest Christian threat to the environment comes from those who hold a view of the future or the end of time (an "eschatological" view) like the one made popular by the Tim LaHaye and Jerry Jenkins's *Left Behind* twelve-book series (published between 1995 and 2003). These stories focus on the tribulations faced by those unfortunate souls "left behind" during the "last days" of Armageddon (judgment day), when they must face the antichrist. Although the books are fictional, the authors insist that they are based on the correct and only valid literal interpretation of biblical prophecy. These Christians may well welcome the destruction of the earth, for it indicates Jesus' "second coming," when he raptures (takes away from the earth) those destined to be saved. If the world ends in a conflagration and such an end is close at hand, why then worry about the environment?

This "premillennial" view was best articulated by James G. Watt, secretary of the interior under the Reagan administration and the cabinet member officially responsible for protecting the environment. He explained that his responsibility "is to follow the Scriptures which call upon us to occupy the land until Jesus returns."[16] Additionally, during a Congressional committee meeting in 1981, he testified, "I don't know how many future generations we can count on until the Lord returns" (Wolf 1981, 58). In short, Jesus is coming soon to rescue the faithful from an earth destined for total destruction. Any attempt to preserve or safeguard the earth is a waste of time.

It seems, though, that our refusal to recognize the damage being committed to the environment constitutes the ultimate form of oppression, for it brings destruction to life (including human life) on this planet. If liberation is to come to the earth's marginalized, then it must also come to the earth. The earth needs to be saved in order for individuals also to receive salvation. If nature is wasted, depleted, and destroyed, then individuals will be unable to control their destiny. Such a sin cannot be easily atoned for, for we cannot resurrect extinct species.

---

16. Bill Prochnau, "The Watt Controversy," *Washington Post*, June 30, 1981.

Scripture articulates that the earth belongs to God. The psalmist boldly proclaims, "The earth is the Lord's, and the fullness of the world and those who live in it" (Ps. 24:1). The God who takes notice of the least of creation, the falling sparrow, is concerned with all of creation. "Man" is not called to dominate the earth; rather, human beings are called to be stewards of the earth's resources, ensuring that each person has sufficient resources to meet his or her needs. Baker-Fletcher insists that the incarnation, God becoming flesh, is the act of the Divine joining the dust of the earth, the very dust from which human beings were created, in order to reconcile the broken relationship between God and creation (1998, 19). The abundant life that Christ came to give cannot be accomplished within a depleted earth. Survival is a key requirement for any form of abundant living.

Most indigenous religions from Africa and the Americas maintain a sacred respect for creation, a respect that has been lost and historically abused by many Western Christian groups. Earth-centered religions, rooted in the abode of ancestors, are unlike Western religions that emphasize a heavenly place or stress the placement of the stars and planets to determine the course of human events. For example, in the religion of the Yoruba people in West Africa as practiced by Caribbean blacks, whites, and biracial Hispanics, the earth is believed to provide all that is needed to live a full and abundant life. Like the oceans that are able to support and sustain all life that exists in its waters, so too is the land able to support and sustain all life that exists upon it. This abundance becomes evident as human beings learn to live in harmony with nature. Shortages occur when humans attempt to impose their own will upon the fair and natural distribution of nature's resources according to the needs of the people (De La Torre 2004, 14).

Step 4. Case Studies

1. Probably the greatest deforestation project presently under way is occurring in the 250,000 square miles of Gran Chaco forest, which covers parts of Brazil, Bolivia, Argentina, and Paraguay. "Chaco" is the Quechua word for "hunting land," and indeed it was. But now, the need for cattle grazing has led German-speaking Mennonite ranchers, descendants of colonialists who arrived over a century ago, to bulldoze and burn down the forest, the home and hunting land of indigenous people. In Paraguay, between 2007 and 2012, these ranchers have cleared about 10 percent of the forest to provide grazing land for their vast herds of cattle, so as to meet the surging demand of beef export (85 percent of all beef is exported). At the present rate of deforestation, a fear exists that the entire Chaco forest will be destroyed by 2040. Already the land's inhabitants are being replaced. For example, in 2004 a subgroup of the Ayoreo people who called themselves

the "Totobiegosode" made contact with outsiders for the first time. Due to the invasion of lands, many were forced to abandon their way of life. According to Nelson Cintra, the Brazilian border town mayor of Porto Murtinho, and among the first ranchers to put down stakes in the Chaco forest in 1997, "Environmentalists complain about deforestation, but the world has billions of mouths to feed. There are now 1 million heads of cattle in Alto Paraguay, whereas 15 years ago there were just 50,000."[17]

— The descendants of the European colonizers continue to profit through the displacement of the original landholders. What responsibility, if any, do they have to the indigenous people?

— Does a link exist between the demand from industrial nations for beef and deforestation in the two-thirds world? If you eat meat, are you responsible for this environmental disaster? If so, what can you do?

— Species and plant life not known to humans are being destroyed. Should this be a concern? Why or why not?

— Is Nelson Cintra, mayor of Porto Murtinho, correct in asserting that feeding the people should take priority over environmental concerns? Should economic development be halted if it negatively impacts the environment? Is some environmental degradation acceptable if it spurs the economy, creating wealth, jobs, and financial independence?

2. Nguyen Van Quy, who suffers from cancer, has had two children born with birth defects. Nguyen Thi Phi has suffered through four miscarriages, while Duong Quynh Hoa suffers from breast cancer and has high levels of dioxin in her blood system. The three women worked in areas sprayed with Agent Orange at the height of the Vietnam War. They blame their physical disorders on the U.S. military.[18] The military is a large, if not the largest, threat to the environment. During the Vietnam War the U.S. military dumped about twenty-five million gallons of assorted noxious chemicals, herbicides, and defoliants. Dioxin (TCDD), a major terato-genic (birth-deforming) contaminant, attaches itself to human and animal fat cells, and it persists in bodies as well as the food chain for decades. According to a 2002 Vietnamese government study, a total of 622,043 individuals have been negatively affected by the chemicals, including 169,693 children and 4,505 grandchildren who suffer from high rates of deformities and mental handicaps.[19] Nevertheless, a direct scientific

17. Simon Romero, "A Forest under Siege in Paraguay," *New York Times*, March 25, 2012.

18. Tini Tran, "Vietnam's Agent Orange Victims File Suit," *Associated Press*, February 4, 2004.

19. "More Than 620,000 Vietnamese Victims of War Herbicides," *Associated Press*, October 23, 2002.

link has yet to be made between dioxin and herbicide exposure and congenital malformations (Schecter and Constable 2006). Still, Vietnamese scientists claim that five out of one hundred children are born with some form of mental or physical abnormality, representing a fourfold increase since the start of the war. The Vietnamese claims are consistent with studies conducted by the U.S. National Institutes of Health that found that Agent Orange's chemical compounds caused birth defects in laboratory animals.[20]

— During war, actions must be taken to protect the lives of the soldiers. In Vietnam the use of Agent Orange defoliated the heavy jungles, exposing enemy troops, hence saving U.S. lives. Does war justify the usage of toxic chemicals to protect our troops? Why or why not? Is preserving the lives of U.S. soldiers of greater value than the lives of future generations of Vietnamese? Why or why not?

— Two of the primary producers of Agent Orange were Dow Chemical Company and Monsanto. What responsibility, if any, do these companies and the U.S. government, which used their products, have toward the people of Vietnam?

— On January 30, 2004, Quy, Phi, and Hoa filed a civil lawsuit at the U.S. District Court in Brooklyn, New York, against ten American chemical companies that produced the defoliant, claiming that these companies committed war crimes for supplying Agent Orange to the military. The suit sought billions of dollars in damages. On March 10, 2005, Judge Jack Weinstein dismissed the suit.[21] And on June 18, 2007, the Second Circuit Court of Appeals upheld Weinstein's ruling and dismissed the case. The Supreme Court, on March 2, 2009, refused to reconsider the Court of Appeals ruling. Is Judge Weinstein correct in siding with the chemical companies, which argued that supplying the defoliant did not amount to a war crime? Are these multinational companies liable? Do Quy, Phi, and Hoa have any legal or moral rights to bring suits against such corporations? Against the U.S. government? Why or why not?

— The dumping of toxic chemicals was conducted secretly, under the cover of national security. Do citizens have a right to know what actions their military has taken, especially when the consequences of those actions have a generational impact on the environment? Or

---

20. Jason Grotto, "Agent Orange: Birth Defects Plague Vietnam; U.S. Slow to Help," *Chicago Tribune*, December 8, 2009.

21. William Glaberson, "Agent Orange Case for Millions of Vietnamese Is Dismissed," *New York Times*, March 10, 2005.

does national security, specifically in the midst of conducting a war, trump environmental concerns?

3. Port Arthur, Texas, has the dubious distinction of being one of the most polluted cities in America. The EPA has listed Port Arthur among the cities with the most dangerous ozone levels, flagging it for excessive amounts of benzene. Toxic chemicals continuously spew from the petrochemical plants, creating health problems for the predominantly poor and of-color residents. And yet government officials fight hard to keep the industry that is literally killing the population. Former mayor Oscar Ortiz framed the conversation in the closing days of his term when he said, "If industry goes away, people might as well go away too because there'll be no money. That's the continued salvation of this city." And while it is true that the refineries and chemical plants contribute through taxes about 67 percent of the city's budget, it is also true that the prosperity brought by these industries bypasses the predominantly black communities. When activist Hilton Kelly campaigned for stricter monitoring of plant emissions, then-mayor Ortiz dismissed him as an alarmist who likes to "stir things up" in communities of color. After all, according to Ortiz, "We've all got to die of something."[22]

    — Does Port Arthur, as former mayor Ortiz maintains, face an "either-or" situation—either the environmental protection of citizens of color or the revenues received from the plants?

    — Does raising the consciousness of the disenfranchised amount to stirring things up in minority communities? Do the mayor's comments sound condescending? Paternalistic? Are there other examples demonstrating how the marginalized are dismissed when they resist their oppression?

    — Are the destructive acts conducted by the chemical companies and oil refineries possibly due to institutionalized racism (impact on communities of color), institutionalized classism (impact on the poor), or a combination of both? Explain your answer.

4. On April 19, 1999, two FA-18 Hornet jets took off from the aircraft carrier USS *John F. Kennedy* during the course of conducting war games in the Vieques Passage off the coast of Puerto Rico. The pilots, training for deployment to the Balkans, flew off course, releasing two five-hundred-pound Mark 82 bombs that detonated near an observation post. Four civilians were wounded, and a security guard, David Sanes Rodriguez, was killed. His death galvanized the islanders to demand an end to the

---

22. Monica Rhor, "Living, and Dying, in a Toxic Town," *Denver Post*, October 28, 2007.

military exercises on the island, whose nine thousand inhabitants had endured naval bombing exercises for sixty years. Protesters trespassed onto the navy base and refused to move. These "People's Zone" encampments were denounced by the navy, which warned of the danger of camping on dangerously contaminated land. At one time, over a thousand protesters gathered on the island to support the encampments, some defiantly sailing into "forbidden waters" to challenge the navy's claim to the seas surrounding Puerto Rico.

Although five decades of bombing stopped in May 2003, the navy left behind tens of thousands of unexploded bombs spewed over a nine-hundred-acre firing range. The fish, crabs, seagrass, and soil are contaminated with toxins. According to Tara Thornton of the Military Toxics Project (MTP), the U.S. Navy "fired enough to poison every man, woman, and child on [Vieques] 420 times over" (Kearns 1999).[23] According to a 2009 U.S. government report, cancer, hypertension, asthma, diabetes, heart disease, and mortality rates (specifically infant mortality) were significantly higher in Vieques then elsewhere in Puerto Rico (U.S. Department of Health and Human Services 2011a, 101, 103, 106). Rather than the tract being cleaned, it will be closed to the public and declared a "wilderness area."

By 2009, the navy began moving unexploded munitions by detonating them in the open air. They have also proposed to burn through nearly one hundred acres of dense tropical vegetation in order to locate and detonate cluster bombs. Island inhabitants worry that the latest actions of the navy will only expose them to newer health risks. The navy cannot guarantee that their cleanup procedure will not expose the population to smoke and contaminants.[24]

— Why are simulated exercises, using live ammunition, not conducted in the U.S. mainland (e.g., New England)?

— What ethical responsibilities does the navy have to the inhabitants of Vieques?

— Are such acts (the protest against the death of Rodriguez) of civil disobedience ethical, even if they disrupt "law and order"? Are such protests during a time when the military is engaged in battle, in effect, an act of treason? Why or why not?

— Military and civilian programs compete for the same national resources. What ethical ramifications exist concerning military spending?

23. Dana Canedy, "Navy Leaves a Battered Island, and Puerto Ricans Cheer," *New York Times*, May 2, 2003.
24. Mireya Navarro, "New Battle on Vieques, over Navy's Cleanup of Munitions," *New York Times*, August 7, 2009.

Part III

Case Studies of National Relationships

Chapter 8

Introduction to National Relationships

When patriotism ("my country, right or wrong") replaces justice, a people are in danger of idolatry. Because the United States can be a strong force for good in the world, it must be confronted and challenged when it fails to live up to its potential. Unfortunately, this nation's quest for economic dominance in the world has usually led down a path that creates poverty not only abroad, but also within our own boundaries. What is lavished abroad to maintain the neoliberal economic order is not available to spend at home to improve social services. Every empire in history has faced diametrically opposed choices: either wield awesome power abroad by strengthening and increasing their military capabilities or improve the living standards of citizens at home. They choose between guns or butter.

Guns versus Butter

Historians such as Paul M. Kennedy have used this zero-sum rule to explain how empires function. The wealth required for military domination stagnates the domestic economy because financial investment in the military is less effective in producing long-term economic growth than such investing in industries geared to meet consumers' needs and desires. In other words, the money spent on "guns" leaves less money for "butter"; it creates a drain on investment capital and raw materials, as well as on the scientists and engineers who would otherwise be engaged in commercial, export-oriented growth (1987, 444–45).

Kennedy's point can be illustrated by an exchange between U.S. governors and President George W. Bush that occurred on the eve of the 2003 war with Iraq. Due partly to national tax policies and also the weak U.S. economy, most states found themselves in their most serious financial predicament since World War II. Mounting deficits in state budgets negatively impacted all state services, especially education. For example, the governor of Missouri ordered every third light bulb unscrewed to save money; teachers in Oklahoma doubled as janitors, cafeteria help, and school bus drivers; some Colorado school districts moved to a four-day week; Nebraska state colleges raised their tuition by 20 percent; and teachers in Oregon worked two weeks without pay. Schools, libraries, and parks were closed, college scholarships eliminated, bus routes dropped, state troopers dismissed, and healthcare for the poor and mentally ill was withdrawn.[1]

So severe was the national crisis that during their annual 2003 winter meeting, governors from both political parties pressed President Bush for fiscal assistance, particularly in the area of education. Bush told the governors that there were no additional funds, and instead he specifically lobbied the governors to support his latest tax-cut proposals.[2] He did not waiver from his earlier promises that tax cuts "will create new jobs . . . generate new wealth . . . and . . . open new opportunities."[3] Unfortunately, the majority of Americans fared poorly due to this era of tax cuts.

Median income grew slowly between 2002 and 2008 (slower than in any other economic expansion) only to fall sharply with the 2008 Great Recession.[4] Economist Emmanuel Saez shows how the incomes of the top 1 percent rose by 11.2 percent since the Great Recession through 2011, but for the bottom 99 percent earnings declined by 0.4 percent. He expects that 2012 will show how the income for the top 1 percent surged due to booming stock prices.[5] The promise that tax cuts would bring a higher rate of economic growth never materialized. Although real GDP (gross domestic product) growth peaked in 2004 at 3.6 percent, it quickly faded. Even before the Great Recession hit, the real GDP was growing at less than 2 percent. Contrast this with the robust growth that occurred with the 1982 and 1993 tax increases. In 1984 real GDP rose 7.2 percent and continued to rise at more than 3 percent a year for the remainder of the 1980s, while in 1994 real growth averaged 4 percent for the remainder of the 1990s.[6]

Recalling that Bush inherited a projected $6 trillion surplus, we are left wondering how we arrived at a $6 trillion cumulative deficit by the close of his presidency. The Bush tax cuts reduced revenue, according to the Congressional Budget Office (CBO), by at least $2.9 trillion below what it would have been between 2001 and 2011. The CBO also notes that lower-than-expected growth furthered reduced revenue by $3.5 trillion; additionally, a higher-than-expected $5.6 trillion in spending helped create the country's fiscal

1. Timothy Egan, "States, Facing Budget Shortfalls, Cut the Major and the Mundane," *New York Times*, April 21, 2003.

2. Robert Pear, "Governors, Hurting Financially, Ask Washington for Assistance," *New York Times*, February 23, 2003; idem, "Governors Get Sympathy from Bush but No More Money," *New York Times*, February 25, 2003; Jonathan Cohn, "Statehouse Pain and the President," *New York Times*, February 26, 2003.

3. George W. Bush, remarks to the U.S. Chamber of Commerce, April 16, 2001, http://www.presidency.ucsb.edu/.

4. David Leonhardt, "Sizing Up the Impact of Tax Cuts (and Their End)," *New York Times*, April 13, 2012.

5. Annie Lowrey, "Incomes Flat in Recovery, but Not for the 1%," *New York Times*, February 16, 2013.

6. Bruce Barlett, "Are the Bush Tax Cuts the Root of Our Fiscal Problems?" *New York Times*, July 26, 2011.

dilemma. It is important to note that the higher interest payments required to finance the deficits caused by the tax cuts are responsible for $3.2 trillion of the higher-than-expected spending. But in spite of the economic damage caused by federal revenue decreases in connection with the 2001, 2002, 2003, 2004, and 2006 tax cuts, politicians such as Senate Minority Leader Mitch McConnell (R-KY), Minnesota Governor Tim Pawlenty (R), Senator Jeff Sessions (R-AL), and Representative Trent Franks (R-AZ) erroneously continued to inform the public that revenues increased due to the Bush tax cuts.[7] In reality, the implementation of the Bush tax cuts from 2001 to 2010 added $2.6 trillion of the public debt, or 50 percent of the total national debt accrued during this period (Fieldhouse and Pollack 2011, 3). It is estimated that if the Bush tax cuts were made permanent, it would cost about $4.6 trillion over the 2012–2021 period (Fieldhouse and Pollack 2011, 1–2).

Why defend tax cuts that were clearly detrimental to the vast majority of Americans? Because those who benefit from the upward transfer of wealth wield tremendous political power. By the end of Bush's presidential term, more than half of the tax cuts benefited the richest 5 percent of Americans, while the middle-class received about 7 percent of the benefits. According to the CBO, fully eliminating the Bush tax cuts for the wealthiest 2 percent of Americans would have immediately increased revenues by about $690 billion over the next ten years, in addition to $140 billion in debt service that otherwise would have been needed to maintain the tax cuts. That comes to a savings of $830 billion (Bogusz et al. 2010, xi–xv).

The Cost of Empire

Empire building costs money. As the governors met in early 2003 requesting federal financial assistance for education, the Pentagon stated that defeating Iraq and occupying the country for six months could cost as much as $85 billion. During the same time, some White House economic advisors estimated that the "police action" could run between $100 and $200 billion.[8] This did not include payments to other nations to join the coalition. Even while the governors were expressing a need for funds to underwrite education, the president was busy negotiating an estimated $15 billion aid package to Turkey in exchange for allowing the military to use Turkey as a staging area in the upcoming war with Iraq.[9]

In reality, the "police action" lasted more than six months and cost much more than what was originally estimated. According to CBO projections, the cost for the so-called Global War on Terror from 2012 through 2020

---

7. Ibid.
8. Donald Hepburn, "Nice War. Here's the Bill," *New York Times*, September 3, 2003.
9. Dexter Filkins, "February 16–22: A Crucial Nod from Turkey," *New York Times*, February 23, 2003.

would total from about $1.56 trillion to about $1.88 trillion (Belasco 2012, 3). However, these government estimates are misleading for what they omit. According to Watson Institute for International Studies at Brown University, the final bill will, on the low end, cost $3.7 trillion and could reach as high as $4.4 trillion. This comes to about $1.4 billion to avenge each person killed in the 9/11 attack. Unfortunately, these numbers will continue to soar as obligated long-term care is provided for wounded U.S. veterans. Absent in calculating the cost of war is the human factor, specifically the 272,727 to 329,745 who directly died due to warfare, the four times that number who indirectly died, the 365,000 who were wounded, and the 7.4 million who were displaced (Crawford and Lutz 2011, 4–9).

Because what occurs in the domestic sphere impacts the foreign sphere, and vice versa, ethics transcends national borders. White supremacy and class exploitation at home are usually linked to aggressive military attacks throughout the two-thirds world as neoliberalism is established. According to Mexican ethicist Enrique Dussel, "The suffering of the conquered and colonized people appears as a necessary sacrifice and the inevitable process of modernization. This logic has been applied from the conquest of America until the Gulf War, and its victims are as diverse as indigenous Americans and Iraqi citizens" (1995, 64).

The global struggle for survival by what Frantz Fanon calls "the wretched of the earth" is the same struggle faced by those who live on the margins within the empire. A correlation does exist between how the United States treats the marginalized throughout the underdeveloped world and how marginalized people within U.S. borders are treated. According to Albert Camus, winner of the 1957 Nobel Prize for literature, the worth of any society is measured by how it treats its marginalized people.

If this is true, what is the worth of the United States? The cost of a postwar Iraq, coupled with the multiple tax cuts of the Bush administration for the wealthy, sapped approximately $10 trillion from the nation's revenue flow over a ten-year period starting in 2001, making it difficult, if not impossible, for those sinking deeper into poverty ever to recover. Can such an ethical system be called "Christian"? Pope John Paul II once called such capitalism "savage." Yet resources exist to end poverty in the United States. What seems to be absent is the will to do it. Could it be because those in control of economic policy benefit from maintaining these economic inequities? In the end, though, does refusing to hear the cry of the poor result in the loss of a nation's humanity or, even worse, its soul?

Although a perfectly just society cannot be achieved here on earth, throughout human history some cultures have proven to be more humane than others. These successes can help track our progress toward a more ethical moral order. Unfortunately, success within the United States continues to be measured by degrees of financial independence. At any twenty-year high school reunion, those who become doctors and lawyers and have six-figure incomes are deemed more successful than those who work as hourly laborers or in other nonprofessional positions. It is no surprise, then, that poverty often is viewed as an individual problem, a consequence of laziness, lack of intelligence or self-motivation, or maybe just plain bad luck. The best and the brightest succeed, while the less-than-capable, through a social process of natural selection, are removed from the responsibility to govern. In order to protect and secure national tranquility, "the best and the brightest" attempt to keep at bay the others: the less worthy and the marginalized, who usually are people of color. Since the early years of this country this process has become institutionalized as part of the very fabric of national life. It works to ensure power and privilege for the few.

From time to time, this attitude clearly manifests itself in the public sphere. The 2012 presidential election provides such an example. Republican candidate Mitt Romney was secretly recorded during a private fundraiser in Boca Raton, Florida, saying this:

> There are forty-seven percent of the people who will vote for [Obama] no matter what. All right, there are forty-seven percent who are with him, who are dependent upon government, who believe that they are victims, who believe the government has a responsibility to care for them, who believe that they are entitled to health care, to food, to housing, to you-name-it. That's an entitlement. And the government should give it to them. And they will vote for this president no matter what. . . . These are people who pay no income tax. Forty-seven percent of Americans pay no income tax. So our message of low taxes doesn't connect. . . . My job is not to worry about those people. I'll never convince them that they should take personal responsibility and care for their lives.[10]

Romney's comments seem to border on class warfare. Yet whenever the poor question the disparity of wealth in this nation, "class warfare" becomes a term used by politicians and political pundits to discredit them. During an interview on the *Today* show in January 2012, Romney, responding to a question concerning economic inequality, said, "You know, I think it's about envy. I think it's about class warfare." When asked if there is ever a time to discuss economic inequalities, Romney continued by stating, "It's

---

10. Rick Ungar, "Romney Fail: Caught on Video Revealing Extraordinary Contempt for 47 Percent of Americans," *Forbes*, September 17, 2012.

fine to talk about those things in quiet rooms and discussions about tax policy and the like."[11]

To raise concerns about the ever-growing economic gap is to risk being accused of formenting social unrest or, worse, being labeled a socialist. When billionaire capitalist Warren Buffett pondered in a *New York Times* op-ed column why he pays a lower tax rate than his secretary,[12] Fox News pundit Eric Bolling called him a socialist.[13] But after hearing candidate Romney's message to major donors, we are left wondering if indeed class warfare is being waged by politicians protecting the super-rich.

From the margins of society, voices like that of Martin Luther King Jr. have arisen to challenge the fairness of the perspective that the nation's poor are freeloaders looking for government handouts. King said, "Any religion that professes to be concerned about the souls of men and is not concerned about the slums that damn them, the economic conditions that strangle them, and the social conditions that cripple them is a spiritually moribund religion awaiting burial" (1986a, 38). The ethics of those privileged by present social structures will be explored in greater detail in this section of the book by examining poverty within the United States, how that poverty is maintained through the political system, and how death plagues those who are marginalized due to healthcare issues and the judicial system.

11. Tami Luhby, "Romney: Income Inequality Is Just Envy," *CNN Money*, January 12, 2012.
12. Warren E. Buffett, "Stop Coddling the Super Rich," *New York Times*, August 14, 2011.
13. Eric Bolling, *Fox News Channel*, aired August 15, 2011.

Chapter 9

National Poverty

Step 1. Observing

A bit of history is needed to understand poverty, as well as the growing distance between the poor and the wealthy in our country today. Beginning with the Great Depression of the 1930s, this nation began a program of funneling large amounts of federal dollars into welfare initiatives. Known as the New Deal, legislation was passed to create a safety net to protect society's most vulnerable members, particularly the elderly at that time. The success of the New Deal could be measured by the return of wage levels to their pre-Depression era and the reduction of unemployment from almost 25 percent to nearly zero on the eve of World War II.

The 1950s witnessed a drop in poverty levels from 32 percent at the start of the decade to 22 percent by decade's end. Meanwhile, median family income was 43 percent higher in 1959 than in 1950. If we ignore sexism and racism for the moment, most families could, with one income, buy a car, take a vacation, and provide a college education for their children. Two-income families were, for the most part, financially unnecessary. During the 1960s, with the war on poverty and the civil rights movement, the income gap (difference between the richest and poorest Americans) continued to narrow as unemployment dropped to a low 4.4 percent and income rose by 38 percent over 1959. Although racial discrimination continued to exclude portions of the population from participating in the booming economy, the unemployment rates of black men still dropped twice as fast as white men. Increased employment opportunities for African Americans contributed to the poverty level falling by 50 percent, closing the 1960s at 12 percent (Cooper 1998, 347–49).

By the 1970s, multiple factors began to widen the income gap. The energy crisis following the Arab-Israeli War brought income growth to a halt. By the close of the 1970s, median family income remained at 1973 levels, while unemployment continued to rise, reaching 7.5 percent by 1980. With economic policies put in place after Ronald Reagan was elected in 1980, the income gap widened dramatically, while the middle class shrank. These new economic policies radically changed the distribution of wealth in this country. During the 1980s the top 10 percent of the population increased their family income by 16 percent, the top 5 percent increased theirs by 23 percent, while the top 1 percent[1] increased their income by 50 percent. Meanwhile, the bottom 80 percent lost income, with the bottom 10 percent down 15 percent, from $4,113 to $3,504. At the beginning of Reagan's administration the income of the top 1 percent was 65 times greater than the bottom 10 percent. By the end of the Reagan administration the income of the top 1 percent was 115 times greater than the bottom 10 percent (Phillips 1990, 12–17).

The economic policies of the New Deal were replaced by a supply-side philosophy that consisted of cutting, if not eliminating, social services and benefits for the poor while providing tax breaks for the wealthy. The hope was that economic benefits given to the wealthy would "trickle down" to the less fortunate. According to figures published by the U.S. Census Bureau, this led to the richest among us seeing their inflation-adjusted income rise by 30 percent from the late 1970s to the mid-1990s, while the poorest saw their income decrease by 21 percent. This so-called Reaganomics pushed unemployment to almost 10 percent, median family income dropped to 6 percent below pre-1973 levels, and poverty rose from 11.1 percent to 14.4 percent. The bottom quintile received 4.7 percent of all income, a full percentage point below the 1973 level. From 1947 through 1979 real income had risen for all segments of society. Since the 1980s "Reagan Revolution," income has risen only for the most affluent families (Cooper 1998, 338–54).

Throughout the 1990s, during the so-called economic boom of the Clinton years, only the top quintile increased its share of the nation's income.[2] According to the Congressional Budget Office, between 1979 and 2000 the gap between rich and poor more than doubled as the United States experienced the greatest growth of wage inequality in the Western world (Wilson 1999, 27). Contributing to the widening income gap was the 1996 Welfare Reform Act, signed by President Bill Clinton.[3] These radical economic changes within the United States have led to the smallest and fastest-shrinking middle class among all industrialized nations.[4]

---

1. In 2012 those belonging to the top 1 percent of taxpayers made at least $352,000 in income.

2. David Leonhardt, "In a Wealthy Country, Who Are the Truly Rich?" *New York Times*, January 12, 2003.

3. Although initial reports indicated that hundreds of thousands of former welfare recipients moved off the rolls into jobs, providing a substantial raise in income, more recent studies indicate a more disturbing trend. By 2003, seven years after the passage of the Welfare Reform Act, state- and urban-policy researchers point to newer studies showing that a significant number of those who left the welfare rolls were unemployed and have sunk to deeper levels of poverty. The Urban Institute in Washington, DC, estimates that one in seven families that left welfare from 2000 through 2002 had no work, spousal support, or government assistance, up from one in ten in 1999. Wade F. Horn, the assistant secretary for families and children within the U.S. Department of Health and Human Services, agreed with these figures. See Leslie Kaufman, "Millions Have Left Welfare, But Are They Better Off? Yes, No, and Maybe," *New York Times*, October 20, 2003.

4. Keith Bradsher, "Widest Gap in Incomes? Research Points to the U.S.," *New York Times*, October 27, 1995.

TABLE 2
Income growth, 1947–1994

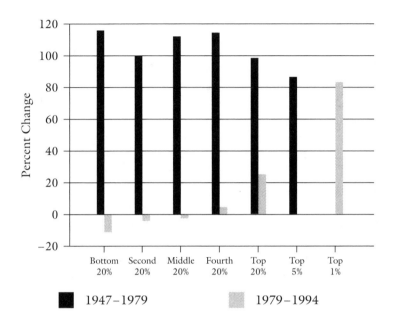

1947–1979   1979–1994

Note: All wages are based on 1979 dollars
Sources: Census Bureau, "Current Population Survey," March 1996;
United for a Fair Economy; and Cooper, 1998:350.

By 1999, at the close of the century, the top 1 percent of taxpayers each had on average $862,700 after taxes, more than triple what they had in 1979. Meanwhile, the bottom 40 percent had $21,118 each, up by 13 percent from their average $18,695 (adjusted for inflation) in 1979. And although median household incomes reached their peak that year at $53,252, the year 2000 proved to have the greatest economic disparity since 1979, when the Budget Office began collecting such data. The National Bureau of Economic Research, a nonpartisan, nonprofit research group, claimed that the top 1 percent enjoyed by the close of the millennium the largest share of before-tax income for any year since 1929.[5] For the next decade all incomes except for the ultra-rich steadily dropped. The top 1 percent garnered 65 percent of the entire nation's growth between 2002 and 2007.[6] By 2010, real median

5. Lynnley Browning, "U.S. Income Gap Widening, Study Says," *New York Times*, September 25, 2003.
6. Steven Greenhouse, "Productivity Climbs, but Wages Stagnate," *New York Times*, January 13, 2013.

household income dropped by 7.1 percent to $49,445 (DeNavas-Walt, Proctor, and Smith 2011, 5), literally wiping out almost two decades of accumulated prosperity, according to the Federal Reserve.[7] The poverty rate in 2010 was 15.1 percent, the highest poverty rate since 1993, with 46.2 million people (the largest number in fifty-two years) living in poverty. Not since the Great Depression has the median family income substantially dropped as it did throughout the first decade of the millennium.[8] During the Obama administration, according to the Social Security Administration, median wages (the midpoint of everyone's wages) grew at a slower rate than the average wages indicating an expanding income gap. During the previous Bush administration, the ratio between median and average wage grew at a rate of 0.28 percentage point a year. Between 2009 through 2011, the ration increased to 1.14 percentage points, indicating an income gap which grew four times faster.[9]

By 2012, during the first full year of so-called recovery from the 2008 Great Recession, 93 percent of income gains went to the top 1 percent, while 7 percent went to the bottom 99 percent. As executive pay soared, the median weekly earning of a full-time worker saw only a 1 percent increase in pay, from $747 to $756; but when we consider this so-called raise in constant dollars, wages actually fell by a little more than 2 percent.[10] The top 10 percent of earners received half of the country's total income in 2012, while the top 1 percent took more than one-fifth of all income earned by Americans; creating a New Gilded Age.[11] Not surprisingly, more Americans find themselves slipping into greater, stomach-wrenching poverty. In New York City alone 50,000 people (21,000 of whom are children) were homeless by 2013, sleeping in shelters or on the streets, driven by a 73 percent increase in homeless families since 2001.[12]

The Great Recession cemented, rather than reversed, the nation's wealth and income inequalities. According to the U.S. Labor Department, before the Great Recession in 2007, 1.7 million workers earned the minimum wage. By 2012, the numbers surged to 3.6 million. President Obama pondered during his 2013 State of the Union address raising the minimum hourly wage from $7 to $9 and indexing it to inflation, a plan that would lift hundreds of thousands of families above the poverty level. But when bills to this effect

---

7. Binyamin Appelbaum, "For U.S. Families, Net Worth Falls to 1990s Levels," *New York Times*, June 12, 2012.

8. David Leonhardt, "Living Standards in the Shadows as Election Issue," *New York Times*, October 12, 2012.

9. Anna Bernasek, "Income Gap Grows Wider (and Faster), *New York Times*, September 1, 2013.

10. Natasha Singer, "C.E.O. Pay Gains May Have Slowed, but the Numbers Are Still Numbing," *New York Times*, April 8, 2012.

11. Annie Lowry, "Top 10 percent Took Home Half of U.S. Income in 2012." *New York Times*, September 11, 2013.

12. "The Forgotten 50,000," *New York Times*, June 17, 2013.

were introduced by Democrats, the Republican-controlled House of Representatives voted them down.[13] And yet while compensation hit a fifty-year low, corporate profits have continued to climb. Nobel laureate Joseph E. Stiglitz (former chief economist of the World Bank) fears the vicious cycle in which the United States finds itself: "Increasing inequality means a weaker economy, which means increasing inequality, which means a weaker economy. That economic inequality feeds into political economy, so the ability to stabilize the economy gets weaker."[14]

Ironically, most Americans are working longer hours to make less money. In 1933, during the height of the Great Depression, the U.S. Senate overwhelmingly voted to establish a thirty-hour workweek. The measure failed in the House. Nevertheless, five years later, in 1938, the Fair Labor Standards Act passed, giving us the statutory forty-hour workweek. By the 1960s, Americans, when compared to their counterparts in Japan and Europe, spent less time on the job. Between 1990 and 2000 the average annual work hours for Americans began to increase. By 2000, Americans were working longer hours than their counterparts overseas. By 2013, about 40 percent of men in professional jobs worked fifty-plus hours a week, as do 25 percent of men in middle-income occupations. Low-income workers are usually forced to have two jobs just to make ends meet.[15]

Organizations not necessarily friendly to the global poor, like the International Monetary Fund (IMF), understand that income inequalities damage the ability of the country to experience long-term growth. Economists interpret this widening gap to mean slower job creation and lower levels of economic growth, mainly because wealth inequalities prevent most of the population from taking advantage of economic opportunities. "Growth becomes more fragile," according to Jonathan D. Ostry of the IMF, in countries, like the United States, that have high levels of income inequality.[16] Even our very democracy is threatened as the few pour riches into political campaigns to elect candidates who will protect and secure the financial interests of a small elite class. How relevant are these words of the prophet Jeremiah: "Woe to those who build their palace on anything but integrity, their upper rooms by injustice, making their compatriots work for nothing, not paying them for their labor" (Jer. 22:13).

Step 2. Reflecting

Liberation theologian Franz Hinkelammert insists that "the existence of the poor attests to the existence of a Godless society, whether one explicitly

13. Annie Lowrey, "Six Faces of the Minimum Wage," *New York Times*, June 16, 2013.
14. Annie Lowrey, "Costs Seen in Income Inequality," *New York Times*, October 17, 2012.
15. Stephanie Coontz, "Why Gender Equality Stalled," *New York Times*, February 17, 2012.
16. Ibid.

believes in God or not" (1997, 27). Nevertheless, most people within the United States hold the assumption that anyone who works hard enough can succeed. That anybody can grow up to become the president is the myth that we install in our little boys (sexism starts young). The only thing that might hold them back is their own lack of initiative. The "Protestant work ethic," a term popularized by sociologist Max Weber, undergirds American society and preaches an equality of opportunities. Hard work in the career (calling) to which God summons every person is rewarded by God with material blessings, while those who fail to work hard are punished for their laziness by poverty.

The Myth of the Work Ethic

Despite this assumption, it seems that generally no matter how hard the poor work, they often continue to slip into greater poverty. The growing disparity of wealth between the poor and the rich leads us to question if it is really a "work ethic" that is at issue or rather a "work ideology" that allows the wealthy and privileged to rationalize classism. Why is it so difficult for the poor to "get ahead"? Is wealth really a reward for hard work, and poverty a punishment for laziness? Or is there another explanation for the accumulation of even greater wealth by those at the top of the economic ladder?

Increasing poverty directly affects the well-being of our society: it leads to a rise in crime, drug and alcohol addiction, family disintegration, child abuse, mental illness, and environmental abuse. Instead of dealing with the causes of poverty and seeking a more equitable distribution of resources, those privileged with wealth seldom make the connection between their riches and the poverty of others. More often they view their wealth as something earned, a blessing from God, or a combination of both. They tend to seek to insulate themselves from the consequences of their riches, moving to gated communities and sending their children to private schools.

In spite of insulating themselves from the affects of poverty, even the rich make less when the poor are scantily paid. Henry Ford, the pioneer manufacturer of automobiles, understood this economic truth. In 1914 the Ford Motor Company paid an unprecedented $5 a day to its employees. Ford believed that low wages made the market weak and the economy sluggish. Paying $5 a day allowed his employees to make enough money to buy the product that they were producing, the Model T automobile. Well-paid workers create greater consumer demand for goods. Economists call this formula for economic expansion "the virtuous circle of growth." Thanks to capitalists such as Ford, a middle class was created throughout the first three-quarters of the last century, before "the virtuous circle of growth" was philosophically replaced with "trickle-down" economics. By the eve of the 2008 Great

Recession, profits of corporations represented the largest share of the national income since 1942, while salaries and wages were at their lowest level since 1929. While CEO salaries increase and record profits are posted, workers are pressured to accept wage freezes (if not cuts), work part-time, and/or work with less employee benefits (i.e., healthcare).

Ethicists from the margins argue that communities that desire a just economic base must place the humanity of their members before economic development. Development today usually means short-term profit, often at the expense of the marginalized. Yet true development, economic as well as sociopolitical, takes place when society's treatment of its most vulnerable members enables them to pass from a less human existence to a more human condition. Conditions faced by the poor are caused by oppressive structures that lead to the exploitation of workers and the creation of material want. The ethical quest for more humane conditions requires a set of social actions, a praxis, designed to overcome extreme poverty, raise consciousness of classism, foster dignity for all people, develop an equitable distribution of the earth's resources, and secure peace—to testify to one's love for God and one's neighbor, a love that binds God with neighbor.

Regardless of how we choose to define this more human condition, it remains threatened by increasing poverty. According to the Department of Agriculture, 14.5 percent of the nation's households suffered chronic hunger in 2013 (Coleman-Jensen, et al 2013: 4-8). Yet Republican House majority leader, Eric Cantor, shepherded the passing of $40 billion in cuts through 2023 in food stamps, blaming the needy, according to a FAQ his office posted, for the lingering costs of the Great Recession. The savings, according to Cantor, can better serve other programs, including tax cuts.[17] The so-called work ethic is debunked when the poor work, often full-time, simply to survive, when there are few if any options for work, and when the work is unrewarding and unfulfilling. Two adults working full-time at the federal legal minimum hourly wage of $7.25 for 2011 equals a before-tax yearly income of $30,160, which is insufficient to meet basic necessities. According to the government, the official poverty level is $22,350 (U.S. Department of Health and Human Services 2011b). Although it appears that this family of four is making $7,810 above the poverty line, these figures are grossly misleading.[18] A family with

17. "Mindlessly Gutting Food Stamps," *New York Times*, September 9, 2013; Ron Nixon, "House Republicans Pass Deep Cuts in Food Stamps," *New York Times*, September 19, 2013; and http://www.scribd.com/doc/168663350/Nutrition-bill-Q-A.

18. The official definition of poverty masks the true extent of poverty in the United States. Poverty was defined fifty years ago by government statistician Mollie Orshansky, who recognized the shortcomings of the definition. The official definition of poverty (PT = 3 x SFB [Poverty Threshold = 3 x Subsistence Food Budget]) fails to consider the radical changes in consumption patterns since the early 1960s. It was originally based mainly on food consumption, which since then has become less expensive in relationship to housing, healthcare, childcare, and transportation. Changes in consumer patterns have converted the original formula into nonsensical numbers (Blank 2008, 233–39, 49–50).

TABLE 3
2011 wage comparisons for the forty-eight
contiguous states and the District of Columbia

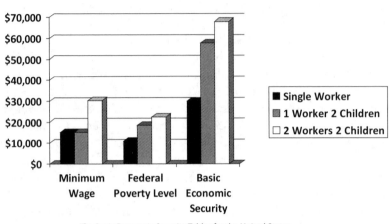

The Basic Economic Security Tables for the United States
(Washington, DC: *Wider Opportunities for Women*, 2011), 1–12.

Source: U.S. Department of Health and Human Services, 2011b.

two working parents and two young children needs $67,920 a year (or about $16.33 an hour per worker) to cover basic expenses and save for retirement and emergencies (McMahon, Nam, and Lee 2011, 1–12).

In 1962 the top 1 percent had a net worth of 125 times that of the median household. By 2010, that net worth shot up to 288 times. The top 1 percent saw their net worth increase from $9.599 million in 1962 to $16.439 million in 2010.[19] Meanwhile, 45 percent of Americans lived in households that lack economic security, representing 39 percent of all adults and 55 percent of all children. This means that one out of every four full-time working-age adults has an annual income that falls below the economic security baseline (McMahon, Nam, and Lee 2011, 1). Not surprisingly, the population groups more likely to live in poverty are children, African Americans and Latino/as, women living alone, noncitizens, single mothers, and those living in urban centers (Becker 2002, 65, 67). Among families of color, 62 percent of African Americans and 66 percent of Hispanics have total family incomes that do not provide economic security (McMahon, Nam, and Lee 2011, 1).

Misrepresenting the true level of poverty within the United States does serve a purpose. Politicians can argue that public spending on the poor has had little effect and therefore should be discontinued. For example, using flawed calculations about the poverty level, Ronald Reagan, during his 1988

19. Tami Luhby, "The Wealthy Are 288 Times Richer Than You," *CNN Money*, September 11, 2012.

State of the Union Address, was able to declare, "My friends, some years ago the federal government declared a war on poverty and poverty won," and thus justify the dismantlement of the social safety net. And yet it is that same safety net (Social Security, food stamps, earned-income tax credits, WIC, and more) that have kept, according to the Center on Budget and Policy Priorities, some forty million people out of poverty.[20] While several government programs have helped reduce poverty, incorrect poverty assessments mask the real extent of poverty in America. If we were to recalculate the definition of poverty to mean less than the figure required for economic security, we would discover that millions of more Americans live in actual poverty than is reported by the government.

Besides misrepresenting the true level of poverty, government statistics also misrepresent the true level of unemployment. Even though the majority of jobs being created are at the bottom of the wage scale, there are not enough jobs to help the poor. From the start of the 2008 Great Recession through the writing of this book, unemployment has hovered at or above 8 percent, or roughly 12.7 million people out of work. This number is misleading when we consider that the real unemployment number is probably greater than 22 million. If we add to the official 12.7 million unemployed those who work part-time because they cannot find a full-time job, or were downgraded to part-time work (7.7 million), plus those who were looking for employment in the past year but stopped looking (2.4 million), we are looking at 22.8 million unemployed—double the official count (Barlett and Steele 2012, 5).

The dismantling of the New Deal has meant over the long haul that working families are unable to earn a living wage. Many are forced to skip meals, forgo paying rent, or postpone needed medical care. A study conducted by the National Low Income Housing Coalition, titled *Out of Reach 2012*, found that even though the 2008 Great Recession temporary stalled the rising cost of housing, it did not result in an increased access of affordable rental housing. In 2012 no state in the country made it possible for a low-income worker to afford a modest one- or two-bedroom rental unit. Most real estate professionals calculate that rents or mortgage payments must be less than 30 percent of total family income to consider housing expenses affordable; yet in 2012, 76 percent of low-income families spent more than 50 percent of their income on housing costs (Bravve et al. 2012, 2–4).

The wealthy, and those who represent them politically, always opposed safety net programs such as Social Security, welfare, Medicare, and the more recent Patient Protection and Affordable Care Act (aka Obamacare), claiming that such government programs interfered with the private market. Nevertheless, the dismantling of other safety net programs has had

---

20. Peter Edelman, "Poverty in America: Why Can't We End It?" *New York Times*, July 29, 2012.

TABLE 4
**Hours a week, at $7.25 hourly minimum wage,
required to afford fair housing rent
in the United States in 2012**

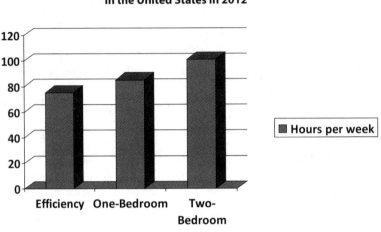

Source: Bravve et al. 2012, 2–4.

devastating effects on the family. A presentation at Harvard University by welfare experts showed a rising number of children, specifically black children in metropolitan areas, live in no-parent households. The lack of adequate childcare has forced parents, specifically single parents, to leave their children with relatives, friends, or foster families. Since the Welfare Act of 1996 was enacted, the number of black children living without parents has more than doubled (from 7.5 percent to 15 percent). Their parents may be working in retail and service industries that pay a fraction of what they used to earn at manufacturing jobs. While these parents put in long hours to earn a poverty-line wage, their children are growing up without a parent present. These children, according to welfare experts, will perform significantly worse in school than children in single-parent homes. They will experience higher rates of school failure, mental health problems, and delinquency, thus contributing to the downward spiral of despair.[21]

From 2000 to 2010, the number of children living in poverty increased by 41 percent.[22] Of the industrial countries, the richest nation in the world is among the few that has a higher percentage of its children living in poverty. Among the thirty-four nation members of the Organisation for Economic Co-operation and Development (OECD), the U.S. poverty rate in

---

21. Nina Bernstein, "Side Effect of Welfare Law: The No-Parent Family," *New York Times*, July 29, 2002.

22. Ezekiel J. Emanuel, "Share the Wealth," *New York Times*, June 24, 2012.

2008 was 21.6 percent, significantly above the 12.6 percent average. Only Chile (22.4 percent), Israel (26.6 percent), Mexico (25.8 percent), and Turkey (23.5 percent) fared worse (OECD 2011, 4). The "American Dream" that children will enjoy a better standard of living than their parents no longer exists. By 2010, the poverty rate of U.S. children (under eighteen years old) rose to 22 percent, representing 16.4 million Americans. While children represent only 24.4 percent of the U.S. population, they disproportionately represent 35.5 percent of those living in poverty. In addition, one out of every four children under the age of six lives below the poverty line (DeNavas-Walt, Proctor, and Smith 2011, 17–18).

With each passing year, the poor sink deeper into despair. Society's most vulnerable find it difficult to simply survive. Many who lost jobs, homes, and retirement funds during the 2008 Great Recession, especially people of color, will never recover. And yet a minority of the population appears to benefit from our culture's economic arrangement. In 2010 the top quintile, the most affluent fifth of the population, possessed 50.2 percent of all household income, while the lowest quintile, the poorest fifth, received 3.3 percent of the total household income (DeNavas-Walt, Proctor, and Smith 2011, 10, 41). Why?

The Rich Get Richer

Who supposedly benefits from the present economic system? Why does the income gap continue to widen? First, the pay schedule of CEOs has increased at the expense of workers' wages. In 1975 corporate leaders made 44 times as much as the average factory worker. During the early 1980s corporate leaders such as Roberto Goizueta of Coca-Cola and Michael Eisner of Disney convinced stockholders to link their compensation to company stock prices. As a result, by 1985 the average CEO salary rose to 70 times that of the average worker; by 1990 it was 100 times.[23] If workers' annual pay during the 1990s had grown at the same rate as that of CEOs, workers' annual earnings in 2000 would have been $120,491. Or if the hourly minimum wage of $3.80 had grown at the same rate as CEOs' earnings, the 2000 hourly minimum wage would have been $25.50 rather than $5.15.[24]

Between 2003 and 2007 the average chief executive's salary increased by 45 percent, compared with a measly 2.7 percent increase for the average worker (Ebert, Torres, and Papadakis 2008, 7). A 2011 report published by the Institute for Policy Studies revealed that corporate leaders in 2008, when the Great Recession occurred, were earning 299 times as much as the average

---

23. David Leonhardt, "The Imperial Chief Executive Is Suddenly in the Cross Hairs," *New York Times*, June 24, 2002.
24. Gretchen Morgenson, "Explaining (or Not) Why the Boss Is Paid So Much," *New York Times*, January 25, 2004.

worker. By 2010, when many workers lost their jobs, were outsourced, or were forced to take pay cuts, the earnings of CEOs increased to 325 times that of the average worker (Anderson et al. 2011, 3). The average pay that year for top executives at the S&P 500 firms was $10,762,304 a year (up by 27.8 percent over 2009), while the average worker made $33,121 a year (up by just 3.3 percent).[25] By 2012, the top two hundred chief executives took home an average pay of $15.1 million, a 16 percent jump since 2011, according to Equilar, ranging from $96.2 million at Oracle to $11.1 million at General Motors.

CEO salaries also outpaced the stock market and corporate profits. From 1985 through 2001 the average worker saw his or her pay increase by 63 percent, while the S&P 500 index rose by 443 percent. Over the same period of time CEOs enjoyed a pay increase of 866 percent.[26] One would have expected CEO incomes to drop as the market took a downturn in 2000. However, this did not occur because of the nature of our economy, one that privatizes profits while it socializes losses (Teninty 1991, 115). At the start of the 2000 down market, compensation rules were rewritten once it became obvious that production goals were not going to be met. For example, at the close of the fiscal year that ended on April 30, 2003, the CEO of H. J. Heinz, the ketchup maker, received a pay package valued at $8.8 million, a 47 percent increase over $6 million the previous year, even though the performance of Heinz stock fell by about 20 percent.[27]

This pattern of increased pay during bear markets was modified after the 2008 recession. While CEOs took pay cuts (11 percent in 2008, 15 percent in 2009, 30 percent in 2010), due in part to stockholder revolts, they still made a major portion of their earnings on the value realized from exercised stock options.[28] Hence, by 2011 top executive pay levels have rebounded nearly all the way back to pre-2008 recession levels (Anderson et al. 2011, 4). The nation's two hundred top-paid CEOs that year enjoyed a median income of $14.5 million, a pay raise over the previous year of 5 percent.[29] In spite of all the news concerning stockholder revolts and holding CEOs accountable leading to cuts in salaries, the fact remains that most CEOs have better financial packages in 2012 than they did in 2007, the year before the Great Recession. Additionally, many executives have created very profitable exit strategies amounting to $100 million (and up). For example, Gene Isenberg of Nabors Industries received $126 million when he exited as CEO; IBM's

25. Among the twenty-five top-paid CEOs, the average compensation was $16,684,071 (Anderson et al. 2011, 4, 31).

26. Morgenson, "Why the Boss Is Paid So Much."

27. Patrick McGeehan, "At Heinz, a Novel Way to Say the Boss Is Worth It," *New York Times*, August 10, 2003.

28. Scott DeCarlo, "What the Boss Makes," *Forbes*, April 28, 2010.

29. Nathaniel Popper, "C.E.O. Pay, Rising Despite the Din," *New York Times*, June 17, 2012.

CEO Sam Palmisano received $170 million; Google's CEO Eric Schmidt received $100 million.[30]

While increases of CEO wages have become tied to the decrease of workers' wages (understood as an expense), those CEOs who announced layoffs of 1,000 or more workers between January 1 and August 1, 2001, earned 80 percent higher compensation than CEOs of 365 top U.S. firms that did not announce layoffs (Anderson et al. 2001, 6–7). For example, the CEO of WorldCom announced layoffs for 6,000 workers while collecting a $10 million bonus. The CEO of Disney earned $72.8 million in 2000 while announcing layoffs for 4,000 people. Such executive raises and worker layoffs took place at a range of companies, including American Express and Cisco Systems (Anderson et al. 2001, 7–8).

Workers suffered in other ways as well. The 1938 Fair Labor Standards Act established a forty-hour workweek, discouraging employers from assigning longer hours by forcing them to pay time-and-a-half on any hours worked above forty. By 1975, exemptions were added by excluding "highly paid executives" who could work up to seventy hours a week with no additional pay. The problem is that "highly paid executive" was defined as anyone who supervises two other employees and is being paid as little as $13,000 a year. This loophole, exploited by the service and retail industries, has meant longer work hours for the average American without an increase in wages.[31]

Racism

According to an affidavit by Beth Jacobson, a former loan officer at Wells Fargo Bank, her employer saw black neighborhoods as fertile ground for high-interest subprime mortgages, pushing customers who could qualify for prime loans into subprime. One of her colleagues referred to the subprime mortgage applicants as "mud people" and to the loans as "ghetto loans." Jacobson, the bank's top-producing subprime loan officer noted, "Wells Fargo mortgage had an emerging-markets unit that specifically targeted black churches, because it figured church leaders had a lot of influence and could convince congregants to take out subprime loans."[32] A racial divide existed as to the type of loan people obtained. Eric Halperin, director of the Center for Responsible Lending, pointed out, "We've known that African Americans and Latinos are getting subprime loans while whites of the same credit profile are getting the lower-cost loans."[33] In 2006 Wells Fargo subprime mortgages charged an

---

30. Gary Strauss, "The Golden Parachute Is Evolving into the Platinum Kiss," USA Today, November 8, 2011.

31. Rose Eisenbrey, "Just What the Worker Needs—Longer Days, No Overtime," Los Angeles Times, February 14, 2003.

32. Michael Powell, "Bank Accused of Pushing Mortgage Deals on Blacks," New York Times, June 7, 2009.

33. Ibid.

interest rate of at least three percentage points above the federal benchmark, financing costs were higher, and prepayment penalties were imposed, making refinancing to lower interest rates to keep one's house out of foreclosure a financial impossibility.[34]

When the housing bubble burst, most of those who took these subprime loans, who were disproportionately of color, were left destitute, widening the wealth gap between them and whites. Furthermore, municipalities such as Baltimore, Cleveland, and Buffalo, faced with waves of foreclosures, experienced as a result reduced tax revenues and increased costs for city services. Abandoned houses cost such cities more as they attempted to ward off crimes such as arson, prostitution, and drug use. The chief solicitor for the Baltimore City Law Department, Suzanne Sangree, best explained the damage that banks such as Wells Fargo has caused in neighborhoods of color: "This wave of foreclosures in minority neighborhoods really threatens to undermine the tremendous progress the city has made in developing distressed neighborhoods and moving the city ahead economically."[35]

Should we then be surprised that for non-Hispanic whites, the 2010 poverty rate was 9.9 percent? Although non-Hispanic whites constitute 64.5 percent of the population, they represented only 42.4 percent of those living in poverty. By contrast, 27.4 percent of blacks, 26.6 percent of Latino/as, and 12.1 percent of Asians lived in poverty (DeNavas-Walt, Proctor, and Smith 2011, 17). According to the U.S. Census Bureau, African Americans and Latino/as experienced an increasing income gap compared to whites, rising to record highs in 2010. Since 2000, Hispanics and blacks have consistently experienced a yearly drop in real median family income (Wessler 2009, 8). Median household income for non-Hispanic whites in 2010 was $54,620. Contrast this with Hispanics, at $37,759, and blacks, at $32,068 (DeNavas-Walt, Proctor, and Smith 2011, 8).

The 2009 median wealth (assets minus debt) of whites ($113,149) is 20 times that of black households ($5,677) and 18 times that of Hispanic households ($6,325). Compare this to 2005, when whites were at $134,992, blacks at $12,124, and Hispanics at $18,359. These numbers reveal that the 2008 Great Recession, triggered by the housing bust, had a far greater toll on the wealth of African Americans and Latino/as than it did on whites. From 2005 to 2009, Hispanics experienced an inflation-adjusted median wealth decrease of 66 percent, while blacks experienced a 53 percent decrease, compared to just a 16 percent decrease for whites. To make matters worse, about a third of African Americans (35 percent) and Latino/as (31 percent) had zero or a negative net worth, compared to 15 percent of white households (Taylor et al. 2011, 1–2).

---

34. Gretchen Morgenson, "Baltimore Is Suing Bank over Foreclosure Crisis," *New York Times*, January 8, 2008.
    35. Ibid.

TABLE 5
Net worth by race before and after
the 2008 Great Recession

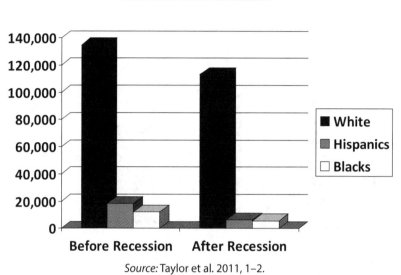

Source: Taylor et al. 2011, 1–2.

People of color are relegated to inner-city poverty and are segregated from the middle class, making it difficult for them to break through barriers that foster and maintain their poverty. Last to be hired, they are also among the first to lose their jobs during downsizing, as was the case with the 2008 Great Recession. By 2009, African American unemployment rates were at 13.3 percent, while Hispanic unemployment rates were at 11.4 percent, compared to whites, at 7.9 percent.[36] These disparities have occurred during economic busts (e.g., 1983, when blacks were at 20.1 percent, Hispanics at 15.6 percent, and whites at 9.1 percent) and economic booms (e.g., 1998, when blacks were at 9.2 percent, Hispanics at 6.9 percent, and whites at 4.0 percent) (Wessler 2009, 4, 14).

Although numerous studies demonstrate the reality of racism, for our purposes it suffices to acknowledge that racism leads toward lower wages, greater financial burdens, and fewer opportunities to transcend the consequences of poverty.

The Unfair Tax Burden

In 1952 corporate taxes represented 32 percent of taxes collected by the federal government; by 2012, the corporate share was only 7.9 percent. According to the Government Accountability Office (GAO), in any given year

---

36. These rates were worst for young workers between twenty and twenty-four years old. Blacks were at 23.0 percent, Hispanics at 16.0 percent, whites at 12.5 percent.

TABLE 6
2009 median yearly earnings by race and gender

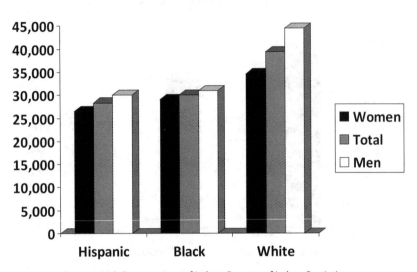

Sources: U.S. Department of Labor, Bureau of Labor Statistics, "Current Population Survey," 2009; Wessler 2009, 13.

seven of every ten major corporations that operate within the United States under "foreign" ownership paid no taxes, companies such as General Electric (GE), Boeing, and Exxon Mobil (Barlett and Steele 2012, 145). The GAO goes on to report that the most profitable American companies (between 2008 and 2010 with over $10 million in assets) that do pay taxes pay but a fraction of what would be owed under official corporate rates. Through the manipulation of deductions and legal loopholes, large corporations pay a 12.6 percent tax rate, as opposed to the 35 percent statutory tax rate imposed by the federal government.[37]

Of the one hundred highest-paid CEOs in 2010, twenty-five took home more compensation than what their companies paid in federal income taxes. In fact, most of the companies that they managed received tax refunds from the IRS to the tune of $304 million each. Take GE as an example. In 2010 GE ranked fourteenth among U.S. firms in global profitability. Although the company reported $5.1 billion in U.S. pre-tax income, the federal government gave it a $3.3 billion tax refund. How does a company like GE receive such preferential treatment? Maybe it is due to the $41.8 million spent in lobbying and campaign spending (Anderson et al. 2011, 1–2). Investment by

37. Nelson D. Schwartz, "Big Companies Paid a Fraction of Corporate Tax Rate," *New York Times*, July 7, 2013.

companies like GE in the political system undermines the fair distribution of U.S. sources (as we will see in greater detail in the next chapter).

Changes in the tax code have harmed the poor. Neoliberal doctrine believes that entrepreneurs and business owners should control the economy, for they are, after all, the so-called job creators. Because the rich supposedly have entrepreneurial skills and experience, they receive greater disposable income through tax cuts. A "trickle-down" effect is supposed to result. Unfortunately, this has not happened. From 1980 to 1990, the poorest 20 percent of the population saw their tax liability increase by 10 percent, while the richest 5 percent of the population enjoyed a 12.5 percent reduction in taxes (Cooper 1998, 345). By 2000, the top four hundred wealthiest taxpayers in the United States represented 1 percent of all income obtained, a figure that had quadrupled in the eight years since 1992. Yet their tax burden dropped from 26.4 percent in 1992 to 22.3 percent by 2000.[38] By 2008, the tax burden of these four hundred taxpayers further dropped to 18.1 percent, lower than the percentage paid by most ordinary workers.[39]

Of the 2009 IRS returns of the 400 super-rich (reporting an average income of $202 million), 6 paid no income tax, 27 paid 0–10 percent, and 89 paid 10–15 percent.[40] The main reason the super-rich pay so little is that most of their income is in the form of capital gains, which is taxed at a maximum rate of 15 percent, far below the maximum tax rate paid on salaries and wages. It was Ronald Reagan who ushered in the tumbling of tax rates, especially for the richest among us, with the passage of the 1986 legislation equalizing the top rate on capital gains (28 percent) with earned income. The real decline of capital gains tax rates began with Bill Clinton in 1997, to assure passage of the Children's Health Insurance Program. The drop of capital gains tax to levels lower than when Herbert Hoover was president occurred under George W. Bush's Job and Growth Tax Relief Reconciliation Act of 2003, whose dividend reduction provision cost us more than $100 billion over seven years. The argument used throughout 2012 against allowing the Bush tax cuts to expire was that it would inhibit the so-called job creators. Yet during Clinton's first term, when the top 400 taxpayers paid close to 30 percent of their income and the capital gains tax was roughly equivalent to the income tax rate, 11.5 million jobs were added to the economy. The Bush administration, during its eight years, never came close to matching these rates of job creation.[41]

38. David Cay Johnston, "Very Rich's Share of Wealth Grew Even Bigger, Data Show," *New York Times,* June 26, 2003.

39. Paul Krugman, "Taxes at the Top," *New York Times,* January 29, 2012.

40. James B. Stewart, "In the Superrich, Clues to What Might Be in Romney's Tax Return," *New York Times,* August 11, 2012.

41. Ibid.

By the tenth anniversary of the Bush-era tax cuts, more than 90 percent of the tax savings went to the taxpayers in the top (fifth) quintile, and nearly half of all the benefits went to the top one-tenth of 1 percent (R. Williams 2011, 1). The Bush tax cuts turned a budget surplus into a deficit, transferring more wealth to the top earners than virtually any act of fiscal policy in American history. The top 0.1 percent of earners (making over $3 million), received an average tax cut of about $520,000, more than 450 times than that received by the average citizen from a middle-income family. Tax filers in the bottom 20 percent (making less than $20,000) received only 1 percent share of the tax cuts, while 75 percent of these low-income families received zero (Fieldhouse and Pollack 2011, 1–2). In addition, the implementation of the Bush tax cuts from 2001 to 2010 contributed $2.6 trillion to the national debt, almost 50 percent of the total debt accrued during this period (Fieldhouse and Pollack 2011, 3). Meanwhile, millions of American children face substandard housing or homelessness, inadequate healthcare and crumbling schools. And yet an independent economic report by the Congressional Research Service (CRS) confirmed the obvious when it concluded that no correlation existed between top tax rates and economic growth: "The reduction in the top tax rates appears to be uncorrelated with saving, investment and productivity growth. The top tax rates appear to have little or no relationship to the size of the economic pie. However, the top tax rate reductions appear to be associated with the increasing concentration of income at the top of the income distribution" (Hungerford 2012, 16). Because it questioned the main tenet of neoliberal economic philosophy of not taxing "job creators," the report, released on September 14, 2012, was pulled from circulation on September 28, immediately after a "conversation" that the CRS had with the Senate Finance Committee's Republicans.[42]

Ignoring research and history, the neoliberal economic philosophy that benefits the wealthiest of Americans continues to be a major voice in the political halls of power. Congressman Paul Ryan (R-WI), 2012 vice-presidential candidate, proposed a budget that would have eliminated all the federal income taxes on capital gain, dividends, and interest income, saving the wealthiest of the wealthy untold billions in taxes. How did he propose offsetting the revenue losses? By slashing the funds allocated to the nation's safety net. According to Ryan, "We don't want to turn the safety net into a hammock that lulls able-bodied people to lives of dependency and complacency; that drains them of their will and their incentive to make the most of their lives."[43]

---

42. Jonathan Wesman, "Tax Report Withdrawn at Request of GOP," *New York Times*, November 2, 2012.

43. Harold Pollack, "A Safety Net, Not a Hammock," *Washington Monthly*, April 9, 2012.

Another way many corporations eliminate paying portions of their taxes is by registering their companies in tax havens such as Bermuda and the Cayman Islands while keeping their working headquarters in the United States. One such tax haven, the British Virgin Islands, is home for 30,000 people and 457,000 companies.[44] The Cayman Islands, with a population of 53,000, has 93,000 companies (Barlett and Steele 2012, 146). One Cayman Islands building, the Ugland House, is the business address for more than 19,000 companies, leading 2008 presidential candidate Barack Obama to exclaim, "Either this is the largest building in the world or the largest tax scam in the world" (2009).

Google provides us with an example on how these tax havens operate. Of Google's $12.5 billion in 2009 sales, 88 percent occurred outside the United States. To save $3.1 billion in taxes from 2007 to 2009, Google created a complicated tax haven in Bermuda that boosted its overall earnings by 26 percent.[45] When a Google search ad is purchased outside the United States, the money is first sent to its office in Dublin. Although Ireland has a 12.5 percent corporate tax rate, Google avoids the tax (it reported a pretax profit of less than 1 percent of revenues in 2008) because it moves the profits to the Netherlands, and Ireland does not tax certain payments made to other European Union nations. The company that Google has in the Netherlands is a shell (Google Netherlands Holding BV) with no employees. Once the profits are in the Netherlands, Google takes advantage of generous Dutch tax laws that allow it to pass 99.8 percent of its profits to Bermuda, which collects no corporate income tax. So what kind of rate did Google pay in taxes from 2007 through 2009? An extremely low one: 2.4 percent.[46]

During the Great Recession, marked by a downward trend in family income and soaring corporate profits, many corporations sought ways to reduce their tax burden. As mentioned earlier, during the 1950s corporate income tax contributed about a third of the total revenue raised by the federal government. By the 2000s, only $1 in $10 of all federal tax dollars collected came from corporations. As of 2012, American companies have close to $2 trillion in profits "permanently reinvested" abroad. According to a report by the CRS, the federal government loses about $10 billion to $60 billion a year from multinational companies shifting their profits to low-tax countries.[47] It appears that the United States does not have a spending problem; it has is a revenue-collecting problem.

44. Robert M. Morgenthau, "These Islands Aren't Just a Shelter from Taxes," *New York Times*, May 6, 2012.

45. David Cay Johnston, "U.S. Corporations Are Using Bermuda to Slash Tax Bill," *New York Times*, February 18, 2002.

46. Jesse Drucker, "The Tax Haven That's Saving Google Billions," *Bloomberg Businessweek*, October 21, 2010.

47. Eduardo Porter, "The Trouble with Taxing Corporations," *New York Times*, May 28, 2013.

Google, of course, is not alone in its quest for the scheme to pay the least taxes possible. The three major corporate abusers of using tax havens are Pfizer, the world's largest drug company, which due to its 172 subsidies in tax havens has reported no taxable income over five years, even though it has $73 billion parked in an offshore account; Microsoft, which avoided paying $4.5 billion in federal income tax over three years, even though it has $60.8 billion parked offshore on which it would have had to pay $19.4 billion in U.S. taxes; Citigroup, beneficiary of the 2008 taxpayer-funded bailout, which maintains twenty subsidies in tax havens, with $42.6 billion sitting offshore on which it would have owed $11.5 billion in U.S. taxes (Baxandall and Smith 2013, 1–2). These foreign subsidiaries are not just for saving money. Halliburton, a major war profiteer, used its offshore tax haven subsidiaries to circumvent U.S. laws and conduct business with Iran during the trade embargo.[48]

According to a study conducted by the CRS, U.S. subsidiaries mainly operate in the top five tax havens,[49] generating in 2008 about 43 percent of their profits in those countries, even though they only had 4 percent of their foreign employees and 7 percent of their foreign investments located in those countries.[50] Apple, the innovator of tax avoidance, funneled over $1 billion worth of iTunes sales to one of the smallest countries in Europe, Luxembourg, making this tax haven the music capital of the world.

iTunes sales is but a portion of $44 billion in taxes that Apple avoided paying due to its web of worldwide subsidiaries. As Senator Carl Levin (D-MI) observed, "Apple wasn't satisfied with shifting its profits to a low-tax offshore tax haven; Apple successfully sought the holy grail of tax avoidance. It has created offshore entities holding tens of billions of dollars while claiming to be tax resident nowhere." By officially being located in Ireland, the firm is exempted from taxes, record-keeping laws, or the need to even file taxes anywhere in the world. Because the United States bases tax liability on where a company is incorporated, while Ireland bases it on where the company is managed, Apple's offshore network is a subsidiary named Apple Operations International, incorporated in Ireland and managed from the United States, hence not needing to file tax returns in the United States, Ireland, or any other country since 2009. Thus, Apple paid no corporate income tax to any national government in overseas income for over four years. Ironically, when Apple CEO Tom Cook testified before the Senate's Permanent Subcommittee on Investigations, senators who the previous day were criticizing Apple instead were tripping over themselves praising the company. Senator John

---

48. Morgenthau, "These Islands."
49. Bermuda, Ireland, Luxembourg, Netherlands, and Switzerland.
50. Steven Rattner, "The Corporate Tax Dodge," *New York Times*, May 23, 2013.

McCain (R-AZ), who the previous day called Apple "a tax avoider," now praised the company's "incredible legacy." Senator Claire McCaskill (D-MO) summed up the mood when she proclaimed, "I love Apple!" Apple is not alone; it is one of six hundred American companies that have set up subsidiaries in Ireland.[51]

Multinational corporations, thanks to numerous loopholes, in effect choose what they want to pay in taxes. According to an academic study conducted by U.S. Public Interest Research Group, tax haven abuses costs the federal government $150 billion a year in tax revenues, with multinational corporations representing $90 billion, and the $60 billion by private individuals (Baxandall and Smith 2013, 1). One of those individual taxpayers who took advantage of these tax havens was Michael Froman. A White House economic aide since 2008, Froman was nominated by President Obama to be his trade representative. According to financial records, he has $490,845 stashed away in the Cayman Islands' infamous Ugland House.[52] Another abuser of the tax haven loophole is Mitt Romney, 2012 presidential candidate, whose tax returns revealed dozens of offshore holdings in places such as Luxembourg and the Cayman Islands.[53] The average taxpayer filling out an IRS 1040 form must pay an additional $1,026 in federal taxes to make up the lost revenue by those who use tax havens. If we assign the $90 billion lost due to multinational corporate tax havens to small businesses, then we can expect each small business to pay an extra $3,067 in taxes (Baxandall and Smith 2013, 1).

Besides taking advantage of tax havens, Michael Froman and Mitt Romney were able to pay low taxes on millions of dollars in income by an accounting technique known as "carried interest." This legal principle allowed private equity fund managers to treat most of the fees that they earn for managing equity funds (management fees usually categorized as ordinary income) as though they were capital gains. As capital gains, even the tax liability can at times be deferred for years. For Romney's company, Bain Capital, this allowed him to convert in 2009 $1.05 billion in management fees from ordinary income into capital gains. If Bain Capital partners paid (rather than deferred) capital gains tax at 15 percent, rather than ordinary income tax at 35 percent, they saved about $210 million in income tax plus $28 million

51. Nelson D. Schwartz and Charles Duhigg, "Apple's Web of Tax Shelters Saved It Billions, Panel Finds," *New York Times*, May 20, 2013; Danny Yadron, Kate Linebaugh, and Jessica E. Lessin, "Apple Avoided Taxes on Overseas Billions, Senate Panel Finds," *Wall Street Journal*, May 20, 2013; Landon Thomas and Eric P. Fanner, "Even before Apple Tax Breaks, Ireland's Policy Had Its Critics," *New York Times*, May 21, 2013.

52. Jonathan Weisman, "U.S. Trade Nominee Has $490,000 in Cayman Fund," *New York Times*, June 4, 2013.

53. Michael Luo and Mike IcIntire, "Offshore Tactics Helped Romney's Increase Wealth," *New York Times*, October 2, 2012.

in Medicare tax.[54] Some legal scholars question the legality employed by Romney and company, believing that if they were challenged, the IRS could win, thus leading to a few private equity firms not taking advantage of this accounting technique.

Some corporations are implementing a new tax strategy designed to aggressively reduce, if not eliminate, federal taxes. Diverse businesses such as Corrections Corporation of America (CCA), a private prison operator, or Penn National Gaming, which operates casinos, are declaring that they are really not ordinary corporations but instead are special trusts that typically are exempted from federal taxes. By using this trust structure, specifically a real estate investment trust (REIT) that has existed for years, CCA is expected to save $70 million in federal taxes in 2013.[55]

As of this writing, the Stop Tax Haven Abuse Act (S.1346, H.R.2669) has yet to pass Congress. If passed, the bill would eliminate many of the abuses of tax havens, resulting in an increase in annual tax revenue of about $100 billion. Furthermore, it would eliminate the incentive for moving jobs and profits offshore. The bill has languished in Congress since 2007; although it passed the Senate, the House has refused to take action. A reason for the House's refusal to move on this legislation might well be the millions of dollars that leaders of private equity firms have spent lobbying to protect their privileged tax status.

During the 2012 presidential election, it could be argued, because candidate Obama made raising taxes on the richest Americans a priority, his successful reelection amounted to a mandate by the majority of the voters. And yet President Obama's original plan of raising marginal tax rates on families with income over $250,000 will have little or no impact on families making up to $300,000, as well as hundreds of thousands of families with even greater incomes, due to the complexity of a tax code littered with tax shelters and loopholes. According to Citizens for Tax Justice, only about 32 percent of families with income between $250,000 to $350,000 will see a tax increase, while 77 percent with income between $300,000 and $350,000 will see a rise.[56] Obama may have pledged to raise taxes on the top 2 percent; nevertheless, the final deal struck in the waning hours of the 112th Congress raised taxes only on the top 0.7 percent, with the very rich still paying vastly lower rates than at any point from the 1940s through the 1970s.[57]

54. Floyd Norris, "A Tax Tactic That's Open to Question," *New York Times*, September 13, 2012.

55. Nathaniel Popper, "Restyled as Real Estate Trusts, Varied Businesses Avoid Taxes," *New York Times*, April 21, 2013.

56. Catherine Rampell and Binyamin Appelbaum, "Obama's Tax Plan Still Spares Large Portion of Nation's Affluent," *New York Times*, December 7, 2012.

57. Annie Lowrey, "After Fiscal Deal, Tax Code May Be the Most Progressive since 1979," *New York Times*, January 5, 2003.

Step 3. Praying

Historically, individuals who commit themselves to a life of Christian service would renounce all earthly possessions so as to be used by God. But are today's Christians required to renounce their riches to become disciples of Jesus? The early church wrestled with issues of wealth, concluding that any riches possessed by Christians were to be used for the betterment of the community.[58] Yet this concept is not well accepted within a capitalist economic structure. Individuals pursue their own economic self-interests, believing that an "invisible hand" will ensure economic benefits for all of society. Perhaps Adam Smith's economic theories of supply and demand may be relevant in a society dominated by small businesses and petty merchants where no one seller can control the market but must compete with others. But in today's economy Smith's theories are outdated. In the United States today the corporation controls the means of production, sets the price for the merchandise or service, and determines the wage for producing the merchandise or service. Prices often are kept artificially high and wages artificially low.[59]

Defenders of our present system of capitalism see no inherent conflict between Christian morality and the pursuit of profit. It is assumed that each person has an absolute right, if not a moral obligation, to follow economic self-interest as a duty in creating a more just society. Yet the biblical text says to us, "Be subject to one another in the fear of the Lord" (Eph. 5:21). We are called to put the needs of the other before our own. How then can these two opposing views be reconciled within a rich Christian community?

Some "prosperity gospel" televangelists have begun to proclaim a "name it and claim it" theology, and some ministers, including Benny Hinn, preach that God wants God's children to be rich. Hinn has actually proclaimed, "Poverty is from the devil, and God wants all Christians prosperous." During several of his sermons he has led his congregation in repeating the phrase "The wealth of the wicked is mine." Another, Kenneth Hagin, founder of Rhema, the Word of Faith Bible School, teaches that "[God] wants His children to eat the best, He wants them to wear the best clothing, He wants them to drive the best cars, and He wants them to have the best of everything" (McConnell 1995, 175). Poverty, then, is the consequence of a lack of faith on the part of the disenfranchised. Should it be surprising that such a theology finds fertile soil within a capitalist "Christian" culture? It even explains why the poor are still with us: obviously, they lack faith in God. Nonetheless, throughout the Gospel of Luke we read the opposite of

---

58. For an excellent text dealing with how the early church handled the issue of riches, see González 1990a.

59. Karl Marx did predict that with the passage of time, small businesses and petty merchants would gradually be absorbed by larger industries until a concentration of industrial power rests in the hands of a few capitalists.

what today's prophets of wealth proclaim. Not only is it the poor who inherit the reign of God, but also they become the instrument by which the rich can discover their own salvation.

In Luke 16:19–31 Jesus tells the story of a poor man, Lazarus. According to the biblical text, there once was a very wealthy man who was accustomed to feasting on only the very best. At the gate of his mansion lay Lazarus, a poor man covered with sores, dreaming of a future that provided him with scraps that fell from the rich man's table. When both men died, Lazarus was carried by the angels to the bosom of Abraham, while the prosperous man was sent to hell to be tormented for all eternity.[60] The rich man, seeing Lazarus held in Abraham's arms, pleaded for mercy. He begged to have a few drops of water placed on his tongue to cool the agony of the flames. But Abraham refused, for a great gulf separated heaven from hell. The rich man then asked to have Lazarus go back to his family to warn them of the danger of their "mammon," their wealth. This too was denied, for as Abraham stated, "If they were not willing to hear Moses and the prophets, even if one from the dead should rise, they will not be persuaded."

Nowhere in the text does it tell us that the rich man's wealth was accumulated unjustly or that he was directly oppressing Lazarus; his judgment and condemnation to hell were based on the fact that he failed to share his resources with those such as Lazarus, who lacked the basics for survival. To ignore the plight of the dispossessed is to deny one's humanity. In this case, God's judgment was not based on anything that the rich man did, or any belief system that he confessed, or any particular church that he attended. He was condemned for failing to give to the very least of God's children. He failed to use his resources so that others could also enjoy an abundant life. If we are truly to love our neighbor, and if this commandment is to be the biblical basis that informs our ethics, then it is immoral to ignore our neighbor's hunger as we continue to store away our riches. To do so is to be called a fool by Christ (Luke 12:16–21).

The Lazarus story condemns the rich, but we must ask, then, who in our time will proclaim the good news of salvation from materialism? While an analysis of this text and others that focus on the plight of the rich has become commonplace, all too often our gaze remains fixed on the wealthy man and not others. Perhaps this is because most of us read the text from the social location of the middle class, and the message of this story in Luke is reduced to a charitable act demanded of the wealthy.

---

60. It is interesting that while the text provides us with the name of Lazarus, the one from the margins, it does not name the rich man, who no doubt was known and honored by the community at large.

But what happens if we read the text from the perspective of Lazarus? We may discover that it was not a sin of commission that resulted in the eternal condemnation of the rich man, but rather a sin of omission. What if Lazarus had been the subject instead of the object of the story? What if instead of sitting by the gate dreaming about the scraps that might fall from the rich man's table, Lazarus had been proactive? What if Lazarus had demanded food, shelter, and clothes, not out of a sense of pity, but based on his human right to survive? What if Lazarus had sought solidarity with others made poor by the prevailing economic structures and joined forces with them to demand structural changes within society? What if Lazarus had confronted the rich man with his sin of greed and hoarding? What if the rich man, upon hearing Lazarus's demands, had repented? Then salvation as liberation from sin would have also come to the rich man, and he too could have found comfort in the arms of Abraham. Even though the rich man forfeited salvation by refusing to fulfill his ethical responsibility to the poor man, the poor are still responsible for acting as moral agents to create a just society. Those who are privileged by the way society is constructed are in need of liberation and salvation because they too are created in the image of God. God desires all, the rich and the poor, to enter into a saving knowledge of God's grace. When the marginalized seek out the liberation of the oppressors, they verify the humanity of both the privileged and themselves (De La Torre 2003a, 99–100).

Jesus of Galilee, coming from the margins, challenged the rich in the hope that they would find their own salvation through solidarity with the poor. To commit one's life to Christ is to commit one's life to those without—those whom Christ opted for. Such a commitment to the poor is not ideological, but rather is an expression of faith. In the Gospel accounts some wealthy persons did find God's salvation, as in the case of Zacchaeus (Luke 19:8–10), who, when confronted with his sin of hoarding wealth, pledged to repay back four times over what he received through fraudulent means; he then split the remainder of his wealth between himself and the poor. These actions led Jesus to proclaim that on that day, salvation had come to the house of Zacchaeus. For others, the path to heaven was impossible to achieve, as in the case of the rich young ruler (Luke 18:24–25), who, though pious and virtuous in keeping the commandments, walked away from salvation out of reluctance to share his wealth with the poor.

Jesus incarnated himself into the lives and plight of the poor. For the church to discover its own salvation, it must do likewise. If not, those who refuse to walk in solidarity with "the least of these," the marginalized, renounce, like the young ruler, a basic principle of Christianity, regardless of how moral they may appear to be. Simply stated: one cannot be a Christian and remain complicit with social structures that privilege whiteness, wealth, and maleness. The gospel message says that it is the people on the margins who are the salvific agents for the recipients of society's power and privilege. In other words, no one gets into heaven without a letter of recommendation from the homeless, the dispossessed, the disinherited, the disenfranchised.

Perhaps the rich man's salvation did not occur because Lazarus failed to demand a place at the banquet table. Those who exist on the margins of society also bear a burden in that they have a sacred trust and ethical responsibility to evangelize the dominant culture about the danger of power and privilege. But how? By coming together, organizing, and demanding that those in power obey God's command not to sell the poor "for a pair of sandals" (Amos 2:6). Not only will the rich find their salvation through their solidarity with the poor, but also the poor will facilitate this process by demanding from the rich their rightful share, working out their own salvation in "fear and trembling" (Phil. 2:12). Additionally, the humanity of the dispossessed is regained as they actively seek the humanity of their oppressors. Through repentance can come salvation.

Step 4. Case Studies

1. The Protestant work ethic is woven into the essence of being an American. According to this ethic, hard work leads to prosperity, while laziness leads to poverty. In the land of opportunity, where the American Dream rules, those who are poor have no one to blame but themselves. They probably lacked industriousness, or simply made poor life choices, as in the case of participating in drug use. For this reason, political conservatives have begun a crusade of insisting that welfare recipients should first pass a drug test before they can receive government assistance. Even 2012 presidential candidate Mitt Romney called the proposal an "excellent idea." He went on to say, "People who are receiving welfare benefits, government benefits, we should make sure they're not using those benefits to pay for drugs."[61] In 2012 thirty states with both conservative and liberal legislators were moving forward with such proposals, with major headway being made in Ohio, Virginia, Florida, Texas, and Kansas.

    — Does the idea of drug testing the poor stereotype an entire people? Does it mask the reasons for poverty in this country? Does it justify cutting back on so-called entitlement programs such as welfare?

    — Federal statistics found that those on welfare are no more likely to abuse drugs than the general public. About 8 percent of the general public and of welfare recipients use drugs illegally.[62] If so, why is this an

---

61. "Growing Support for Drug Testing of Welfare Recipients," *New York Times*, February 26, 2012.

62. Ibid.

issue? Why are states pursuing this course of action, especially since a similar law on the books in Michigan was struck down in 2003 by the U.S. Court of Appeals as unconstitutional, a violation of the Fourth Amendment?

— Who is mainly on welfare? Why? Should they first be proven innocent before receiving assistance from the government?

2. In a 2011 op-ed in the *New York Times*, billionaire capitalist Warren Buffett wondered why he paid a lower tax rate than his secretary.[63] Since then, the "Buffett Rule" became a popular political proposal requiring that all millionaires pay at least 30 percent of their income in taxes. If implemented, the Buffett Rule would raise an estimated $50 billion over ten years. The 2013 budget proposed by the Obama administration contained the Buffet Rule. As of the writing of this book, Republicans have continued to refuse considering changes to increase revenue, arguing that money raised from closing loopholes should be used to bring down overall tax rates. Additionally, if the Bush tax cuts would have expired on those making over $250,000 a year, as Obama campaigned for, the additional revenue over ten years would have been closer to $800 billion.

— What would have been a fair taxation policy? Preserving the Bush tax cuts on everyone? Adopting the Buffett Rule? Implementing Obama's campaign promise? Closing loopholes? Should any of the tax revenues added to the coffers due to the wealthy paying more taxes be used to bring down tax rates? Should extra tax revenues pay down the national deficit? Or should these revenues be used to strengthen the social safety net?

— Was the Buffett Rule simply a symbol, a distraction? Was the failed attempt of House Speaker John Boehner to implement "Plan B" during the "fiscal cliff" negotiations with President Obama an earnest attempt to implement the Buffett Rule?

— Is it just for Buffett, a job creator, to pay a lower tax rate than his secretary? Why should Buffett, who contributes to the growth of the economy, not pay less than those who contribute nothing? The middle-class tax burden in 2010 was 16 percent. Mitt Romney paid 14 percent, but he did so on $21 million of income. Thus, he provided more dollars than the average taxpayer. Is this not just? Will taxing the job creators hurt the economy while it is in the midst of a slow recovery from recession?

---

63. Warren E. Buffett, "Stop Coddling the Super Rich," *New York Times*, August 14, 2011.

3.   Angelica Gonzales, Melissa O'Neal, and Bianca Gonzalez are three poor
     Latinas who wanted to escape the poverty of their native Galveston,
     Texas. Believing that education was their ticket to socioeconomic suc-
     cess, they devoted their high school weekends and summers to becom-
     ing college-ready. Attending Ball High School (among the 2 percent of
     Texas high schools ranked "academically unacceptable"), they refused to
     be among the third of the girls who failed to graduate on schedule. Their
     hard work paid off. Angelica (GPA of 3.9, SAT of 1240) was accepted
     into Emory University, Melissa left for Texas State College, and Bianca
     went to a local community college. Each was smart and excelled while
     in college. But after four years none of them had a degree. Lack of funds,
     campus alienation, and ties to boyfriends not going to college compli-
     cated their trajectory. Angelica left Emory with $60,000 in student loans
     and ended up working as a clerk at a Galveston furniture store.[64] Bianca
     finished her two-year associate degree and is working as a beach-bar
     cashier and a spa receptionist. Only Melissa, a fifth-year senior, although
     undergoing great hardships, is planning to graduate in 2013.

     — Education was once seen as the great equalizer. It is becoming difficult,
       if not impossible, for low-income students, regardless as to how smart
       they might be, to move up the socioeconomic ladder. Has education
       become the preserver of class divisions? Is a college education simply
       beyond the reach of the poor? Especially if the poor are of color? Espe-
       cially if the poor of color are female?

     — Even after accounting for financial aid, the cost of attending a public
       university has increased by 60 percent from 1990 to 2010.[65] Has the
       cost of college become a means of blocking the poor from upward
       mobility? Do elite universities have any obligation to low-income stu-
       dents who cannot afford to attend their prestigious institutions? Do
       state universities hold any responsibilities? What about community
       colleges?

     — By eighth grade, white students surpass blacks by three grade levels;
       meanwhile, upper-income students surpass poor students by four grade
       levels. Fewer than 30 percent of students whose families belong to the
       bottom quarter of incomes ever enroll in a four-year college, and of
       those who do, fewer than half graduate.[66] Considering the high rate
       of tuition that can further aggravate a lifetime of financial ruin, why

---

64. Jason DeParle, "For Poor, Leap to College Often Ends in a Hard Fall," *New York Times*, December 23, 2012.
65. Ibid.
66. Ibid.

should the poor bother obtaining a college degree? Would it be better for them simply to learn a trade? Has college become a financial trap for the poor?

4. Anger, angst, and anxiety have filled the streets since the 2008 Great Recession, fueled by an existential despair faced by most Americans concerning their economic future. In 2011 this anger took form as the Occupy movement among those on the left, placing blame for the economic meltdown on unfettered capitalism, specifically big corporations and the top 1 percent. In 2009 some on the right organized as the Tea Party, blaming economic troubles on government spending, maximized by the Obama administration. Both movements emerged seemingly out of nowhere, quickly becoming political forces. Among the left, Zuccotti Park in lower Manhattan was physically occupied (leading to similar acts throughout the U.S. and global cities). Their major concern was income inequality, best captured by the slogan, "We are the 99 percent." For the right, the debate over the Patient Protection and Affordable Care Act (referred to as Obamacare) led to an attack against a "welfare state," where the slogan of resistance was best captured by the 1776 Revolutionary War battle cry, "Don't tread on me." Although one side demands greater regulations while the other clamors for none, both are suspicious and distrustful of politicians. Yet while the Occupy movement refused to deal with, let alone try to elect, sympathizers of their views, the Tea Party became active in the political system. By 2013, forty-nine members of the House of Representatives and five members of the Senate constituted the Congressional Tea Party Caucus. No one in Congress claims any connection with the Occupy movement. While the Occupy movement is mostly defunct, the Tea Party successfully led the October 2013 government shutdown. Still, both movements have raised interesting questions.

— Is anger a sufficient motivator for political action? Can it be sustained? If not, what alternatives can be employed? What happens to the movement once the anger dissipates?

— Even though the Occupy movement is largely defunct, did it succeed in raising consciousness concerning income inequality, introducing the term "99 percent" into the discourse? Can purists involved in the Occupy movement ever succeed without dirtying their hands in politics? Can nonhierarchal, leaderless, and consensus-based movements effectively bring about social, political, or economic change?

— Was part of the success of the Tea Party due to the wealthy benefactors (such as the Koch brothers) who poured money into the movement? What did the movement forfeit for political gains? Was the movement captured by those paying the bills? Are movements that begin in anger and frustration easily hijacked by those with clearer political agendas? Christians were found in both movements. Should they participate in such protests? Is this a violation of the separation of church and state?

— Both movements lacked racial and ethnic diversity. Why? Most protestors were not the poor who were hurt the most by social injustices, but rather were from the middle class. Who are the "we" whom both movements are protesting for? Was the Occupy movement a class struggle between the rich and the well-off? In response to the Occupy movement, municipal legislation was passed preventing overnight stays, thus hurting the homeless the most, long after occupiers left their tents for their more secure home. How were the poor ultimately helped by the Occupy movement?

Chapter 10

Political Campaigns

Step 1. Observing

Since the early 1900s, corporations have been banned from making campaign contributions to federal candidates in an attempt to prevent their "deep pockets" from subverting the democratic process. The coercive impact of money on the democratic process became obvious during the Watergate era, leading to political reforms such as public financing of presidential elections. From 1976 until 2008, both Republicans and Democrats took public money for the general election, adhering to spending limits that reduced the influence of campaign contributions. This changed in 2008, when Barack Obama became the first presidential candidate since the Watergate era to refuse public financing during the general election so as to be able to raise as much funds as possible without any restrictions or limitations. By the 2012 election, the post-Watergate reforms were dead as both presidential candidates unashamedly raised hundreds of millions more than the public system. It was the public financing of elections that made the candidacies of Ronald Reagan (who challenged Gerald Ford in 1976), Jimmy Carter (1976), George H. W. Bush (1980), Jesse Jackson (1988), and Pat Buchanan (1992) possible.[1] Our electoral process has been transformed from trying to limit the role that money plays in determining who will be president to one of super-PACs, unlimited contributions, secret donors, and voter suppression.

This is not to say that public financing was a panacea. Individuals within corporations, and/or their families, were still allowed to make individual donations. In many cases, this was, and continues to be, accomplished through a process known as "bundling," whereby a multitude of individual checks written by executives and their families within a corporation are bundled together and presented to the candidate. In addition to bundling, the Federal Election Campaign Act in 1974 allowed large corporations to form "political action committees" (PACs) for the express purpose of pooling funds from a group of individuals who voluntarily join together to support a candidate.

The express purpose of a PAC is to influence the political sphere by helping elect public officials friendly to the PAC's ideology.[2] PAC contribu-

---

1. "An Idea Worth Saving," *New York Times*, May 5, 2012.
2. The law does not allow PAC contributions for federal candidates to exceed $5,000 per candidate per election ($15,000 in the event of a primary, a runoff, and a final election). However, no limits exist in spending as long as the PAC operates independently from the candidate's campaign organization.

tions are made to those aligned with the interest of the corporation, or as a reward to incumbents who have continuously acted in the best interest of the corporation. Although somewhat eclipsed in the 1990s by direct contributions to candidates' campaigns through "soft money," PACs are still an important component in influencing political officials. PAC monies do not necessarily guarantee that the recipients will vote a specific way, although how they vote on public issues can determine how much PAC monies they will receive during the next electoral cycle. And while laws do exist to prevent corporations from unfairly influencing elected officials, enough loopholes also exist to weaken such regulations.[3]

The laws concerning corporate contributions to political campaigns were radically changed on January 21, 2010, with the Supreme Court's 5-4 decision *Citizens United v. Federal Election Commission*. Corporations were no longer prohibited from making contributions to candidates during elections. The decision was based on a broad interpretation of the First Amendment principle of free speech. Those who support the decision, which overturned earlier court precedent,[4] argued that campaign contributions constitute political speech, and thus the government has no right to regulate any form of free speech. According to Justice Anthony Kennedy, in his majority opinion, "When government seeks to use its full power, including the criminal law, to command where a person may get his or her information or what distrusted source he or she may not hear, it uses censorship to control thought. This is unlawful. The First Amendment confirms the freedom to think for ourselves."[5] In effect, political reliance on large corporate donations posed the probability that the influence of the average voter would be overwhelmed.

---

3. During the mid-1980s I was chairperson of the Real Estate Political Action Committee for the Miami Board of Realtors. My job was to serve as a pseudo-lobbyist, traveling to the state's and the nation's capitals, to relay our organization's positions on specific legislation and target candidates to whom we would give support and provide funding. It was very common to "hedge one's bets" by giving monies to both candidates. Regardless of who won, we would be on the winning team. When there was a particular candidate whom we really liked, we were always able to funnel additional monies to that person through "bundling." Our support bought us access. I always had a direct line to the representatives whom we supported with a phone call or visit, access that I lost when I was no longer representing the PAC. It was common for me to hear, in my position, candidates say, "Just tell me what you guys want, and I'll support it." One candidate in particular who was running for reelection once threatened to vote against a measure that we supported because he had not yet received our organization's financial endorsement. We quickly stated that an oversight was made and cut a check to his reelection committee. Within hours, he voted for the bill that we supported. While this was not the norm, still it is the way the system legally operates.

4. *Citizens United v. Federal Election Commission* in effect overturned the earlier Supreme Court precedents: *Austin v. Michigan Chamber of Commerce*, which decided in 1990 to uphold campaign spending decisions that supported or opposed candidates, and *McConnell v. Federal Election Commission*, which in 2002 upheld the Bipartisan Campaign Reform Act (aka McCain-Feingold), which restricted corporations and unions from campaign spending.

5. Adam Liptak, "Justices, 5-4, Reject Corporate Spending Limit," *New York Times*, January 21, 2010.

Those opposing the decision argued that the flood of corporate money would corrupt the democratic process. At the time of the decision, President Obama called it "a major victory for big oil, Wall Street banks, health insurance companies and the other powerful interests that marshal their power every day in Washington to drown out the voices of everyday Americans."[6] Despite his protestations, Obama created his own super-PAC, Priorities USA Action, which raised $78 million. The quest for campaign contributions, over and against connecting with voters, was demonstrated during the last week of the 2012 election, with Obama attending 221 fundraisers in 24 states, as opposed to 101 campaign rallies in 9 states.[7]

The 2010 midterm electoral contest was the first post–*Citizens United* election. By March 8 of the electoral cycle, $15.9 million in outside campaign contributions was spent, compared to just $1.8 million during the pre–*Citizens United* 2006 midterm election. Similar explosions in campaign contributions occurred in the first post–*Citizens United* presidential election. By March 8, 2012, $88 million was spent, compared to $37.5 million on the same date during the 2008 presidential election.[8] By Election Day 2012, corporate business interests spent about $2 billion, making it the most expensive campaign in U.S. history, with a final price tag of more than $6 billion.[9] Outside spending organizations reported $1.28 billion in campaign spending, more than a 200 percent increase over the pre–*Citizens United* 2008 presidential election, outspending the candidate's own campaign war chest (Lioz and Bowie 2013b, 1; 2013c, 1).

A review of the Federal Election Commission filings for the 2012 presidential election, conducted by Demo and U.S. Public Interest Research Group, showed that each of the top 32 super-PAC donors gave an average $9.9 million, matching the $313 million that Barack Obama and Mitt Romney raised from all of their small donors combined. This means that the presidential election was mainly funded by about three thousand very rich individuals and companies with very specific, not-so-hidden agendas. Almost 60 percent of super-PAC funding came from only 159 donors, each of them contributing at least $1 million. More than 93 percent of the money that super-PACs raised came in contributions of at least $10,000, from just 3,318 donors, or 0.0011 percent of the U.S. population. The impact of this money is best seen in Congress. During the 2012 election 83.9 percent of House

---

6. Ibid.
7. Nicholas Confessore, "Results Won't Limit Campaign Money Any More Than Ruling Did," *New York Times*, November 12, 2012.
8. Matt Bai, "How Much Has Citizens United Changed the Political Game?" *New York Times*, July 17, 2012.
9. Eduardo Porter, "Get What You Pay For? Not Always," *New York Times*, November 7, 2012; Nicholas Confessore and Jess Bidgood, "Little to Show for Cash Flood by Big Donors," *New York Times*, November 8, 2012.

candidates and 66.7 percent of Senate candidates who outspent their opponents won their races. During the general election House incumbents won, outspending major opponents by 108 percent, and Senate incumbents won, outspending by 35 percent. House incumbents outraised major challengers $1,732,000 to $319,000, for a 443 percent advantage. Senate incumbents outraised major challengers $7.02 million to $1.69 million, for a slightly smaller 316 percent advantage. This translates to 95.2 percent of incumbent senators and 91.2 percent of incumbent representatives winning reelection (Lioz and Bowie 2013a, iii–iv).

But what if a corporation does not want the public to know its political leanings? Think of the negative publicity that engulfed Target in 2010 when it contributed $150,000 to a Minnesota candidate for governor, Tom Emmer, who opposed same-gender loving marriage.[10] Today, corporations can influence elections while remaining outside the public gaze by passing their contributions through trade associations, such as the U.S. Chamber of Commerce. Companies such as Prudential Financial, Dow Chemical, and Merck (pharmaceutical manufacturer) poured millions into the Chamber of Commerce, which pledged to spend $50 million in political advertising during 2012. Other trade associations that benefited from this arrangement included Founding Fund, which received $1 million from the nation's largest utility, American Electric Power; and American Action Network, which received $3 million from the insurance giant Aetna. These companies were united in their attempt to push for a pro-business, limited government.[11]

But how has the *Citizens United* decision made it possible to funnel money to a candidate that remains untraceable to the corporate benefactor? Because 2012 was the first presidential election since the *Citizens United* ruling, we are able to see how the ruling made it possible to give in secret. Even though public support exists for public disclosure of campaign giving and decades of legal precedent support the right for the public to know who is funding campaigns, 2012 saw the rise of "dark money." Dark money comes from innocuously named nonprofits engaged in "social welfare" (designated as "civic leagues, social welfare organizations, and local associations of employees" under section 501[c][4] of the U.S. Internal Revenue Code) that do not disclose their funding sources. And even when such groups that do disclose their donors receive millions, it can still be kept anonymous by the funneling of funds through fake corporations designed to cover the money trail. During the 2012 election, shell corporations that did not disclose the funding sources funneled at least $17 million to super-PACs. Contributions to super-PACs via identified shell corporations

---

10. Meena Hartenstein, "Target Boycotted for Donating $150,000 to MN Right-Wing Republican Tom Emmer's Campaign for Governor," *New York Daily News*, August 3, 2010.

11. Mike McIntire and Nicholas Confessore, "Groups Shield Political Gifts of Business," *New York Times*, July 8, 2012.

represented almost 17 percent of all business contributions. During 2012, dark-money nonprofits reported spending over $299 million, running "issue ads" that need only be reported when aired just before primaries or the day of election. Thanks to both dark-money nonprofits and shell corporations, it is now almost impossible to identify violations of election or tax law, such as the infiltration of foreign funds (Fischer and Bowie 2013, 1).

Political contributions might easily influence who gets government jobs. Since 1940, federal government contractors were prohibited from contributing to political campaigns or parties. Known as the Hatch Act, this law eliminated two common practices: companies using political contributions as kickbacks or bribes to obtain lucrative federal contracts, and politicians extorting money from companies hoping to conduct business with the government. The ban on contractors was broken when candidate Romney's super-PAC, Restore Our Future, accepted $890,000 from at least five government contractors based on how it interpreted the *Citizens United* decision, differently from the super-PACs of Barack Obama, Rick Santorum, Newt Gingrich, and Ron Paul.[12]

Additionally, large sums of political contributions might influence how a candidate votes, specifically by supporting the mission of the corporation. Take the example of Amgen, the world's largest biotechnology company, which was able to have inserted into the "fiscal cliff" bill of 2013 a provision that financially benefited the firm, even though the company's name never appeared on the provision. The provision delayed a set of Medicare price restraints on a class of drugs that Amgen produces for an additional two years (even though the company previously obtained a two-year delay). The cost of the legislation to the taxpayers is calculated at $500 million and runs counter to Washington's supposed effort to reduce medical cost.

Amgen was successful because it employed an army of seventy-four lobbyists who pushed for the provision, and because of its financial ties to three influential senators: Senate Minority Leader Mitch McConnell (R-KY) and Senate Finance Committee leaders Max Baucus (D-MT) and Orrin Hatch (R-UT). Besides the $73,000 in campaign contributions to McConnell between 2007 and 2012, $67,750 to Baucus, and $59,000 to Hatch, additional hundreds of thousands of dollars went to charitable contributions connected with the senators, along with large donations to Glacier PAC, sponsored by Baucus, and Orrin PAC, controlled by Hatch. Some Amgen employees even obtained important jobs within the Capitol, such as Dan Todd, who found employment as Hatch's top Finance Committee staff member responsible for supervision over his former employer.[13]

Political support need not be so brazen as the Amgen example. In most cases, the return on corporate political contribution investment can be

---

12. "The Wall between Contractors and Politics," *New York Times*, March 25, 2012.

13. Eric Lipton and Kevin Sack, "Fiscal Footnote: Big Senate Gift to Drug Maker," *New York Times*, January 20, 2013.

received in matters that do not appear to be quid pro quo. A beneficiary of campaign contributions might choose to abstain from voting altogether if the corporation and the political official disagree on how they were originally planning to vote on the proposed legislation. Or the beholden politician can, behind the scenes, encourage certain witnesses to testify at a committee hearing or block those whose testimony may be perceived as harmful. Corporations can greatly benefit when public officials whom they support encourage or block someone's appointment to a post that oversees or regulates the benefactor's industry. In effect, the corporation transforms the relationship from regulator and regulated to a more symbiotic one between parties with mutual interests.

Citizens United has done more than legalize the influencing of politicians with unlimited funding; it has also opened the door to the financing of ballot initiatives by the wealthy few. Once considered a progressive exercise in direct democracy, ballot initiatives, in a post–*Citizens United* era, have become a means by which laws can be challenged with private funding. For example, of the eleven ballot propositions faced by California voters in 2012, four were initiatives of single wealthy individuals, while others were challenged by the millions of dollars of the few. Tom Steyer, founder of the hedge fund Fallon Capital Management, poured $22 million into Proposition 39, which rescinded a three-year-old tax benefit given to out-of-state companies. Billionaire insurance executive George Joseph funneled $16 million to change, singlehandedly, the state's automobile insurance laws. Whereas in the past the wealthy have used their money to advance pet projects, now it has become a more common method of setting governmental policies.[14]

If corporations are to be treated as humans, then should humans be silenced so as not to be an electoral counterpoint? For the vast majority of the history of this U.S. democracy, methods were legally employed to disenfranchise a major portion of the electorate through the legal means of literacy tests, competency tests, or poll taxes. Until the 1960s, politics, especially in the southern states, was the means of ruthlessly disenfranchising nonwhites in every facet of daily life. Unfortunately, such Jim and Jane Crow suppression of votes is not necessarily a thing of the past.

For example, during the 2012 presidential election Florida's Republican State House cut back on early voting and imposed onerous identification requirements. Additionally, the Florida State House passed legislation to scrub from its voting rolls those whom they suspected might not be U.S. citizens, claiming that such action was to ensure the prevention of illegal voters, even though no evidence exists whatsoever that undocumented immigrants

---

14. Norimitsu Onishi, "California Ballot Initiatives, Born in Populism, Now Come from Billionaires," *New York Times*, October 17, 2012.

are registering to vote, or that anybody fraudulently registered to vote. A *Miami Herald* study showed that 58 percent of those purged from the voting list were Hispanics, and 14 percent were blacks.[15] White Republicans were least likely to appear on the list. Some thirty-one states (mainly those located in battleground states and controlled by Republican legislatures) passed some form of voter-identification law. The Brennan Center for Justice at New York University estimated that such laws could disenfranchise some five million voters, the majority of whom voted for Obama in 2008.[16]

In addition, draconian rules (e.g., a forty-eight-hour limit to turn in new registrations) were enacted to burden those organizations that register voters, thus creating a sharp decline. Since the law took effect in May 2012, 81,471 fewer Floridians registered to vote than during the same period before the 2008 presidential election.[17] Those most affected by such legislative actions are blacks, the poor, and especially Hispanics. Prior to the 2012 electoral outcome Florida, with its twenty-nine electoral votes, which, according to an NBC-Marist poll had Obama barely ahead of Romney at 48 percent to 44 percent, was a crucial state if Romney hoped to remain viable (Obama went on to win Florida).[18] One tactic that might have increased Romney's chances of success was to eliminate from the voting rolls those more likely to vote for Obama: blacks, Hispanics, and the poor. After all, in 2000 whoever actually won Florida probably did so by just hundreds of votes. Under the leadership of then-governor Jeb Bush, Florida purged from its rolls some 173,000 eligible voters.[19]

According to the U.S. Census Bureau, minorities accounted for 92 percent of the nation's population growth in the decade that ended in 2010. By July 2011, births of white babies ceased being the majority for the first time since the European colonization of what would become the United States. These white births accounted for 49.6 percent of all births during the previous twelve months.[20] This raises questions concerning the motivation for implementing restrictive electoral laws. Could it be the rapid change in national demographics? A relationship cannot be denied between voter suppression and the race or ethnicity of those mainly suppressed. Through voter suppression, can a shrinking white minority hold on to power and use it to the detriment of the emerging "colored" America?

---

15. "Florida's Discriminatory Voter Purge," *New York Times*, May 31, 2012; Charles Blow, "Darkness in the Sunshine State," *New York Times*, June 1, 2012.

16. Corey Dade, "Political Battle Brewing over New Voter ID Laws," *NPR News*, January 12, 2012.

17. Blow, "Darkness in the Sunshine State."

18. Ibid.

19. Lizette Alvarez, "Search for Illegal Voters May Violate Federal Safeguards, U.S. Tells Florida," *New York Times*, June 1, 2012.

20. Sabrina Tavernise, "Whites Account for Under Half of Births in U.S.," *New York Times*, May 17, 2012.

Take the example of Viviette Applewhite, a ninety-three-year-old African American woman who had her Social Security card stolen from her. Unable to provide a state-approved photo ID, she was prevented from voting in the 2012 election because she lives in Pennsylvania, which requires such identification. Obtaining a state-issued ID is not easy, and for the poor it is sometimes costly. Although partisan politics is regularly dismissed as a motivation for such ID-required laws, we must consider Pennsylvania State House majority leader Mike Turzai, who listed as one of his legislative accomplishments the following: "Voter ID—which is going to allow Governor Romney to win the state of Pennsylvania—done." Almost every one of the thirty-three states that passed legislation requiring identification had a Republican-controlled legislature.[21] Coincidence? In response to this new Jim and Jane Crow, the NAACP appealed to the U.N. Human Rights Council in Geneva to support the rights of U.S. minorities against voter suppression. And although the United Nations has no jurisdiction over the United States, this international denouncement might serve as an effective way of shaming creators of such legislation.[22]

It should be noted that on June 17, 2013, the Supreme Court ruled (7-2) that the Arizona law requiring documentary proof of citizenship for those seeking to vote in federal elections impinged on the federal government's jurisdiction of controlling borders and regulating federal elections. The law disenfranchised 31,550 (mostly Hispanic) citizens from their ability to vote because they failed to present the required evidence when they registered. Still, the way the majority decision was written by Justice Scalia left the door open for Arizona to reinstate the voter-suppression maneuver. In October 2013 Arizona joined Kansas in creating a separate registration system requiring proof of citizenship for local and state elections. Thousands of eligible U.S. citizens will be prevented from participating.[23]

The strategy used on those who do have a proper ID has been to create longer waiting lines for voting in order to discourage the casting of votes. Studies show that long waiting lines depressed voter turnout during 2012. What is highly problematic is that blacks and Hispanics wait longer than whites. A Massachusetts Institute of Technology analysis found that Latino/as and African Americans waited, on average, twice as long in line to vote than whites. We must ask why. Take Florida as an example. The state had the dubious honor of having the nation's longest lines, at forty-five minutes.

21. Ethan Bronner, "Legal Battles Erupts as Voters Fear Exclusion by Tough ID Laws," *New York Times*, July 20, 2012.

22. Corey Dade, "The Fight over Voter ID Laws Goes to the United Nations," *NPR News*, March 9, 2012.

23. Adam Liptak, "Vote Law Can't Require Proof of Citizenship," *New York Times*, June 18, 2013; and Fernanda Santos and John Eligon, "2 State Plan 2-Tier System for Balloting," *New York Times*, October 12, 2013.

An analysis conducted by the *Orlando Sentinel* and an Ohio State University professor concluded that more than 200,000 voters "gave up in frustration" without voting. Considering that Obama won Florida by just 74,000 votes, any net loss due to long lines clearly can negatively impact the integrity of any election.[24]

People of color were not the only ones targeted during the 2012 election. College students, who typically vote Democratic, also found it harder to register to vote. In some states college IDs were no longer valid for registration, or out-of-state drivers' licenses made their holders ineligible, and even paying out-of-state tuition when having a proper in-state driver license prevented proper voter registration.[25]

Consider that Obama was elected in 2008 in part by a surge of new-voter support. Is, then, a nineteenth-century registration method that relies on filling out a form, which disenfranchises millions of eligible voters, another technique employed to shrink the voting rolls?

Probably the most interesting proposition being considered in some Republican-controlled legislatures (Michigan, Ohio, Pennsylvania, Virginia, and Wisconsin) after the 2012 election is replacing the Electoral College winner-take-all system with a proportional allocation based on congressional districts, thus privileging rural areas by diminishing the voting power in urban areas. In the 2012 Congressional election, more cast votes for Democrats than for Republicans, meaning that the 113th Congress, if majority ruled, would have been controlled by Democrats, but due to gerrymandering it instead was controlled by Republicans. In the states where this reallocation is being discussed, Obama, who won the popular vote in each of those states, would have lost the vast majority of the Electoral College vote. Had such a system been in place nationwide, Romney would have been the forty-fourth president of the United States.

What cannot be suppressed legislatively is done through the threat of losing one's livelihood. Prior to the *Citizens United* ruling, corporations were prohibited from urging employees from supporting specific candidates. Since the ruling, a disturbing trend developed. Several major companies sent letters and packages to employees suggesting (instructing?) whom they should vote for during the 2012 presidential election. Some of these letters warned that an Obama reelection could jeopardize their jobs. Take the example of David A. Siegel, chief executive of Westgate Resorts, who wrote to his seven thousand employees, "The economy doesn't currently pose a threat to your job. What does threaten your job, however, is another four years of the same

---

24. Jeremy W. Peters, "Waiting Times at Ballot Boxes Draw Scrutiny," *New York Times*, February 5, 2013.
25. "Keeping Students from the Polls," *New York Times*, December 26, 2011.

presidential administration. If any new taxes are levied on me or my company as our current president plans, I will have no choice but to reduce the size of this company." Would employees feel comfortable placing on their cars a bumper sticker opposing the views of their employer? Or a yard sign if they live in a small community where the company is the major employer? Georgia-Pacific, a subsidiary of Koch Industries, also sent out an information packet to more than thirty thousand of its employees, warning (threatening?) of the consequences of another Obama administration while providing a list of candidates acceptable to the conservative billionaire Koch brothers.[26]

Corporate attempts to influence the political process are not limited to quasi-coercive letters to employees. Using the libertarian industrialist Koch brothers as an example provides an entry into observing how access to major corporate funding skews the democratic process. In 2010 Charles and David Koch, two of the richest men in the world, with a calculated net worth of $50 billion each (per *Forbes* calculations, up from $532 million in 1982), held a seminar for wealthy donors at the St. Regis Resort in Aspen, Colorado, where they laid out a three-pronged, ten-year strategy to shift the United States to a smaller and less regulated country with fewer taxes. The first two pieces of the strategy played out during the 2012 election. First, they conducted grassroots activist education, best demonstrated in financing the formation of Americans for Prosperity, the political action group responsible for galvanizing Tea Party organizations and their causes. Second, they influenced the political electoral process, contributing more than $60 million during the 2000s ($275 million since 1986) to foundations, think tanks (e.g., the Cato Institute, founded by Charles Koch in 1974), and front groups (e.g., Americans for Prosperity, founded by David Koch in 2004) to mold public opinion along the lines of libertarian positions (Barlett and Steele 2012, 29–30). The third piece, which began to be implemented in 2013, is controlling the media through the purchasing of major newspapers.[27] Concern should exist when the free press becomes a commodity to be purchased and sold to advance the special interests of the wealthy few.

Corporations and the wealthy, like the Koch brothers, are less interested in the religious issues of past conservative movements (e.g., the Religious Right) than they are in the economics of less government and taxes. What truly matters are their economic goals, and their contributions move the center of the discourse closer to this corporate ideology. Differences between candidates may be noticeable on social issues, but on the goals and aims of big business, differences are measured by minor degrees. We should

---

26. Steven Greenhouse, "Bosses Offering Timely Advice: How to Vote," *New York Times*, October 27, 2012.

27. Amy Chozick, "Conservative Koch Brothers Turning Focus to Newspapers," *New York Times*, April 30, 2013.

not forget that it was the liberal president Jimmy Carter, not the conservative Ronald Reagan, who deregulated the trucking and airline industries. Before the airline deregulation, ten large airlines contended for customers, making airfare competitive. Today, only three large airlines remain (American, United, and Delta), offering substandard services at much higher rates, providing the lowest wages ever to its pilots and flight crews, and overseeing lost pensions.

Deregulation may be great for corporate leaders, but it can prove deadly to average persons. Consider the explosion at a fertilizer plant in West, Texas, on April 17, 2013, that leveled a large portion of the town and killed fifteen citizens. Just five days later, after the worst industrial accident in decades, Texas governor Rick Perry was in Illinois wooing businesses, selling them on his state's limited regulations and low taxes. When questioned, the governor declared that more government regulation or increased safety inspections would not have prevented the disaster. Texas takes pride in being the only state that exempts companies from contributing to workers' compensation coverage; also, there is no state fire code, the state prohibits smaller counties from developing a code, and cities such as Houston have no zoning laws. This is great for companies that move to this laissez-faire paradise, but the average citizen works in a state that has the nation's highest number of workplace fatalities (more than four hundred annually) and in which more than 1,300 chemical and industrial plant fires and explosions from May 2007 through 2012 have cost more property damage than in the other forty-nine states combined.[28]

Maybe the ultimate paradox is that entrepreneurship capitalism, which rewards the one who can build a better mousetrap and get it to market quicker, is being destroyed by monopolistic capitalism, whose "winner take all" philosophy is sustained through a bought government whose electability is dependent upon corporate donations received. In return, less government and lower taxes are advocated to the detriment of average citizens, who develop a false consciousness that blames government and those on the margins for their difficulties rather than the elite.

Step 2. Reflecting

"Class warfare" is a term used by politicians and political pundits whenever the public (rich or poor) questions the disparity of wealth in this nation. To raise concerns about the ever-growing economic gap in this nation is to risk being accused of fomenting social unrest or, worse, labeled a socialist. As mentioned earlier, even when billionaire capitalist Warren Buffett pondered

---

28. Ian Urbina, Manny Fernandez, and John Schwartz, "After Plant Explosion, Texas Remains Wary of Regulation," *New York Times*, May 9, 2013.

in a *New York Times* op-ed why he pays a lower tax rate than his secretary,[29] Fox News pundit Eric Bolling called him a socialist.[30]

Many may wish to avoid the term "class warfare" lest they too be labeled a socialist (as if the term "socialist" was synonymous with evil); yet the truth remains that the massive infusion of corporate political contributions, thanks to *Citizens United*, only strengthened the class warfare waged by politicians protecting the super-rich. This war began in 1980 when Ronald Reagan, followed by George H. W. Bush, occupied the White House. Deregulation and massive tax cuts to the richest Americans—the new economic political mantra—were most responsible for the greatest transfer of wealth in human history from the poorest Americans to the richest, as discussed in the preceding chapter.

When Bill Clinton was elected, the national deficit was at $300 billion. And while he worked to control this, ending his term with a surplus (the first in decades), he still participated in the transfer of wealth, specifically in his "ending welfare as we know it." More important was his administration's role in deregulating the banking industry, a charge led by his third treasury secretary, Larry Summers, and Senator Phil Gramm (R-TX) in the form of the 1999 Financial Services Modernization Act. The safeguards put in place to prevent another depression like that of the 1930s were basically gutted. Not surprisingly, nine years later, our nation began and, as of 2013, continues to experience the Great Recession. Aggravating the situation was a greater transfer of wealth that has come to be known as the Bush tax cuts of 2001.

In spite of the budget surplus inherited, Bush's $1.3 trillion tax cuts for the richest Americans grew the deficit by $400 billion a year. Also aggravating the situation are the two wars started under Bush, funded by borrowed money. When the Obama administration began, during the worst economic crisis since the Great Depression (a crisis whose roots are in deregulation), he signed an $800 billion spending increase to stimulate the economy. The growth in spending needed to stave off the Great Recession and a drop in revenue due to the Bush tax cuts exploded the deficit to $1.4 trillion (down to $1.1 trillion in 2012).

These words to public officials found in the book of Deuteronomy remain relevant for our times: "You shall not pervert justice, nor show partiality, nor take bribes, for a bribe blinds the eyes of the wise and perverts the words of justice" (Deut. 16:19). The ability of incumbents to raise great sums of money for a "war chest" sufficiently large enough to scare off potential rivals, coupled with sophisticated gerrymandering designed to create safe district seats for the party in power, has contributed to 90 percent of the House and 91 percent

29. Warren E. Buffet, "Stop Coddling the Super Rich," *New York Times*, August 14, 2011.
30. Eric Bolling, Fox Business's *Follow the Money*, aired August 15, 2011.

percent of the Senate being reelected in 2012 (a reelection increase from 2010 of 85 percent and 84 percent, respectively).[31] In spite of a 10 percent approval rating for Congress three months prior to the 2012 election, the vast majority sailed toward electoral victory.[32] Thus, not surprisingly, most members of Congress are beholden, more or less, to those responsible for raising the funds needed to mount successful campaigns. Once elected, most politicians indebted to the corporate leaders who placed them in power advocate the neoliberal policies favorable to the corporations, policies that usually maintain the status quo and safeguard privilege.

As discussed in the preceding chapter, neoliberalism has succeeded greatly in transferring wealth from the bottom of society to the top, as evidenced by the growing income disparity between the poor and the rich—a process brought about by reducing available social services (such as welfare, support for education, and healthcare) and increasing tax breaks for the wealthiest. Neoliberalism poses a distinct threat to democracy. When concentrated wealth influences legislation, it is only a matter of time until political inequality follows. True democracy is replaced with a democratic façade, and the public is led to believe that it is exercising its right to choose leaders. Because corporations funnel large sums of money to candidates from both parties, the corporations win regardless of who wins the election.

For example, many celebrated the 2008 election of our first biracial president, creating an illusion that we live in a postracial society. But is there truly a difference between Barack Obama and Hillary Clinton, on the Democratic side, and John McCain, on the Republican side, all of whom vied for the presidency in 2008? Because of unregulated campaign contributions, all three can be considered to be ontologically white males. One cannot become the leader of the world's most powerful country (empire?) without being committed to what male whiteness symbolizes within the colonial process. Barack Obama's "whiteness" and Hillary Clinton's "maleness" raise concerns and questions and, as such, make their ascension in the political process an issue of class. The power of corporate monies contributed to candidates subjugates the collective will of both feminists and the black community regardless if "one of their own" wins the election.

Campaign contributions can easily negate the importance of electing a black man or a white woman as president. If the national politics and economics of the captains of industry were to be threatened by the needs of U.S. marginalized communities, be they blacks, women, or poor whites, the future president would rally all the forces at his or her disposal to maintain the

31. Catalina Camia, "Analysis: 90 percent of Congress Wins Re-election," *USA Today*, December 13, 2012.

32. Greg Giroux, "Voters Throw Bums in While Holding Congress in Disdain," *Bloomberg News*, December 12, 2012.

prevailing economic power structures that exist, even if those structures are detrimental to communities that share his or her gender or skin pigmentation. This raises a major concern. Has the democratic system been reduced to a choice among pro-empire individuals who throughout political campaigns show no significant difference in their commitments to protecting the rights of multinational companies to expand globally? Will future presidents, regardless of race or gender, protect the interests of Exxon, Microsoft, and Walmart even at the expense of establishing justice, and even at the cost of committing U.S. troops?

Any presidential candidate who questions free-market policies or seriously addresses the undemocratic distribution of wealth, resources, and privileges in this country would never be considered a serious contender, since he or she would be unable to attract the corporate campaign contributions needed to mount a viable run for the office. Campaign contributions from multinational firms have the corroding power to transform hopeful politicians such as Obama and Clinton into the black or female face of a global neoliberalism that continues to privilege the few at the expense of the vast majority of the world's population.

We have created a social structure where politicians, with a keen eye on special interests, determine what is ethical. We allow politicians to construct the social order in which we live when we are politically irresponsible. This happens when we call politics "dirty" and flee from it and/or we concentrate solely on supporting politicians who learn to expound certain "Christian" jargon without seriously considering the ramifications of their political actions. Yet throughout the Bible God shows concern and love for the disenfranchised. God cares about the political order.

The question seldom pondered is, who would benefit by less government regulation? The answer is obvious: large corporations would benefit the most by less labor, environmental, and/or safety regulations and by lower taxes, thus explaining why *Citizens United* is such a bonanza; it opens the political donation floodgates needed to peddle libertarian political goals. Given the continuing influence of corporations through super-PACs, we are now moving away from a representative democracy toward a plutocracy, a system in which unequal wealth creates political inequality. The excessive wealth enjoyed by the privileged few provides them the right, through the funneling of campaign contributions, to influence and, in some cases, to determine laws and regulations, often to their own benefit. Wealth funneled to political campaigns, especially through super-PACs, serves to conceal the will of the privileged few and to fuse and confuse it with the will of the majority. And who suffers most from *Citizens United*? It is the vast majority, whose ability to influence the political process is greatly diminished.

The marginalized's concept of ethics is far different from that of politicians beholden to PACs. Any law or regulation is ethical if it produces a more human existence as a response to *agape*—unconditional love. Proper public policy promotes a more human existence by providing opportunities for all citizens to participate in the abundance of life promised by Christ, and specifically those citizens who are the most vulnerable within a society. PACs, whose purpose is to have laws and regulations reflect private interests rather than public interests, prevent the societal goal of *fiat justitia ruat coelum*—"Let justice be done though the heavens should fall." Although the elimination of super-PACs will not usher in a new dawn of justice, their continuation prevents the disenfranchised from participating equally in what society has to offer.

According to American sociologist and civil rights activist W. E. B. Du Bois (1868–1963), the best way to prevent the rich from controlling the political process is for democracy to be allowed to modify industry. In seeking an alternative to the present disjointedness between economics and electoral democracies, Du Bois advocated a proper relationship between the two. He wrote, "While wealth spoke and had power, the dirtiest laborers had voice and vote." Or, as restated by Dwight Hopkins, "The power of wealth submits and succumbs to the will of a collective, conscious, common folk" (2000, 136). The ethical question to ponder is this: How do super-PACs subvert and pervert the proper relationship between economics and electoral democracies? Hopkins may very well be correct in stating,

> The federal government (the presidential, judicial, and legislative branches) often appears to be a competing system of objective checks and balances. But if the national politics and economics were threatened with a reversal, that is, if the pyramidal monopoly capitalists structure in the United States began to move bottom to top, then the so-called checks and balances system would rally to prevent such a movement. The present system would immediately stop the realization of genuine democracy in which the majority of the citizens—the people at the bottom in the United States—would own all the economic resources as well as the military industrial complex, and would, therefore, control the federal government. (2000, 187)

Step 3. Praying

God calls political leaders to do justice by linking justice with how the disenfranchised are rescued from the oppressor's hand, with how the least in society are treated,[33] and with how those who are innocent are protected.

---

33. The biblical phrase "alien, orphan, and widow" can be understood as a way to refer to the marginalized.

None of us will enter through those pearly gates without a letter of recommendation for the wretched of the earth. Speaking to the prophet Jeremiah, God said,

> Go down to the house of the king of Judah, and there speak this word, and say: Hear the word of God, O king of Judah who sits on the throne of David, and also your servants and your people who enter through these gates. Thus says God: Do justice and practice righteousness; deliver the one wronged from the hands of the oppressor; do not oppress the alien, the orphan, or the widow; do no violence; and do not shed innocent blood in this place. (Jer. 22:1–3)

Today it has become standard practice for special-interest groups to contribute funds through super-PACs to those charged with establishing justice. We seem to have become so accustomed to this form of political order that it has become normative in our eyes. Theologians from the margins of society, however, offer a different political model, a model based on the concept of the Trinity.

Whether one accepts the theological concept of the Trinity is unimportant. What is important is the model that the Trinity provides. For the dominant Christian culture, the concept of the Trinity is a cosmic religious mystery that explains how a monotheistic deity can be understood as three entities: Father, Son, and Holy Spirit. Although it is emphasized that these three separate entities are an equal composition of one, many Christians still perceive a hierarchy, with the Father being first, followed by the Son, and trailed by the Spirit. For those doing ethics from the margins of society, the relationship existing within the Trinity, between Father, Son, and Holy Spirit, is not a cosmic puzzle in need of solution, but rather is a paragon to be emulated by humanity. Father, Son, and Spirit do not exist in a hierarchy; rather, all three share equally in substance, power, and importance. The Trinity represents a Godhead whose very existence is that of a sharing Being, co-equal in power, awe, and authority. As Justo González reminds us, the fourth-century theologians (e.g., Ambrose, Jerome, Basil, and Gregory Nazianzen) who developed the doctrine of the Trinity were staunch critics of greed and argued for economic justice (1990b, 113–14).

The triune God provides a pattern of sharing for those who claim belief in the doctrine of the Trinity, a pattern that subverts any economic system that requires an undereducated and underskilled army of laborers so that the few can disproportionately hoard the majority of the wealth (De La Torre and Aponte 2001, 91). Each person of the Trinity fully participates in divinity, sharing God's power and nature while maintaining their distinct functions. This teaching of the Trinity maintains that it is God's nature to share. God invites all to share divinity and power with God and each other, or as Paul would promise, to become "coheirs with Christ" (Rom. 8:17). Luis Pedraja writes,

> God reveals to us how to live with one another and in God's image by calling us to engage in a life of sharing. The communal nature of the early church as exemplified in the Book of Acts also points us in this direction. What the Trinity reveals to us is a God who exists by sharing both power and divinity. If God does not hoard power, then neither should we hoard power. If God shares the very property of divinity and the essence of the divine is in sharing with others, then should we not live in the same fashion? (2004, 56)

Implementing the Trinity model significantly impacts how economics and politics should be done by a people attempting to establish a just distribution of power. The model calls for the dismantling of social structures that maintain economic injustices and also for all power to be shared, destroying structures of dominance and oppression that foster marginalization. How, then, can those who insist on maintaining their power and privilege become part of the body of Christ?

Throughout his ministry Jesus proclaimed that God's reign was at hand. What did he mean by this? Those doing ethics from the margins believe that Jesus, and all the prophets before him, understood God's reign to mean a striving toward establishing the Trinity model as the foundation for a social order where justice prevails for all. God's reign is not limited to the otherworldly; it also exists in the here and now. This reign of God can best be understood by what Jesus did: he fed the hungry, he healed the sick, he proclaimed the good news to the poor. But while Jesus anchored his good news with the experience of the disenfranchised of his time, he still emphasized the ethical responsibilities of those who possess power and authority over others, warning of the importance of moral diligence.

During Jesus' earthly ministry he and his disciples lived from a common purse (John 13:29). The early church continued by creating a church in which "all the believers were together, and held all things in common; they sold their goods and possessions and distributed them to all, each according to their need" (Acts 2:44–45). Nonetheless, there were those who tried to create a façade of Christianity while holding on to the material possessions that secured their privilege. The apostle Peter challenged Ananias and Sapphira, who publicly agreed to participate in the Trinity model of community but privately attempted to secure their wealth. Their sin was not that they withheld a portion of the proceeds of the sale of their property, for, as Peter said, it was their property to keep or dispose of as they saw fit (Acts 5:1–11).

Their sin was that they claimed to be part of the faith community while attempting to maintain an uneven distribution of the power that comes from wealth. In a similar way, we can conclude that our present political process, which establishes an uneven distribution of power and wealth, thanks in great part to super-PAC money funneled to politicians, is irreconcilable with the sharing model of the Trinity.

Step 4. Case Studies

1. In 1789 state-backed revolutionary bonds became worthless. Alexander Hamilton, secretary of the treasury, moved to strengthen the values of the bonds. But before word got out, Congressional members secretly obtained thousands of bonds from unsuspecting veterans and farmers, paying pennies on the dollar. Many became rich, benefiting from insider trading. It was not until April 4, 2012, that Congress passed the Stop Trading on Congressional Knowledge (Stock) Act, which prevents lawmakers profiting from insider information. Still, the Stock Act does not restrict elected officials from owning stock in industries they oversee.[34]

    — Lawmakers exempt themselves from insider trading regulations because as "citizen legislators" their investment portfolios should mirror those of their constituents, and because they, unlike federal workers, are elected, and voters could vote them out if they become involved in a conflict of interests. Are these good reasons? Are these reasons outdated? Unethical? Should those who make the laws live under those same laws?

    — While healthcare overhaul was in process, lawmakers invested in medical supply companies that would be impacted by provisions in the bill. Senators on the Armed Services Committee own stock in companies that do business with the Defense Department. Should the Stock Act have eliminated these abuses? Why or why not? Two provisions were eliminated from the Stock Act prior to its vote. The first would have regulated "political intelligence" from political insiders for the use of other investors, and the second would have given prosecutors tools to pursue corruption. Should these provisions have remained in the Stock Act? Why or why not? Should the Stock Act have been made more stringent?

    — A year later, on April 15, 2013, Congress passed and the president signed legislation introduced by Senator Harry Reid (D-NV) that removed the required online electronic filing of reports, making it

---

34. Kimberly Kindy, "Congressional Rules on Trading Had Their Start in 1789," *Washington Post*, June 23, 2012.

almost impossible for watch groups to verify if congressional members are benefiting from insider trading. The reason given was a fear that electronic disclosures might be a risk to "national security." Does this new legislation gut the 2012 Stock Act? Although congressional insider trading is still illegal, does this new provision make it impossible to enforce?

2. A major triumph of the civil rights movement was the passage of the Voting Rights Act of 1965, the heart of which is Section 5, which required local governments, mainly in the South,[35] to acquire preclearance from the U.S. Justice Department before making changes that affect voting. In *Shelby County v. Holder*, the opponents of Section 5 argued that the provision outlived its purpose of protecting minority voters, especially in an era when a biracial man occupies the White House. On June 25, 2013, the Supreme Court, by a 5-4 vote, struck down the heart of the Voting Rights Act, freeing nine states to change their election laws without federal preclearance. In effect, local officials will face less scrutiny on thousand of decisions made each year concerning the redrawing of district lines, specifically racial gerrymandering, imposing voter IDs, moving or closing polling places, and changing voting areas in areas that have a history of disenfranchising voters.[36]

— Was the Supreme Court decision correct? Have we outlived the need for the Voting Rights Act? Does not the election of President Obama prove that we are living in a postracial America? Were white southerners being discriminated against by having their states rights impinged and having to get permission from the Justice Department in determining their political future, a requirement not imposed on other states? Is it problematic that Section 5 is considered to be a badge of shame for those whom it covers?

— During oral arguments Justice Scalia said that Section 5 is a "perpetuation of racial entitlement." Is he right? Are voting rights an entitlement? Why or why not?

— Do the tactics that arose during the 2012 election to disenfranchise voters, such as voter IDs, dropping names from voter rolls, and changing and shortening voting hours, raise concerns about the need for the Voting Rights Act? According to Morgan Kousser of the California

---

35. The law applied to nine states: Alabama, Alaska, Arizona, Georgia, Louisiana, Mississippi, South Carolina, Texas, and Virginia, and also to parts of other states with records of extreme discrimination toward minorities.

36. Adam Liptak, "Justices Void Oversight of States, Issue at Heart of Voting Rights Act," *New York Times*, June 26, 2013.

Institute of Technology, "Five-sixths or more of the cases of proven election discrimination from 1957 through 2013 have taken place in jurisdictions subject to Section 5 oversight."[37] Is this significant? Why? Should the Voting Rights Act have applied to all fifty states?

— The Supreme Court's decision freed a number of states with a history of discrimination, mostly in the South, to change election laws. Within hours of the Supreme Court's ruling, Texas announced that the decision to implement voter identification recently federally blocked by the Voting Rights Act on the grounds that it would disproportionately affect Latino/a and black voters would immediately go into effect. Mississippi, North Carolina, and Alabama, which passed their own voter identification laws but have not received federal approval, vowed to proceed with enforcing the laws.[38] Is this problematic?

3. From 1990 through 2010 the financial industry spent about $2 billion in donations to members of Congress. One major legislation piece, the Financial Services Modernization Act of 1999, provided the financial industry a profitable return on their investment. The law, whose major architect was Senator Phil Gramm (R-TX), removed the regulatory barriers between securities companies, banks, and insurers, allowing them to sell each other's financial products. Banks became stockbrokers as stockbrokers became banks. In effect, the new law repealed the Glass-Steagall Act of 1933, which was passed to rein in the excesses of the financial industry that led to the Great Depression. For decades, Glass-Steagall kept banks, which wanted to sell mutual funds and stocks, in check—a regulation that banks despised. Prior to the Financial Services Modernization Act, lenders would service mortgages until they were paid off, earning their profits on the interest. Hence, they were motivated to ensure the ability of homeowners to repay their mortgage loans lest they be saddled with a foreclosed house. Deregulation of the banking industry occurred simultaneously with the transformation of the mortgage industry. Independent mortgage brokers would now originate the mortgage, collect their fee, then pass the loan to someone else, who would bundle it with other mortgages to be sold to investors. Mortgage brokers got paid regardless if the homeowner could pay the mortgage. Failure to make mortgage payments became the problem of someone else. Deregulation led to fraudulent credit reports, hidden fees, and usurious loan rates (Barlett and Steele 2012, 187, 208–11).

37. Morgan Kousser, "The Strong Case for Keeping Section 5," *Reuters*, February 15, 2013.
38. Michael Cooper, "After Ruling, States Rush to Enact Voting Laws," *New York Times*, July 6, 2013.

— Were the housing crash and the 2008 Great Recession consequences of the political donations from the financial industry? Are company donations socializing corporate losses while privatizing gains? Does the United States have a capitalist economy, or are corporate political contributions creating a new economic order? If so, what is it?

— In May 2013 a bill that was essentially written by Citigroup's lobbyists sailed through the House Financial Services Committee (over the objections of the Treasury Department) that would exempt broad swathes of trades from new regulations. Citigroup recommendations could be found in seventy lines of the eighty-five-line bill. It helps when the banking industry provides large political campaign donations to committee members on both sides of the aisle.[39] Bob Ney (R-OH), former chair of the House Financial Services Committee's housing subcommittee, oversaw the rise of the subprime market (which grew by 600 percent in the first five years since passage of the Financial Services Modernization Act). He was also a major figure in the lobbying scandal involving Jack Abramoff, who pleaded guilty and served prison time for conspiring to defraud the federal government and falsifying financial disclosure forms. Still, no Wall Street titan who financially benefited from the Great Recession has gone to jail, let alone been charged with a crime. Why? The "too big to fail" doctrine triggered the greatest economic meltdown since the Great Depression; and yet the deregulation that caused this financial crisis is still in place. Why? Are our current political leaders prisoners of the industries that they are supposed to regulate and protect citizens from? How can the system change? To what?

— Huge bailouts saved the financial institutions, but in the process an estimated 12 million foreclosures have been filed since the Great Recession, some 4 million people lost their homes, and millions more are at risk of also losing their homes. Close to $5 trillion in home equity evaporated. Should there have been a bailout for average Americans? What about a sales tax on all Wall Street transactions? For a tax lower than most states' sales taxes, hundreds of billions in revenue can be collected.

4. Many members of Congress or office holders in former administrations become lobbyists when they leave office, or they obtain lucrative jobs in the very industries that they once regulated. For example, when Senator Phil Gramm left office, he became vice president of UBS, a Swiss bank-

---

39. Eric Lipton and Ben Protess, "Banks' Lobbyists Help in Drafting Financial Bills," *New York Times*, May 23, 2013.

ing giant and a benefactor of the Financial Services Modernization Act, the banking deregulation legislation that Gramm championed.

— Was this ethical? Can this be construed as bribery? Should former public officials be allowed to become lobbyists or obtain employment in the industries that they once regulated? If not, is this restricting their rights to employment? Lobbyists can be paid $200,000 at the low end and over $1 million on the high end. Should limits be placed on what a lobbyist can earn? Why or why not? Why are firms willing to pay lobbyists such high fees? Are these reasons ethical, even if they are detrimental to those who cannot afford lobbyists?

— At times, family members benefit from the lobbyist-politician relationship. A 2012 study conducted by Citizens for Responsibility and Ethics in Washington found that the family members of more than half of all House members received payments or some sort of financial benefit (in the tens of millions) due to their affiliation with a lawmaker during the 2010 and 2012 elections.[40] For example, Representative Alcee Hasting (D-FL) paid his girlfriend $622,574 between 2007 and 2010 to be deputy district director of his congressional office.[41] Should family members of politicians be paid lobbyists or campaign workers? Does this restrict their right to employment? Do their salaries provide a legal means for corporations to funnel funds that are not tied to political contributions into the private financing of the politician and his or her family?

— At other times, it is the representative's aide who financially benefits. When the food chain McDonald's, the tobacco giant Altria, or the alternative energy company Sapphire Energy wanted to protect their tax incentives, they retained firms that employed former aides to Max Baucus (D-MT), chairman of the Senate Finance Committee. Some twenty-eight of his former aides were registered lobbyists on K Street by 2013. They saved financial firms $11.2 billion in tax deferments and secured $222 million in tax benefits for the liquor industry. Some of these former aides earn over half a million dollars due to their access to Baucus. Their presence on K Street becomes a major source for fundraising; many of them join Baucus for his weekend fundraising retreats.[42] Should lobbyists participate in politicians' fundraising? Should the time required before former aides can lobby for their former boss—one year—be expanded? Is it ever proper for former aides or relatives of a member of Congress to lobby for that person?

---

40. Eric Lipton, "Study Shows House Members Profit," *New York Times*, March 22, 2012.

41. Dan Christensen and Erika Bolstad, "South Florida Lawmakers Used Jobs to Benefit Family, Themselves," *Miami Herald*, March 23, 2012.

42. Eric Lipton, "Tax Lobby Builds Ties to Chairman of Finance Panel," *New York Times*, April 6, 2013.

Chapter 11

Life and Death

Step 1. Observing

Although disagreement exists about what actions should be taken on most political and economic issues, there is general agreement on the basic human right to good health. Nearly everyone would argue that human beings have a right not to have their well-being threatened by exterior forces. Although we may disagree as to how this might happen, still, human beings can expect not to have governments or businesses impose upon them conditions that produce illness or death. In fact, it could be argued that when this occurs, it undermines Jesus' promise to provide an abundant life. Yet for many in the United States, the quality of healthcare ranges from poor to nonexistent. The United States spent in 2013 about 18 percent of its gross domestic product on healthcare, twice as much as most industrialized countries, mainly because most nations set the rates for healthcare as if it were a public utility.[1] But we operate under a capitalist belief that the private market is the best way to provide healthcare and coverage to Americans. In addition to a lack of adequate health, specifically for the poor, who are disproportionately people of color, those with darker skin also face a greater risk of being incarcerated and/or executed by the state. This chapter will explore how issues of life (adequate healthcare) and death (capital punishment) impact marginalized communities.

The Quality of Healthcare

Why do African Americans live thirteen years fewer than Asian Americans? Why do Native peoples in South Dakota have a shorter lifespan in 2010 than the average American citizen fifty years earlier (UNDP 2010, 76)? What role do race and ethnicity play in the quality of U.S. healthcare? Even when insurance coverage and access to medical treatments are compatible, the quality of care received varies depending on one's race or ethnicity. According to a 1999 study appearing in the *New England Journal of Medicine*, the race and gender of a patient complaining of chest pain affect the physician's decision about whether or not to refer the patient for cardiac catheterization (Schulman et al. 1999, 623). In another study conducted in 2000 published

---

1. Elisabeth Rosenthal, "The $2.7 Trillion Medical Bill," *New York Times*, June 1, 2013.

by the same journal, pharmacies in predominantly nonwhite neighborhoods were significantly less likely to stock medication to treat patients with severe pain than those pharmacies located in predominantly white neighborhoods (Morrison et al. 2000, 1026). Several articles published by the *Journal of the American Medical Association* seem to indicate that poverty, along with race and ethnicity, influenced the quality of care received by acutely ill insured patients in a hospital. Even when the patient's income and insurance benefits are the same, racially and ethnically disenfranchised persons receive a lower quality of healthcare (Kahn et al. 1994, 1174).

The first comprehensive study of racial disparities in healthcare was conducted by the Institute of Medicine, an independent research agency that advises Congress on healthcare issues. Reviewing over a hundred studies conducted from 1992 to 2002, the report concluded that the disparities in healthcare due to race and ethnicity contribute to higher death rates among people of color from cancer, heart disease, diabetes, and HIV infections. To illustrate the point, the report cites a study conducted by Medicare that shows that African Americans suffering from diabetes are 3.6 times more likely than whites to have their limbs amputated instead of receiving more sophisticated treatments.[2] The empirical evidence overwhelmingly indicates that, all things being equal, those from nonwhite racial and ethnic communities receive a lower quality of healthcare than their white counterparts.

Not much has changed since the start of the millennium, when these studies were first conducted; in some cases the situation worsened. Race, ethnicity, and place of residency have a major impact on the quality of healthcare received. By 2008, blacks with diabetes or vascular disease were nearly five times more likely than whites to have a leg amputated. Women in Mississippi were less likely to have a mammogram than those in Maine. African Americans covered by Medicare were less likely to receive recommended mammograms and other important medical tests than white patients.[3] By 2012, Euroamerican children were more likely to be given CT scans at hospital emergency rooms for minor head trauma than Hispanic or black children. When low risk of trauma was involved, 17 percent of Euroamerican children received CT scans as opposed to 10 percent of black and Latino/a children.[4] While black women have a lower incidence of breast cancer than white women, their death rate is 41 percent higher. In some areas, such as Denver,

2. Sheryl Gay Stolberg, "Minorities Receive Inferior Care, Even If Insured, Study Finds," *New York Times*, March 21, 2002.

3. Kevin Sack, "Research Finds Wide Disparities in Health Care by Race and Region," *New York Times*, June 5, 2008; Anna Wilde Mathews, "Health Care Has Racial, State Disparities," *Wall Street Journal*, June 5, 2008.

4. Kate Yandell, "CT Scans More Likely for White Children," *New York Times*, August 14, 2012.

black women are dying at a 74 percent higher rate than white women.[5] African Americans living in segregated counties are 20 percent more likely to die of lung cancer than those living in less-segregated counties.[6] These examples raise questions concerning the link, if any, between living a healthy life and the race or ethnicity of those who get to live that healthy life.

Two studies published in 2012 examined whether stereotypes still unconsciously influence the thinking and behavior of physicians. The first study assessed what diseases and treatments physicians associated with African Americans. The second study explored doctors' computerized reaction time to images of African Americans and Euroamericans in association with specific medical terms. These two studies revealed that when presented with a black face, white doctors reacted quicker in diagnosing stereotypical diseases, indicating an implicit association in the physician's mind between certain diseases and race. These studies suggest that the diagnosis and treatment of African Americans may indeed be biased (Moskowitz, Stone, and Childs 2012, 996).

Physicians' stereotypes were also evident among pediatricians in prescribing treatment recommendations for pain management, urinary tract infections, attention deficit hyperactivity disorder, and asthma among children of color. Specifically, prescribed narcotic medications decreased for children of color but not for Euroamerican children (Sabin and Greenwald 2012, 998).

In another study, Latino/a and black children who visited emergency rooms complaining of abdominal pain were less likely than white children to receive pain medication. According to the study with a 2,298 sample size, 27.1 percent of Euroamerican children received analgesics while only 15.8 percent of African Americans, 18.9 percent of Hispanics, and 7.1 percent of other races did. Additionally, children of color spent more hours in the emergency room than white children. Children of African Americans were 68 percent more likely than children of Euroamericans to spend more than six hours waiting in an emergency room (Johnson et al. 2013, 851–58).

These forms of implicit stereotyping among physicians can be detected in the revelations of multiple studies published in 2012 showing that patients of color, overall, receive poorer quality of healthcare than Euroamericans. For example, African American patients are less likely than Euroamericans to be recommended for oral cancer surgery, Chinese and Latina women are less likely than Euroamerican women to receive adjuvant hormonal therapy, physicians recommend more advanced and potentially more effective medical procedures (e.g., coronary bypass surgery) for Euroamericans than

5. Nicholas Bakalar, "Racial Differences in Breast Cancer's Toll," *New York Times*, November 20, 2012; Michael Booth and Colleen O'Connor, "Study Finds Racial Gap in Denver Breast-Cancer Deaths," *Denver Post*, March 23, 2012.

6. Sabrina Tavernise, "Segregation Linked in Study with Lung Cancer Deaths," *New York Times*, January 17, 2013.

African Americans, and racial and ethnic minorities are more likely than Euroamericans to be recommended for and undergo unnecessary surgery. A decade into the new millennium still shows that people of color within the United States have greater health problems than Euroamericans, including suffering substantially higher mortality rates. African Americans' mortality rates for strokes, prostate cancer, and cervical cancer is 50 percent higher. Making matters worse, the mortality rate gap between Euroamericans and African Americans for heart disease, female breast cancer, and diabetes has significantly widened in recent years (Dovidio and Fiske 2012, 945, 948).

Not surprisingly, patients of color rate the interpersonal quality of care received from physicians more negatively than Euroamerican patients. Patients of color experience poorer communication with medical providers, particularly in race-discordant patient-clinician relationships. One study revealed that physicians have more negative conscious attitudes toward blacks than they do toward whites. This negative attitude correlates with and mediates disparities in treatment decisions (Cooper et al. 2012, 979). Even the suspicion held by patients of color concerning prejudices of healthcare providers lead to exacerbated psychological and physiological stress, specifically threat cognitions, threat emotions, and increased cardiovascular reactivity. According to the study, over time, such stress can lead to coronary and carotid atherosclerosis and hypertension. The study concluded that the mere anticipation of prejudice from the care provider leads to health hazards for the patient (Sawyer et al. 2012, 1020).

How bodies of color are seen and defined also has negative effects upon the advancement of medical professionals. A seventeen-year study of faculty promotion rates of professors of color within academic medical centers across the United States revealed that rates for Euroamerican, Hispanic, and black faculty were, respectively, 30.2 percent, 23.5 percent, and 18.8 percent from assistant to associate professor. And from associate to full professor, they were 31.5 percent, 25.0 percent, and 16.7 percent. The study concludes that if a more equitable faculty promotion rate existed, improved healthcare access and quality for all patients could ultimately develop (Nunez-Smith et al. 2012, 852).

Discrimination within the medical profession cannot easily be dismissed as the consequence of some individual discriminatory actions. Racism and ethnic discrimination within the medical profession is not limited to individual whites' biased acts toward people of color; it must also include a discriminatory ethos that is internalized and institutionalized throughout all levels of the medical profession, an ethos that has a negative health effect on patients of color. In short, the present-day healthcare system in the United States is structurally designed in such a way that it brings better health to the white middle and upper classes than it does to people of color. One could go so far as to say that it tends to bring ill health or even death to poor people of color.

This reality has historical roots. The most infamous example is the forty-year-long (1932–1972) Tuskegee experiment in which the U.S. Public Health Service conducted an experiment on 412 poor black sharecroppers in the late stages of syphilis. They were told by government researchers that they were being treated, when in fact they were not. The data that the experiment sought to obtain was gathered from autopsies. Consequently, these poor black men were deliberately left to degenerate under the ravages of tertiary syphilis, whose symptoms included tumors, heart disease, paralysis, blindness, insanity, and finally death.

U.S. medical experiments such as these were not limited to domestic subjects. From July 1946 through December 1948, U.S. doctors, with the full backing of U.S. health officials and then–surgeon general Thomas Parran, deliberately infected 1,300 unsuspecting Guatemalans (out of the 5,500 in the study) with venereal diseases to learn of ways to control STDs. Take the example of Federico Ramos, just one of the thousands who, as a low-ranking soldier in the Guatemalan army, was ordered to report to a clinic run and operated by U.S. doctors. There, over two visits, he was injected with what he now suspects was syphilis and gonorrhea. After leaving the armed forces, he returned to his rural village, where for decades he suffered from the effects of disease, unable to pay for medical treatment. Worse, he infected his wife and children. These medical human experiments were uncovered in 2010. Ramos and others sued the U.S. government, and although President Obama's official apology contained flowery words, the U.S. Department of Justice requested that the compensation case be dismissed. In June 2012 the case was rejected by the U.S. District Court. Instead of settling with those whose personhood was violated, the U.S. government pledged $1 million to study new rules protecting medical research volunteers and $775,000 to help fight STDs in Guatemala.[7]

Race and ethnic identity were a major component in the Tuskegee and Guatemalan experiments; yet ironically, they were conducted at the time white Americans were prosecuting Nazi officials at the Nuremberg trials immediately following World War II for carrying out medical experiments on human beings (Jews). The conclusion of the trials of Nazi doctors led to the establishment of what came to be called the Nuremberg Code of medical ethics. Medical practitioners cannot participate in human experimentations without first obtaining voluntary consent from participants. Additionally,

---

7. Matthew Walter, "First, Do Harm," *Nature*, February 9, 2012; Brian Vastag, "U.S. Pledges $1.8 Million in Response to Unethical Guatemalan Medical Studies," *Washington Post*, January 10, 2012.

unnecessary harm to the subject should be avoided. Accounts of U.S. medical experiments on humans are troubling in the shadow of the Nuremberg trials.

Nonetheless, it also remained common to conduct medical experiments on prison inmates and the disabled. Reports exist of mental patients in Connecticut being infected with hepatitis, prisoners in Maryland having pandemic flu virus squirted up their noses, and the chronically ill at a New York hospital being injected with cancer cells. At least forty such cases of human medical experiments were carried out by the U.S. government within the United States from the 1940s through the 1960s. It was legitimate in the minds of health professionals to experiment on those who lacked full rights within society, specifically prisoners, the mentally disabled, and poor people of color.[8]

More recently, about fifteen hundred six-month-olds, predominantly black and Hispanic babies in Los Angeles, were used as human guinea pigs in June 1990. They were given an experimental measles vaccine developed by Kaiser Permanente. The parents of these children were never informed that the vaccine, which was used before in two-thirds-world countries with devastating results, was experimental.[9] Another troubling example of human testing also occurred in the 1990s at the Kennedy Krieger Institute, which is affiliated with Johns Hopkins University. The prominent Baltimore medical institute knowingly exposed more than a hundred black children as young as a year old to lead poisoning so as to periodically test their blood to study the cumulative hazards of lead poisoning. The children were endangered in homes with high levels of lead dust, even while the Kennedy Krieger Institute assured parents that the houses were "lead safe." The six-year program of human testing led to permanent neurological injuries among some of the children.[10]

Just as troubling is the fact that human medical experiments continue to occur using the world's poor as subjects. Developing nations with lower medical standards lack the means to enforce the rules already on the books effectively. At such places, foreign drug companies have been accused of often testing their experimental drugs on the poor and illiterate without obtaining their consent or properly explaining the risks involved. For example, in 2009 the pharmaceutical giant Pfizer agreed (without admitting any wrongdoing) to a $75 million settlement over the death of Nigerian children who participated in testing a new antibiotic called Trovan.[11] A U.S. Department

8. Mike Stobbe, "Past Medical Testing on Humans Revealed," *Washington Post*, February 28, 2011.

9. Marlene Cimons, "U.S. Measles Experiment Failed to Disclose Risk," *Los Angeles Times*, June 17, 1996.

10. Timothy Williams, "Racial Bias Seen in Study of Lead Dust and Children," *New York Times*, September 16, 2011.

11. Walter, "First, Do Harm."

of Health and Human Services report reveals that between 40 percent and 65 percent of clinical studies of federally regulated medical products were conducted in foreign countries in 2008, a percentage that more than likely continues to grow. Yet problematically, U.S. regulators were able to inspect less than 1 percent of these foreign clinical trial sites.[12] Is it any wonder that the world's poor and nonwhites have a healthy suspicion of Euroamerican medical professionals?

Disparities in the Legal System

Like the health system, the U.S. legal system also negatively impacts marginalized communities of color. A disproportionate number of people of color face prison and capital punishment. At the close of the twentieth century, the United States incarcerated more than two million of its citizens, of which 70 percent were people of color. The first ten years of the new millennium revealed that not much has changed. According to statisticians with the U.S. Department of Justice, 67.8 percent of the 2010 prison population was nonwhite. Black non-Hispanic males and Latino males had, respectively, an imprisonment rate of 6.7 and 2.7 times higher than Euroamerican men, while the rate of imprisonment for black non-Hispanic and Latina females was, respectively, 2.8 and 1.6 times that of Euroamerican women. These trends have remained consistent throughout the first decade of the millennium (Guerino, Harrison, and Sabol 2011, 1, 7, 26–29). That people of color unduly fill our prisons should not be surprising when we consider that a 2009 study conducted by the Pew Center showed that compared to non-Hispanic whites, Latino/as, as a percentage, are two to three times more likely to experience unjustifiable stops, insulting language, excessive force, or corrupt activities by police. This finding holds true for repeated experiences as well, especially verbal abuse, excessive force, and unjustifiable stops (López and Light 2009, 1–4).

Complicating the Hispanic experience within the penal system are those who lack proper documentation. A study conducted by the advocacy group No More Deaths, based on 4,130 interviews with 12,895 individuals held in U.S. Border Patrol custody from the fall of 2008 to the spring of 2011, paints a disturbing portrait of the depth of human rights abuses presently occurring.[13] According to the study, U.S. Border Patrol agents denied food to 2,981 people and gave insufficient food to 11,384 people who were held in custody. Only 20 percent of those in custody for more than two days received a meal.

---

12. Stobbe, "Past Medical Testing."

13. Although I did not participate in this particular report, my own work on the border, interviewing in Mexico deported migrants also held by the Border Patrol, collaborates the rampant abuses that exist. I too spoke to many migrants, saw the recent scars and bruises on their bodies, and heard their testimonies of physical and psychological abuses.

Water was denied to 863 people, and 1,402 individuals received insufficient water. Children were more likely to be denied water or not given enough. It is important to remember that these individuals were recently picked up traversing a desert; hence, many were suffering from moderate to severe dehydration when apprehended.

Physical abuse was reported by 10 percent of those interviewed, including teenagers and children. Of the 433 incidents in which emergency medical treatment or medications were needed, the U.S. Border Patrol provided access to care in only 59 cases. The study recorded 2,926 incidents of failure to return personal belongings. The U.S. Border Patrol deported 869 family members separately. This means that families were deported through different ports of entry, a costly practice designed to separate families by distance. More disturbing is that 1,051 women, 190 teenagers, and 94 children were repatriated in the middle of the night, with no money, to dangerous border towns when Mexican humanitarian service agencies are closed. Increasing reports of psychological abuse were also noted, including threatening detainees with death, depriving them of sleep, keeping vehicles and cells at extremely hot or cold temperatures, playing traumatizing songs about people dying in the desert, and forced holding of strenuous or painful positions for no apparent reason other than to humiliate (No More Deaths 2011, 4–9).

Because most cannot tell the difference between a documented and an undocumented Latino/a, all Hispanics face discrimination in the hands of law enforcers. Take the egregious charges brought against Sheriff Joe Arpaio of Maricopa County, which encompasses Phoenix, Arizona. In May 2012 a federal lawsuit asserted a "pattern of unlawful discrimination" against Hispanics by the sheriff's office. The suit claims that Latino/a drivers were five to nine times more likely to be stopped or searched than non-Hispanics. Some were detained for appearing dirty, disheveled, or nervous. Those arrested were subjected to coarse ethnic slurs and degrading language.[14] Sheriff Arpaio's jails are notorious for feeding Latino/a prisoners green baloney and forcing male prisoners to wear pink underwear so as to humiliate them.[15] In early 2008 he unveiled a hotline that citizens can call to report those whom they suspect of being undocumented.[16] This begs the question: What does a person who is undocumented look like so as to raise suspicion?

Seeing people as suspicious is not limited to those who appear undocumented along the border. In New York City the Bloomberg administration

---

14. Fernanda Santos and Charles Savage, "U.S. Suit Says Arizona Sheriff Discriminated against Latinos," *New York Times*, May 11, 2012.

15. Randal C. Archibold, "Challenges to a Sheriff, Both Popular and Reviled," *New York Times*, September 28, 2008.

16. Miriam Jordan, "Arizona Seizes Spotlight in U.S. Immigration Debate," *Wall Street Journal*, February 1, 2008.

has reduced the homicide rate to its lowest levels since reliable data was kept in the early 1960s. Credit for this accomplishment is given to programs such as the controversial "Stop, Question, Frisk." As the name of the initiative implies, supposedly suspicious individuals are stopped by the police, questioned, and then frisked. However, of the 685,724 street stops conducted in 2011, 41.6 percent of them were of young black and Hispanic males (ages 14 through 24), who, combined, represent only 4.7 percent of the city's population.[17] This question must be asked: What is it that makes black and Latino youth look more suspicious than other youth?

Being seen as more dangerous by those who have the power of life and death over you is highly problematic. Take, for example, the comments of Judge Edith H. Jones of Houston, who sits on the U.S. Court of Appeals for the Fifth Circuit and served as its former chief justice. During a speech at the University of Pennsylvania Law School in February 2013, she said that blacks and Latinos were "predisposed to crime." According to an affidavit concerning the event, Judge Jones went on to state, "Sadly, some groups seem to commit more heinous crimes than others. . . . [There is] no arguing that blacks and Hispanics far outnumber Anglos on death row. . . . Sadly, people from these racial groups do get involved in more violent crimes." Judge Jones further suggested that a death sentence would be a service to them because it allows them to "make peace with God." Arguments against capital punishment based on mental retardation or systemic racism were dismissed by the judge as "red herrings."[18]

Not only can bodies of color not be trusted because, as per Judge Jones, they are more prone to commit violent crimes, but also a Michigan State University College of Law study revealed that persecutors found these bodies of color to lack trustworthiness when sitting on a capital-offense jury. The 2011 study revealed that, in every analysis conducted within the state of Michigan, race was a significant factor in the prosecutorial decision to exercise peremptory challenges to strike qualified blacks from juries dealing with death penalty proceedings. Between 1990 and 2010, prosecutors were twice as likely to strike qualified blacks from juries than members from other races (O'Brien and Grosso 2011, 17).

Greater worth is placed on the body of a white person, whether that body sits on a jury or on death row, than the body of a person of color. While most murders in this country are intraracial (the murderer and victim are of the same race), of the 1,283 prisoners executed from 1976 through 2012, 42 cases (of the 724 whites executed), or 5.8 percent, were of a white defendant

---

17. Al Baker, "New York Police Release Data Showing Rise in Number of Stops on Streets," *New York Times*, May 13, 2013.

18. Ethan Bronner, "Complaint Accuses U.S. Judge in Texas of Racial Bias," *New York Times*, June 4, 2013.

killing a victim of color, while 332 (of the 559 people of color executed), or 57.6 percent, were of defendants of color executed for killing white victims (Death Penalty Information Center 2012, 1–2). These figures unmask society's subconscious way of "seeing" bodies of color as having less worth than white bodies.

Disproportionate percentages among those who are executed within the United States have led Amnesty International to conclude, "Beyond any reasonable doubt, the U.S. death penalty continues to reflect the deep-rooted prejudices of the society that condones its use. Amnesty International cannot find any evidence that current legal safeguards eliminate racial bias in the application of the death penalty." The organization demonstrates how the United States places a greater worth on the life of a white person than it does on the life of a person of color. When blacks are brought to trial for murder, prosecutors routinely dismiss black jurors. Hence, we should not be surprised that at least one out of every five executed African Americans was convicted by an all-white jury (Amnesty International 2003, 3). A 2011 Duke University study collaborated Amnesty International's findings. Examining felony trials in Florida between 2000 and 2010, the study showed that all-white jury pools convict black defendants 16 percent more often than white defendants. This gap in conviction rate is entirely eliminated when the jury pool includes at least one black member (Bayer, Anwar, and Hjalmarsson 2011, 23–24).

When racism and ethnic discrimination play such a prominent role in who is executed and who is not, we should expect the innocent also to be put to death. Since 1973, a total of 142 people on death row have been freed after being exonerated due to DNA or some other type of evidence. One can only wonder how many innocents were executed based on the inherent racism and ethnic bigotry of the judicial process. The arbitrary and discriminatory manner by which the death penalty is imposed has meant that even if it could be argued that the state has the right to execute our worst criminals, the state has lost its moral authority to do so because of how our judicial system enforces executions based on race and ethnicity. Black leader Jesse Jackson declares,

> Who receives the death penalty has less to do with the violence of the crime than the color of the criminal's skin or, more often, the color of the victim's skin. . . . The death penalty is essentially an arbitrary punishment. There are no objective rules or guidelines for when a prosecutor should seek the death penalty, when a jury should recommend it, and when a judge should give it. This lack of objective, measurable standards ensures that the application of the death penalty will be discriminatory against racial, gender, and ethnic groups. (1996, 96–97)

Not only is the imposition of capital punishment dependent on a person's race or ethnicity, but also it is highly dependent on a person's economic class. The economically privileged are simply not executed. U.S. Supreme Court associate justice William O. Douglas bemoaned the fact that "one searches our chronicles in vain for the execution of any member of the affluent strata of this society" (Costanzo 2002, 174). Why have people of color, specifically blacks, historically been disproportionately represented in our prison system, most specifically on death row? Mark Lewis Taylor suggests that our present judicial system is rooted in the former institution of slavery, thus explaining its apartheid character. He writes, "Especially after the Civil War and the announced abolition of slavery, the prisons became the major locus for the continual enforcement of slave conditions for black Americans. In short, today's prison is enmeshed in the legacy of slavery just as today's capital punishment is in the legacy of lynching" (2001, 45).

Whether it involves the healthcare system or the legal system, the underlying assumption is that life can be reduced to a commodity whose value can be determined. But in this country not all human life has equal value. The life of a white person has historically been more valuable than that of a dark-skinned person, the life of a wealthy person more valuable than that of a poor person, and the life of a heterosexual man more valuable than the life of a woman or a gay person. A quick perusal of life insurance rates indicates the differentiating worth of individuals. In the past, nonwhites were charged about 25 percent higher premiums for the same coverage of life insurance paid by white people. Companies such as MetLife have been ordered by a U.S. district court judge to respond to accusations of consistently charging African Americans higher premiums than whites. Other companies, such as Prudential and American General, chose to settle, refunding up to $206 million to policyholders.[19]

Numerous studies also show that people of color pay more for house and automobile insurance. For example, while automobile insurance rates can dramatically vary, those living in poor communities and communities of color pay much higher premiums, beyond any additional risk, even after accounting for individual characteristics, driving history, and coverage (Ong and Stoll 2006, 21–24). A lawsuit brought against Geico, the fourth-largest U.S. automobile insurer, charged that the company based car rates on the client's level of education and occupation. Low-wage earners paid about 41 percent more than high-income earners. The end result was that blacks paid more on average for automobile insurance because African Americans were less likely

---

19. Scott J. Paltrow, "In Relic of '50s and '60s, Blacks Still Pay More for a Type of Insurance," *Wall Street Journal*, April 27, 2000; "MetLife Ordered to Respond to Rate Discrimination Suit," *Insurance Journal*, June 27, 2001. For a study detailing the history of blacks paying higher insurance premiums, see Heen 2009.

to have a college degree. The lawsuit argued that a store clerk is not inherently a worse driver than a college-educated professional, an assumption that makes education and occupation a proxy for race.[20]

This nation's judicial system seems to be rooted in the violent birth of the country, influencing how the very definition of justice is determined. For Mark Lewis Taylor, the very foundation of the United States and the forging of its economic life designed to benefit a small segment of the dominant culture were achieved through the violent appropriation of the land of the indigenous people and the cultivation of that land by the imposition of African slavery (Taylor 2001, 50–51). Thus, those who have suffered under the unjust U.S. justice system cannot rely on or look toward the dominant culture for guidance on defining justice. The persistence of discriminatory social structures like the healthcare system or American legal system remains an indictment of the dominant culture.

Step 2. Reflecting

Why is it that for many within the United States, the quality of healthcare has consistently ranged from poor to nonexistent, a phenomenon disproportionately experienced by the poor and people of color, although in the past few years many middle-class whites have been rapidly joining their ranks? The reason is that the U.S. healthcare system has historically been structured along a neoliberal philosophy. In other words, healthcare was, and continues to be, a profit-making venture. And yet the question ignored during the debates that led to the Health Care and Education Reconciliation Act of 2010 (which amended the Patient Protection and Affordable Care Act, aka Obamacare) was this: Are affordable healthcare and profit-making mutually exclusive? Attempting to offer universal healthcare within a capitalist paradigm means that low-income workers will find the cost of health insurance cost-prohibitive. For example, Stay Green Inc., a landscaping service in Santa Clarita, California, will begin offering coverage to its 230 low-wage workers in 2014 in order to comply with the new laws. The company expects, however, that most of its employees will opt out of the program, preferring to receive the employer's portion of the premium in cash than having to pay the employee's portion of the premium. One employee, Salvador Martínez, a fifty-year-old grounds-crew worker who makes about $10.50 an hour, believes that he will be unable to afford the estimated $140 a month to cover his share of the premium. "I make too little to spend on insurance," he said in Spanish. "How am I going to pay for food?"[21]

---

20. "Geico Bases Rates on Race, Twin Cities Lawsuit Charge," *Twin Cities Pioneer Press*, April 5, 2006.

21. Emily Maltby, "Will New Health Insurance Be Too Expensive for America's Lowest-Paid?" *Wall Street Journal*, June 6, 2013.

If we decide that healthcare should be provided through so-called free-market forces, then it is moral for an insurance company to refuse to insure those individuals who provide a higher risk of accruing medical expenses, or to drop individuals from coverage if they get ill, or to refuse the treatment recommended by the patient's physician because the cost outweighs profit. If we decide that healthcare should create a profit, then it is ethical when pharmaceutical companies charge whatever the market can bear for life-saving medicine, or to provide through PACs donations to politicians who would legislate against preventing the same medicine sold cheaper in other countries to be sold in the United States. If healthcare should be ruled solely by market forces, then we should be satisfied with a system under which healing is available to those who can afford it. Complaining about the affordability of healthcare betrays our capitalist economic structures.

Rather than philosophically questioning the principles upon which we, as a society, determine who gets to live and who gets to die based on who receives healthcare and who does not, Obamacare attempted to reform a system that for some might be beyond reform, a system whose very purpose is to make money and thus must inherently remain unattainable to large segments of the population. As of the start of the sweeping national effort in October 2013 to extend health coverage, two thirds of poor blacks and single mothers and half of low-wage workers will be ineligible because they live in Republican controlled states that have declined to participate in the expansion of Medicaid even though the federal government will pay for 100 percent of the expansion till 2016, and 90 percent thereafter.[22] Jesus tells us that no person can serve two masters; nevertheless, that is exactly what Obamacare has tried to do: heal all who are ill and still make money.

There are areas within society where principles of entrepreneurship may better serve society, and likewise there are areas where a more communal approach might be needed. Could it be that a communal approach to healthcare (socialized medicine) provides the greatest number with more affordable healthcare than Obamacare is able to do? If there exists a basic human right to good health, then a conversation that determines under which economic structures healthcare should be framed is needed.

One of the consequences of the economic structure of the United States is the subjugation of its own citizens, particularly the marginalized, to social structures such as our healthcare and our legal systems that do not foster abundant life. The social structures of a society are established around or to support certain social and moral values. But there are questions that must be asked. Whose or what social and moral values form the foundation of these

22. Sabrina Tavernise and Robert Geheloff, "State Medicaid Decisions Leave Millions Uninsured," *New York Times*, October 3, 2013.

structures? Is the morality of any given society determined by whatever the dominant culture of that society decides is correct social behavior? To a great extent, any judicial system that is established by the dominant culture exists to legitimize the social and moral values of that culture, which usually is privileged by whiteness and economic class. These values are then imposed upon the marginalized, who may well perceive them to be unjust and oppressive.

We should therefore not be surprised when ethical issues concerning healthcare or the legal system represent the perspectives of the dominant culture. Seldom explored are the perspectives of the disenfranchised, usually those ill-treated by the present systems. A clear example lies within the field of bioethics, where the roles played by racism, classism, and sexism within the medical establishment are rarely discussed. When bioethicists focus on the ethical issues raised by scientific and technological advances, advances that may prolong or secure a richer quality of life, little attention is given to how or why those on the margins fail to benefit.

Generally, the marginalized are excluded from the benefits of medical advances or from the fair application of justice within the legal system mainly because of how they are seen. "Seeing" can transform human beings into things, into objects. Once social structures adopt this form of seeing, it becomes normalized and legitimized within society. Seeing (or defining) dark-skinned bodies as dangerous occurs unconsciously. This is demonstrated by simply consulting a dictionary for a definition of the word "black." When the dominant culture gazes upon a dark-skinned male body, that body is automatically defined as something evil, wicked, harmful, and dangerous. If the act of "seeing" is used to mask the power and privilege of those who benefit from how reality is constructed, then seeing dark bodies as dangerous is the first crucial step in maintaining a system that continuously seeks to punish or confine those dangerous dark bodies.

Actions taken upon people of color based solely on appearance are illustrated by a study conducted at the department of psychology of the University of Colorado, whose findings were published in the *Journal of Experimental Social Psychology*. The research was inspired by the shooting of Amadou Diallo, an unarmed, twenty-two-year-old West African immigrant killed in the Bronx in 1999 by police officers who mistook his wallet for a gun. The subjects of the study played a video game in which they were instructed to shoot human targets that were armed. Some of the targets were white, others black. The subjects, who in all but one sample were primarily white, were more likely to mistakenly conclude that black men were armed and shoot them. When confronted by blacks holding cell phones, wallets, soft-drink cans, or cameras, the subjects were more likely to shoot than when confronted by whites. When confronted by white targets with guns, subjects were less likely to fire than if the targets were blacks with guns. The study concluded,

> Ethnicity influences the shoot/don't shoot decision primarily because traits associated with African Americans, namely "violent" or "dangerous," can act as a schema to influence perceptions of an ambiguously threatening target. . . . [Hence] participants showed a bias to shoot African American targets more rapidly and/or more frequently than White targets. The implications of this bias are clear and disturbing. (Correll et al. 2002, 1325, 1327)

How our culture teaches us to "see" dark bodies shapes the behavior of people responding quickly and automatically when confronted by those from the margins who are dark-skinned.

But in most cases, racist behaviors are seldom conscious. No doubt, many within the medical profession in the aforementioned studies or those involved in law enforcement are not necessarily intentional racists who subscribe to white supremacy. The face of racism and ethnic discrimination has changed from a more direct bigotry toward an ambivalence characterized by many who probably are well-intentioned, liberal, highly educated white persons whose unexamined attitudes nonetheless disenfranchise communities of color. Studies show how socialization practices and normal cognitive biases contribute to aversive racist and discriminative perspectives that exist under the surface of consciousness, even though this aversive racism conflicts with consciously held, positive, life-affirming beliefs concerning justice and equality.

Aversive racism is more likely expressed in the form of prejudice and discrimination during ambiguous situations, when attitudes and/or behavior that negatively impact people of color can be attributed to causes other than discrimination or could be justified on nonracial grounds. Aversive racism can also be manifested in terms of pro-ingroup bias that favors one's own group versus the more recognizable anti-outgroup bias that negatively affects people of color (Hodson, Dovidio, and Gaertner 2009, 2). A politically correct racism that is seldom personally recognized is no less damning to communities of color and the society as a whole.

Step 3. Praying

The *imago Dei* (image of God), created by God in every person, establishes the infinite worth of each human being. To ignore this *imago Dei* violates the inherited rights of all humans. Because the spark of the Absolute exists within every human, all possess dignity. Even so, social structures are constructed to deny the worth of those who are relegated to the margins or, worse, to cause the oppressed to question if they even possess the *imago Dei*. As Desmond

Tutu observed, "The ultimate evil is not the suffering . . . which is meted out to those who are God's children. The ultimate evil of oppression . . . is when it succeeds in making a child of God begin to doubt that he or she is a child of God" (1991, 131). How is the *imago Dei* denied? By assigning more worth to one human life than to another human life because of race, class, orientation, or gender. To ignore the *imago Dei* of the least among us is to reject the God of life.

Taking capital punishment as an example, we can note that biblical texts, specifically in Leviticus, prescribe capital punishment for crimes such as murder and rape. But Leviticus also prescribes that a disobedient, stubborn child who curses his or her parent is subject to the death penalty (Lev. 20:9). So is one who commits adultery (Lev. 20:10), one who lays with a man as with a woman (Lev. 20:13), one who curses God (Lev. 24:16), and one who breaks the Sabbath (Exod. 31:14–15). Still, biblical texts also provide examples of murderers and rapists who were not condemned for their transgressions. Moses, who killed an Egyptian (Exod. 2:11), is chosen to lead his people to liberation. King David, a man chosen by God, uses his power as king to force himself on Bathsheba and then, to cover his transgression, has her husband murdered (2 Sam. 11). In this particular case, not only is David acquitted (2 Sam. 12:13), but also the ancestry of Jesus can be traced back to this adulterous union (Matt. 1:6). Such apparent contradictions between God's law and how those chosen by God fell short of the law yet were greatly used by God can be understood through the affirmation of the basic principle of the sacredness of human life due to its reflection of the *imago Dei*.

The *imago Dei* finds fullest expression in the personhood of Jesus as he turned many "rules" upside down. For example, Jesus said, "You have heard that it was said, an eye for an eye and a tooth for a tooth, but I say unto you, do not resist an evildoer" (Matt. 5:38–39). It could be argued that Jesus was "unjust" as that term is defined by our present culture, for he refused to punish the wrongdoer. Rather than accommodating the current definition of justice by meting out deserved punishment, he was quick to provide undeserved mercy. In John 8 he is confronted with an adulterous woman caught in the very act (where was the man?), a capital offense. Asked to judge her, he instead balanced justice and mercy with the famous line, "Whoever is without sin should cast the first stone." Throughout the New Testament Jesus provides a model that should prompt us not to look toward the law for justice principles, but rather to ground moral guidance and principles upon relationships, always cognizant that all human beings contain the image of God.

Step 4. Case Studies

1. During the 1950s, the United States ranked third among all nations in its ability to prevent infant mortality.[23] By the 1990s, the United States had a higher infant mortality rate than all of the Western European countries. In 2004 infant mortality within the United States rose for the first time since 1958.[24] By 2012, the United States ranked fiftieth among all nations in its ability to prevent infant mortality. Developing countries such as Slovenia and Cuba were among the many that had lower infant mortality rates.[25] More disturbing is the finding that among communities of color, the infant mortality rate was higher than those of many nations of the two-thirds world. In fact, among the largest disparities found in healthcare, according to the U.S. Department of Health and Human Services, are the racial and ethnic differences found in infant mortality. In 2007 the infant mortality rate for non-Hispanic black women (13.31 per thousand) was 2.4 times the rate for non-Hispanic white women (5.63). Native American (9.22) and Puerto Rican women (7.71) also had relatively high infant mortality rates (MacDorman and Mathews 2011, 1). Your chances of survival being born black in the United States, the richest country known to humankind, are worse than if you were born in economically struggling countries such as Libya, Romania, and Botswana. Part of the problem is the absence of prenatal care among some communities of color. In 2009 Native American women were the group most likely to receive late (third trimester) or no prenatal care (11.4 percent of births), followed by African Americans (10.6 percent) and Hispanics (8.8 percent); by contrast, the rate for white women was 4.5 percent (Child Trends Data Bank 2012, 3).

   — Do these statistics indicate that the value of white infants' lives is greater than that of infants of color? If not, how do we explain the continuously growing gap between the mortality rate of white infants and infants of color? If women of color are unable to afford prenatal care or vaccination shots once the child is born, due to lack of insurance or having low wages, should they be provided by the state?

   — Are white babies simply more valuable than black babies? Consider that the cost of adopting a white child is approximately $35,000, plus some legal expenses, while the cost of adopting a fully black child is

---

23. The infant mortality rate indicates the number of deaths occurring among children under the age of one per thousand live births in a given year.

24. Rob Stein, "U.S. Infant Mortality Rate Rises 3 percent: First Increase Since '58, Surprises Officials as Other Health Indicators Keep Improving," *Washington Post*, February 12, 2004.

25. Central Intelligence Agency World Factbook as of 2013 (available at https://www.cia.gov/).

$18,000, and that of a biracial child being $24,000 to $26,000.[26] If the value of life is not correlated by skin pigmentation, how do we explain the cost difference?

— The United States has the highest infant mortality rate among industrial countries, and the costliest maternity care. For substantially less, other developed countries provide similar access to high-tech care. In 2012 the cost for conventional delivery in the United States was $9,775, and $15,041 for cesarean section. Compare this cost with the second-highest country, Switzerland, at $4,039 and $5,186, respectively; or France at $3,541 and $6,441, Great Britain at $2,641 and $4,435, New Zealand at $2,386 and $4,717, Argentina at $1,188 and $1,541.[27] Why does the richest nation have the most inferior healthcare system among industrial nations? Who benefits from a privatized healthcare system? Is the marketplace the best means of providing adequate healthcare? Should healthcare remain privatized? Should the United States have universal healthcare insurance? If so, who would pay for it?

2. Pavle Mircov and his partner, Daniella, live in Serbia, a nation battered by war and financial crises that have gripped the continent. Both of them are selling their kidneys online for $40,000 each. Unemployed, they survive on one meal per day and are in desperate financial need. They are not alone. If they succeed, their organs will be among the 15,000 to 20,000 kidneys illegally sold globally each year. Other Europeans are selling their bone marrow, corneas, or other needed body parts. A lung can go for as much as $250,000. And yet according to the World Health Organization, only 10 percent of the global need for organ transplantation is being met. Although illegal, advertisements for such practices have appeared in Spain, Italy, Greece, and Russia. These European countries have joined more traditional countries such as China, India, Brazil, and the Philippines as centers for illegal organ trafficking.[28]

— Is selling one's organs a way for the poor to gain financial security? In a commoditized global economy, why not let supply and demand among willing adults operate unfettered? According to Mircov, "It's my body, and I should be able to do what I want with it." Is he right? Should any governmental authority restrict what a consenting adult can do

---

26. "Six Words: 'Black Babies Cost Less to Adopt,'" *NPR News*, June 27, 2013.

27. Elisabeth Rosenthal, "American Way of Birth, Costliest in the World," *New York Times*, July 1, 2013.

28. Dan Bilefsky, "Black Market for Parts Spreads among the Poor in Europe," *New York Times*, June 29, 2012.

with his or her own body, especially in deciding a medical procedure? If we own our bodies, why should we not be able to sell parts of them?

— Wang (surname only), a seventeen-year-old high school student in China, sold his kidney for $3,500 so that he could buy an iPad and an iPhone.[29] Should economic safeguards exist to prevent this sort of thing? Is this an indication that something is wrong with our global economy?

3. Gordon "Randy" Steidl was freed on May 28, 2004, from an Illinois prison after serving seventeen years on death row, wrongly convicted in 1986 for the murder of Dyke and Karen Rhoads. This means that the real murderers were not brought to justice. Cameron Todd Willingham was executed in 2004 for setting fire to his house, killing his three children. Experts today claim that the arson theories used during the investigation were outdated, meaning that Willingham was executed for what probably was an accidental fire. Between 1973 and 2012, a total of 142 individuals were freed from death row due to DNA evidence or other new evidence. This comes to about one exonerated person for every ten executed. By 2013, seventeen states abolished the death penalty, and thirteen states have not executed anyone in the past five years. Thus, some thirty states are leading the nation in a new national consensus recognizing that the implementation of capital punishment is morally ambiguous and financially prohibited.

— What obligations does the state have toward the wrongfully convicted? Should the state provide counseling, job placement, and so on to these individuals? If so, who should pay for it? Should the state's legal liabilities for wrongful convictions be limited? Is the fact that most of those people wrongfully convicted are poor and of color relevant or significant? Why or why not?

— Even if capital punishment was equitably applied, it is financially unsustainable. A California study revealed that from 1978 to 2012 the state spent $4 billion to carry out thirteen sentences of capital punishment. Two individuals in 1978, John V. Briggs and Donald J. Heller, are most responsible for the success of Proposition 7, which reinstated the death penalty. Today, Heller, along with Briggs's son Ron, are the two most ardent advocates of reversing what they have come to recognize as the biggest mistake of their lives, mainly due to the fiscal cost.[30]

---

29. "Five Face Charges in China over Sale of Youth's Kidney," New York Times, April 8, 2012.

30. Adam Nagourney, "Seeking an End to an Execution Law They Once Championed," New York Times, April 7, 2012.

If not for moral reasons, should capital punishment be abolished for the sake of budgetary prudence?

— What about those who are rightfully convicted of a felony and serve their time? Upon being released, in most states, they are barred from receiving welfare or food stamps, public housing, voting, or obtaining certain jobs in plumbing, education, barbering, or healthcare (to name but a few). Should such restrictions exist, even after such persons have paid their debt to society? Are these former prisoners simply getting what they deserve for their crimes? What consequences, if any, exist for society if these former felons are not reintegrated into society?

4.   Operation Streamline is designed to quickly move undocumented immigrants charged with "illegal entry," a federal petty offense that is a lesser charge than a misdemeanor, through the legal system. According to Heather Williams, supervisor of the Federal Public Defender Office for the District of Arizona, an equivalent act for a U.S. citizen to commit would be "shoving someone on federal land with the intent to shove." In the large courtroom the defendants sit silently, unbathed and dressed in the same clothes that they wore when arrested by the U.S. Border Patrol during the past week. Prior to their trial, they are held in a converted military base never meant to function as a prison. Not surprisingly, there are no beds (just benches), which forces most to sleep on concrete floors, with only a few receiving blankets. The water fountain does little to quench the thirst of those who recently attempted to cross the desert, and the lack of cooking facilities at the base offers little nourishment. If they were carrying any medicine, it was confiscated, placing several (e.g., diabetics) at grave risk. According to newspaper accounts, a few have died while in detention for lack of access to their medications, a clear violation of the Geneva Conventions. Prior to the hearing, the court-assigned attorneys meet with the defendants, usually in groups, to explain complex legal procedures in a few minutes. The exploration of possible grounds for asylum or derivative citizenship (having a parental citizen connection) is either skipped or misunderstood during these huddles. Also, since the consultation occurs in the same courtroom where all the defendants will be convicted, in the presence of court officials, U.S. Border Patrol personnel, and U.S. marshals, the attorney-client privilege is violated.

I witnessed a day when there were ten defense attorneys in the courtroom representing about seven migrants each. For their full day of service (morning consultation and afternoon conviction) they were paid $125 an hour. According to Williams, Tucson pays $3 million a year just to reimburse these attorneys. Similar trials for those caught entering the United

States occur five days of the week. Prior to 2005, those who entered the country without proper documentation were not prosecuted, but simply expatriated. However, since then an elaborate legal procedure has been created ensuring that before the undocumented migrant is deported, a criminal record is established. Of course, not every migrant caught crossing the border experiences Operation Streamline. An undocumented number of them are simply deported without any trial, raising concerns that numbers are being manipulated in order to demonstrate fewer convictions (hence incorrectly associating these numbers with fewer immigrants crossing), which falsely justifies how militarizing the border since 1994 is indeed working.

The penalty for entering the United States without proper documentation is a maximum of six months in jail and/or a $5,000 fine, which is routinely plea-bargained for time served. All the defendants on this day pleaded guilty, as do 99.9 percent of all who ever go through Operation Streamline. They were charged, tried, convicted, and sentenced in groups of five. Using a stopwatch to time how "efficiently" justice en masse works, each defendant on this particular day received 1 minute and 44.2 seconds, or about 20.4 seconds per person, raising grave concerns about due process as enshrined in the Fifth and Sixth Amendments of the U.S. Constitution. Additionally, Operation Streamline seems to violate the Federal Rule of Criminal Procedure 11.

About forty of the defendants on this day were charged with a misdemeanor because this was their second attempt to enter the United States. Each received some jail time, usually longer than a month. To house one of them, according to Williams, costs taxpayers $2,000 a month, more than the approximately $850 that we spend to educate a child in our public schools. Housing all forty convicted on this day would cost $80,000. Realizing that this procedure is repeated each day, taxpayers can expect to spend $1.6 million a month for the Tucson district alone. Multiply this by all the federal districts on the border with Mexico, and we are talking about a billion-dollar industry.[31]

— Regardless of one's views on immigration, is Operation Streamline problematic? Does it violate basic human rights? Can this be construed as a fair and just judicial procedure?

— Is Operation Streamline a cost-effective governmental expense? Who financially benefits from Operation Streamline? Should we be

---

31. Comments are based on an interview that I conducted on November 30, 2012, and I witnessed the procedures described.

concerned that the prison corporations that benefit by incarcerating undocumented immigrants are spending millions on lobbying politicians to pass strict anti-immigrant legislation? Can a more equitable way to live up to the rhetoric "and justice for all" be employed?

— On any given day, about three hundred undocumented immigrants are in solitary confinement, of which half are housed for fifteen or more days, the point at which psychiatric experts say the inmate is at risk for severe mental harm. About thirty-five of them are kept for longer than seventy-five days.[32] Is this "cruel and unusual punishment"? Given that these immigrants are being held on civil, not criminal, charges, they are not supposed to be punished. They are confined in order to ensure their appearance at an administrative hearing. Why, then, are they punished? Most undocumented who are LGBT are routinely placed in solitary confinement, supposedly for their own protection. Is this justifiable? Sending an immigrant to solitary confinement triples the daily cost of housing an inmate. Does this provide a financial incentive for these private corporations?

---

32. Ian Urbina and Catherine Rentz, "Immigrants Held in Solitary Cells, Often for Weeks," *New York Times*, March 24, 2013.

Part IV

Case Studies of Business Relationships

Chapter 12

Introduction to
Business Relationships

Each society must determine for itself how goods and services needed and/ or wanted by the community are to be produced, who will be responsible for producing these goods or providing these services, where production will occur, and how the goods and services will be distributed within the community. Within the present global marketplace the responsibility for making these decisions generally belongs to multinational corporations. In theory, an employee has a right to accept or reject employment at a given company. If a corporation treats its employees poorly or refuses to pay a living wage, the employee is free to find a job elsewhere. But if the two parties negotiating are not equal, which is true of the average worker and the typical company, what happens then? Or what if through monopolistic dealings and political connections one company can determine how a particular good or service is to be produced, who will produce it, where it will be produced, and how it is to be distributed? What effects will this have on employees and consumers?

Corporations, which are legal entities with limited liabilities, consist of three groups of people. First come the stockholders who provide capital; their liabilities are limited to the money invested. In theory, the raison d'être of the corporation is to create profit for these shareholders. Second are the directors and officers charged with administrating the corporation's assets and running the day-to-day activities. Finally, there are the employees who provide the labor necessary to produce the goods or provide the services.

Corporations are recognized by society as "artificial persons"; they are able to enter into agreements and to be sued when those agreements are broken. Mitt Romney, while campaigning for president in Iowa, best captured this sentiment in his now famous retort to a heckler, "Corporations are people, my friend."[1] In effect, the corporation is a "soul-less" person. Can it, then, be expected to follow moral dictates and practices? Even if it were to operate according to some moral standards, we are again forced to ask, whose or which standards? If a multinational corporation has offices in the United States, the Middle East, and Asia, should it follow Christian, Muslim, or Buddhist ethics? Should it adhere instead to a system of secular humanist ethics?

---

1. James Oliphant, "Romney in Iowa: 'Corporations are People' Too," *Los Angeles Times*, August 11, 2011.

How should it operate if it has a branch office in a society that believes that women have a moral obligation to stay at home and raise children? Should the corporation hire no women, or if does hire them, pay them less? Should corporate ethics be defined by what is customary or legal in the country in which it operates? Should "When in Rome, do as the Romans do" be the basic rule to follow?

For example, laws regulating the disposal of corporate byproducts, which are stringent in the United States in order to protect the environment, are lax in many countries of the two-thirds world. Likewise, the safety regulations in the United States that protect employees from physical hazards at the workplace are nonexistent in some other countries. Yet, on the other hand, a practice such as bribing government officials to facilitate the navigation of bureaucratic red tape, while illegal in the United States, is considered an acceptable and necessary business procedure elsewhere. Because certain safety and environmental regulations that are mandatory within the United States cut into corporate profits, relocating to nations of the two-thirds world with less stringent laws may be desirable for a corporation. Do these practices in different countries require a system of business ethics in which what is moral depends on where one does business?

Nobel Prize economist Milton Friedman argues for restricting moral obligations, limiting corporate responsibilities to obeying the laws in whatever nation a corporation finds itself pursuing profit:

> There is one and only one social responsibility of business—to use its resources and engage in activities designed to increase its profits so long as it stays within the rules of the game, which is to say, engage in open and free competition, without deception or fraud. . . . Few trends could so thoroughly undermine the very foundations of our free society as the acceptance by corporate officials of a social responsibility other than to make as much money for their stockholders as possible. (1962, 133)

Friedman ignores any connection between corporate profitability and the quality of life of the general public or of the corporation's employees. Corporations are legally created entities responsible for abiding by the law to ensure individual legal rights, but their participation within society also subjects them to certain moral rights beyond simply making "as much money for their stockholders as possible." Corporate responsibility that goes no further than making as much money as possible can produce a vacuum in ethics and clearly lead to abuse. According to business ethicist Manuel Velasquez, "Unlike legal rights, moral rights are not limited to a particular jurisdiction. If humans have a moral right not to be tortured, for example, then this is a right that human beings of every nationality have regardless of the legal system under which they live" (1998, 87).

Nonetheless, a danger exists if such moral rights are established from the perspective of the dominant culture, which has a vested interest in corporate profit, in securing "as much money as possible." Moral rights must be a product that includes the disenfranchised community, from which many employees are drawn. And if we speak of Christian moral rights, then it is the responsibility of the marginalized faith community to spearhead the formulation of what these moral rights should be.

The definition of moral rights should never be too tightly limited and should include positive actions as well as proscriptions. As Joel Feinberg notes, moral rights mean that other agents have a positive duty to assist the holder of moral rights with what is needed to freely pursue those rights (1980, 224). Conservatives generally reject the concept of positive duty, maintaining that the government should not demand that businesses become responsible for the welfare of their employees, but simply that businesses not interfere with the employees' pursuit of their rights.

For example, if it is determined that individuals who work for a corporation have a moral right to a wage that supports the basics of human existence (food, clothes, and shelter), then the concept of positive rights would insist that corporations have a duty to pay a living wage. The employer cannot be absolved of such duty simply by pointing to the worker's right to freely choose to work elsewhere, for although workers may indeed have the right to reject a job, they cannot reject every job if they hope to survive. Because workers cannot bargain as equals with multinational corporations to arrive at mutually beneficial arrangements, they are limited to the type of wages that corporations are willing to pay. When the heads of corporations increase their wealth at the expense of the labor pool because they have the power to control wages, the corporation, even though it is an artificial person, is acting immorally. By extension, those who are privileged by the actions of the corporation are also acting immorally, whether they are the officers, directors, stockholders, or consumers.

In part II of this book we considered case studies that explored the impact of neoliberalism upon the global stage. Part III provided case studies that narrowed our exploration to the field of national policies. In part IV we will consider case studies that explore the ethics of business within a global marketplace by focusing on four areas: the moral accountability of corporations, affirmative action, the overall treatment of women, and private property.

Chapter 13

Corporate Accountability

Step 1. Observing

In his classic text *The Wealth of Nations*, first published in 1776, Scottish economic philosopher Adam Smith wrote, "It is not from the benevolence of the butcher, the brewer, or the baker, that we expect our dinner, but from their regard to their own self-interest" (1976, 13). The fictional character Gordon Gekko (played by Michael Douglas) in the 1987 movie *Wall Street* best summarizes Adam Smith's sentiments in his now famous speech: "The point is, ladies and gentleman, that greed, for lack of a better word, is good. Greed is right, greed works. Greed clarifies, cuts through, and captures the essence of the evolutionary spirit. Greed, in all of its forms—greed for life, for money, for love, knowledge—has marked the upward surge of mankind."

Real-life personality Fabrice P. Tourre, better known as "Fabulous Fab," captures fictional Gordon Gekko's mantra. This former Goldman Sachs trader became infamous for an email that he wrote to his girlfriend as the U.S. economy approached the brink of economic collapse in 2008 due to the rapidly expanding mortgage crisis. In the email he bragged about unloading toxic real estate bonds to "widows and orphans."[1]

Trading Money for Influence

At the start of the twenty-first century the American business community was rocked by corporate scandals. The business shenanigans that occurred in corporations such as Enron, Arthur Andersen, Global Crossing, and Adelphia Communications (to name but a few) revealed how a privileged elite was able to amass great fortunes by subscribing to greed. Unfortunately, these fortunes usually were made on the backs of shareholders, the middle class, and the poor.

We begin with the example of Enron CEO Ken L. Lay, who had close ties with the Bush family. The Texas energy giant hired prominent members of the first Bush administration (such as James Baker and Robert Mosbacher) and was also among the largest donors to the second Bush presidential campaign. Newly elected president George W. Bush appointed two of Ken Lay's nominations to the Federal Energy Regulatory Commission (FERC), and

---

1. Susanne Craig and Ben Protess, "After Goldman and before Trial, a Global Education for Fabrice Tourre," *New York Times*, July 14, 2013.

one, Pat Wood, was named chair of the commission. FERC has oversight of the nation's electricity and gas markets, markets in which Enron made most of its money. FERC failed to act during the winter of 2000–2001 when Enron manipulated the price of gas and electricity during California's energy crisis. Enron's price-gouging maneuvers ensured that the company made the bulk of its profits ($7 billion in net trading profits during the energy crisis) at the expense of Californians, who endured rolling blackouts and higher energy prices.[2] The demise of Enron after the company was caught in massive financial fraud cost thousands of jobs, more than $60 billion in market value, and more than $2 billion in pension plans. Investors hoping to recoup some of their losses through the legal system were dealt a setback when the U.S. Supreme Court refused to review the investors' lawsuit.[3]

Then again, we should not be surprised by the decision of the Supreme Court. After all, those who appoint and confirm Supreme Court justices (as well as all other federal justices) are the same politicians beholden to corporate political contributions needed to mount election or reelection campaigns. The court under Chief Justice John Roberts (which started in 2005) has been the most pro-neoliberal, pro-corporate court since World War II. In the first eight years of the Roberts court, corporations have been given the human right of free speech, allowing them to spend freely during elections (*Citizens United v. Federal Election Commission*), have been provided with extra protection from class action and human rights litigation (*Dukes v. Wal-Mart*), and have succeeded in getting arbitration as the method of choice for resolving disputes (*AT&T Mobility v. Concepcion*). These rulings allow business to operate without fear of litigation by those harmed by their actions, products, or wrongdoing, be they employees, customers, or the public at large. Studying over two thousand business-related court decisions between 1946 to 2011, political scientists discovered that all five of the 2012 more conservative justices sitting on the bench ranked among the top ten most pro-business justices out of thirty-six.[4] The study concludes that the "Roberts Court is indeed highly pro-business—the conservatives extremely so and the liberals only moderately liberal" (Epstein, Landes, and Posner 2013, 1449–50).

While the peddling of political favors in return for campaign support continues to plague and threaten U.S. democracy, it is important to note that

---

2. David Barboza, "Despite Demand, Enron Papers Show Big Profit on Price Bets," *New York Times*, December 12, 2002; Adam Zagorin, "The Trail out of Texas," *Time*, February 18, 2002, 41.

3. "Supreme Court Won't Hear Complaint by Enron Investors," *New York Times*, January 23, 2008.

4. Justice Alito, appointed by George W. Bush, ranked first. Justice Roberts, also appointed by George W. Bush, ranked second. Justice Thomas, appointed by George H. W. Bush, ranked fifth. Justice Kennedy, appointed by Ronald Reagan, ranked sixth. Justice Scalia, also appointed by Ronald Reagan, ranked ninth.

corporate scandals that enrich the privileged are not limited to accounting shenanigans or trading money for influence. More grievous is the commodification of human beings for the sake of profit, a process that at times results in the loss of human life, usually the life of the less fortunate. Some of the practices of Bayer pharmaceutical company illustrate this point.

The Commodification of Human Life

Cutter Biological, a division of Bayer, profited handsomely from the sale of a blood-clotting medicine for hemophiliacs. By 1982, the Center for Disease Control (CDC) warned that medicine using blood products, like the one produced by Cutter, might transmit the AIDS virus. In February 1984, as evidence mounted that the earlier version was infecting hemophiliacs with AIDS, Cutter introduced a safer medicine. By October of that year, a joint study conducted by Cutter and the CDC found that the newer medicine eradicated the threat of transmitting the AIDS virus because it was heat-treated. However, 74 percent of hemophiliacs who had used the older, untreated version of the medicine tested positive for HIV. Not surprisingly, the study, once made public, made the old version of the medicine unmarketable within the United States and Europe. The company, holding an overstocked inventory of the old medicine valued at $4 million, distributed its surplus of the untreated medicine to Asia and Latin America.[5]

In November of that same year, Cutter informed its Hong Kong distributor that "we must use up stocks" of unheated medicine before making "safer, better" heat-treated products available. Not only was the old medicine sold, but Cutter also continued to produce untreated medicine for foreign distribution because it held several fixed-price contracts that made the old medicine more profitable. It is estimated that more than ten thousand overseas hemophiliacs who used Cutter's untreated medicine have since died of AIDS. When the company raised the ethical question of whether it could "in good faith continue to ship nonheat-treated coagulation products" abroad, the company's task force that studied the issue responded in the affirmative. In the twenty years since then, how has Bayer, the parent company, responded to the task force's ethical decision? Bayer continues to claim that Cutter "behaved responsibly, ethically and humanely" in selling its old product abroad. Bayer was not alone in its ethical reasoning. Three other American-based companies, Armour Pharmaceutical, Baxter International, and Alpha Therapeutic, also continued to sell the untreated medicine, citing the same reasoning as Bayer.[6]

---

5. Walt Bogdanich and Eric Koli, "2 Paths of Bayer Drug in 80s: Riskier One Steered Overseas," *New York Times*, May 22, 2003.

6. Ibid.

In late 2010, Bayer, along with Baxter, Behring, and Alpha, agreed to a multimillion-dollar settlement with HIV- and hepatitis C-infected hemophiliacs from twenty-two countries. However, as part of the settlement, victims and their lawyers were prohibited from speaking about the arrangement. When contacted to confirm the settlement, a company spokesperson said, "The company accepts no responsibility" in this case and "continues to insist it has always acted responsibly and ethically." Ironically, news of the settlement barely appeared in English-language presses. Philipp Mimkes, of the German-based Coalition against Bayer Dangers, asks, "Why is Bayer concealing these payments? Why are the media not able to report on this precedent? It is outrageous that the companies who knowingly infected thousands of hemophiliacs are blackmailing the victims not to talk about this important development!"[7]

It is easy to assume that Asians and Latin Americans received the life-threatening medicine because their lives were considered to be worth less than those of Americans or Europeans. It is also true that companies such as Bayer are more concerned with making a profit than with discriminating against certain groups. With mounting pressure to discontinue the untreated medicine, Bayer continued to question the study's findings, although most scientists agreed with the CDC that the heat-treated medicine prevented AIDS.

If a corporation decides that its first responsibility is to create profit for its stockholders, then it may need to redefine what is just and ethical in order to allow the maximum profit to be made. If people are hurt in the pursuit of profit, it matters very little whether they are white or of color or their nationality. This does not mean that racism and ethnic discrimination do not continue to play a role in deciding who benefits from corporate decisions; it simply reiterates that classism can at times be color-blind if it means greater power and privilege for the dominant culture's elite. And yet when we explore where power lay, it is hard to argue classism's color-blindness. The lack of diversity in corporate boardrooms where decisions are made that financially benefits those sitting around the conference table remains highly problematic. If we look solely at those who in 2011 were Fortune 500 CEOs, we discover that only twenty-one of them were persons of color (4.2 percent). Four were black (0.8 percent), nine were Asian (1.8 percent), and six were Hispanic (1.2 percent).Additionally, four of these CEOs of color were women (0.8 percent). And while women of all races and ethnicity represent nearly half of the labor force, only eighteen (3.6 percent) were CEOs (Burns, Barton, and Kerby 2012, 5). The question remains that if the CEOs were

---

7. Jim Edwards, "Bayer Admits It Paid 'Millions' in HIV Infection Cases—Just Not in English," CBS News, January 28, 2011; Coalition against Bayer Dangers, "Bayer, Baxter Pay Multimillion Indemnity to Hemophiliacs," press release confirmed by Agence France-Presse, January 24, 2010 (see http://www.cbgnetwork.org/367.html).

as racially and ethnically diverse as the nation, would classism continue to trump sexism, racism, and ethnic discrimination? Would it matter if the CEO is of color or is female if greed continues to be good?

Corporate Welfare

The term "welfare queen" entered the U.S. lexicon during the 1976 presidential campaign when then-candidate Ronald Reagan described an alleged case from Chicago's South Side of a Cadillac-driving person who through the use of fraud received excessive welfare assistance. Reagan's welfare queen, who was never found by the media to prove his point, had twelve Social Security cards, received benefits from four faked dead husbands, and collected food stamps—all to the tune of $150,000 a year. Another race-based fictitious accusation made by Reagan was of the "strapping young buck" using food stamps to buy T-bone steaks at a local grocery store. For southern whites, "young buck" usually denoted a large black man. These pejorative terms, meant to conjure up images of lazy blacks taking institutional advantage of hard-working whites, were used to prove to the conservative base that the so-called welfare state has run amok.

While Americans focus on social-welfare programs, few discuss where most tax dollars go: to corporate welfare in the form of subsidies and tax breaks, totaling some $80 billion a year. States and cities that compete against each other to lure businesses in the hope that new jobs will be created dole out large financial breaks to corporations. Unfortunately, the jobs promised seldom materialize. For example, the movie industry receives about $1.5 billion each year in tax breaks. Pontiac, Michigan, a city declared in 2009 to be in financial crisis, hoped to attract Hollywood studios in an attempt to become a "cool city." The city virtually waived all property tax; the state provided $14 million in tax credits, and a state pension fund guaranteed $18 million in bonds to lure a studio that created only twelve permanent jobs by 2011. More problematically, the studio defaulted in August 2012 on the entire $630,000 bond payment, leaving state pension retirees on the hook.[8]

Rather than providing $80 billion in tax breaks to corporations, investing these funds in education, rebuilding infrastructures, or providing incentives for local entrepreneurs could prove more profitable, possibly leading to greater long-term economic growth and stability. Many cities and states are dealing with budget deficits. Is it wise to provide such incentives to major corporations that simply pit one government agency against another to obtain

---

8. Louise Story, "The Empty Promise of Tax Incentives," *New York Times*, December 2, 2012; idem, "Michigan Town Woos Hollywood, but Ends Up with a Bit Part," *New York Times*, December 4, 2012.

the greatest incentive? Complicating the situation is the impact of well-paid lobbyists for these large corporations, who through generous political contributions get the ears of politicians who ultimate decide on what the incentive package would look like.

Corporations also receive welfare when they are able to cheaply finance major business projects through government bonds that are exempt from federal taxes. While these types of low-interest, tax-exempt bonds were once employed by cities and states for public works such as building bridges, roads, and schools, now for-profit corporations take advantage of these instruments. Corporate gains come at the expense of taxpayers, who in effect subsidize the interest paid to bondholders. Between 2003 and 2012 more than $65 billion in bonds were issued on behalf of corporations. Through tax subsidies, a museum dedicated to the Corvette automobile was built in Kentucky, a winery was planted in North Carolina, a golf resort was created in Puerto Rico, and offices for Barclay and Goldman Sachs were constructed in Brooklyn and Manhattan, respectively. The major benefactor of this program has been Chevron Corporation, which in 2012 reported a $26 billion profit.[9]

Corporate welfare is not limited to municipalities competing with each other to attract major companies; it is inherent in our tax codes in the form of loopholes. For example, Walmart, the world's biggest retailer, pays billions of dollars a year in rent for its stores. In about twenty-five states Walmart pays rent to itself and then deducts the rent from its state taxes. In effect, taxpayers have been subsidizing the retailer's rent to the tune of several hundred million dollars. Obviously, Walmart is not the only corporation that takes advantage of this loophole.[10] These types of subsidy programs become a form of socialism in reverse, where profits are privatized while risk is spread among the general public. "Too big to fail" has become the new norm as government bailouts of mismanaged corporations become the responsibility of taxpayers.

Step 2. Reflecting

The exploitation of labor dehumanizes workers by reducing their existence to expendable commodities. Workers become nonpersons who are prevented from living the abundant life promised to them by Christ. What the economic order values is how cheaply their labor can be extracted, even if their wages are insufficient to acquire the necessities of clothing, food, and shelter. Hence, what are perceived as moral vices (stealing and lying) may appear more as virtues than vices to the marginalized when dealing with those with power and privilege. As mentioned in previous chapters, since the twelfth

---

9. Mary Williams Walsh and Louise Story, "A Stealthy Subsidy Aiding Big Businesses Is Growing," *New York Times*, March 5, 2013.

10. Jesse Drucker, "Wal-Mart Cuts Taxes by Paying Rent to Itself," *Wall Street Journal*, February 1, 2007.

century, theologians have recognized the rights of the poor, specifically "theft arising from necessity." This right to steal for survival's sake was proclaimed within the context of the famines and plagues common in that era (Boff and Pixley 1989, 165).

Ethicist Cheryl Sanders continues this understanding of ethics in her analysis of slave testimonies. Slave masters would hire ministers to preach to the slaves about the virtues of speaking honestly and of not stealing from the owners of their bodies (1995, 14–15). A former slave, commenting on a sermon preached against stealing, said,

> I did not regard it as stealing then, I do not regard it as such now. I hold that a slave has a moral right to eat and drink and wear all that he needs, and that it would be a sin on his part to suffer and starve in a country where there is plenty to eat and wear within his reach. I consider that I had a just right to what I took, because it was the labor of my hands. (Raboteau 1978, 296)

The ethics of the slaveholder, which defined the stealing of food by slaves as a vice, was a socially constructed ethics designed to protect the slaveholder's privilege within the social order. The appropriate question to ask is this: Did the slaves have a moral right to steal from their masters? Do the oppressed, whose labor is stolen from them, have an ethical right, perhaps even a duty, to take what is produced through their labor to feed themselves and their families? Updating this question leads us to ask if employees today who are not paid a living wage also have a right to "steal" from their employers for the purpose of meeting their basic needs for food, clothes, and shelter.

For former slaves, stealing items necessary for survival (food and clothing) was justified on the grounds that they had been victimized by a worse sin: the theft of a human being. This is why an ethics developed among the disenfranchised of "stealing from thieves and deceiving the deceiver." But stealing and lying had their own constraints. It was understood that such actions were to be done only against those who were privileged. Stealing from a fellow slave led to the accusation of being "just as mean as white folks" (Sanders 1995, 14–15). Scripture scholar Brian Blount observes that although there was agreement among slaves not to steal from each other, it was "not only appropriate but also moral to 'take' from an owner . . . because owners often fed their slaves as little as possible in order to increase their margins of profit, [and thus the slave had no] other means of assuaging the hunger of their children and kin" (2001, 40–41).

Although the institution of slavery cannot be equated with the situation of marginalized employees, the same motivation of maximizing profit at the expense of others exists. When the economy experiences a downturn, as was the case with the 2008 Great Recession, some companies continued to grow and prosper on the backs of their employees. Not receiving a living wage contributes to individuals living a less-than-human existence. In effect, denying workers a living wage is stealing. Corporations steal from employees when they extract a full week of labor and refuse to compensate them with what is needed for basic necessities for the week.

In her book *Nickel and Dimed: On (Not) Getting By in America*, Barbara Ehrenreich took several jobs at wages available to the unskilled in an attempt to discover if she could live as a low-wage worker. She worked at three different jobs, none of which provided enough income for her to attain the basic necessities: decent housing, sufficient food, basic clothing, and proper healthcare. She worked as a waitress in Florida, a house cleaner in Maine, and a Walmart employee in Minnesota. During her orientation as a new Walmart employee, she was warned of the dangers of unions and why she would be worse off if they were to organize Walmart employees. Even more significant was the admonition against "time theft," which is doing anything other than working while on company time (2001, 144–46). While employees are guilty of the sin of "time theft" when they take a five-minute break to go to the bathroom (as defined in the supercenter where Ehrenreich worked), Walmart participates in grand-scale time theft by understaffing stores and forcing employees to work off the clock. Reminiscent of sweatshops in countries of the two-thirds world, several Walmart superstores even lock the doors at closing time and force employees to work additional hours at no pay.

Walmart, the world's largest retailer, with over 4,601 stores throughout the United States in 2012 and employing more than 1.4 million workers (Walmart likes to call them "associates"), provides a good example of unfair practices. Walmart's total worldwide sales of $444 billion during 2012 was greater than the economies of the majority of the world's nations. The retail outlet employed 800,000 "associates" in 6,085 stores operating under 69 different banners in 27 countries, bringing the total number of employees to 2.2 million.[11] Although for purposes of this chapter we will focus on Walmart, it is important to acknowledge that the practices employed at Walmart exist, in varying degrees, in other corporations that predominantly employ the marginalized.

On December 20, 2002, a federal jury in Portland, Oregon, found Walmart guilty of forcing its employees to work unpaid overtime. Employees in twenty-seven other states have filed similar class-action suits against the giant retailer. These employees were pressured to clock out after working forty hours but to continue working, in violation of the Federal Labor Standards Act, which requires that employees receive time-and-a-half pay for all hours worked over forty within a week. According to testimony given during

---

11. Based on information from Walmart's website (http://www.walmart.com/).

the Oregon trial, time cards were falsified by erasing hours worked in order to keep those hours below forty and thus avoid paying time-and-a-half. Failure by employees to comply negatively affected promotions, raises, and employment security.[12]

Why would an employee willingly work off the clock? Take the example of Liberty Morales, a woman with limited job skills and only a high school diploma. She states that she routinely worked off the clock without complaining. She knew through the experience of others who did complain that if she did not comply, she would be given fewer hours, demoted, reassigned to the night shift, or even fired. Compliance, on the other hand, led to desired schedules and promotions. In her words, "I put up with it because I needed to work."[13]

In 2010 Walmart agreed to a settlement that provided about $4 million to about 28,000 former Oregon employees. In spite of agreeing to the settlement, Walmart maintained its innocence. Of the $4 million agreed upon, claimants could expect to receive payouts ranging from $50 to $241. This is not the first time Walmart has faced such accusations. In 2000 Walmart settled a class-action suit in Colorado for $50 million that asserted that its laborers were also forced to work off the clock.[14] As with the Bayer settlement previously mentioned, victims, under the terms of the settlement, were limited to what they could say.[15]

In addition to the practice of forcing employees to work off the clock, the retailer also faced a sex-discrimination lawsuit that accused it of denying equal pay and promotions to 700,000 of its female employees from 1996 to 2001. The suit claimed that female employees made $1,150 less per year than men in similar jobs, while female managers made $16,400 less. According to one of the women testifying, her department manager in South Carolina explained that Walmart pays men more than women because the Bible says that God made Adam before Eve.[16]

In June 2011 the U.S. Supreme Court threw out the employment discrimination class-action suit (*Dukes v. Wal-Mart*) on behalf of 1.5 million female employees against Walmart. In a 5-4 decision along ideological lines, the court ruled that the suit failed to satisfy the requirement that "there are questions of law or fact common to the class" of female employees. The court

---

12. Steven Greenhouse, "U.S. Jury Cites Unpaid Work at Wal-Mart," *New York Times*, December 20, 2002.

13. Steven Greenhouse, "Suits Say Wal-Mart Forces Workers to Toil off the Clock," *New York Times*, June 25, 2002.

14. Ibid.

15. Laura Gunderson, "Wal-Mart Sets Aside up to $4M to Settle Oregon Class-Action," *The Oregonian*, May 26, 2010.

16. Laura Gunderson, "Wal-Mart Faces Lawsuit over Sex Discrimination," *New York Times*, February 16, 2003.

did not decide if Walmart discriminated against women; it only stated that the suit could not move forward as a class action because the case was improperly certified. Specifically, writing for the majority opinion, Justice Scalia said that the women who brought the case failed to point to any specific company-wide policies that had a common effect on all the women covered by the class action, even though Justice Ginsburg noted that the overwhelming evidence and testimonies demonstrated that "gender bias suffused Walmart's corporate culture." Not only does the Supreme Court decision immediately impact the claim of Walmart's female employees negatively, but it also makes it more difficult for employees or consumers to join together and challenge institutionalized biases that do not arise from a clear company policy. Joseph M. Seller, attorney for the plaintiff, explained that the court's decision "reversed about forty years of jurisprudence that has in the past allowed for company-wide cases to be brought challenging common practices that have a disparate effect, that have adversely affected women and other workers."[17]

In addition to Walmart's blatant sexism, an internal audit under court seal revealed that, between 2000 and 2003, employee records at 128 stores showed extensive violations of child-labor laws and state regulations requiring time for breaks and meals. Child-labor violations are estimated to be in the tens of thousands each week, with more than a million violations of regulations involving meals and break, according to the Shipley Audit. Walmart at that time dismissed the audit as meaningless. Nevertheless, by 2005, the company agreed to pay $135,540, while denying any wrongdoing, to settle federal charges of violating child-labor laws in Connecticut, New Hampshire, and Arkansas. Part of the settlement, which was written mainly by Walmart lawyers while leaving the U.S. Department of Labor's legal division out of the settlement process, included a peculiar concession. In violation of its own policies, the Department of Labor is prohibited by the settlement from beginning any new investigation on any other "wage and hour" accusation against Walmart without notifying the company fifteen days in advance.[18]

Rather than dealing with the reported missing meal and rest breaks, the company simply implemented a new policy that stopped employees from clocking out and in, thus eliminating any systematic method for determining whether employees were receiving their breaks. Not surprisingly, unions and workers brought (as of 2007) 292 cases against Walmart with the National Labor Relations Board, which found 101 of those cases to have merit. Those

---

17. Adam Liptak, "Justices Rule for Wal-Mart in Class-Action Bias Case," *New York Times*, June 20, 2011; Joan Biskupic, "Supreme Court Limits Wal-Mart Sex Discrimination Case," *USA Today*, June 21, 2011.

18. Steven Greenhouse, "Wal-Mart Agrees to Pay Fine in Child Labor Cases," *New York Times*, February 12, 2005; idem, "Labor Dept. Is Rebuked over Pact with Wal-Mart," *New York Times*, November 1, 2005.

cases were consolidated into thirty-nine complaints, with seventeen administrative law judges ruling that Walmart violated labor laws.[19] By 2008, the retail firm was facing more than seventy lawsuits across the company for failing to award meal or rest breaks and forcing employees to work off the clock.[20] To avoid continued national embarrassment, Walmart that same year agreed to pay $352 million (which could reach $640 million) to settle sixty-three cases claiming that the retailer forced employees to work off the clock that were pending in federal and state courts across forty-two states, making this the largest court settlement over wage violations.[21]

When employees at Walmart attempted to unionize in order to have more leverage with management, union supporters were fired, intimidated, and threatened with the loss of bonuses. A union supporter at a store in Jacksonville, Texas, was fired for supposedly stealing a banana. The only successful effort at organizing Walmart employees occurred in the meat department in a Texas store, but within two weeks of the unionizing, the company disbanded the department. When a Walmart outlet unionized in Jonquière, Quebec, becoming the first store to be unionized on the North American continent, the headquarters in Bentonville, Arkansas, closed that store's doors a few months afterward. A former Walmart store manager who now works as a union organizer summed up the company's attitude: "They go after you any way they can to discredit you, to fire you. It's almost like a neurosurgeon going after a brain tumor: We got to get that thing out before it infects the rest of the store, the rest of the body."

According to Walmart's then–senior vice president, Jay Allen, the reason Walmart remains nonunion is that the company has done a great job in keeping its employees happy and paying them competitive wages.[22] Human Rights Watch disagrees, asserting that Walmart's aggressive tactics to keep out labor unions have often violated federal laws while infringing on workers' rights. The retail giant, when faced with the threat of unionization, often broke the law by, for example, eavesdropping on workers, turning surveillance cameras on them, infiltrating anti-Walmart organizational meetings, and/or firing those who favored unions.[23] A favorite technique, which administrative

19. Laura Gunderson, "Trying to Overcome Embarrassment, Labor Launches Drive to Organize Wal-Mart," *New York Times*, November 8, 2002; Steven Greenhouse, "Report Assails Wal-Mart over Unions," *New York Times*, May 1, 2007.

20. Mark Friedman, "Walmart's Own Audit Documented Constant Violation of Labor Laws," *Arkansas Business*, July 28, 2008.

21. Steven Greenhouse and Stephanie Rosenbloom, "Wal-Mart Settles 63 Lawsuits over Wages," *New York Times*, December 24, 2008.

22. Laura Gunderson, "In-House Audit Says Wal-Mart Violated Labor Laws," *New York Times*, January 13, 2004; Anthony Bianco, "No Union Please, We're Wal-Mart," *Business Week*, February 12, 2006.

23. Greenhouse and Rosenbloom, "Wal-Mart Settles 63 Lawsuits"; Ann Zimmerman and Gary McWilliams, "Inside Wal-Mart's 'Treat Research' Operations," *Wall Street Journal*, April 4, 2007.

law judges ruled as illegal, is transferring out or firing pro-union workers and replacing them with anti-union employees to skew the vote whether or not to unionize, as was successfully done at the Walmart tire-and-lube shop in Loveland, Colorado.[24]

Walmart's refusal to unionize negatively impacts its workers and threatens to undermine the wages being paid by other competitors such as Sears, K-Mart, and Costco, which also can demand contract concessions from unions so that they can compete with Walmart. They cite their inability to compete with Walmart's wages and benefits, which are 20 percent lower than theirs. In effect, Walmart, the nation's largest corporate employer, is lowering the living standards for everyone by aggressively and artificially keeping wages depressed for the sake of profit. According to a 2007 study conducted by the UC Berkeley Labor Center, empirical evidence exists that Walmart employees earn lower average wages and receive less generous benefits than comparable employees working for other large retailers (17.4 percent earning gap with other general merchandising employees, 25 percent gap with large general merchandise companies). Research indicates that better-paying jobs are replaced with lower-paying jobs whenever a new Walmart store opens in a community. Walmart openings drive down wages of competing industry segments within the new store's proximity. When Walmart enters a new marketplace, the total county's wage bill declines along with the average wage. Similar effects also appear on the state level. Fifty new Walmart stores in any given state means a 10 percent reduction of average wages (Dube, Lester, and Eidlin 2007, 1, 3, 6).

Because Walmart is able to cut the cost of operations by paying employees less, the retail giant has been able to push over two dozen national supermarket chains into bankruptcy. The list of now defunct chains includes Grand Union, Bruno's of Alabama, Homeland Stores of Oklahoma, and Winn Dixie, and F.A.O. Schwarz, to name but a few. In February 2004 Walmart opened its first of an expected forty supercenters in California. In California, unionized stockers and clerks averaged at the time $17.90 an hour, with health benefits after two years, solidly placing them within the middle class. Walmart's employees, with an average starting pay at that time of $8.50 an hour with little or no health insurance, found themselves living in poverty. Since then, competition with Walmart was and continues to be used as a ploy during contract negotiations with unions for lowering wages and cutting benefits.[25] The Walmartizing of America means that in order to compete,

24. Steven Greenhouse, "At a Small Shop in Colorado, Wal-Mart Beats a Union Once More," *New York Times*, February 26, 2005.

25. Gunderson, "Trying to Overcome Embarrassment"; idem, "Wal-Mart Driving Workers and Supermarkets Crazy," *New York Times*, October 19, 2003; Abigail Goldman and Nancy Cleeland, "An Empire Built on Bargains Remakes the Working World," *Los Angeles Times*, November 23, 2003.

other supermarkets must race against Walmart to the bottom of the labor pool or else face their own demise.

Walmart's corporate ethos of disenfranchising and marginalizing workers is not limited to North America; the giant retailer is having a negative global impact. For example, in Mexico, Walmart, the country's largest private employer, wanted to build a store barely a mile from the ancient pyramid of Teotihuacán. What stood in their way was a 2003 zoning map that prohibited commercial development close to the ancient site. So a $52,000 bribe was paid to change the zoning map in Walmart's favor before it was published in the newspaper. Months later, Walmart broke ground on its new store, which opened in 2004. Additional bribes amounting to about $221,000 were paid to ensure that the store was built. Total bribes paid in Mexico: more than $24 million.[26]

By 2005, Walmart CEO Mike Duke found out about the bribes. An internal Walmart investigation into the affair was begun; but by April 2006, it was shut down, and steps were taken to conceal what was discovered. In fact, the driving force behind years of bribery, Eduardo Castro-Wright, was promoted to vice chairman of Walmart in 2008. What eventually became-apparent is that Walmart was not some reluctant victim of a corrupt Mexican culture in which bribes are an inherent cost of doing business; rather, Walmart aggressively and routinely used bribes as the means to subvert governance so as to procure what the law otherwise prohibited. For example, a $341,000 bribe made it possible to build a Sam's Club in a densely populated Mexico City neighborhood without a construction license, an environmental permit, an urban impact assessment, or a traffic permit. A $765,000 bribe facilitated the building of a refrigerated distribution center at a Mexico City environmentally fragile flood basin where electricity is so limited that smaller developers were not permitted to build at the site.[27] Even if the company got caught and was found guilty of bribing officials, it was still worth breaking the law because, as the company saw things, the repercussions were unlikely to have a "material adverse effect" on its business. In a note to investors, Janney Capital Markets analyst David Strasser wrote, "This is clearly a bad action, if found guilty, but we believe these issues and penalties will not dramatically impair their balance sheet and its ongoing business model," especially in the United States.[28]

Not surprisingly, Mexico is not the only location where briberies are a common occurrence. In China, at a Uniden plant in Shenzhen, young

---

26. David Barstow, "Vast Mexico Bribery Case Hushed Up by Wal-Mart after Top-Level Struggle," *New York Times*, April 22, 2012; David Barstow and Alejandra Xanic von Bertrab, "The Bribery Aisle: How Wal-Mart Used Payoffs to Get Its Way in Mexico," *New York Times*, December 18, 2012.

27. Barstow and Xanic von Bertrab, "The Bribery Aisle."

28. "Wal-Mart Says Loss Likely from Bribery Probe," *Denver Post*, March 27, 2013.

women recruited mainly from China's poor interior provinces make the wireless phones supplied to Walmart. These women claim that they are required to work eleven hours a day plus three hours of mandatory overtime for a monthly salary of about $58, half of which must be returned to the company in payment for the drab company dormitories in which they must live. These women accuse the company of hiring many minors and of being forced to pay about half of a monthly salary as a job-finder fee in order to be hired.[29]

In India, regulators began in 2012 an informal inquiry into allegations that Walmart violated rules restricting foreign investments. Specifically, they are investigating $100 million invested by Walmart in the countrywide Indian supermarket chain Bharti Retail. The interest-free, so-called debt security converted into a 49 percent ownership stake thirty months after issue, in violation of India's law. This has allowed Walmart to enter a retail sale market estimated at $500 billion annually that presently is dominated by small, family-owned stores. Political pressure of irregularities has led Walmart in November 2012 to expand an internal bribery investigation, originally focused on Mexico, to include India, as well as China and Brazil.[30]

Probably the most grievous complicity of Walmart with life-threatening business practices occurred in Bangladesh, the world's second-leading garment exporter after China. On November 24, 2012, at the Tazreen Fashion factory, 112 workers lost their lives in a factory fire. The fire was started by mounds of flammable yarn and fabric illegally stored next to electric generators on the ground level. This is not the first time lives were lost to violations of fire codes. From 1990 to 2012, more than one thousand laborers have died in hundreds of fires or accidents, without a single factory owner ever being charged with any crime.[31] When the fire broke out at the Tazreen Fashion factory, two managers blocked the exits, ordering everyone to get back to work and ignore the alarm. Sadly, two Walmart officials who attended an April 2011 meeting in Bangladesh to discuss factory safety in the garment industry played lead roles in blocking any effort to improve fire and electrical safety at these factories. Despite the minimal cost involved in improving safety against fire, minutes from the meeting record officials stating, "It is not financially feasible for the brands to make such investments."[32]

29. Howard W. French, "Workers Demand Union at Wal-Mart Supplier in China," *New York Times*, December 16, 2004.

30. Vikas Bajaj, "India Puts Wal-Mart Deal with Retailer under Scrutiny," *New York Times*, October 19, 2012; idem, "India Unit of Wal-Mart Suspends Employees," *New York Times*, November 24, 2012.

31. Jim Yardley, "Justice Elusive in a Bangladesh Factory Disaster," *New York Times*, June 30, 2013.

32. Steven Greenhouse, "Documents Indicate Walmart Blocked Safety Push in Bangladesh," *New York Times*, December 6, 2012; idem, "2nd Supplier for Wal-Mart at Factory That Burned," *New York Times*, December 11, 2012; Jim Yardley, "Recalling Fire's Horror and Exposing Global Brand's Safety Gap," *New York Times*, December 7, 2012.

At least three American apparel makers supplying garments to Walmart were using the Tazreen Fashion factory at the time of the fire. Nevertheless, Walmart has taken a defensive posture, claiming that it was a victim of a rogue supplier who used the factory without Walmart's knowledge, even though several documents recovered from the fire indicate the opposite. Although Walmart has aggressively moved since the fatal blaze toward a no-tolerance stance, the fact remains that serious and continued safety violations were reported from May 2011 through April 2012 at this factory. An audit conducted in May 2011 gave the factory a rating of "high-risk violations." These violations included barred windows that prevent workers from escaping in case of an emergency, lack of fire alarms in key areas, and shortage of fire extinguishers. Even today, after the tragic Tazreen fire, Walmart's new no-tolerance policy does not require its factories to have fireproof staircases or external fire escapes.[33]

Walmart's failure (along with those of other European and American companies) to safeguard garment workers at factories that produce its brand name was amplified just months after the horrific fire when another factory in Rana Plaza collapsed due to structural deficiencies, crushing some 1,250 workers. As mentioned earlier, in January 2013 Walmart refused to join other Western retailers in financing fire-safety efforts and structural upgrades in Bangladeshi factories, offering instead the less expensive course of pledging $1.8 million to train some two thousand factory managers in fire safety. The failure to provide sufficient compensation by Western retailers is one reason why factory owners are forced to cut corners on fire and structural safety.[34]

Walmart purchases over $1 billion worth of Bangladesh's garments. The factory workers who died at the Tazreen Fashion and Rana Plaza factories were mainly young, rural women with limited education, earning as little as $37 a month in minimum wages (lowest in the world) in an industry that in 2012 accounted for $19 billion in Bangladesh's exports. Compare the plight of these marginalized workers for Walmart with the financial situation of their top executive officer, Michael Duke, whose total compensation for 2012 was $20.7 million (a 14 percent increase from the previous year).[35] The connection between the privileged elite and the poor and marginalized workers is maintained through a corporate system that enriches the former at the expense of the latter. The privilege of top executives is protected through the

---

33. Steven Greenhouse, "Wal-Mart Toughens Fire Safety Rules for Suppliers after Bangladesh Blaze," *New York Times*, January 23, 2013; Jim Yardley, "Recalling Fire's Horror and Exposing Global Brand's Safety Gap," *New York Times*, December 7, 2012.

34. Jufikar Ali Manik, Steven Greenhouse, and Jim Yardley, "Western Firms Feel Pressure as Toll Rises in Bangladesh," *New York Times*, April 25, 2013.

35. Anne D'Innocenzio, "Wal-Mart's CEO Paid $20.7 Million in 2012," *Associated Press*, April 22, 2013.

creation of a professional-managerial class that then serves as a buffer zone between top management and those employees living in poverty due to low wages.

The function of a professional-managerial class was ignored by Marxist economic theorists, who focused their analysis on only two classes: the bourgeoisie and the proletariat. Barbara and John Ehrenreich have argued that the middle class, composed of technical workers, managerial workers, "culture" producers, and so on, must be understood as comprising a distinct class in an advanced capitalist society. They call this group the "professional-managerial class" (1972, 8–11). Middle-class managers, who are responsible for ensuring that employees work at the lowest possible wage, with few or no benefits, consist of salaried employees who do not own the means of production but function within the social division of labor as the reproducers of capitalist culture and class relations. Not surprisingly, the relationship between this professional-managerial class and the employees usually is antagonistic.

This professional-managerial class is, in effect, a contradictory class. Although, like the poor, they are excluded from owning the means of production, their interests are still opposed to the workers because of their managerial positions within the corporate organization. Although supposedly materially comfortable, they remain associated with the processes of exploitation (Wright 1985, 285–86). The excessive profits made by the heads of multinational corporations makes it possible to "bribe" this contradictory class, through higher salaries, into maintaining the status quo and thus strengthening the marginalization of the disenfranchised.

The rise of the professional-managerial class has contributed to two sets of business ethics, both constructed to benefit the economic elite. The marginalized, who work at the bottom rungs in companies such as Walmart, are expected to be upright, honest, and loyal. They must pass drug tests to prove that they are responsible and take personality tests to ensure their submissiveness. As business ethicist Alex Michalos pragmatically points out, it is good for corporations to promote ethical behavior among its personnel, for the business cannot survive if its employees are not maintaining the company's best interests. It also becomes profitable for companies to maintain a public persona of being ethical, and while no doubt some firms are ethical, for others it is simply an issue of public relations (1995, 54–57). The professional-managerial class is responsible for maintaining the ethical façade for the benefit of the top executives, who ultimately are responsible for "the bottom line," even at the expense of those upright, honest, and loyal employees.

The professional-managerial class can take comfort in knowing that while things may be economically bad, at least they are not the marginalized.

Nevertheless, the professional-managerial class is also susceptible to unemployment, underemployment, and low wages. Those losing jobs during the 2008 Great Recession are not so much the uneducated poor; rather, they are predominantly middle-class people with college degrees, years of experience, and seemingly impeccable credentials. A downwardly mobile professional-managerial class presents an additional problem. The distinction between them and the marginalized is being blurred. Not surprisingly, the no longer upwardly mobile are angry. Rather than blaming the elite, who sit above them, they blame those under them, specifically the marginalized. "Illegal" immigration or affirmative action easily becomes the scapegoat for the economic conditions that have led to their economic reversals.

It would be erroneous to caricature the top executives of Walmart as demonic or wicked people. In fact, many are considered virtuous, upright, leading citizens and churchgoers. "Is Wal-Mart a Christian company? No," said a former Walmart executive during a prayer breakfast. "But the basis of our decisions was the values of Scripture." The stores cater to churchgoing customers, sanitizing questionable products (like keeping *Cosmopolitan* magazine covers out of view) while being the largest retailer of Christian-themed merchandise.[36] Nevertheless, in his exposé of Walmart culture, Bob Ortega reveals the disconnect between the Christian virtues expounded by top officials and their corporate practices. He concludes,

> David Glass [then Walmart's president] was considered by his friends to be a fine, upstanding, morally correct, and honest man. Don Soderquist [then Walmart's vice chairman] was a devout Christian once named lay churchman of the year by a national Baptist organization. And yet these two ran a company that profited from the exploitation of children—and, in all likelihood, from the exploitation of Chinese prisoners, too. Time and again it was put before them, by *Dateline* [NBC revealed that some Walmart products made in Bangladesh used illegal child labor], by Harry Wu [former Chinese political prisoner for nineteen years who alleged that some Walmart products were made with slave labor], by the *Wall Street Journal*, by others. And yet their response was to do the very least they could, to hold up, time and again their feeble code, as if its mere existence—forget monitoring, forget enforcement—was enough; as if by uttering once more "our suppliers know we have strict codes" would solve any problem. And nothing would change. (1998, 258–59)

---

36. Jeff M. Sellers, "Deliver Us from Wal-Mart?" *Christianity Today*, May 2005.

It is of little comfort to the marginalized that these top officials, while ignoring the Hebrew Bible's condemnation of "those who cheat workers of their wages" (Mal. 3:5) or the New Testament rebuke of those who "cheated the worker who mowed [the employer's] fields" (James 5:4), have certain personal virtues. Just as faith without works is dead (James 2:20), right virtues without right praxis is meaningless.

Step 3. Praying

In teaching about the day of final judgment, Jesus tells a parable of two stewards in charge of the master's household—one conscientious, the other self-absorbed. The conscientious steward fulfilled his ethical obligations to both his master and his fellow servants. The self-absorbed steward instead beat those under his authority. Rather than providing his fellow servants with their fair share of profits from the work performed, the steward ate and drank what was stolen from the laborers. The master came home unexpectedly and, seeing how both stewards had behaved, rewarded the conscientious one and condemned the oppressive one, casting off the latter to where there is "constant weeping and grinding of teeth" (Matt. 24:45–51). Through the parable Jesus prescribes the ethical responsibilities of those with power over workers. Increasingly, laws and government regulations tend to legitimize the power and privilege of multinational corporations, which have become the stewards of today's world. Because these new oppressive stewards "lord it" over the disenfranchised majority and contribute to their poverty, salvation becomes ever more elusive for them.

Rather than looking at the CEOs responsible for setting the wages of the employees, as well as their own compensation, our culture teaches us to blame the workers for their lot. Sometimes we justify this callousness through an ideology based on Charles Darwin's findings that argue for a natural selection that supposedly ensures the "survival of the fittest." Some economic philosophers, misreading Darwin's assertions, have proposed that just as animals compete with each other to survive, so too do human beings. Social Darwinists maintain that free markets guarantee that only those who are aggressive enough will survive because they are the fittest—in effect, the best human beings. Hence, those who fail deserve to fail because they are neither the fittest nor the best. There is no reason then for the government to provide them with assistance (such as welfare, unemployment compensation, and so on), because preserving these economic "losers" or "moochers" would perpetuate inferior qualities in the next generation.

The Spirit of God runs counter to the exploitation of labor. When corporations create conditions that contribute to the poverty of workers, whether such actions are disguised as a defense of democracy, open economic markets,

or Christian virtues, these corporations in reality are complicit in establishing and maintaining institutionalized violence. Violence is never limited to
the use of physical force; it also incorporates power used to achieve wealth
and privilege at the expense of others. Violence is anything that prevents an
individual from fulfilling the purpose of Christ's mission, which is to give life
and give it abundantly (John 10:10).

Such violence (usually manifested as racism, classism, heterosexism, and
sexism) becomes institutionalized when it is built into the very structure of
the corporation. The violence experienced by the working poor through inadequate food, clothing, healthcare, and shelter brings profit to those within
the corporation, specifically its officers, directors, and, to a lesser extent, the
stockholders. Such exploitation of workers dehumanizes them, turning them
into just another resource. Contrary to such common practices, biblical texts
call for workers to be treated humanely and justly:

> You shall not oppress a poor and needy hired servant, neither
> among your compatriots nor an alien who is in your land or
> within your gates. You shall pay them for their work on the same
> day. The sun shall not set upon them, for they are poor, and
> upon these wages their heart is lifted up. Let them not cry out
> against you to God and it be sin against you. (Deut. 24:14–15)

As we survey the plight of the global poor, the connection between the
global privileges enjoyed in the so-called first world is linked to economic
disenfranchisement elsewhere. The prophet Amos warns us not to "sell the
just for silver, or the poor for a pair of sandals" (Amos 2:6). Those who get to
live in the West, along with the few within the global South, who are able
to enjoy a middle- and upper-class lifestyle do so because the just are sold for
silver and the poor for a pair of sandals—or more exactly, a pair of sneakers.

Consider the rural farmers harvesting rice on the island of Java in Indonesia. Those wielding the sickle are usually barefoot. Men who are over sixty
spend the entire day stooped over harvesting rice for about the equivalent
of $3.19 a day, which is barely above the lower range of Indonesian wages,
which average from $2.93 to $5.35 a day. Of course, there is an underground
economy that relies on trading goods and services, thus complicating the liv-
ability of the people; nevertheless, the day's wage of an Indonesian rice farmer
is equivalent to the pocket change that most Americans carry.[37]

If these rural workers have children wishing to go to college, they would
be unable to pay tuition costs for a year at a low-end school that would cost
less than a pair of Nike sneakers. Add the cost of books, housing, and meals,
and it becomes impossible. Their children are relegated to finding similar

---

37. Information concerning rice farmers in Indonesia is based on my fieldwork in Java.

types of employment on farms or in the city. But what would happen if this field hand were to get a job at one of the Nike's factories in Indonesia? He or she could expect a salary of about 1,285,000 rupiahs a month, which translates to about $4.80 a day. What can $4.80 buy you in Indonesia? Barely enough to pay rent for a tiny, bare room, buy two meager meals a day, and bus fare to get to work. One thing the worker would not be able to buy is the Nike sneakers that he or she is producing.[38]

Westerners get to buy $100 sneakers because the poor of the earth make them at slave wages. When in May 27, 2013, some three thousand workers (mostly women) at a Nike factory in the Kampong Speu province of Cambodia blocked a road outside their factory to protest wages, the police, using stun batons, were called to break up the protest. Twenty-three workers were hurt. The workers were demanding a $14-a-month raise (above their monthly minimum wage of $74) to help cover the cost of their transportation to the factory, rent, and healthcare.[39]

The riches of so-called first-world nations are directly connected to the poverty in the global South. But the ones who truly benefit are the CEOs and the stockholders in such companies, who directly are rewarded by keeping expenses (salaries of those who make the product, not the CEO's leadership team) as low as possible. And here is the internal contradiction of capitalism. As corporations search throughout the globe for the lowest possible wage to pay, the day will come (if it has not already come) when workers will not be able to purchase what they produce, causing an abundant surplus of goods whose weight could crush capitalism. Could it be that the 2008 Great Recession is the beginning of the death pangs of this global economic system that we created—death pangs that may signal the end in just a few more generations? The great irony of all this is that the U.S. Congress has moved to protect the so-called job creators from taxation, when in reality their bonuses are calculated on how many jobs they can eliminate, outsource, or maintain at the lowest possible wage. In effect, they receive large bonuses when they sell the poor for a pair of sandals.

Step 4. Case Studies

1. One possible reason that the United States has a dysfunctional immigration system is that imprisoning the undocumented is a billion-dollar industry. By 2011, nearly half the beds in the nation's civil detention systems were in private facilities. The two major corporations that benefit from this arrangement are Corrections Corporation of America

---

38. J. W. Keady, "Wage Slavery: Are Nike's Workers Paid a Living Wage?" *CNN iReport*, October 20, 2011.

39. "Cambodia: Protest at Factory for Nike," *New York Times*, May 27, 2013.

(CCA) and the GEO Group. The average nightly cost to detain an undocumented immigrant is about $166 in 2012, up from $80 in 2004. Additionally, these companies rake in additional profits from subsidiaries that provide healthcare and transportation. Because these facilities are paid by the day, there exists no motivation to quickly repatriate these immigrants, just detain them. In 2000 CCA was on the verge of bankruptcy. At the time, the Federal Bureau of Prisons signed contracts worth $750 million to house 3,300 immigrants. By 2012, the agency paid private companies $5.1 billion to house more than 23,000 immigrants. The corporate desire to maintain, if not increase, the bottom line has led to fierce competition on Capitol Hill (and state houses throughout the nation) to increase incarceration. CCA and GEO have spent at least $45 million on campaign donations and lobbyists during the first decade of the millennium to maintain and introduce laws that ensure that a steady stream of undocumented aliens flows though detention centers.[40]

— Should we feign surprise that the undocumented face inhuman conditions during their U.S. incarceration? Over the years, Amnesty International has documented how these inmates are routinely denied food, water, and medical attention, while being exposed to verbal, physical, and psychological abuse. Many human rights organizations, legal scholars, and the United Nations have meticulously documented how the United States consistently violates international human rights. Do undocumented aliens deserve such treatment because they broke the law and entered the United States illegally? What should be our response to such human rights violations?

— Should prisons, a responsibility of the government, be privatized? Are there certain tasks that only the government should do? Should other governmental tasks be privatized? Military? Environmental protection? Mail service? If not, should some companies profiting at the government's expense be nationalized?

— If detention numbers were to decrease, their stock values would drop. The main concern, then, is not to provide humane living conditions, but rather to increase corporate profits. This can occur only when basic services are cut so as to reduce actual costs. Substandard living conditions can be maintained because there are no substantive legislative or regulatory standards governing detention conditions. Those more likely to complain, or even bring legal proceedings against these firms, are deported from the country. Are these corporations at fault

---

40. Garance Burke and Laura Wides-Munoz, "Immigrants Prove Big Business for Prison Companies," *Associated Press*, August 2, 2012.

for seeking the highest profits for their stockholders? Should noncitizens be protected by U.S. laws? Is it problematic that these facilities
that house the undocumented lack proper oversight?

2. Scores of companies, leading up to the 2008 Great Recession, froze the
    pension plans of their employees. Simultaneously, unbeknownst to the
    workers, some of these companies converted the pension plans into
    resources that financed the retirement benefits and pay of top execu-
    tives. Hundreds of millions of dollars in obligations for executive benefits
    were quietly moved into the rank-and-file pension plans, even though
    this remains a dubious employment of tax law. More importantly, said
    actions weaken the sustainability of the pension plans, creating the risk
    of draining pension assets. Companies that enact this procedure are able
    to capture tax breaks intended for pensions of regular workers. For exam-
    ple, in 2005 Intel (the computer-chip manufacturer) moved more than
    $200 million of its deferred compensation to executives into its rank-
    and-file pension fund plus at least $187 million in cash to the plan. So
    when the executive retires, Intel need not pay, the pension plan does.
    Intel's contribution to the plan resulted in an immediate $65 million tax
    saving the first year. What this means is that taxpayers helped finance
    Intel's executive compensation package. The move also allows Intel
    to book an extra $136 million of profits over the next ten years, which
    reflects the investment return that Intel assumes on the $187 million
    contribution on the pension plan. Taxpayers continue to fund executive
    retirement plans years from now because the deferred executive salaries
    and bonuses are part of a pension plan; thus they can be rolled over into
    an IRA, taking advantage of another tax perk.[41]

    — Does corporate welfare really exist? Is this an example or simply a tax
      incentive to help corporations save funds that can then be reinvested
      to create jobs?

    — For years, attempts have been made to close loopholes such as this,
      and yet they have usually been framed as tax hikes. Is closing this
      loophole a tax hike? If loopholes are closed, will it negatively impact
      the market?

3. The self-serving activities of banks "too big to fail" that led to the cat-
    astrophic losses that in turn triggered the 2008 Great Recession con-
    tinue to be practiced, as made evident by JP Morgan Chase, the nation's
    largest bank, revealing a $6.2 billion trading fiasco. CEO James Dimon

---

41. Ellen E. Schultz and Theo Francis, "Companies Tap Pension Plans to Fund Executive Benefits," *Wall Street Journal*, August 4, 2008.

admitted that the same complex derivatives that brought down several big financial institutions such as Bear Stearns, Lehman Brothers, and American International Group, as well as much of the U.S. economy in 2008, were at play in JP Morgan losses in 2012. The Dodd-Frank banking reform laws that were enacted in 2010 were supposed to curtail banks' bad behaviors; however, according to a 2013 U.S. Senate inquiry, the reform laws failed to cut down on reckless banking activities. JP Morgan ignored internal controls, manipulated documents, and withheld information from regulators. Besides engaging in problematic business practices, the bank made attempts to influence the regulations established to police its practices. JP Morgan alone spent $7.41 million in lobbying to undermine the new regulations set in place to prevent another meltdown. Specifically, Dimon worked to water down the Volcker Rule, which would impose strict limits on what type of trading risk banks are allowed to take with their own money, thus curbing banks from making speculative bets. Before the Volcker Rule was finalized in October 2011, JP Morgan, along with other banks, spent money to lobby Congress in creating a loophole in the rule (known as "portfolio hedging") that allows banks to make large bets in their portfolios, including the types of betting that led to billions of dollars in losses. According to Senator Carl Levin (D-MI), this is a "loophole that a Mack truck could drive right through."[42]

— Although JP Morgan is big enough to absorb the $6.2 billion loss, other banks are not. Does the watering down of the Volcker Rule create an opportunity for other banks to incur similar losses? If so, and enough banks lose money, could we see another economic meltdown? Should not laws be passed to protect taxpayers from such Wall Street risk? If another crisis occurs, should taxpayers be concerned that there are still financial institutions too big to fail? Should the government step in and break up these intuitions too big to fail into smaller companies that can be allowed to go under if they engage in risky business dealings?

— The Senate report indicated that JP Morgan Chase is too big to regulate, too big to fail, and too big to prosecute. And yet the banking industry's attempt to water down the Volcker Rule found sympathetic ears among the main overseers of banks—officials at the Treasury Department and the Federal Reserve, as well as the Office of the

---

42. Peter Eavis and Susanne Craig, "Risk Management Failed at JP Morgan, as It Has So Often for Others," *New York Times*, May 12, 2012; Edward Wyatt, "JP Morgan Chase Fought New Rule on Risky Trade," *New York Times*, May 12, 2012; Jessica Silver-Greenberg and Ben Protess, "Senate Inquiry Faults JP Morgan on Trading Loss," *New York Times*, May 15, 2012; Gretchen Morgenson, "JP Morgan's Follies, for All to See," *New York Times*, March 17, 2013.

Comptroller of the Currency. Are government regulators captives of the corporations that they are supposed to regulate? If so, how can they be stopped from being allies to the industry that they regulate? Should a push be made to simply close all loopholes in banking? What about industries other than banking?

— Are banks that are too big to fail also too big to go to jail? According to the U.S. attorney general in 2013, the answer is yes. Eric Holder said, "The size of some of these institutions becomes so large that it does become difficult for us to prosecute them. . . . If we do bring a criminal charge, it will have a negative impact on the national economy, perhaps even the world economy." Is Holder right? Does this mean that Dodd-Frank reforms fail to end the "too big to fail" dilemma? Is this a cause for concern? Should the size of a company influence a prosecutor's decision to bring criminal charges? When the accounting firm of Arthur Andersen was charged with obstruction of justice in the bankruptcy of Enron, the firm went out of business, and twenty-eight thousand employees lost their jobs. Was prosecution the correct course of action?[43]

4. When the BP Corporation spent $37.2 billion in cleanup expenses after the 2010 Gulf of Mexico oil spill, it received a $10 billion tax windfall by writing off the expense. Corporations reap tax benefits from payments made to correct their wrongdoings while taxpayers lighten corporations' responsibilities. A report by the Government Accounting Office in 2005 suggested that this practice is prevalent. Examining more than $1 billion in settlements made by thirty-four companies, the report discovered that twenty of them deducted part or all of the settlements from their tax bill.[44]

— Should taxpayers subsidize the cost of corporations paying to correct egregious wrongs? In the past, Congress has tried to require that payments made for actual or potential violations of a law would not be tax-deductible. Unfortunately, such bills have died. Why? Should such legislation be passed?

---

43. Andrew Ross Sorkin, "Big Banks Go Wrong, but Pay Little Price," *New York Times*, March 12, 2013.

44. Gretchen Morgenson, "Paying the Price, but Often Deducting It," *New York Times*, January 13, 2013.

Chapter 14

Affirmative Action

Step 1. Observing

Carter G. Woodson, son of African slaves and among the first to study black history, reminds us,

> The opponents of freedom and social justice decided to work out a program which would enslave the Negroes' mind inasmuch as the freedom of body had to be conceded. . . . If you can control a man's thinking, you do not have to worry about his action. When you determine what a man shall think, you do not have to concern yourself about what he will do. If you make a man feel that he is inferior, you do not have to compel him to accept an inferior status, for he will seek it for himself. If you make a man think that he is justly an outcast, you do not have to order him to the back door, he will go without being told; and if there is no back door, his very nature will demand one. (1933, 84)

During the antebellum period (prior to the Civil War) it was illegal to teach African Americans to read. Even after the ratification of the Fourteenth Amendment to the U.S. Constitution (equal rights for all citizens), traditions, customs, and local ordinances conspired to prevent blacks from receiving an adequate education. Consequently, whites became the interpreters of reality. Those who could read were in a position of power over those who could not because those privileged with an education maintained and manipulated the flow of information. During this time there was widespread fear, particularly in the South, of educated persons of color, and so schools were segregated, job opportunities withheld, and resources to correct these injustices denied.

If knowledge is indeed power, then marginalization can be maintained by limiting, censuring, or fabricating "truth," not just for African Americans, but for any who fall short of the white ideal, an ideal maintained in turn by the dominant culture. As the dominant white majority sees it, the post–civil rights era has corrected most of the grievances of people of color. The election of the first black president in 2008 serves as proof that we now live in a postracial America. But for many of the marginalized, though some advances have occurred, institutionalized violence, specifically in education, continues to exist because social structures are designed to preserve the racism, sexism, heterosexism, and classism that have historically benefited those privileged by the status quo.

In spite of affirmative action and some legal gains, people of color continue to be ignored by institutions. As we have already seen, statistics of the U.S. Census Bureau reveal that African Americans and Latino/as earn substantially lower wages than white Euroamericans.[1] Blacks and Hispanics are more likely than whites to become victims of homicide,[2] be discriminated against when looking for a home in which to live,[3] pay higher interest rates for homes,[4] be racially profiled,[5] be arrested for drug charges,[6] and suffer from higher unemployment levels.[7] The presence of racism and ethnic

---

1. A 2010 comparison of non-Hispanic white households with households of color shows that the ratio of blacks' income to that of non-Hispanic whites was 0.59, and the ratio of Hispanics' income to that of non-Hispanic whites was 0.69 (DeNavas-Walt et al. 2011, 9).

2. In 2008 the homicide victimization rate for nonwhites was six times higher than for whites. The offending rate for nonwhites was seven times higher than for whites. These trends held steady in 2009 and 2010, for which detailed data were not yet available (Cooper and Smith 2011, 1, 11–13).

3. While the most blatant forms of housing discrimination (refusing to meet with home seekers from minority communities or provide information to them about any available units) have declined since 1977, when the first national study was conducted, subtle forms of discrimination (providing information about and/or being shown fewer units) persist in 2012, raising the costs of a housing search for minorities and restricting their housing options. For example, black renters who contact agents concerning advertised housing units learned about 11.4 percent fewer available units than equally qualified whites and were shown 4.2 percent fewer units; Latino/a renters learned about 12.5 percent fewer available units than equally qualified whites and were shown 7.5 percent fewer units; and Asian renters learned about 9.8 percent fewer available units than equally qualified whites and were shown 6.6 percent fewer units. When it came to purchasing houses, black homebuyers who contact agents about advertised houses for sale learned about 17.0 percent fewer available houses than equally qualified whites and were shown 17.7 percent fewer homes; Asian homebuyers learned about 15.5 percent fewer available homes than equally qualified whites and were shown 18.8 percent fewer homes. These practices lead to whites being more likely to own their homes, occupy better-quality homes, and live in safer, more opportunity-rich neighborhoods (Turner et al. 2013, 1–2, 5, 7).

4. According to a study conducted by the Center for Responsible Lending, during the height of the fast-growing subprime mortgage market prior to the bubble busting in 2008, Latino/as and African Americans who had credit ratings similar to those of whites were 30 percent more likely to be charged higher interest rates (Gruenstein Bocian, Ernst, and Li 2006, 5). Not surprisingly, those who ended up losing their homes to foreclosures disproportionately comprised black and Hispanic households. Nearly 8 percent of both African Americans and Latino/as lost their homes to foreclosures, compared to 4.5 percent of whites (Gruenstein Bocian, Ernst, and Li 2010, 2).

5. Transportation Security Administration agents are more likely to racially profile Middle Easterners, Hispanics traveling to Miami, and blacks wearing baseball caps backward, stopping, searching, and questioning them for "suspicious" behavior. See Michael S. Schmidt and Eric Lichtblau, "Racial Profiling Rife at Airport, U.S. Officers Say," New York Times, August 12, 2012.

6. In 2010, blacks were four times more likely than whites to be arrested on marijuana possession charges, even though both groups use the drug at similar rates. In some states (Iowa, Minnesota, Illinois) blacks were around eight times more likely to be arrested. See Ian Urbina, "Blacks Are Singled Out for Marijuana Arrests, Federal Data Suggests," New York Times, June 3, 2013.

7. Unemployment rates in 2010 were 18.4 percent for black men and 12.3 percent for black women, for a combined rate of 16 percent. The rate was 12.7 percent for Latinos and 12.3 percent for Latinas, for a combined rate of 12.5 percent. Compare this with 9.6 percent for white men and 7.7 percent for white women, for a combined rate of 8.7 percent (Editors Desk 2011, 1). New York City, for example, has by 2012 recovered all the jobs lost during the 2008 Great Recession. Nevertheless,

discrimination, however, is not limited to those who are passed over for a job or not admitted into college; racism and ethnic discrimination are also an expression of the reality of institutionalized violence in an economic and social system that fosters violence upon the disenfranchised because of the pigmentation of their skin or the nationality from which they derive. Discrimination is a system-wide phenomenon that affects employment and advancement within the society. It often decides who gets decent housing, education, and healthcare, who gets to live in "safe" neighborhoods, and who is stigmatized as sinful (as in Max Weber's *Rise of Capitalism*) because they are unable to "pull themselves up by their bootstraps," never realizing, as so many people of color have said, that they have no boots.

Racism, sexism, and ethnic discrimination mean that people of color often lack the same skills as white males because they have been locked out of education and/or employment opportunities. Because of past racism, ethnic discrimination, and sexism, people of color and women are conspicuously absent from the more desirable and prestigious jobs within society today. Not surprisingly, almost all of the heads of the Fortune 500 companies are white males. How, then, can society mend this structural flaw? One of the means used is affirmative action.

Noting the inadequacy of the 1964 Civil Rights Act to remedy institutionalized racism, President Lyndon B. Johnson signed Executive Order 11246, requiring government contractors to implement a type of affirmative action to ensure that people of color get hired. On June 4, 1965, during his commencement address at Howard University, titled "To Fulfill These Rights," Johnson argued, "You do not take a person who, for years, has been hobbled by chains and liberate him, bring him up to the starting line of a race, and then say, 'You are free to compete with all the others,' and still justly believe that you have been completely fair."

Some, however, believe that President Johnson's action itself was discriminatory. For example, Supreme Court Justice John Roberts argued in a 2007 decision, "The way to stop discrimination on the basis of race is to stop discriminating on the basis of race."[8] Yet ethicist Manuel Velasquez wonders,

> If a racial group, for example, has been unjustly discriminated against for an extended period of time in the past and its members consequently now hold the lowest economic and social positions in society, does justice require that members of that

---

more than half of all African Americans and other non-Hispanic blacks living in the city were still unemployed, even though on average they spent a full year looking for work. See Patrick McGeehan, "Blacks Miss Out as Jobs Rebound in New York City," *New York Times*, June 21, 2012.

8. *Parents Involved in Community Schools v. Seattle School District No. 1.*

group be compensated by being given special preference in hiring, training, and promotion procedures? Or would such special treatment itself be a violation of justice by violating the principle of equal treatment? (1998, 119)

Although a thorough discussion of how affirmative action impacts employment, housing, and social services would be valuable, we will focus here solely on its impact within the education system, specifically higher education. Ironically, while a majority of Americans (over 68 percent) support the general principles of affirmative action in 2013, few (29 percent) support minorities receiving preferences for college admission based on race or ethnicity. Even among those who support affirmative-action programs, in May 2013 only 38 percent supported its usage in college admission, while 57 percent were in opposition (Public Religion Research Institute 2013, 1). A *New York Times–CBS News* poll conducted the following month revealed that large margins of those who favored affirmative action believed that the goal of achieving diversity was a stronger rationale than making up for past discrimination.[9]

In the period of Reconstruction following the Civil War, people of color began to attend school, but due to a racially segregated society, a community would have a white school and a "Negro" school. In the early 1950s a process began to end segregation, which until then had been the norm, based on a U.S. Supreme Court ruling that justified the "separate but equal" rule. In Topeka, Kansas, a black third-grader, Linda Brown, had to walk one mile to get to her black elementary school, even though a white elementary school was only seven blocks away. When her father attempted to register his daughter at the white elementary school, the principal refused to admit her. The U.S. District Court for Kansas heard the case on June 25–26, 1951. The school argued that because segregation in Topeka and elsewhere pervaded many other aspects of life within the United States, segregated schools simply prepared "colored" children for life in America. Losing the case in the U.S. District Court, advocates appealed to the Supreme Court, which did not rule until 1953.

Today that ruling is known as *Brown v. Board of Education*. Although the court neither abolished segregation in public areas nor placed a time limit on when schools had to desegregate, it did declare segregation to be unconstitutional. In spite of the court's decision, most public schools simply ignored the ruling and continued racial segregation. It would take four years and the dispatching of federal troops to Central High School in Little Rock, Arkansas, to provide a few black students access to a white school. Through the

---

9. Sheryl Gay Stolberg and Dalia Sussman, "Same-Sex Marriage Is Seen in Poll as an Issue for the States," *New York Times*, June 6, 2013.

1960s and 1970s a battle raged throughout our nation's public school systems, which fought tooth and nail against the will of the Supreme Court.

What role did Christian churches play? Many of the same Christian churches, particularly in the South, that preached that the saving grace of God is for all people, regardless of race or ethnicity, responded to the moral crisis of segregation by establishing their own "Christian" schools. Members could now send their white children to a school where they would not have to sit next to black or brown children. Many Christian schools established during these times were founded for the sole purpose of circumventing the Supreme Court's mandate to desegregate. Although such schools were a response to a political situation, their motivation supposedly was religiously based.

At the beginning of the new millennium, half a century after *Brown v. Board of Education*, there are still many "Christian" schools with a faculty, administration, and student body that are predominantly white. The role played by these Christian schools to maintain the "separate but equal" mindset raises suspicions among people of color about the moral commitment of the dominant culture to create a truly desegregated learning environment. Ironically, the students within a predominantly white educational system also suffer because they acquire an education devoid of diversity, limiting their ability to function or succeed in the new global marketplace. The new global system of neoliberalism means that our present generation will have to deal with, purchase from, sell to, negotiate with, work for, and supervise people from different races, cultures, and ethnicities.

Although those who are denied a competitive education mainly are students of color, it would be an error not to consider the link between this nation's disparity in wealth and skin pigmentation. In 2010, according to the U.S. Census Bureau, while 22 percent of American children live in poverty, a disproportionate number of children of color live in poverty (39 percent for blacks, 35 percent for Hispanics).[10] In spite of President Bush's No Child Left Behind initiative, which set unrealistic goals that ultimately proved to be self-defeating, and President's Obama attempted fix by which teachers are evaluated by their students' test scores, both failed to consider the driving force behind school failures: class. According to data from the National Assessment of Education Progress, more than 40 percent of the variation in average reading scores and 46 percent of the variation in average math scores are directly correlated with variation in child poverty.[11] A 2013 study demonstrates that on an 800-point SAT-type test scale, a child whose family income is $165,000 will score 125 points higher than a child whose family income is $15,000.[12]

10. Valerie Strauss, "Public Education's Biggest Problem Gets Worse," *Washington Post*, September 14, 2011.

11. Helen F. Ladd and Edward B. Fiske, "Class Matters. Why Won't We Admit It?" *New York Times*, December 11, 2011.

12. Sean F. Reardon, "No Rich Child Left Behind," *New York Times*, April 27, 2013.

TABLE 7
2009 SAT scores and family income

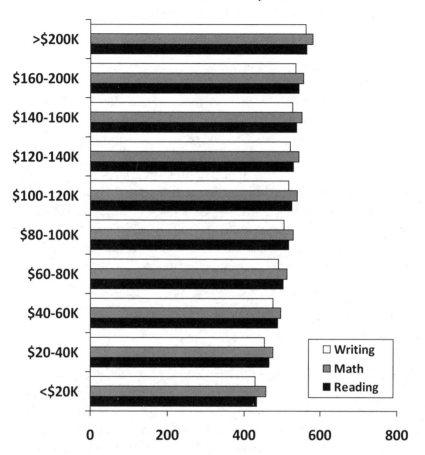

Sources: College Board 2009 data; Catherine Rampell,
"SAT Scores and Family Income," *New York Times*, August 27, 2009.

Could it be that ignoring class issues while setting high standards for all students undermines public education by leading many to fail or leading states to lower standards, thus justifying the need for privatization and creating support for a voucher system?

In her 2011 presidential address to the Association for Public Policy Analysis and Management, Helen L. Ladd argued that the current initiatives to improve the U.S. education system, such as No Child Left Behind, are misguided because they ignore the body of evidence that documents how students from disadvantaged households on average perform at a lower level than those from more advantaged families. Ignoring class-based data means that educational policy initiatives, thus far, have contributed little and more than likely will not contribute much in the future in dealing with the educational gap that exists between those attending schools in poor areas and those attending schools in more affluent communities (Ladd 2012).

Step 2. Reflecting

Is it possible to be color-blind in a society where color still matters? For the past half millennium, racial and ethnic forms of oppression were normalized and legitimatized in the eyes of the overwhelming majority of Euroamericans, an entrenched understanding that found legal (eugenics was constitutional, upheld by the U.S. Supreme Court) and religious justification.

The 1960s civil rights movement (and other antiracist, anticolonial, and democratizing movements throughout the world) ushered in a new way for nonwhites to be seen that radically challenged and changed the legitimized norm. Nevertheless, a racial hegemony was preserved by advancing a new racial project that repackaged white supremacy and secured structural inequalities and injustices under the concept of "color-blindness." In spite of the presence of racism in every aspect of life in the United States, the dominant culture insisted on the construct of color-blindness and the rhetoric of reverse discrimination.

When color-blindness is claimed, the Euroamerican ideal of the segregated life that they have carved out for themselves is masked. Simply examine the racial demographics of most neighborhoods, schools, and social gatherings. Obviously, color is evident. But by claiming color-blindness, whites need not be bigots; in fact, they could be very politically correct, even unmercifully stigmatizing with righteous indignation those who utter bigoted comments. No longer is there a need to believe in white supremacy, because the social structures are racist *for* them, protecting white privilege even while providing the opportunity to lament the lack of diversity.

To claim the ideal of color-blindness allows some Christians, specifically conservative and evangelical Christians, to approach racism on an individual, rather than communal, level. Under the lordship of Christ, they believe, different races can come together as true brothers and sisters. Because Christ is Lord, Euroamerican Christians can downplay, if not outright ignore, the importance of initiating sociopolitical acts that challenge the present social structures that are detrimental to communities of color, which remain embedded within the United States. For them, reconciliation is achieved through personal relationships across racial and ethnic lines. Stressing individual-level actions over and against changing social structures allows those who are privileged by those same structures to feel righteous because of public apologies for past racist acts—apologies usually accompanied by crocodile tears. Meanwhile, they can continue to benefit from the status quo due to their Eurocentric privilege.

Sociologist Howard Winant argues that the construction of color-blindness has moved the conversation from addressing institutionalized racism (as evident in the education system) to creating a political correctness that attempts to expunge individual bigotry. The "new right" racial project, according to Winant, differs from the more racist "far right" by not vocally espousing white supremacy. Unlike the far right, the new right embraces mainstream political activities. The new right can accept a few nonwhites to politically and socially participate within the prevailing power structures as long as they are willing to expound color-blindness. A face of color is usually placed on a pedestal to prove that minority individuals who work hard enough can be as successful as white people. Participants in this movement differ from outright racists by their willingness to manipulate whites' fear of people of color through "coded language" (2004, 56–57). This was best demonstrated during George H. W. Bush's 1988 campaign ads featuring Willie Horton, California governor Pete Wilson's 1994 attack on immigrants for electoral purposes, or Mitt Romney's 2012 postelection remarks concerning "gifts" promised by President Obama for blacks and Hispanics.

Winant goes on to describe the "neoconservative" racial project as a discourse seeking to preserve white advantages through the denial of racial differences, which for this group, as for the new right, is best accomplished by advocating color-blindness (2004, 57). White resentment toward the consequences of neoliberalism is blamed on unfair advantages given to nonwhites (affirmative action), which can be remedied only when everyone is treated the same, regardless of how social structures continue to privilege whites. Establishing a color-blind society is the expressed goal of many powerful and influential leaders from the Religious Right, including Richard Viguerie, Tom DeLay, Phyllis Schlafly, Gary Bauer,[13] Joseph Coors,[14] James Dobson (whose Focus on the Family website celebrated former Chief Justice Rehnquist for upholding the "intent of a color-blind civil rights law"),[15] and Paul Weyrich (who sits on the board of the Houston-based Campaign for a Color Blind America),[16] to name but a few. The problem with expounding color-blindness is that regardless of Euroamericans' best intentions, the disparities between whites and people of color show that social structures are not color-blind.

13. Stephen Dinan and Ralph Z. Hallow, "Conservatives Slam Split Race Rulings; Urge Bush to Pick Supreme Court Nominee with Care," *Washington Times*, June 25, 2003.

14. Timm Herdt, "Groups Ask: Who Gave the Money?" *Ventura County Star*, July 10, 2002.

15. http://www.family.org/cforum/citizenmag/features/a0036727.cfm (website no longer active).

16. David Lerman, "District Lawsuit Arguments to Begin; Black-Majority District Challenged," *Newport News*, September 11, 1996.

The civil rights movement is hailed as a success for eliminating most of our racist past as we speak about living in a postracial world. But somehow racism and ethnic discrimination persist. Why? Because the radicalness of the civil rights movement was toned down in order to obtain some significant and important concessions from the dominant culture. Unfortunately, these compromises simply replaced racial domination with a racial hegemony that poses questions concerning the struggle for justice on a universal rather than on a corporate plane by integrating the opposition so as to nullify their more radical demands of the movement. Even Martin Luther King Jr.'s dream that his children be judged by the "content of their character" and not by "the color of their skin" is co-opted to insist that affirmative action violates the spirit of King's "dream," and that true followers of King should also advocate color-blindness. The reconciliation attempting to be forged is a color-blind one that enacts antiracist laws while failing to fundamentally change or transform the social structures that maintain and sustain racism. The more radical demands of the civil rights movement (equitable distribution of wealth, resources, and opportunities) were sacrificed in favor of limited economic, political, and cultural access to some power and privilege for a minority of middle-class people of color.

Ironically, whenever those who suffer disenfranchisement raise their voice in protest due to the oppression caused by the segregated society in which they live, they are dismissed as "racist" by those who claim to be color-blind. It is indeed a curious thing that those who have spent most of their lives advocating legislation and policies detrimental to communities of color are usually among the first to accuse people of color of being racists. Take the 2009 example provided by former congressman and Speaker of the House Newt Gingrich when he echoed the earlier comments of radio personality Rush Limbaugh. Gingrich was calling for then–Supreme Court nominee Sonia Sotomayor to withdraw her nomination to the Supreme Court because she was, in his words, "A Latina woman racist."[17] She was attacked for lacking sufficient intelligence (although she graduated summa cum laude) or for being too abrasive (a euphemistic way of saying that she is a nondocile Latina who speaks her mind). Some of the comments bordered on the absurd, as was the case with former Republican presidential candidate Tom Tancredo, who called the National Council of La Raza (the Latino equivalent to the NAACP), an organization to which Sotomayor belonged, a "Latino KKK without the hoods or the nooses."[18]

17. Sheryl Gay Stolberg, "Two Sides Start Plotting Confirmation Strategies," *New York Times*, May 28, 2009.

18. Oscar Avila, "Controversy Precedes Latino Conference; Economics in Focus amid Criticism for Immigration Stance," *Chicago Tribune*, July 26, 2009.

Euroamericans who pine for the "good old days" lament the loss of their own affirmative action that assured whites, regardless of qualifications, of filling every empty slot in the workplace, the marketplace, and academic institutions. In a perverse zero-sum rule, every position earned by a person of color was interpreted as a slot "given" to a less deserving applicant—a birthright taken away from a member of the dominant culture. The level of intellectual acumen possessed by students of color matters little, because they are never considered as good as or as likely to succeed as a white student. Racism reinforces the societal belief that people of color are inferior because they lack white skin. Affirmative-action initiatives were put in place to combat the mindset that people of color, specifically blacks and Latino/as, present a threat to the dominant culture. Affirmative action has little if anything to do with correcting past wrongs.

It has been charged that affirmative action itself is a form of "reverse discrimination." Yet the acceptance to a college of Latino applicant "A" does not mean that white student "B" with a higher SAT score was not accepted because he or she was displaced by Latino A. In reality, if Latino A was denied admittance, it would be more likely that another white student with a lower SAT score than that of white student B might be accepted because he or she might belong to one of several subgroups that receive preferential consideration, such as children of parents who attended the school, athletes, or low-scoring children of possible future donors. Or perhaps the spot going to Latino A might instead go to another student of color who scored higher than white student B, or the position might be given to a foreign student.

Affirmative action is not another form of racism—"reverse racism"; rather, it recognizes a historical white privilege that reserved all slots in higher education (and jobs) for whites. Even today, whites continue to have the advantage, holding a disproportionate number of more desirable jobs and attending more prestigious educational institutions than people of color. No one contends that whites are excluded from getting a college education simply because they have white skin. The same cannot be said about students of color. Affirmative action is an attempt to provide an equal opportunity for all, regardless of race, to achieve the advantage currently reserved for white males. Its purpose is not to exclude whites, but rather to serve the missions of colleges and universities to create diverse learning environments for the betterment of the overall student body and for the good of the general public.

And yet "reverse discrimination" masks the domestic economic disparity caused by neoliberalism that is racialized so as to blame affirmative action, which, in the minds of many among the white working class, gives blacks and Hispanics an unfair advantage. "Welfare queens" and those who "do not play by the rules" are conjured up to serve as scapegoats. Reverse discrimination is created so as to explain why whites get a raw deal. And while reverse dis-crimination is an illusion for which no empirical data exists, it provides "the answer" for why whites are disadvantaged by neoliberalism. Rather than looking upward toward the top 1 percent as a possible cause for the nega-tive consequences of neoliberalism, the majority of white Americans have learned to direct the blame downward.

Although the United States cannot return to its past of white supremacy, nor is it willing to challenge neoliberalism, it can advocate color-blindness to address the downwardly mobile, white middle class. Of course, most would not make the error of voicing racist comments or appearing to violate the rules of political correctness (at least not in the presence of people of color). Nevertheless, wishing to preserve white advantages through the denial of racial differences has led to the advocacy of color-blindness. Frustration with the present economic crisis has caused many whites to blame the so-called "unfair advantages" given to nonwhites (affirmative action), which can be remedied only when everyone is treated the same, ignoring how social struc-tures continue to privilege whites.

Rejecting the assumption that people of color are inferior, those on the margins of society recognize that they are locked out of educational and employment opportunities because white males, the guardians of society's power structure, either consciously or unconsciously bias their decisions in favor of other white males. Affirmative action was designed as a correc-tive measure. Nonetheless, numerous studies show that even when people of color and/or women are more qualified, white males in power will grant higher salaries and positions to their fellow white men (Velasquez 1998, 405). If the goal of affirmative action was to racially and ethnically diversify college campuses, it has failed. Attendance of students of color and those economically disadvantaged has fallen off since the early 1970s. Even under current affirmative-action policies, students of color continue to be under-represented. The underrepresentation of low-income students is even greater. By 2003, African Americans and Hispanics each comprised 6 percent of the freshman classes of the 146 "most" and "highly" selective four-year colleges, a drop from 15 percent and 13 percent, respectively, of all eighteen-year-olds in 1995. Because attending a selective institution provides advantages, specifi-cally greater likelihood of graduating, greater access to graduate schooling, and higher wages (Carnevale and Rose 2003, 6), homogeneous campuses, whether or not consciously designed as such, serve to further institutionalize racism, sexism, and classism within society.

Ironically, affirmative action is beneficial for neoliberalism, and the "establishment" generally recognizes this fact. This was made evident during the legal case concerning the University of Michigan. *Grutter v. Bollinger* involved admission to the university's law school, while *Gratz v. Bollinger* dealt with admission to the university's undergraduate program. Both cases were filed in 1997 on behalf of white female applicants who were denied admission. They argued that promoting racial and ethnic diversity was not a compelling enough reason to justify the university's admission policies. They also argued that admission policies at the University of Michigan were too broad to promote diversity, hence failing to meet the compelling-interest exemption that the court applies to the Constitution's equal-protection clause.

A record-setting sixty-six friend-of-the-court briefs were filed in support of the University of Michigan's admission policies. Those filing amicus briefs in the Supreme Court cases *Grutter v. Bollinger* and *Gratz v. Bollinger* were not liberal or activist organizations, but rather the defenders of the conservative establishment, such as the military, including twenty-one retired generals and admirals and three former superintendents of military academies, and some titans of corporate America such as General Motors, Viacom, Microsoft, IBM, Bank One, American Express, Boeing, Shell, General Electric, Coca-Cola, and fifty-four other Fortune 500 companies. They maintained that race should be one of many factors used to achieve a more diverse student body.[19] Because selective universities train the future leaders of society, a society marred by racial and ethnic tension will benefit from a diverse and integrated leadership corps. Ironically, again, it was a conservative U.S. Supreme Court that agreed to uphold the law school admission policies of the university. It was acknowledged that in order for the United States to compete aggressively on the global stage, its white students must understand and work with diversity.

The Michigan cases were decided in 2003, with the Supreme Court invalidating the practice of awarding points to minority students. At the time, Justice O'Connor expressed the hope that within twenty-five years of the decision, there would no longer be a need for affirmative action. Unfortunately, at least three obstacles prevent Justice O'Connor's vision from being realized. First, there is a reluctance to eliminate class preferences in college admissions, specifically the legacy-type programs that function as affirmative action for privileged middle- and upper-class whites. Legacies began to be implemented at the more prestigious institutions of higher education following World War I as a reaction against the influx of immigrant students (particularly Jews). This un-American racist system exists only in the United States, preserving an aristocratic right virtually unheard of at universities throughout

---

19. Justice Powell's written opinion in the court's landmark 1978 case *Regents of the University of California v. Bakke* allowed colleges to consider race in determining admission for the sake of diversity, as long as quotas were not used.

the world. Today, legacies continue to be used to keep out students of color. In 2008, while African American and Hispanic students constituted more than 30 percent of the traditional college-age population, they represented about 10 percent of the enrollees of the top fifty national universities.[20]

Legacy programs, a relic of white supremacy, give admission preference to the sons and daughters of alumni, who, due to historical racism and ethnic discrimination, are disproportionally white. Legacy preference is employed at almost three-quarters of selected research universities and at virtually every elite liberal arts college. While their importance is usually downplayed by colleges and universities, research suggests that their weight in selecting students is significant, on the order of adding 160 SAT points to prospective students' scores (on a 400–1600 scale). Research done by the Andrew W. Mellon Foundation discovered that legacy increased one's chances of admission by 19.7 percent within a given SAT score. A classist quota system is maintained at selected institutions where legacies comprise 10 to 25 percent of the student body. Compare this to the 1.5 percent of legacies found at California Institute of Technology, which has no legacy preference.[21]

In addition, many selective colleges treat applicants from very wealthy families as legacies because the families are able to make major financial contributions to the institution. Portraying affirmative action solely as a race issue fails to consider the affirmative action, accepted as normative, that benefits wealthier white students on a regular basis. Neoliberalism continues to influence all aspects of human life, where today white privilege is more than ever trumped by class privilege. One of the major class struggles occurring today is being fought in the admission buildings of the highly selective colleges and universities. Children of the wealthy can afford the SAT tutors and top prep schools that groom their children for marquee colleges. But as the income gap continues to widen, as discussed in chapter 9, the once protected privilege of whiteness becomes less secure for the lower and middle classes and creates a backlash of legislation, referendums, and court decisions attempting to limit affirmative action. Protection is sought for white privilege, specifically through college legacy programs.

During the oral arguments on the University of Michigan cases, Justice Breyer asked the attorney representing white students suing the university about the difference between legacy preference and affirmative action. According to the lawyer, the equal-protection clause of the U.S. Constitution prohibits race discrimination, not discrimination based on alumni affiliation.

---

20. Joyce Hesselberth, "10 Myths about Legacy Preference in College Admission," *Chronicle of Higher Education*, September 22, 2010.
21. Ibid.

Yet because students of color were historically discriminated against when applying to predominantly white universities, few of today's students of color have parents who attended Ivy League institutions. Students of color are thus locked out of legacy opportunities, continuing the racism that privileges white applicants who claim legacy. In fact, five of the nine U.S. Supreme Court justices (or their children) who determined the *Grutter v. Bollinger* and *Gratz v. Bollinger* cases themselves were "affirmed" into the legacies of Ivy League schools.[22]

It is a given that among students with better grades, those who made the mistake of not being born white and wealthy have difficulty entering such selective colleges. According to an analysis of the 1999 entering graduate class at leading private research universities, a considerable number of high-scoring minority students were not admitted. For example, among male students of color with SAT scores well within the top 10 percent of minority test-takers and the top 20 percent of all test-takers, only 35 percent were admitted (Bowen and Levin 2003, 232–39, 250). Because race and class privilege trump merit, affirmative action serves as a counterbalance to legacy preference.

A second obstacle preventing Justice O'Connor's vision from being realized is the unequal distribution of funds for K–12 education. O'Connor recognized this obstacle during a rare interview with the *Chicago Tribune* in which she said, "I hope it looks as though we don't need artificial help to fill our classrooms with highly qualified students at the graduate level. . . . And if we do our job of educating young people, we can reach that goal."[23] Yet in spite of Justice O'Connor's optimistic hope for the future, the reality is a national refusal to provide a basic public education for all its children.

In the early 1990s Jonathan Kozol described schools in predominantly poor and nonwhite districts as functioning with outdated, secondhand books, gaping holes in their roofs, overcrowded classrooms, inadequate climate control, nonfunctioning restrooms, running sewage, and in one case a classroom conducted in an abandoned swimming pool (1991, 23–37). The financial situation faced by these marginalized schools has worsened with the passage of time and has been exacerbated by how school financing continues to be distributed. According to a study conducted in 2006 by the Educational Trust, a nonpartisan group, school districts that are predominantly black and

---

22. Justices Breyer and Kennedy have ties to Stanford University that span three generations; Justice O'Connor's two children benefited from legacy at Stanford University. Stanford admits one-fourth of all legacies compared to just one-eighth of the overall applicant pool. Justice Stevens attended the University of Chicago and Northwestern Law School, as did his father, and Justice Ginsburg's daughter benefited from legacy at Harvard Law School. See Daniel Golden, "For Supreme Court, Affirmative Action Isn't Just Academic," *Wall Street Journal*, May 14, 2003.

23. Jan Crawford Greenburg, "O'Connor Voices Hope for Day Affirmative Action Not Needed," *Chicago Tribune*, June 25, 2003.

Hispanic spent on average $908 less per student than mostly white school districts (Wiener and Pristoop 2006, 6).

In major urban centers such as New York City, students of color received about $2,241 less per student than white students during the 2007/2008 academic year (Hall and Ushomirsky 2006, 2). The study showed that in twenty-six of the forty-nine states that submitted financial data to the federal government, those schools with the smallest representation of poor students (predominantly students of color) got substantially more than districts with high concentrations of poor students (Wiener and Pristoop 2006, 6). Schools outside of the prosperous suburbs must contend with less funding than their white counterparts. Studies have shown that, historically, reduced tax bases in communities predominantly of color were created mainly by the flight of the white middle class and the exodus of businesses (and I would add white churches) to more prosperous neighborhoods, resulting in lower school quality (Wilson 1987, 56). With limited access to computers and microscopes, nonsuburban schools struggle with overcrowding, decaying infrastructure, and outdated resources. In short, schools with the greatest financial needs get the fewest resources.

Even if the federal and state governments were committed to eliminating the financial discrepancies between white and minority schools, they would be unable to do so. On average, state and federal governments provide less than 56 percent of the schools' revenues over the past decades—8.9 percent from the federal government, 47.1 percent from the state (Pristoop 2006, 14). The remainder comes from local sources, specifically property taxes.[24] The financial structures created to fund K–12 education are tied to the neighborhoods, which in turn have historically been and continue to be segregated. Because the neediest schools are located in predominantly poor neighborhoods, where most of the residents are of color, K–12 educational funding will never be equitable unless the financial structures are radically changed. This present system of unequal educational opportunities in K–12 means that most students of color will be unable to compete with white students for college admission, not because they are intellectually inferior, but because institutionalized racism and classism in education have ill-equipped them.

An analytical study that explored how school and neighborhood contexts are jointly related to high school and graduation showed that the level of neighborhood resources positively predicts earning bachelor degrees, while neighborhood socioeconomic status predicts high school graduation. Blacks and Hispanics who attend predominantly black and/or Hispanic poor schools

---

24. Steven A. Holmes and Greg Winter, "Fixing the Race Gap in 25 Years or Less," *New York Times*, June 29, 2003.

have lower test schools and are more likely to drop out of school, contributing to the black/Hispanic–white gap in test scores. In other words, neighborhood characteristics remain the main indicator for educational attainment. However, simply shipping economically deprived students to predominantly white and affluent schools is not the answer, since the study showed that their odds of educational attainment were reduced (Owens 2010, 287, 289, 307). Difficulties in predominantly white and affluent schools might be due, at best, to the inability of teachers and administrators (85 percent of whom are white), possibly because of lack of training, to know how to educate in integrated settings, or, at worst, to lingering conscious or unconscious racism. Taking this study into consideration leads to the alternative that educational success for students of color in poor neighborhoods is not only a path to the economic revitalization of these neighborhoods, but also a more equal distribution of educational resources among the schools.

A third obstacle to Justice O'Connor's vision is the recent trend toward a more segregated educational system. According to the Civil Rights Project/Proyecto Derechos Civiles at UCLA, the proportion of blacks and Hispanics in white-majority schools has significantly dropped, making them more isolated from their white counterparts. Forty-four percent of public school children are non-Euroamerican, of which the largest share—African Americans and Latino/as—are more segregated today than at the assassination of Martin Luther King Jr. (Orfield 2009, 6). Starting with *Board of Education of Oklahoma City v. Dowell* in 1991, the Supreme Court authorized a return to segregated neighborhood schools, maintaining that desegregation was but a temporary measure, not a school system's lasting responsibility. Contributing to the resegregation of the nation's schools are dozens of court-ordered desegregation plans (specifically busing), an increase of students of color within the overall population, continuing white flight from urban centers, and redlining real estate.

Whites, who represent the majority of the population, are the most segregated group, attending schools where 76.6 percent of their classmates are white. By contrast, blacks and Hispanics are in schools with almost 75 percent minority students, while about 40 percent find themselves in intensely segregated schools (Orfield 2009, 13). But this is as much a class issue as it is a race issue, linking segregation by race with segregation by poverty. Blacks and Latino/as attend schools where, respectively, about 58.8 percent and 57.4 percent of the students are poor, compared with the majority of white students, who attend schools where the percentage of poverty ranges from 0 percent to 30 percent (Orfield 2009, 13). To rectify this, 62 percent of blacks and 48 percent of Latino/as (based on U.S. Census Bureau data) would have to move in order to eradicate segregation (Goldsmith 2009, 1913). Unfortunately, multiple studies based on in-depth interviews with Euroamericans and on white flight indicate that the majority of Euroamericans will not freely integrate with Hispanics or blacks (Renzulli and Evans 2005, 398). Nonetheless, Justice O'Connor's colleague Anthony Kennedy best articulated the new approach to education in a seminal opinion. Writing about a Georgia school district, he said, "Racial balance is not to be achieved for its own sake. . . . Where resegregation is a product not of state action but of private choices, it does not have constitutional implications." From Missouri to Oklahoma, similar court decisions are reversing *Brown v. Board of Education*, so that once-integrated schools are again becoming segregated.[25]

Lisa Navarette, vice president of the National Council of La Raza, commenting on Justice O'Connor's vision of affirmative action ending by 2028, said it best: "If all we do over the 25 years is affirmative action, then we will still need affirmative action."[26] Unfortunately for Navarette, her dismal appraisal of 2028 came early. In 2012, just nine years after the Michigan decision, the Supreme Court again heard arguments concerning affirmative action. Abigail Fisher, a white female student, brought suit against University of Texas at Austin when the institution, which her father and sister attended, rejected her application. Using zero-sum logic, she claimed that her white race was held against her, even though the university clearly stated that she would not have been admitted even if race played no role in the process. But even if race did play a role (which it did not), the university insists on the flexibility needed to assemble a varied student body as part of its academic mission.[27] The majority of educators and administrators maintain that students from diverse backgrounds learn from each other, making them better prepared to overcome biases and assume leadership positions within society.[28]

White privilege known as legacy is not the issue that the justices considered. Rather, the Supreme Court's 7-1 ruling in *Fisher v. University of Texas* on June 24, 2013, continued its skeptical assessment of affirmative action. Although the narrow ruling was a reprieve that allows for the continuation of the program, the justices ordered the appeals court to reconsider the case under standards that appear to doom affirmative action in the future. Justice Kennedy, writing for the majority, said that schools must demonstrate that

---

25. Allen G. Breed, "Separate but Equal?" *New York Times*, September 29, 2002.
26. Holmes and Winter, "Fixing the Race Gap."
27. The University of Texas at Austin admits about 80 percent of its students by automatically accepting the top 10 percent of students from every high school in the state. The remaining 20 percent are chosen through individual assessments, taking into account many factors, such as legacy, diversity, grades, life experiences, and activities in which the applicants engaged.
28. Adam Liptak, "Race and College Admissions, Facing a New Test by Justices," *New York Times*, October 9, 2012.

"available, workable race-neutral alternatives do not suffice" before considering race in admission decisions. Universities must "verify that it is necessary . . . to use race to achieve the educational benefits of diversity."[29] The "strict scrutiny" to be employed by universities considering race allows opponents of affirmative action an easier path to bring new cases before the court, thus providing an opportunity to continue its drift away from the ideal goals that began with *Brown v. Board of Education.*

Regardless of the Supreme Court ruling, most schools of higher education will continue to find ways of increasing the admission of students of color that do not directly conflict with judicial decisions. As Ada Meloy, general counsel of the American Council on Education, said prior to the *Fisher v. University of Texas* decision, regardless of limited options imposed by the Supreme Court, universities and colleges will "be seeking diversity by any means possible."[30] And while strategies differ among the states, enrollment increases still fall short from when affirmative action was more overt.

Probably the best strategy that can be employed is an affirmative action based on class rather than race. A 2012 study shows that most low-income students with top test scores do not apply to any selective college or university, contributing to greater economic inequality within the country. A 2013 Georgetown University Study found that at most competitive colleges, only 14 percent of students come from the lower 50 percent of families by income.[31] And worse, these low-income students who excelled in high school seldom graduate from the less selective colleges that they do attend (Hoxby and Avery 2012, ii). Regardless of the rhetoric of selective colleges expressing the desire to recruit a diverse student body, most have failed to do so. A shift from race preference to class preference, if done correctly, appears to have a better chance of achieving the goal of diversity without the distractive discourse of race-conscious admission. According to former Amherst College president Anthony Marx,

> We claim to be part of the American dream and of a system based on merit and opportunity and talent. Yet if at the top places, two-thirds of the students come from the top quartile and only 5 percent come from the bottom quartile, then we are actually part of the problem of the growing economic divide rather than part of the solution.[32]

---

29. Adam Liptak, "Justices Step Up Scrutiny of Race in College Entry," *New York Times*, June 25, 2013.

30. Richard Pérez-Peña, "To Enroll More Minority Students, Colleges Work around the Courts," *New York Times*, April 2, 2012.

31. Richard Pérez-Peña, "Elite Colleges Differ on How They Aid Poor," *New York Times*, July 31, 2013.

32. David Leonhardt, "Top Colleges, Largely for the Elite," *New York Times*, May 24, 2011.

But caution must be taken before rushing to solely a class-conscious admission policy. Where implemented, it has reduced the numbers of black and Hispanic students because the largest portion of low-income families is white (Carnevale and Rose 2003, 6). For a shift toward class-conscious admission to also guarantee racial and ethnic diversity, then, special attention must be based on how social location of students of color can complement criteria for class-based admission policies.

By 2012, ten states have no race-conscious affirmative action. California was the first to outlaw affirmative action in 1996 with the passage of Proposition 209. Voters in Washington banned the use of affirmative action in 1998. Nevertheless, Washington became one of the few states to employ a more holistic approach that reduces the emphasis on test scores and grades while paying more attention to life experiences and challenges overcome. One way the state accomplished this was by giving additional credit to those students who have overcome poverty, low-performing schools, language barriers, and/ or troubled neighborhoods. The outcome of this approach speaks for itself. Black and Latino/a enrollment at state universities in Washington initially dropped but quickly rebounded, providing a long-term effect of minute impact once the ban went into effect.[33] A similar drop in racial and ethnic diversity after banning race-conscious admission followed by a rebound to previous levels occurred in Florida, the University of Georgia, and the University of Nebraska, although the University of Michigan did not fare well (Kahlenberg 2012, 20). In California, public universities have spent more than $7 million a year to embed themselves into disadvantaged communities so as to provide assistance to students in choosing courses, completing classwork, preparing for standardized tests, filling out scholarship and college applications, and making visits to campuses.[34]

Because those within the United States who are more likely to be poor or who have attended troubled schools are of color, a more racially and ethnically diverse student body can still be created. Classism is linked to racial and ethnic discrimination; it is not its cause. A class-based approach could foster a more just approach to those situations where poor whites are forced to compete against students of color who come with class privilege and can afford costly SAT tutoring. At selective colleges, 86 percent of African Americans were either middle or upper class, while at Ivy League institutions 41 percent of black freshmen were immigrants, a group that is more socioeconomically privileged than nonimmigrant blacks (Kahlenberg 2012, 5).

Class integration should not start at the college level. In Wake County, North Carolina (which includes Raleigh and the surrounding suburbs),

---

33. Pérez-Peña, "To Enroll More Minority Students."
34. Ibid.

a concerted effort was made to economically integrate the school system, ensuring that no school had a proportion of low-income students exceeding 40 percent. Some of the districts best schools, contrary to the national norm, were located in its poorest neighborhoods. The end results have been a dramatic increase in reading and math scores for blacks and Hispanics since 2000. Only 40 percent of African Americans in grades three through eight read at grade level in 1995. By 2005, 80 percent scored at grade level. But these successes were not restricted to African Americans: 91 percent of students, regardless of race, ethnicity, or economic status, scored at grade level, up from 79 percent a decade earlier.[35] These results seem to validate multiple studies that show academic benefits in economically diverse schools. Not surprisingly, other schools throughout the country started looking into how this model can be replicated.

Wake County's public school system, for a brief moment in time, provided a glimpse of a more just education system; unfortunately, it is now reverting to its segregated past. A newly elected school board in 2011, backed by the national Tea Party Americans for Prosperity, pledge to "say no to the social engineers." The school district returned to neighborhood schools, arguing that the concentration of poor students, who are predominantly of color, in a few schools has merit. The Tea Party–backed, Republican-controlled school board believes that promoting diversity is no longer a proper or necessary goal for public schools.[36] Failure to diversify, from grade school to graduate school, runs the risk of continuing the sorry history of our education system as the primary engineer of inequalities within the United States.

Step 3. Praying

At times, the dominant culture believes that inclusion is an adequate ethical response to structural oppression. Diversity and multiculturalism do not equal justice; they equal political correctness. Even if society were to abide by some politically correct decorum and thus eliminate the appearance of bigotry and prejudices, it still could not reverse the damage of centuries of racism wrought upon those relegated to the margins. Nor could it eliminate the consequences of (mis)education, which have led to poverty and all the misery, bitterness, and hatred that it produces. Ethics, when done from the margins, attempts to move beyond political correctness, that Disney-like façade where different cultures, races, and ethnicities are presented as "a small world after all."

Affirmative action must be understood as a product of love rather than political correctness. Basing ethics upon the concept of love is not new. Many

---

35. Alan Finder, "As Test Scores Jump, Raleigh Credits Integrate by Income," *New York Times*, September 25, 2005.
36. Stephanie McCrummen, "Republican School Board in NC Backed by Tea Party Abolishes Integration Policy," *Washington Post*, January 12, 2011.

Eurocentric ethicists have attempted to base their deliberations upon such a concept (e.g., Joseph Fletcher). However, many have fallen short because they have applied love primarily to interpersonal relations while ignoring issues of social injustices, such as segregation within education. Martin Luther King Jr., more so than any other love ethicist, made love the essential theme for both the private and public sector (P. Williams 1990, 18–23). Nevertheless, for many ethicists of the dominant culture, such as Reinhold Niebuhr, unconditional love (*agape*) as an essential theme for the public sector is seen as problematic as a standard for moral behavior, or as Niebuhr said, an "impossible possibility" (1943, 76).

However, by failing to make love the primary motive for social actions such as affirmative action, the good intention to love remains separated from the action of love. The transformative power of love remains restricted to the inner soul rather than moving in the outer social environment. While admirable theoretical models are constructed to explain varied nuances in conceptualizing love, those on the margins complain that at times it is difficult to see the connection between the complex models and their practical application within the "everyday" of the disenfranchised. For so many who deal with the daily struggle for dignity, ethical deliberations founded upon love as an abstraction provide little help for those marginalized by the educational system.

For example, in his book *Christ and the Moral Life*, James Gustafson states, "Love as a disposition needs love as an intention, as a purpose, and also love as a norm" (1968, 256). This provides no help for the marginalized. Although Gustafson goes on to define intention as a "basic direction of activity," one is hard-pressed to find examples in his book of praxis for justice based on love in facing the greatest injustices of his time. When we consider that his book was published in 1968, during the black community's struggles for civil rights, we are left asking why he failed to connect his ethical perspectives with the moral crises unfolding before him and the Christian community. Did his silence confirm the power of those within the center to determine what is, and what is not, to become a topic for moral discourse?[37] As James Cone reminds us, white ethicists (Gustafson is just one example) reflect the racism prevalent in society. The "invisibility" of racism is maintained by suggesting that the problem of racism is only one social expression of a larger ethical concern (1975, 201).

If it is true that God is love (1 John 4:8), then the only absolute that can be claimed is love. Therefore, love ought to be the prime motive behind

---

37. In all fairness, Gustafson does include Martin Luther King Jr.'s essay "Letter from Birmingham Jail" in a collection of essays that he co-edited with James Laney in another book published that same year (1968, 256–74).

every decision taken, including affirmative action. But is the biblical concept of love sufficient? Because of the prevalent racism in higher education, those from the margins remain leery of basing any ethics upon a fixed law or regulation formulated by society, specifically the dominant culture. In the end, relying on how the dominant culture defines love (either paternalistically or as "tough" love) can mask the self-interest of those with power. The basic flaw of relying solely on love as defined by the dominant culture is one of trust. Can the dominant culture be trusted to act in love? If the past history of how people of color have been treated in the United States is to serve as a guide in answering this question, then obviously the answer is no.

In addition, love coming from the centers of power and privilege usually focuses on how "they" can love those who are marginalized. But unconditional love is never limited to one direction (in other words, love from the privileged toward the marginalized), lest it reduce the disenfranchised to objects by which those in power can express their paternalistic charity. Love must be mutual. To love the marginalized is to serve them and receive in return God's love through them. Thus, the privileged and powerful find their salvation by discovering God, through Christ, in the lives of "the least of these," their neighbors. In this way, God's love can be experienced, a love manifested in the establishment of just relationships that can lead toward just social structures such as affirmative action. Only then can community be established and the possibility of hope arise for a just social order.

Step 4. Case Studies

1. Arizona school districts, which are largely composed of Mexican Americans, were forced to eliminate ethnic studies programs because they were un-American, apparently teaching hatred and ethnic unrest. To facilitate the process, the Tucson Unified School District released the titles of banned books that were "biased, political and emotionally charged." Teachers are encouraged to stay away from any works where race, ethnicity, and oppression are central themes.[38] Hispanic-based books cannot be read because they are in violation of Arizona House Bill 2281, which specifically states,

    > A school district or charter school in this state shall not include in its program of instruction any courses or classes that include any of the following: (1) Promote the overthrow of the United States government; (2) Promote resentment toward a race or class of people; (3) Are designed primarily for pupils of a par-

---

38. Rheana Murray, "Ethnic Book Ban in Arizona School District Includes All Books about Mexican-American History, Even Shakespeare's 'The Tempest,'" *New York Daily News*, January 16, 2012.

ticular ethnic group; (4) Advocate ethnic solidarity instead of the treatment of pupils as individuals.

If history is any guide, banned books usually become more popular among those who were told not to read them. The Roman Catholic Church's *Index Librorum Prohibitorum* (List of Prohibited Books), the Nazis' book-burning campaign of 1933, and the Soviet Union's censorship by the Goskomizdat agency failed to curb the human mind's quest for free thought.

— Does the Arizona book ban undermine freedom of thought, no matter how repulsive that thought might be? Does freedom of expression mean that individuals have the right to hold abhorrent ideas such as denying that the Holocaust existed, or that blacks and Latino/as are inferior people (e.g., *The Bell Curve*, by Richard J. Herrnstein and Charles Murray), or that protesting an unequal and immoral distribution of resources amounts to class warfare? If so, why? If not, which books and ideas can or cannot be taught?

— Does a school district have a right to include books such as the Bible, the Quran, *Mein Kampf*, and *Nat Turner's Diary* on a school reading list? Must all works and perspectives be included, especially contrary views, if enlightenment is truly sought? Does humanity flourish when no book is banned? Is the banning of any book, no matter how detestable it may be, a return to a darker age?

— Is Arizona's law an appeal to xenophobic and nativist sentiments that can help neoconservatives win elections? Can Hispanic reality be ignored just because the state legislature passes a law?

2. Erika Medina, Miguel Puente, and Rita Garcia were turned down for admission to California Polytechnic in San Luis Obispo, California. They since have sued the state university, contending that its admission system illegally discriminated against students of color by giving undue weight to SAT scores. Their case, however, was dismissed, and in 2005 the Court of Appeals affirmed the dismissal. Nevertheless, the lawsuit is based on the claim that California laws prohibit discrimination by institutions that receive state funds. The plaintiffs insisted that SAT scores are being used as a means by which students of color are denied higher education.[39] The SAT is widely accepted as a measure of scholastic achievement or merit. Each question is carefully pretested by the Educational Testing Service (ETS), and as a result, testers can determine in advance how

---

39. Peter Y. Hong, "Lawsuit Accuses University of Admissions Bias," *Los Angeles Times*, January 9, 2004.

members of one ethnic group will fare on any particular question. Whites consistently pick the correct answer to some questions; on other questions, minorities perform better. Yet according to Jay Rosner, executive director of the Princeton Review Foundation, the only questions that appear on SAT exams are the white-preference questions.

In an article published in the *Harvard Educational Review* in the spring of 2003, a former ETS researcher, Roy Freedle, maintained that black students often performed better on harder verbal questions than whites because words used in common vocabulary are understood differently by members of different racial/ethnic groups. Yet these harder questions were not incorporated into SAT exams; in fact, every one of the 138 questions on the 2000 SAT exam favored white students, with not one of the pretested questions favoring minority students appearing.[40] As could be expected, Freedle's findings received extensive media attention and an onslaught of criticism from ETS experts. Nevertheless, in 2010 Maria Veronica Santelices and Mark Wilson, replicating and updating Freedle's methodology with more recent SAT datasets, confirmed that the SAT does indeed function differently for African American and white subgroups in the verbal test. In their own words, "The SAT, a high-stakes test with significant consequences for the educational opportunities to young people in the United States, favors one ethnic group over another" (Santelices and Wilson 2010, 106, 126). Do merit-based scholarships, determined in most states by SAT scores, discriminate against Latino/a and black students? Against poorer students? If so, should SAT scores be the means of determining merit?

— Do Erika Medina, Miguel Puente, and Rita Garcia have a case against California Polytechnic? Why or why not? What would be an ethical way to determine admission to state colleges that are funded by the state taxpayers to serve all citizens of that state?

— What about economically privileged students who can afford tutors who help them improve scores? For example, in the Hamptons, New York, tutors rent $10,000 to $15,000 "shacks" for two summer months to tutor the privileged at $200 to $400 an hour.[41] Should the

---

40. Jeffrey R. Young, "Researchers Charge Racial Bias on the SAT," *Chronicle of Higher Education*, October 10, 2003. A question chosen for the SAT favors white students because of how "reliability" is defined by the test designers. A question intended to be difficult is considered reliable if those who score highest consistently do well on the exam, and those who score low on that particular question consistently do poorly on the exam. Thus, the highest achievers among test-takers, who historically have been white students, set the standards. Questions on which they do well become, by definition, reliable, and questions on which they do poorly become unreliable and thus are eliminated from consideration, even though students of color may score higher.

41. Jenny Anderson, "A Hamptons Summer: Surfing, Horses and Hours of SAT Prep," *New York Times*, August 14, 2012.

marketplace determine how students do on their SATs, or should there be a move toward creating a more level playing field?

3. During the 2012 race for a U.S. Senate seat in Massachusetts between Democrat Elizabeth Warren and Republican Scott Brown, it came to light that Warren, who taught at several law schools, including Harvard's, for several years had listed herself in a legal directory as having Native American ancestry. She did not. During a time when Harvard was under pressure to diversify, it appears as if she benefited from what she claimed was a belief held based on family lore.

— Should Warren be held accountable if it is proven that she is not of Native American ancestry? If so, how could she be held accountable?

— If "passing" as a minority assists a white person in getting a job or admission into a school, should that person provide misinformation if he or she believes that affirmative action is morally wrong?

Chapter 15

War on Women

Step 1. Observing

In 2012 the House Oversight and Government Reform Committee was debating if insurance plans should contain a mandate for covering the cost of contraceptives.[1] One of the scheduled speakers, Sandra Fluke, a Georgetown University law student, was not allowed to testify by the Republicans on the committee. She instead later testified before Democratic members. Rather than debating her assertions, radio personality Rush Limbaugh labeled her a promiscuous "anti-Catholic plant" and called her a "prostitute." According to Limbaugh, Fluke is a "slut" who "wants to be paid for sex." Fluke, Limbaugh said, is "having so much sex, it's amazing she can still walk." Confusing contraceptives with Viagra (which is covered by most insurance policies), Limbaugh accused Fluke of "having sex so frequently that she can't afford all the birth-control pills that she needs."[2] It seems that whenever so-called uppity women refuse to stay in their places, men attempt to shame them into silence, at times by using misinformation as though it were fact.

During the 2012 election, we learned from Missourian senatorial candidate Todd Akin that "legitimate" rape does not result in pregnancy because "the female body has a way to try to shut that whole thing down." And while many conservatives from Akin's own party rejected and rebuffed his understanding of rape, it was still disturbing that some supported him, specifically the Family Research Council (FRC)—the political arm of Focus on the Family. Connie Mackey, the president of FRC Action PAC, released a statement stating, "We support [Akin] fully and completely."[3]

Akin was not the only politician during the 2012 election cycle holding views that most women and many men found offensive. Richard Mourdock, candidate for a U.S. Senate seat in Indiana, while discussing why he opposed abortion, even in case of rape or incest, said, "I think even if life begins in that horrible situation of rape, that it is something that God intended to happen."[4] Another U.S. Senate candidate, Tom Smith of

---

1. This chapter includes discussion of sexual assault, rape, and other forms of violence against women; thus, be aware of potential triggering language.
2. Brian Stelter, "Limbaugh Apologizes for Attack on Student in Birth Control Furor," *New York Times*, March 3, 2012.
3. Rosalind S. Helderman, "A Todd Akin Defense," *Washington Post*, August 20, 2012.
4. Annie Groer, "Indiana GOP Senate Hopeful Richard Mourdock Says God 'Intended' Rape Pregnancies," *Washington Post*, October 24, 2012.

Pennsylvania, compared pregnancy due to rape with "having a baby out of wedlock."[5] These insensitive gaffes made about issues that primarily concern women (although these issues should concern all people) were prevalent during the 2012 election. But the end of the election did not end the ignorance and misconceptions on the part of some male and even female politicians as to how a woman's body operates.

Celeste Greig, president of the conservative California Republican Assembly, told the *San Jose Mercury News* that pregnancies by rape are rare "because it's an act of violence, because the body is traumatized."[6] Another example came from Arizona representative Trent Franks (R-AZ), who during a July 2013 House Judiciary Committee meeting that was considering banning abortions after twenty weeks of pregnancy, argued against a Democratic amendment to make exceptions for rape and incest. According to Franks, pregnancy from rape is rare. He said, "Before, when my friends on the left side of the aisle here tried to make rape and incest the subject—because, you know, the incidences of rape resulting in pregnancy are very low."[7]

It is important to note and make abundantly clear that there exists no scientific evidence whatsoever that those who are victims of rape or incest are less likely to become pregnant—quite the contrary. A St. Lawrence University study published in 2003 concluded that because women do not plan on being sexually assaulted, pregnancy resulting from rape occurs at significantly higher levels than it does in other cases (Gottschall and Gottschall 2003, 1). A 2011 San Francisco State University study conducted in Colombia confirmed that young women who experienced sexual violence resulted in significantly higher levels of unintended pregnancies (Gómez 2011).

As troublesome as misogynist comments made by politicians and pundits against women are, more damning is the legislation that is proposed based on politicians' beliefs (in most cases their religious beliefs). This war on women can easily be mapped out by the political, economic, social, and traditional acts taken in multiple areas of daily life; however, due to limited space, this chapter will concentrate only on: (1) U.S. workplace opportunities (equal pay), (2) violence toward women (rape) within the United States, (3) control over American women's bodies (reproductive rights), and (4) the global manifestation of this war on women.

---

5. Christine Roberts, "Pennsylvania Senate Hopeful Says Pregnancy from Rape 'Similar' to 'Having Baby out of Wedlock,'" *New York Daily News*, August 27, 2012.

6. Steven Harmon, "Leader of California Republican Group Steps into Rape Pregnancy Controversy," *San Jose Mercury News*, March 1, 2013.

7. Aaron Blake, "GOP Congressman: Rate of Pregnancies from Rape Is Very Low," *Washington Post*, June 12, 2013.

Workplace Opportunities

Sexism has historically been the norm in the workplace. "Sexism" is the name given to social structures and systems in which the "actions, practices, and use of laws, rules and customs limit certain activities of one sex, but do not limit those same activities of other people of the other sex" (Shute 1981, 27). This becomes obvious when we compare the wages of women to those of men. Women (5.52 million) are twice as likely as men (2.3 million) to work in occupations that pay poverty wages. Even though women represented almost half (47 percent) of the U.S. labor force, in every work category and at every education level they were paid less than men (Hegewisch, Williams, and Harbin 2012, 6). On June 10, 2013, fifty years to the day since the Equal Pay Act was signed into law, women still earned an average wage ratio of 77 cents for every dollar earned by a man.[8] At our present rate of progress pay parity eventually will be achieved in the year 2057, almost a century after the law was originally passed (Dobuzinskis 2013, 1). Not surprisingly, women of color fared worse, with African American women making 64 cents for every dollar paid to a white man, and Latinas making 55 cents (National Partnership for Women and Family 2013a, 1; 2013b, 1). According to 2012 data from the U.S. Census Bureau, nearly 40 percent of all households headed by African American and Latina women live below the poverty level (National Partnership for Women and Family 2013a, 1; 2013b, 2).

Although the situation has improved for white women since the law was signed in 1963, at which time women earned 60 cents for every dollar a man made, the narrowing of the gap over the past half-century, according to the Council on Contemporary Families, had more to do with wage losses among men rather than wage gains among women. This continuing disparity, according to economist Stephanie Seguino, means that women must work for 52 years to earn what a man will make in 40 years.[9] Another way to calculate this disparity is: if the wage gap was eliminated, a full-time working woman would have enough for approximately (1) eighty-nine more weeks of food, (2) more than seven months of mortgage and utilities payments, (3) more than a year of rent, or (4) more than three thousand additional gallons of gasoline (Hegewisch and Matite 2013, 1).

Most of the progress made in income parity occurred among single women, making a woman with children the greatest predictor of wage inequality. Mothers earn 5 percent less per hour per child than comparable childless women and are less likely to be hired (Hegewisch and Matite 2013,

---

8. The wage gap, according to the U.S. Census Bureau, differs from state to state, with Wyoming paying women the least, at 67 cents for every dollar made by a man, and Vermont paying the most, at 87 cents for every dollar paid to a man (Hegewisch and Matite 2013, 1).

9. Stephanie Coontz, "Progress at Work, but Mothers Still Pay a Price," *New York Times*, June 8, 2013.

1). This becomes especially problematic when we consider that 40 percent of all households in 2013 with children under the age of eighteen include mothers who are either the primary source or the sole source of income for the family, an increase from 11 percent in 1960. While 5.1 million (37 percent) of these mothers are married with higher incomes than their husband, the vast majority, 8.6 million (63 percent), are single mothers with an annual median family income of $23,000. These single mothers are more likely to be Latina or black and less likely to have a college degree (Wang, Parker, and Taylor 2013, 1).

When we consider only white-collar employment, women fare no better. The median wage of female managers in 2012 was 73 percent of what male managers earned. A Catalyst survey revealed that female MBAs received on average $4,600 less in wages than male MBAs' starting salaries, a trend that continues throughout their career as they witness men outpace them in salary and rank growth even if the women remained childless. Among the one thousand top Fortune 500 companies, only 4 percent of CEOs are women. The highest-paid female CEO is Marissa Mayer of Yahoo, who in 2012 earned $36.6 million. Compare this to the highest-paid male CEO, Lawrence J. Ellison of Oracle, who made $96.2 million.[10]

Studies also indicate that as an occupation becomes more dominated by women (e.g., social workers and primary school teachers), wages for those jobs begin to decline when compared with similar job skills associated with occupations dominated by men.[11] Women can also expect to be among the last hired. According to John Challenger, CEO of a Chicago-based global outplacement firm, men snagged three out of every four of the 2.4 million new jobs created between 2009 and 2012, leading him to nickname the recovery from the 2008 Great Recession as the "he-covery" or "mancovery." The threat of a continuing mancovery is that gains that women made in the workplace could be reversed, as occurred in the 1940s, when men returning from war pushed women out of jobs.[12]

Disparity does not exist solely with wages and recovery hires. When it comes to health insurance, women can expect to continue paying more for the same health coverage as men, even though the new healthcare laws known as Obamacare prohibit such "gender rating" starting in 2014. The gap will persist in most states, with no indication that insurance companies will take action to reduce the gap. For example, in 2012 a thirty-year-old woman in Chicago can expect to pay 31 percent more than a man of similar age for the same coverage ($375 a month versus $258.75). A forty-year-old

10. "The Unstoppable Climb in C.E.O. Pay," *New York Times*, June 30, 2013.
11. Stephanie Coontz, "The Myth of Male Decline," *New York Times*, September 30, 2012.
12. Aldo Svaldi, "Men Winning More Jobs Than Women in Economic Recovery," *Denver Post*, August 10, 2012.

nonsmoking woman in Louisville, Kentucky, can expect to pay 53 percent more for the same coverage as a nonsmoking man of the same age ($196 a month versus $128). In Arkansas a twenty-five-year-old woman can expect to pay 81 percent more than a man, even though a similar plan in the same state, but with a different company, charges women only 10 percent more. Maternity cost does not explain the rate differential, because it seldom is included as part of the standard package; rather, it is covered as an optional benefit with a hefty additional premium, also known as an insurance rider.[13]

Discrimination against women, especially in the workplace, has been based on the popular adage that women could not be fulfilled wives and successful mothers while pursuing a career. In 1962 psychiatrists maintained that "normal" women renounced aspirations outside the home so as to meet their feminine need for dependence—a view that two-thirds of Americans, according to a University of Michigan survey at the time, agreed with. The survey revealed that the most important family decisions "should be made by the man of the house."[14]

Since then, a revolution of attitudes concerning women in the home and workplace took place. Consider that in 1977 two-thirds of Americans believed that it was "better for everyone involved if the man is the achiever outside the home and the woman takes care of the home and family"; but by 1994, two-thirds of Americans rejected this notion. And yet this 1994 trend of thinking began to reverse. From 1994 to 2004, the model of male breadwinner and female homemaker rose in popularity among Americans from 34 percent to 40 percent. From 1997 to 2007, the number of full-time working mothers who would have preferred to stay at home increased to 60 percent from 48 percent.[15]

The historical patriarchal assumption that women's domain is within the domestic sphere while men are charged with being the primary breadwinners continues to be challenged in today's age. And yet 28 percent of Americans believe that it is worse for marriages if wives earn more than husbands. Economists discovered that wives with higher education and possible better earning potential are less likely to work.[16] The economic challenges that women face in the workplace (e.g., lack of paid paternity leave and minimal maternity leave) are forms of institutional violence. Unfortunately, they also face physical violence.

13. Robert Pear, "Gender Gap Persists in Cost of Health Insurance," *New York Times*, March 19, 2012.

14. Stephanie Coontz, "Why Gender Equality Stalled," *New York Times*, February 17, 2013.

15. Ibid.

16. Catherine Rampell, "U.S. Women on the Rise as Family Breadwinners," *New York Times*, May 29, 2013.

Violence against Women

On average, more than four women a day are murdered by their husbands or boyfriends in the United States (Catalano et al. 2009, 2–3), with one out of every four women experiencing violence at the hands of their boyfriend or spouse (current or former)—some two million injuries from intimate partners each year (Centers for Disease Control and Prevention 2008, 113–17), and one in fifty experiencing stalking victimizations (Baum et al. 2009, 3). Black women were four times more likely than white women to die at the hands of a boyfriend (Catalano et al. 2009, 3). Homicide is the second leading cause of traumatic death for pregnant women, accounting for 31 percent of maternal injury death, with black women experiencing seven times more fatalities when pregnant than white women (Chang et al. 2005).

According to one statistic, about five hundred rapes occur per day in the United States (Rand 2008, 1). One in six U.S. women have, at some time, experienced an attempted or completed rape, with more than 300,000 women being "forcibly"[17] raped and more than 4 million being assaulted—(Foshee et al. 1996). All women are at risk of abuse, but those experiencing the highest rate of rape or sexual abuse are women between the ages of twenty and twenty-four (Rand 2008, 4). Native American women experience the highest rates of violence at the hands of their partners (Catalano 2007, 12–13). Violence, specifically sexual violence, all too often occurs early, before adulthood is reached. The second-highest age range for women who experience sexual assault or rape are those between sixteen and nineteen years old (Rand 2008, 4). In the graduating U.S. high school class of 2013, 28 percent of the students have survived some sort of sexual assault, 10 percent are survivors of dating violence in the past year, and 10 percent are survivors of rape (Murphey 2013, 1–2). And yet according to the U.S. Department of Justice, only three out of every one hundred rapists ever serve prison time (Cohen and Kyckelhahn 2006, 3).

Violence is the means by which control is maintained over the conduct, thoughts, beliefs, and actions of the Other, specifically women. The possibility of violence is sufficient for the one abused to docilely obey. The internalization of power teaches those who are abused to police themselves. As a form of survival or self-preservation, the one on the receiving end of the violence (more often than not women, but also girls and boys) learns to behave in the appropriate manner—a manner that reinforces her status of imposed inferiority. Self-disciplining leads to justifying one's oppression ("I deserved to be punished"), thus undermining one's sense of self-worth and dignity, which is crucial for the development of well-adjusted personhood.

---

17. Although all rapes are, in a sense, forcible, making the usage of this adjective troublesome, it is used nonetheless so as to remain faithful to the legal distinction used in the data collection.

One common form of violence that usually is categorized as benign by men is sexual harassment. Sexual harassment occurs whenever sexual favors are demanded to ensure professional and/or economic gain or when refusing to provide sexual favors threatens one's professional and/or economic security. Sexual harassment is not limited to physical violence; it also encompasses economic deprivation, intentional degradation, public humiliation, spiritual manipulation, and verbal intimidation. The abuse of women, whether it is manifested physically, sexually, spiritually, or psychologically, and whether committed by a family member, acquaintance, or total stranger, is first and foremost about power. Sexual harassment and/or violence (even in the case of rape) have nothing to do with sex, even though sex becomes the means by which power is enhanced.

We should recognize that sexual abuse encompasses more than harassment carried out by economically powerful men against women in their employ. Sexual abuse is also a threat to wives and young children, prostitutes and prison inmates, college students, the elderly and young teenagers, and it crosses all economic, gender, orientation, and racial lines. And while all men are not sexual predators, almost all women have experienced sexual harassment at least once. Although a thorough and comprehensive analysis of violence toward women in the workplace could prove productive, for the purposes of this chapter we will focus on just one institution, the military forces of the United States.

The acceptance of women within the military has been resisted by many means, perhaps most disturbingly by sexual assault. That warriors rape women is nothing new. The U.S. liberators (known as the greatest generation) who landed in Normandy on D-Day to oust the Nazis instituted their own "regime of terror." According to historian Mary Louise Roberts's archival research, soldiers were "sold" on the invasion by its portrayal of an erotic adventure among oversexed Frenchwomen. But the so-called adventure was an excuse to unleash a "tsunami of male lust" (2013, 9). According to Roberts,

> Rape posed an even greater threat to the myth of the American mission as sexual romance. In the summer of 1944, Norman women launched a wave of rape accusations against American soldiers, threatening to destroy the erotic fantasy at the heart of the operation. The specter of rape transformed the GI from rescue-warrior to violent intruder. Forced to confront the sexual excess incited by its own propaganda, the army responded not by admitting the full range of the problem, but by scapegoating African American soldiers as the primary perpetrators of the rapes. (2013, 10)

Sexual assault remains part of a military culture of sexual violence; only now, female military personnel are the targets.[18] According to a Pentagon report, some twenty-six thousand service members were sexually assaulted in 2012, a 35 percent increase since 2010.

The climate of fear reigning in the military branches led then defense secretary Leon Panetta to acknowledge that the number of sexual assaults probably is far higher in the military than what official statistics show. The Defense Department believes that one in three women in the military has been sexually assaulted, compared to one in six civilian women. About 20 percent of female soldiers who served in Iraq and Afghanistan experienced a sexual assault. And yet only 3,374 in 2012 reported their abuse, likely due to the fact that fewer than one in ten sexual assault reports results in court-martial convictions (U.S. Department of Defense 2012, 3, 12, 71). For a woman to come forward with an accusation can be a career-ender; worse yet the victim could face administrative retribution and reprisals, especially given that reports are handled within the military chain of command. A woman choosing to report an assault or abuse within the military is very often forced to continue to serve under the command of her assailant. Not surprisingly, many refuse to report their abuse. And if they do report their rape, as did Sergeant Kimberly Davis, it usually is covered up, at times by the officer assigned to the case, leading her to conclude, "The sexual assault program in the Air Force is a joke."[19]

Tragically, two days after the 2012 Pentagon report on sexual violence was released, Lieutenant Colonel Jeffrey Keusinski, the officer responsible for the Air Force's sexual assault prevention programs, was arrested and charged with sexual battery. A couple of weeks later, Sergeant Michael McClendon of the U.S. Military Academy at West Point was accused of videotaping female cadets, without their consent, as they showered or undressed in the bathroom.[20] Senator Susan Collins (R-ME) probably said it best: "If I were a parent with a daughter who is thinking of going into the military today, I would think twice about whether the environment is safe for her, not from the enemy, but from sexual assault from her fellow military members."[21]

---

18. The focus here will remain on women, but it should be recognized that men too are victims of sexual violence. According to a Pentagon report, 6.1 percent of active women in the military and 1.2 percent of active men experienced sexual assault in 2012, an increase over the 2010 report, which documented that 4.4 percent of women and less than 0.9 percent of men experienced sexual assault. Because men represent the largest proportion of armed service personal (85 percent), the majority of the twenty-six thousand service members who experienced unwanted sexual contact were men (U.S. Department of Defense 2012, 2).

19. James Risen, "Military Has Not Solved Problem of Sexual Assault, Women Say," *New York Times*, November 2, 2012; idem, "Air Force Leaders Testify on Culture That Led to Sexual Assaults of Recruits," *New York Times*, January 24, 2013.

20. Thom Shanker, "Women Were Secretly Filmed at West Point, the Army Says," *New York Times*, May 22, 2013.

21. Jennifer Steinhauer, "Sexual Assaults in Military Raise Alarm in Washington," *New York Times*, May 7, 2013; idem, "Military Courts Are Called Outdated on Sex Crimes," *New York Times*, May 8, 2012.

Sexual assault is not restricted to the military. According to the U.S. Department of Justice, 8 percent of all rapes occur at the workplace (Duhart 2001, 1–2). But a violent attack at work is not the only way a woman suffers while on the job; many times she is held responsible for what occurs during her off hours. At times society, especially religious institutions, tends to "blame the victim" who suffers physical abuse. Take the example of Carie Charlesworth, a second-grade teacher in El Cajo, California. Following a domestic-violence incident involving her ex-husband, Holy Trinity School, where she worked, fired her. Although she did nothing wrong in the classroom, her school district viewed her as a liability and thus, due to the domestic-violence dispute, too unsafe to have around. Diocesan officials are concerned about her ex-husband's "threatening and menacing behavior," and as a result they will not allow her to teach. Charlesworth, the one who was abused, is punished with loss of employment by the religious institution for which she worked.[22]

Other times, a woman is punished for whom she loves. Take the example of Carla Hale, who was fired as a teacher from Bishop Watterson High School. When her mother passed away, the obituary noted that the survivors included Hale and her partner. As a result, the Roman Catholic Diocese of Columbus fired her for being in a committed, loving, same-gender relationship. Although, according to Bishop Frederick Campbell, Hale was fired on "moral issues," she maintained, "I've never thought my sexual orientation is a sin."[23] Women who leave their relegated domestic space of the household have faced, and continue to experience, all forms of abuse solely because they are seen as invading the male public domain.

Control over Women's Bodies

A study conducted by the Guttmacher Institute reveals that issues related to reproductive health and rights received unprecedented attention in 2011 at the state level. State legislators in all fifty states introduced more than 1,100 reproductive health- and rights-related provisions, a sharp increase from the 950 in 2010. By year's end, 135 of these provisions had been enacted in thirty-six states, an increase from the 89 enacted in 2010 and the 77 enacted in 2009 (Guttmacher Institute 2012, 1). By 2012, an additional 43 provisions were enacted in nineteen states (Guttmacher Institute 2013, 1). When can heartfelt opposition to abortion on moral and ethical grounds be separated from a larger campaign to assert control over women's sexual lives?

---

22. Steven Luke, "San Diego Domestic Violence Victim Fired from Teaching," *NBC7 San Diego*, June 13, 2013.

23. Denise Yost, "Hale: 'I've Never Thought My Sexual Orientation Is a Sin,'" *NBC4 Columbus*, May 24, 2013.

For many politicians, the present strategy seems to be to incrementally narrow abortion rights on the state level (where Republicans gained control of many legislatures) until a sympathetic Supreme Court is in place that can overturn *Roe v. Wade*. For example, as of 2012 twenty-six states require a waiting period for a woman seeking an abortion; thirty-five states require mandatory counseling; three states established stringent regulations that affect abortion providers, but not other providers of outpatient surgical and medical care;[24] three states require abortion providers to have hospital admitting privileges, but not other providers of outpatient surgical and medical care;[25] and eight states mandate invasive ultrasound prior to having an abortion.[26] Attempts have been made in several states either to declare legally that life begins at conception or to grant human rights to embryos as a pathway to legally overturn abortion.

By 2012, ten states had banned abortion at or beyond twenty weeks' gestation. In 2013 Texas joined these states by also banning abortions after twenty weeks. Furthermore, Texas now holds abortion clinics to the same standards as hospital-style surgical centers. Although supporters claimed that the new regulations on abortion clinics were put in place to provide better health protection for women, opponents argued that the stringent restrictions were designed to place an exorbitant financial burden on these clinics in the hopes of shutting them down.[27]

The most restrictive bans, and strongest challenges to *Roe v. Wade*, were passed in North Dakota, calling for a ban on abortions after six weeks, when a fetal heartbeat can first be detected using a transvaginal probe, and in Arkansas, calling for a ban at twelve weeks, when the fetal heartbeat can be detected with an abdominal ultrasound.[28] On May 21, 2013, a federal appellate court panel struck down Arizona's abortion ban, claiming that it was unconstitutional "under a long line of invariant Supreme Court precedents" that guarantee a woman's right to end a pregnancy any time before a fetus is deemed viable outside her womb, generally at twenty-four weeks.[29] By July 22, 2013, a federal judge blocked the enforcement of North Dakota's ban calling it "invalid and unconstitutional."[30]

---

24. Arizona, Michigan, Virginia.
25. Arizona, Mississippi, Tennessee. The Mississippi law closes down the state's only remaining abortion clinic, which relies on traveling doctors.
26. Alabama, Arizona, Florida, Kansas, Louisiana, Mississippi, Texas, Virginia.
27. John Schwartz, "Texas Senate Approves Strict Abortion Measure," *New York Times*, July 14, 2013.
28. Erik Eckholm, "Arkansas Passes a 12-Week Limit in Abortion Law," *New York Times*, March 7, 2013.
29. Fernanda Santos, "Arizona Law Struck Down as Restricted," *New York Times*, May 22, 2013.
30. Erik Eckholm, "Abortion Restrictions Go Too Far, Judge Rules," *New York Times*, July 23, 2013

Within twenty-four hours, Congressional House Republicans proposed federal legislation that would ban all abortions after twenty weeks' gestation (the twenty-second week of pregnancy).[31] After the bill, the Pain-Capable Unborn Child Protection Act was approved by the House Judiciary Committee in June 2013 along party lines (20-12); it was passed by the House that same month, mainly along party lines (228-196).[32] In an attempt to frame the conversation, bill supporter Kristi Noem (R-SD) proclaimed, "I'm not waging a war on anyone."[33]

Of course, not all opponents of abortion are engaged in a war on women, but this is not the first time the House has tried to pass legislation that abortion rights supporters argue would endanger the lives of women.[34] In 2011 the House attempted to allow hospitals receiving federal funds from refusing to perform emergency abortions even when the life of the mother was at stake.[35] Regardless of one's view on abortion, the political system seems to be moving toward a stance that the reproductive organs of women must be regulated by the government (if not state, then federal), the majority of whose legislators are men.

Similar struggles have taken place around sex education and the availability of birth control. A woman who is sexually active but is not using contraception has an 85 percent chance of becoming pregnant within a year (Trussell 2011, 398). Nearly one in five female teenagers who are at risk for an unintended pregnancy were not using any method of contraception during their last intercourse (Mosher and Jones 2010, 7, 22). Eighty-two percent of teen pregnancies were unplanned, accounting for one-fifth of all unintended annual pregnancies (Finer and Zolna 2011, 478). Of all these teen pregnancies, 17.8 percent ended with an abortion, the lowest since abortion was legalized (Kost and Henshaw 2012, 2, 7).

The 2008 rate of 68 pregnancies per 1,000 teens represented a 42 percent decline from 117 per 1,000 since 1990 (Kost and Henshaw 2012, 3). The

---

31. "House Republicans, Taking on Own Leaders, Promote Legislation to Ban Abortion after 20 Weeks," *Washington Post*, May 22, 2013.

32. Jeremy W. Peters, "House Panel Advances Bill to Restrict Abortions," *New York Times*, June 13, 2013; idem, "Unfazed by 2012, G.O.P. Is Seeking Abortion Limits," *New York Times*, June 18, 2013. It should be noted that because Democrats control the Senate and the White House, the bill had no chance of becoming law; nevertheless, its purpose was to satisfy a vocal constituency of the Republican base. Also, Republican-controlled legislatures in Arkansas and North Dakota already passed more restrictive bans on abortions, while South Carolina, Texas, and Wisconsin are considering bans similar to the one proposed by the U.S. House.

33. Jeremy W. Peters, "In Partisan Vote, House Approves Ban on Abortions after 22 Weeks," *New York Times*, June 19, 2013.

34. Abortion rights supporters argue that women's lives are endangered not only by the difficulty, if not the refusal, to perform medically necessary terminations to save the lives of women, but also by the lack of safeguards for women who would resort to unsafe solutions if they are unable to access safe and legal abortions.

35. "The Campaign against Women," *New York Times*, May 19, 2012.

main reason for this decline (86 percent) was due to improved contraceptive use among teenagers; the rest was due to teenagers deciding to delay sexual activity (Santelli et al. 2007, 150). Despite this decline, the United States continues to have one of the highest rates of teen pregnancy among industrial nations (McKay and Barrett 2010, 45–46, 49–50). And yet proponents of sex education note that those most opposed to abortion are also usually opposed to the availability of contraceptives and sex education.

Title X, the main federal family planning program created in 1970 with the support of Republican president Richard Nixon and Congressman George H. W. Bush, does not pay for abortions. A 2009 Congressional Research Service report cited Title X with preventing nearly a million annual unintended pregnancies. Experts also estimate that Title X helps prevent about four hundred thousand abortions a year. The majority of Title X's funds also provide about five million women, especially poor women, with life-saving cervical and breast cancer screening, HIV and STD testing, adolescent abstinence counseling, and infertility counseling. Some of its funds cover birth control. About a quarter of Title X's $300 million budget went to Planned Parenthood, which serviced about a third of Title X's patients in 2011.[36]

For example, the poor women of San Carlos, an impoverished town in southern Texas, have relied on Planned Parenthood to obtain breast cancer screenings, free birth control pills, and pap smears for cervical cancer. Maria Romero, a housecleaner with four children, is one of those women. Before the clinic closed in the fall of 2011, a lump was discovered in her breast. The San Carlos clinic closed, along with over a dozen others throughout the state, when financing for women's health was slashed by the state's Republican-controlled legislature by about two-thirds. Some four hundred thousand women, including Maria Romero, were left without services. The next-closest clinic to Romero is in Edinburg, sixteen miles away. She has no means by which to get there, and even if she did, the wait time for an appointment is four weeks. To make matters worse, she cannot afford the $20 for a monthly supply of birth control tablets, which she previously obtained for free. Ironically, even though none of these clinics performed abortions, the supporters of the cutbacks were motivated mainly by their opposition to abortion. Governor Rick Perry rejected receipt of $35 million in federal funds that would have financed women's health programs in order to ensure that Planned Parenthood received none of those funds. Other states are following Texas's lead in one way or another.[37] But these tactics are not limited to the

---

36. Pam Belluck and Emily Ramshaw, "Women in Texas Losing Options for Health Care," *New York Times*, March 8, 2012. It should be noted that Presidents Truman, Eisenhower, and Johnson served as honorary co-chairmen of the fundraising committee of Planned Parenthood.

37. Since 2011, Kansas, Indiana, New Hampshire, North Carolina, and Wisconsin have tried to

state level. Since 2011, the Republican-controlled House of Representatives has attempted to pass legislation that would have eliminated all funding for Title X, mainly because of its connection to Planned Parenthood.[38]

Additionally, seven states moved to disqualify family planning providers from eligibility for funding.[39] Two states in 2012 added new restrictions,[40] effectively barring family planning clinics not operated by health departments from being eligible for grant funds. Even though new private health plans that are written on or after August 1, 2012, are mandated to cover contraceptive counseling and services with no out-of-pocket costs to patients, twenty states allow certain employers and insurers to refuse compliance with the mandate. Finally, five states since 2010 have enacted legislation concerning sex education; all but one supported abstinence-only education. By 2013, twenty-six states stressed abstinence in sex education (Guttmacher Institute 2013, 1).

The opposition to contraceptives by religious organizations can be noted by the 2012 actions of thirteen Roman Catholic dioceses, evangelicals, Mennonites, several related religious groups, and some private corporations (i.e., Hobby Lobby) that filed more than forty-five lawsuits across a dozen federal courts claiming that the inclusion of contraceptives in basic healthcare coverage was a violation of their religious freedoms (though the contraception-coverage mandate does exempt houses of worship).[41] But should religiously affiliated organizations (hospitals, schools, charities) that believe that the use of contraceptives is a sin be forced to provide them via their insurance coverage to their female employees? A study conducted by the *American Journal of Obstetrics and Gynecology* discovered that besides abortion restrictions, the most frequent issues associated with religiously affiliated hospitals revolve around the lack of birth control and sterilization for women seeking it after giving birth.[42] This raises some interesting questions. Are religious hospitals imposing their religion upon women's bodies, or are they simply being faithful to their convictions? Can a pharmacy refuse to fill contraceptive medication because the pharmacist's personal convictions consider its usage to be a sin?

David Green, founder of Hobby Lobby, who pays his employees almost twice the minimum wage, forsakes profits on the Sabbath, and provides comprehensive health insurance, has no objection to covering contraception, but he considers the "morning-after pill" to be an abortion-inducing procedure. Green, who considers himself a conscientious Christian capitalist, believes

stop family planning and cancer screening funds.

38. Pam Belluck and Emily Ramshaw, "Women in Texas Losing Options for Health Care," *New York Times*, March 8, 2012.

39. Kansas, Wisconsin, North Carolina, New Hampshire, Tennessee, Indiana, Texas.

40. Arizona, North Carolina.

41. "The Politics of Religion," *New York Times*, May 27, 2012.

42. Julie Rover, "When Religious Rules and Women's Health Collide," *NPR News*, May 8, 2012.

that the morning-after pill is irreconcilable with the Christian principles upon which he operates his company. If Green adheres to his conscience and does not cover the morning-after pill, he could eventually face a fine of $1.3 million a day.[43] But can a corporation have a soul? If the Supreme Court ruled in the *Citizens United* case that corporations are protected by the First Amendment's freedom-of-speech clause, then does the First Amendment's freedom-of-religion clause also protect the corporation's conscience? After all, the First Amendment allows churches and religious organizations to preach and speak against the use of contraceptives, declaring it to be a sin. Still, in a 1990 decision Justice Scalia wrote that to make "the professed doctrines of religious beliefs superior to the law of the land [would allow] every citizen to become a law unto himself. Government [w]ould exist only in name under such circumstances."[44]

When the Obama administration declined to renew the contract with the U.S. Conference of Catholic Bishops to aid victims of human sex trafficking, the administration was charged for being anti-Catholic. The contract, however, lost renewal because the bishops required its subcontractors not to use federal monies to pay for contraceptives and abortion referrals and services, thus failing in the government's eyes to meet the needs of those who were sexually abused.[45] Furthermore, according to federal district court judge Richard Stearns, the bishops' requirements violate the First Amendment because they impose religion-based restrictions on the use of taxpayer dollars.[46]

Global Sexism

The phenomenon of the oppression of women, which is based on male supremacy, is a problem not only in the United States, but also globally. The danger when making comparisons between the United States and other cultures is the tendency to conclude that "our" sexism is not as bad as "theirs," and that "our" women are treated better than "theirs." Although the concern of making the racial or ethnic Other more misogynist exists, the fact still remains that other cultures and societies engage in their own wars on women. Although sexism may appear differently with varying degrees of oppression, we must avoid the temptation of ranking sexist acts in such a way that redeems Eurocentric expressions as not being so bad in comparison to

---

43. On June 28, 2013, U.S. district judge Joe Heaton ruled that Hobby Lobby would not be subjected to the $1.3 million in daily fines until its hearing scheduled for July of that year. See "Judge: Hobby Lobby Won't Have to Pay Fines," *NPR News*, June 28, 2013.

44. *Employment Division, Department of Human Resources of Oregon v. Smith.*

45. It should be noted that the Hyde Amendment bars the use of federal money for abortions except in the case of rape, incest, or when the life of the woman is endangered.

46. "Sex Trafficking and the First Amendment," *New York Times*, April 3, 2012.

those of Others. To the oppressed and repressed victims of the war on women, all forms of marginalization are damning.

Many may look in horror at the case of a twenty-three-year-old student in India who was so viciously gang raped in 2013 on a bus ride home from the movies that it led to her death two weeks later. Such stories reinforce some latent belief that those people "over there" are somewhat uncivilized, if not barbaric, all the while ignoring our own form of uncivilized and barbaric behavior. Consider another case, that of the Steubenville, Ohio, high school football players who on August 11, 2012, reportedly raped an unconscious sixteen-year-old girl as they lugged her from party to party. In both cases, the "victims were blamed." In a poll conducted in India, 68 percent of judges listed "provocative attire" as an "invitation to rape." Probably the most barbaric act of all is the failure of the U.S. Congress, as of this writing, to pass the International Violence against Women Act,[47] which would name and shame those countries that tolerate acts of violence toward women. Congress has also failed to pass the Trafficking Victims Protection Act.[48] As we turn our attention to the war on women overseas, it is important to remember that we in the United States are not necessarily on the side of women during the global war on them.[49]

That being said, we begin by recognizing that women around the world face life-threatening situations simply because they were born as women. Millions of women and girls worldwide suffer from some form of violence on a daily basis. Violence can manifest itself as rape, as sexual abuse, as a tool of repression in war-ravaged regions, as early arranged marriages, as dowry-related murder, as honor killing, as sex trafficking, as female infanticide, as female genital circumcision, and as acid attacks. The violence can be physical, but it also can be manifested verbally, economically, spiritually, and psychologically. Women from all cultures, all religious faiths, all economic strata, and all racial and ethnic groups are at risk of experiencing violence.

Violence against women is a common phenomenon. According to a 2013 briefing paper from the United Nations, one in five women throughout the world will become a victim of rape or attempted rape at some point in their lifetime; as many as 70 percent will experience violence sometime during their lives. Women subjected to sexual violence (according to the World Health Organization) ranges from 6 percent in Japan to 59 percent in Ethiopia. Half of all women worldwide who are victims of homicide are killed by

---

47. The International Violence Against Women Act (I-VAWA) is proposed legislation intended to address violence against women through the foreign policy of the United States, specifically by providing practices that prevent violence, protect victims, and prosecute offenders.

48. The Trafficking Victims Protection Act provides the U.S. government with the tools to combat worldwide and domestic trafficking of persons.

49. Nicholas D. Kristof, "Is Delhi So Different from Steubenville?" *New York Times*, January 13, 2013.

their current partner or husband. For example, in Australia, Canada, Israel, South Africa, and the United States it is estimated that 40 percent to 70 percent of female deaths by homicide came at the hands of their partner.[50] Fear of stigma prevents many women from reporting the violence that they face; hence, we can expect current data to underrepresent the situation. Rather than concentrating on the men who perpetuate this violence, the historical trend has been to "blame the victim."

Women, in the minds of some, are to blame for their victimization because of the way they dress (showing too much skin by wearing revealing clothes), because they drink alcoholic beverages, because they work outside the home, or because they entice men by flirtation (flirtation as perceived and defined by men). When women who participated in public protests in Tahrir Square spoke out in Cairo, Egypt, about their rapes, the police general and lawmaker Adel Abdel Maqsoud Afifi responded by stating, "Sometimes a girl contributes 100 percent to her own raping when she puts herself in these conditions." Sheik Abu Islam, a television cleric who is a political powerbroker responded, "You see those women speaking like ogres, without shame, politeness, fear or even femininity. . . . [Such a woman] is like a demon. . . . [They] went there to get raped."[51]

Women have always faced abuse at the hands of the military, as rape is used as an instrument of war. For example, during the military conflict in the Democratic Republic of Congo, some 1,100 rapes were reported each and every month. It is estimated that over 200,000 women suffered from sexual assault since the start of military conflict. The region of Darfur has also seen rape used as a military tactic. The Rwanda conflict of 1994 witnessed 250,000 to 500,000 rapes, while the Bosnia conflicts of the 1990s reported between 20,000 and 50,000 rapes.[52] In addition to rape as a tactic, women are forced into sex slavery. According to Toru Hashimoto, leader of a populist political party in Japan, sex slavery during war is a necessary evil. Referring to the usage of "comfort women" during World War II, he upheld the popular belief among many Japanese (including Prime Minister Shinzo Abe) that no evidence exists that women were forced to serve in brothels, thus ignoring the voices and testimonies of women from many countries who claimed to have been sexual slaves. Historians estimate that two hundred thousand women were rounded up to serve as "comfort women" by the Japanese imperial forces.[53]

50. U.N. Resources for Speakers on Global Issues, "Ending Violence against Women and Girls" (available at http://www.un.org).

51. Mayy El Sheikh and David D. Kirkpatrick, "Rise in Egypt Sex Assaults Sets Off Clash over Blame," *New York Times*, March 26, 2013.

52. U.N. Resources for Speakers on Global Issues, "Ending Violence against Women and Girls."

53. Hiroko Tabuchi, "Japanese Politicians Reframes Comments on Sex Slavery," *New York Times*, May 27, 2013.

Rape is not confined to war. The custom of early marriage (male adults marrying girls) is a common practice worldwide, especially in African and South Asian countries. Rape of children in these cases is masked under the term "marriage." Arranged marriages that are against the wishes of the bride are also a form of rape. More problematic is when such marriages end in the death of the wife. For example, dowry murder occurs predominantly in South Asia. In India a woman harassed for years by her husband and his relatives was finally kidnapped, raped, strangled, and tossed into a ditch. Her father, Subedar Akhileshar Kumar Singh, an army officer, has tried for over a year to have her husband arrested, but to no avail. He believes that she was killed by her in-laws, who were unsatisfied with her dowry. In India alone it is estimated that 25,000 to 100,000 women a year are killed over dowry disputes, many of whom are burned alive. One way to avoid paying a dowry is to have no daughters, accomplished by aborting female fetuses.[54]

Honor killings of women (as many as five thousand in 2012) occur when a family's honor has been damaged by premarital sex, the accusation of adultery of a woman or girl, or rape.[55] For a woman in Afghanistan to be alone with a man who is not her relative constitutes sufficient grounds for arrest on the charge of attempted adultery. Among those jailed for "moral crimes," based on the testimonies of their abusers, are Asma, who ran away from her husband after he beat her, threw boiling water on her, gave her a sexually transmitted disease, and announced his engagement to his mistress; fifteen-year-old Fawzia, who took refuge with a family that drugged her and forced her into prostitution; sixteen-year-old Farah, who eloped with her brother's friend; and Gulpari, also sixteen, who was kidnapped by a stalker who wanted to marry her.[56]

For a woman to choose her own spouse can be, in some regions, sufficient grounds for a death penalty. Take the example of Nusrat Mochi of Karachi, Pakistan. She ran away from home to marry a man of her own choosing rather than the husband, who is fifteen years her senior, selected by her parents. For four years her parents' wrath has trailed her, forcing Mochi and her husband to flee towns where they settled after receiving death threats. Mochi's parents are willing to call off the feud if her husband pays them $2,110 (he earns $2.11 a day).[57] Such threats are real when we consider what recently occurred to another couple, Almas Khan and Shamim Akhtar, who defied their parents

54. Gardiner Harris, "India's New Focus on Rape Shows Only the Surface of Women's Perils," *New York Times*, January 13, 2013.

55. U.N. Resources for Speakers on Global Issues, "Ending Violence against Women and Girls."

56. Rod Nordland, "Moral 'Crimes' Land Afghan Women in Jail," *New York Times*, March 29, 2013; Graham Bowley, "Afghan Prosecutor Faces Criticism for Her Pursuit of 'Moral Crimes,'" *New York Times*, December 29, 2012.

57. Meghan Davidson Ladly, "Defying Parents, Some Pakistani Women Risk All to Marry Whom They Choose," *New York Times*, September 12, 2012.

and married. They were killed over the Id al-Fitr weekend marking the end of Ramadan. They were lured back home with promises of forgiveness, then shot, and their bodies were strung up in trees.

Only through the death of these women can honor be restored to the family. Honor can be maintained by keeping women ignorant. In some places the desire of women to become educated (the first step toward any hope of liberation) is met with violence. Take the example of Malala Yousafzai, the fifteen-year-old Pakistani pupil who in October 2012 was shot point-blank in the head and neck by the Taliban in order to silence her. Her crime? Not only did she dare to defy the Taliban's ban against girls going to school, but also she was vocal about the rights of girls to an education. According to UNESCO, 66 million girls are out of school worldwide, many more than boys, who do not face the same discrimination and obstacles.[58] Six months after the attack on Malala Yousafzai, in June 2013, eleven students were killed and twenty wounded in a bomb blast on a Sardar Bahadur Khan Women's University bus in the city of Quetta, in western Pakistan. As the victims were taken to the hospital, gunmen appeared and continued the assault. The region has been experiencing a surge of militant violence by Islamist groups that oppose women's education.[59]

It is estimated that as many as 27 million men, women, and children around the world are the victims of human trafficking, of which 4.5 million are sexually exploited, an estimated 98 percent of whom are women and girls (U.S. Department of State 2012, 7, 45). One of those women forced into prostitution is Valentina, from Romania. She was promised a job in La Jonquera, Spain, working at a hotel. When she arrived, she was forced into prostitution. If she refused, the man who made the travel arrangements, whom she thought was her boyfriend, threatened to beat her and kill her children. She now spends her life, working from a roundabout, charging $40 for intercourse and $27 for oral sex. Valentina is one of the 200,000 to 400,000 trafficked women forced to work as prostitutes just in Spain.[60]

On the other side of the world, in China's Yunnan Province, women become a major export, shipped off by their families to the thriving sex businesses of Thailand or Malaysia to work in the brothels. Previously, these women used to be kidnapped and forced into sex slavery, but since 2005 the trade has become largely voluntary, motivated mainly by the poverty of Yunnan Province. If they stay at home, they become a liability, another mouth to feed; if they leave, they can provide their family with a relatively affluent lifestyle.[61]

---

58. Kyle Almond, "Malala's Global Voice Stronger Than Ever," *CNNWorld*, June 17, 2013.
59. "Pakistan Blast Kills Female Students," *BBC News*, June 15, 2013.
60. Suzanne Daley, "In Spain, Enslaved by a Boom in Brothel Tourism," *New York Times*, April 6, 2012.
61. Howard W. French, "A Village Grows Rich Off Its Main Export: Its Daughters," *New York Times*, January 5, 2005.

In the United States we have the case of thirteen-year-old Maria Elena, from a small village in Mexico. A family acquaintance assured her family that she could make ten times more money waiting tables in the United States. Maria Elena, along with other girls, was smuggled across the border, walking for four days through the desert. They finally arrived at a run-down trailer in Texas where they were forced into prostitution. Maria Elena was compelled to have sex with up to thirty men a day. When she got pregnant, she was forced to have an abortion and sent back to work the next day (U.S. Department of State 2012, 8).

Violence against females occurs early in the form of female infanticide, prenatal sex selection, and the systematic neglect of girls, a problem in South and East Asia, North Africa, and the Middle East. For some 3 million girls a year who survive infancy, the horror of genital mutilation awaits them. It is estimated that 100 to 140 million girls and women alive in 2013, mainly in Africa and some Middle Eastern countries, have undergone genital circumcision.[62] As these girls mature, they still face grave dangers if they rebuff the advances of a potential suitor or become the imaginary cause of a husband, lover, or boyfriend's jealousy. Afghanistan, Bangladesh, India, Pakistan, and more recently Colombia report acid attacks (throwing sulfuric or nitric acid into a woman's face to disfigure her) as a cheap and quick way of destroying a woman's life.[63]

As horrific as these global situations are, we would expect some worldwide outcry, some attempt by international institutions to band together in solidarity with the half of the world's population that faces life-threatening situations in the conduct of their daily activities. In March 2013 the work of the U.N. Commission on the Status of Women was hampered by delegates from Iran, Russia, and the Vatican who attempted to eliminate from the final communiqué an admonition to states to refrain from invoking custom, tradition, and religious considerations as a way of avoiding their obligations to condemn all forms of violence against women.[64] Delegates from Poland, Egypt, several Muslim states, and conservative Christian groups in the United States objected to other parts of the document, including, but not limited to, references to abortion rights and references to the term "rape" when used to describe forcible sexual behavior by a woman's husband or partner.[65] It appears that as long as women are kept from participating in education, society, and the political arena, men who dominate these spheres of human life will continue to define what is abuse and what is liberation for women.

---

62. U.N. Resources for Speakers on Global Issues, "Ending Violence against Women and Girls."
63. Juan Forero, "Acid Attacks in Colombia Reflect Rage," *Washington Post*, August 3, 2012.
64. Iran, Russia, and the Vatican failed in their attempts to exclude the language that appears as paragraph 14 of the 2013 document, "The Elimination and Prevention of All Forms of Violence against Women and Girls."
65. "Unholy Alliance," *New York Times*, March 11, 2013.

Step 2. Reflecting

Since ancient times, the woman's domain was the home, while the man's domain was the public sphere. Even in 2013 half of Americans believed that children are better off if their mothers stay at home without employment, while only 8 percent say the same thing concerning the father.[66] The roots of these modern-day assumptions are found in the ancient honor-shame code. The family's place and reputation within any given society was based on either acquiring honor or inducing shame. Honor is a male-centered activity. It was the responsibility of men to maintain or improve the honor of their family while simultaneously avoiding anything that might bring shame upon their family name. Through the man's participation in the public sphere, honor can be increased or decreased by his interactions with other men. While honor is achieved in the public sphere, the domain of men, shame is created within the private sphere, the domain of women.

Because of patriarchy, a woman who belonged to one man yet was used by another brought shame to the "owner" of her body. So to protect one's honor, men confined women to the household, where they could remain secure and protected from enemies wishing to bring shame upon the good name of the one who owned their bodies. This honor-shame code helps explain the binding of feet in some Asian countries, the societal pressure to wear a burka in some Islamic countries, the forced medical procedure of female circumcision in some African countries, or simply the required custom of chaperoning unattended women.

The residue of this ancient honor-shame value system can be seen throughout the development of Christianity. Eve's association with the fall makes her the counterpoint to Mary, the mother of Jesus and the perpetual virgin. Eve represents the ultimate temptress who leads men, and by extension all of humanity, astray. Mary, on the other hand, signifies the ideal model for all Christian women to emulate. Christian women have historically been given a choice between the purity that comes with motherhood or the wantonness that comes with independence from benevolent male authority—in short, between the virgin and the whore, and thus between the pivotal values of the ancient world: honor and shame.

Not surprisingly, merchants and soldiers during the fifteenth and sixteenth centuries who left for business or crusades to liberate the Holy Land would protect the family's honor by fashioning chastity belts on their wives. A man could leave in peace knowing that his sexual property was locked and protected from trespassers (with the possible exception of the local locksmith). Remaining tied to her domestic habitation forestalled shame. "As the

---

66. Catherine Rampell, "U.S. Women on the Rise.".

snail carries its house with it," Martin Luther informs us, "so the wife should stay at home and look after the affairs of the household, as one who has been deprived of the ability of administering those affairs that are outside and that concern the state" (1995, 203). Women's redemption from Eve's influence, and from the shame that she herself could bring upon the honor of her man's name, was to seek virtue, either through chastity, which becomes solely her responsibility, or by becoming a prolific mother. If she is a mother, her worth and respect increase proportionately to the number of males that she births.

Yet regardless of how much honor the woman brings to her husband's name, she remains inferior, someone who is less than a male. But women are not the only ones who can be designated as feminine; seeing Others as feminine (whether they be female or male) justifies their subjugation, helping us to better understand the underpinnings of both colonialism and imperialism. Sexism also serves as a paradigm for the subjugation of all people groups that fall short of the white male ideal. Because inferiority has historically been defined as feminine, all who are oppressed, be they females or males, are feminized. While this is not an attempt to minimize oppressive and violent structures toward women in communities of color, it is an attempt to stress that all forms of oppression are identical in their attempt to domesticate the feminine (i.e., inferior) Other, to place the Other in a subordinate position (De La Torre 2010, 222).

The danger that sexist comments made by politicians and pundits poses to society goes beyond some ignorant misogynist remark; they provide us with a blueprint for maintaining and sustaining the racist, elitist, classist, and imperialist structures of society through sexist paradigms that these structures advocate. Theologian Mary Daly quipped, "If God is male, then the male is God" (1973, 19). And probably this truth is what undergirds the historical war on women. Because God is male—in other words, because God, like males, has a penis—then the male is a god lording over all who lack a penis. Women, as well as non-whites (females and males) and the poor (regardless of skin pigmentation), are subordinated to those who possess a penis.

Throughout Judeo-Christian history God has been thought of as a male, consistently referred to as a "he." But if the function of a penis is to urinate and/or copulate, why would God need a penis? Or does the penis have societal meaning? If women were castrated by the Almighty He, envious of what only God and men possess, should it not be natural, then, for women to submit to men, who, unlike women, are created in the very image of God? Is Sigmund Freud's theory of "penis envy" therefore accurate?

With this in mind, we can understand why Abraham and Israel placed great spiritual value on their penises, swearing oaths upon their genitals (Gen. 24:2–3; 47:29–31), or why King David wins Michal as his wife through the gift of a hundred foreskins from Philistine penises (2 Sam. 3:14). More importantly, the very sign of the covenant between God and man begins with the penis, specifically cutting off its foreskin through the ritual of circumcision (Gen. 17:10–14). How, then, do women enter into a covenant with God if there is no penis to circumcise (De La Torre 2007, 16–17)?[67]

To use a psychological analysis, when "the Man" looks into Lacan's mirror, he constructs his male identity through a distancing process of the negative, defining himself through the archetype of "I am what I am not." For example, because women are emotional, when the man looks into a mirror, he does not see a woman, and therefore he is not emotional. Because women are inferior and weak, when he looks into a mirror, he does not see a woman, and therefore he is not inferior or weak. In the formation of the subject's ego, an illusory self-representation is constructed through the negation of a penis, which is projected upon Others, those who would be identified as non-men.

Ascribing femininity to the Other, regardless of gender, forces feminine identity construction to originate with the domesticating man. In fact, the feminine Object, in and of itself, is seen as nothing apart from a masculine Subject, which provides unifying purpose (Grosz 1990, 115–45). The resulting gaze of the white, elite male inscribes effeminacy upon Others who are not man enough to "make" history, or "provide" for their family, or "resist" their subjugation. Ironically, no one really has a penis. The man lives, always threatened by possible loss, while the non-man is forcibly deprived. The potent symbolic power invested in the penis both signals and veils heterosexual male domination, as well as white supremacy and socioeconomic power. Constructing those oppressed as feminine allows men with penises to assert their privilege by constructing oppressed Others as inhabitants of the castrated realm of the exotic and primitive. Lacking a penis, the Other does not exist, except as designated by the desire of the one with a penis. While non-men are forced to flee from their individuality, the white man must constantly attempt to live up to a false construction (De La Torre 2012, 125).

When Sandra Fluke attempted to speak for herself, Rush Limbaugh attempted to define her as an oversexed slut while defining himself through the self-negation of his construction of her. Publicly discrediting women is not a new strategy; historically, whenever women have attempted to declare their own agency, they have been shamed into silence. Consider Mary of

---

67. Paul Tillich and Paul Ricoeur assert that one can speak of or describe God only through the use of symbols, connecting the meaning of one thing recognized by a given community that is comprehensible (e.g., father) with another thing that is beyond our ability to fully understand (God) (see Tillich's *Theology of Culture* [1959] and Ricoeur's *Interpretation Theory* [1976]). As important as symbols are to better grasp the incomprehensible essence of the Divine, they are incapable of exhausting the reality of God. Taking symbolic language literally (God is exclusively male or female) leads to the absurd (God has a penis or a vagina) and borders on idolatry (the creation of hierarchies in relationships based on who is closer to the Divine ideal).

Magdala, who, for many within the church, was believed to be a prostitute. Yet nowhere in the biblical text is Mary of Magdala referred to as a prostitute. All three Synoptic Gospels (Matt. 27:55–56; Mark 15:40–41; Luke 24:10) instead refer to Mary of Magdala as first among Jesus' female disciples. Contrary to tradition, which credits Peter as the first to witness the resurrection (1 Cor. 15:4–6), it was Mary of Magdala who first saw the risen Lord and the first to proclaim the good news of the resurrection (Mark 16:9–10; John 20:1–18). The biblical text and the early writings of the first church[68] testify to the leadership position that she held. Nonetheless, as the early Christian church reverted to patriarchal structures, Mary of Magdala had to be discredited so as to disqualify her position of authority within the church. Hence, the church tradition constructed by men, protecting male privilege, arose that she was a prostitute, an attempt to question her contribution to the establishment of Christianity.

Step 3. Praying

The biblical text has historically been interpreted within Christianity in such a way that it has contributed to the creation and propagation of abuses toward women that remain not so well masked within many churches today. Probably the best biblical way to maintain control over women is through the construction of the traditional biblical marriage, as defined by most religious conservatives, even though such a concept is foreign to the biblical text. In fact, it would be hard to find a modern-day Christian who would actually abide by a biblical marriage in practice, for the biblical understanding of marriage meant that (1) women are property owned by men, (2) women are human incubators, (3) women are the weaker sex, and (4) women are the cause of evil.

Male ownership of women meant that women, as the property of men, existed for male desires. Early in the biblical text we are told that the woman's desire would be for her husband, while he would rule over her (Gen. 3:16).[69] Upon marriage, a woman's property and her body became the possession of her new husband. Women became available for male possession soon after they reached puberty (usually eleven to thirteen years old)—that is, when a woman became physically able to produce children. Throughout the Hebrew Bible it is taken for granted that women (as well as children) are the possessions of men. The focus of the text does not seriously consider or concentrate

---

68. For example, in the *Gospel of Mary*, Mary of Magdala is referred to as the "apostle of the apostles," specifically for her rousing sermon to the despondent disciples after Christ's ascension.

69. Historically, men have argued that this hierarchy is the divine order of things. Others maintain that the man and the woman being naked yet feeling no shame (Gen. 2:25) is the correct pre-fall divine order of things, and the verse stating that the man will rule over the woman (Gen. 3:16) refers to the consequence of sin, not the will of God.

upon the women's status, but instead constructs their identity by their sexual relationship to the man: virgin daughter, betrothal bride, married woman, mother, barren wife, or widow. A woman's dignity and worth as one created in the image of God is subordinated to the needs and desires of men.

As chattel, women became the extension of a man, thus any trespass against the man's possession becomes a direct violation of the man. Not surprisingly, women often are equated with a house or with livestock (e.g., Deut. 20:5–7), which is demonstrated in the last commandment: "You shall not covet your neighbor's house, wife, slave, ox, or donkey" (Exod. 20:17). Because women are excluded from being the subject of this commandment, the woman, like a house, slave, ox, or donkey, is reduced to an object, just another possession, another piece of property that belongs to the man, and thus should not be coveted by another man. This is why regulations concerning sexual activities appear in the biblical text under the category of property law. If a daughter was raped, the perpetrator had to either pay her father (who owned her virginity) three times the original marriage price for the loss in value of his property or marry the young girl (Exod. 22:16–17, 23–29).

A man could have as many sexual partners as he could afford. Patriarchs of the faith, such as Abraham, Jacob, and Judah, had multiple wives and/or concubines and delighted themselves with the occasional prostitute (Gen. 38:15). King Solomon alone was reported to have had over seven hundred wives of royal birth and three hundred concubines (1 Kings 11:3). The book of Leviticus, in giving instructions to men wishing to own a harem, provides only one prohibition, which is not to "own" sisters (Lev. 18:18). The Hebrew Bible is clear that men could have multiple sex partners. Wives ensured legitimate heirs; all other sex partners existed for the pleasures of the flesh. A woman, on the other hand, was limited to just one sex partner who ruled over her, unless, of course, she was a prostitute. Sins such as adultery never applied to men, but only to women, which explains why the man involved with the woman "caught in the act of adultery" (John 8:3) did not need to be brought to Jesus, but she did. After all, if she was caught in the very act, was there not also a man present (De La Torre 2007, 18–22)?

Second, the biblical understanding for the purpose for marriage has historically been reproduction; women were understood to be human incubators. A barren Sarai offers her slave girl Hagar to Abram for rape so that she, Sarai, can give him an heir (Gen. 16:2). Rachel, Jacob's wife, demands of her husband, "Give me children, or I shall die" (Gen. 30:1). If the woman was unable to bring forth a child, the marriage could be dissolved by the man. Besides reproduction, marriage within a patriarchal order also served political and economic means. To ensure that offspring were the legitimate heirs, the woman was restricted to one sex partner, her husband. Biblical marriages were endogamous; that is, they occurred within the same extended family or clan, unlike the modern Western concept of exogamy, where unions occur between outsiders.

The early shapers of Christian thought believed that the only purpose for a woman's existence was her ability to procreate. Only through child-bearing could a woman be saved, a disturbing understanding of salvation as reiterated by Paul: "It was not Adam who was led astray, but the woman who was led astray and fell into sin. Nevertheless, she will be saved by childbearing" (1 Tim. 2:14–15). Paul, the promoter of salvation solely through grace, not works, implied that unlike men, women are saved through childbearing, a concept rooted in patriarchy. Birthing children took precedence over the life of the mother. Or as Martin Luther instructed women, "Bring that child forth, and do it with all your might! If you die in the process, so pass on over, good for you! For you actually die in a noble work and in obedience to God."[70]

On a side note, if the only natural reason for participating in sex is pro-creation, then all sexual activities that do not lead to children are, by defi-nition, unnatural. Hence, for a man to engage in intercourse with a barren woman, a menopausal woman, or menstruating woman becomes an abomi-nation because of her inability to conceive (Lev. 15:24). Any sexual act that does not directly lead to human conception automatically becomes defined as "unnatural," be it oral sex, anal sex, homosexual sex, using condoms during sex, or sex solely for the sake of pleasure. Hence, the admonition from the early Christian thinker Clement of Alexandria (ca. 150–215): "To indulge in intercourse without intending children is to outrage nature" (De La Torre 2007, 22–24).[71]

Third, an underlying assumption found throughout the biblical text is that men are physically and morally superior to women, the weaker sex. According to 1 Peter, "Husbands must treat their wives with consideration, bestowing honor on her as one who, though she may be the weaker vessel, is truly a co-heir to the grace of life" (1 Pet. 3:7). Although equal in grace, still the purpose for the woman as the "weaker vessel" is to be ruled by the man. In his first letter to the Corinthians Paul insisted that women cover their heads because the woman is the "glory of man." Specifically, he writes, "For man . . . is the image and glory of God. But the woman is the glory of man. For man did not come from woman, but woman from man. And man was not created for woman, but woman for man" (1 Cor. 11:7–9).

Because man is closer to the spirit, he is a rational subject ordained to rule; and because woman is closer to the flesh, she is an emotional object

---

70. Martin Luther, *The Estate of Marriage* (1522), part 3.
71. Clement of Alexandria, *Christ the Educator* 2.10.95.

ordained to be ruled. Thus, subjecting woman to man becomes the natural manifestation of subjecting passion to reason. Paul makes this view obvious when he writes, "But as the church is subject to Christ, so also are wives to be subject to their husbands in everything" (Eph. 5:24). Just as the body must submit to the spirit, which is superior, and the church must submit to Christ, so too must the wife submit to her husband. Ephesians (along with Col. 3:18–19) sets up the marriage relationship in which husbands are commanded to love their wives, while wives are commanded not to love, but rather submit to, their husbands. This makes women, according to Thomas Aquinas, a "defective and misbegotten male"—probably due to "some external influence, such as that of a south wind, which is moist" (De La Torre 2007, 24–27).[72]

Fourth and finally, another assumption of the biblical tradition can be summed up as the following: because women are responsible for the evil in the world, they must be controlled for their own good. Their shapely curves incite passion among holy men. Thus, they are the cause of man's disgrace and downfall. One of the major Christian themes is that women, represented by Eve, are the cause of sin, and consequently they are the reason mankind was led astray from God's perfect will. She was first to be deceived and was responsible for deceiving the man. Like their mother Eve, all women today are the incarnation of temptation. Connecting Eve with all women, the early Christian thinker Tertullian (ca. 165–220) proclaimed, "You [woman] are the one who opened the door to the devil. . . . You are the one who persuaded [Adam] whom the devil was not strong enough to attack. All too easily you destroyed the image of God, man. Because of your desert, that is, death, even the Son of God had to die"[73] (De La Torre 2007, 27–29). In conclusion, the use of the biblical text in the war on women becomes somewhat problematic in the quest for liberation.

Step 4. Case Studies

1. Since 1979, China has had a one-child policy, an attempt to deal with a growing population that is placing a strain on national and global resources and on the environment. Village officials are charged with charting the menstrual cycle of every childbearing woman and providing pelvic exams within their rural region. Women who are impregnated without government permission must pay an exorbitant fine or risk a forced abortion. Feng Jianmei, who was carrying a second child in violation of the national policy, was forced by local officials to abort a seven-month-old fetus. Until she ceded to official demands, peasants in her village of Yuping were led

---

72. Thomas Aquinas, *Summa Theologica* 1.92.1.
73. Tertullian, *The Apparel of Women* 1.1.2.

in a march that denounced family members as "traitors." Her husband was even beaten. She could have kept the second child if she would have paid the $6,300 fine (anywhere from three to ten times a household income, depending on the province).[74] Compare her plight with that of Zhang Yimou, the celebrated film director and arranger of the Beijing 2008 Summer Olympics opening ceremony. He also violated the one-child policy by fathering seven children with four different women.[75] But unlike Feng, Zhang is wealthy and thus can easily afford the penalty. What is a ferocious tiger for Feng is but a paper tiger for Zhang.

— Are mandatory abortions ever ethical? Even for the common good? State officials argue that without the one-child policy, the economy would falter and the population would explode. Do the needs of the state trump the rights of the individual? Does the one-child policy reduce women to a means of production? Could this be why China has the highest rate of female suicide in the world?

— Should family planning be determined by ability to pay? Should those who are successful be allowed to have more children, who will have the economic means of also succeeding?

— If it is determined that the fetus is female, do parents have a right to abort in hopes that the next pregnancy might produce a boy? Sex-selection abortions have skewed China's sex ratio to 118 boys for every 100 girls. Is this problematic? Why or why not? In the United States the House of Representatives rejected a measure that would have imposed fines and prison terms on doctors who performed sex-selection abortions.[76] Was the rejection of this legislation moral? Why or why not?

— In the western state of Rakhine, Myanmar, which has the highest Islamic population within a Buddhist-majority country, local authorities have imposed a two-child limit for Muslim families.[77] How problematic is this regulation? Although Muslims represent 4 percent of the country's population, the state argues that this policy will reduce sectarian violence. In 2012, Buddhists armed with machetes razed thousands of Muslims' homes, leaving hundreds dead and forcing 125,000 to flee. Is securing future peace by controlling Muslim women's bodies worth considering such regulations? Why or why not?

---

74. Edward Wong, "Forced to Abort, Chinese Woman under Pressure," *New York Times*, June 27, 2012.

75. Ma Jian, "China's Brutal One-Child Policy," *New York Times*, May 21, 2013.

76. Jennifer Steinhauer, "House Rejects Bill to Ban Sex-Selective Abortions," *New York Times*, June 1, 2012.

77. "One Region in Myanmar Limits Births of Muslims," *New York Times*, May 25, 2013.

2. Melissa Nelson, a ten-year dental assistant for Dr. James Knight, was fired from her job because he found her attractive. Both he and his wife were concerned that the woman might become a threat to their marriage, so he fired her to save his marriage. Nelson sued and lost. The all-male Iowa Supreme Court ruled that employers could fire employees whom they found to be an "irresistible attraction," even if the employee did nothing warranting termination. Justice Edward M. Mansfield wrote that such firings are lawful under state law because they are motivated not by gender, but rather by feelings and emotions. Knight's attorney interpreted the decision as a victory for family values. Nelson's attorney, Paige Fiedler, on the other hand, said that the courts failed to recognize the discrimination that women consistently experience in the workplace. She went on to say, "These judges sent a message to Iowa women that they don't think men can be held responsible for their sexual desires and that Iowa women are the ones who have to monitor and control their bosses' sexual desires."[78]

    — Should Knight be praised for his fidelity to his wife in going to extreme lengths to save his marriage? Is it better for men to admit their "irresistible attraction" for certain beautiful female employees rather than to subject them to unwanted attention or sexual harassment? What responsibility, if any, does Nelson hold in her dismissal? Was the ruling fair and just? Why or why not?

    — Can a married female employer fire an attractive man whom she finds attractive? What about an employer who finds an employee of the same gender attractive, even if the employee is a heterosexual? Does the ruling objectify bodies based on desirability? Can the argument of sexual desire be used as an excuse to dismiss unwanted employees?

3. Taj Mohammad, who lives in a sprawling refugee camp in Kabul, Afghanistan, is unable to repay a debt to a fellow camp resident and elder. He makes $6 a day, when he can find work as an unskilled laborer. He borrowed the money to pay for his wife's hospital treatment and medical care for some of his nine children. If the debt is not paid, he is at risk of losing what he put up as collateral, his six-year-old daughter, Naghma. Unless he repays the $2,500 loan, Naghma will be forced to leave her home and marry the creditor's seventeen-year-old son. Unfortunately, Mohammad does not have the money. He is so poor that his three-year-old daughter, Janan, froze to death during the bitter winter because he could not afford enough firewood.[79]

---

78. "Iowa: Court Upholds Firing of Woman Whose Boss Found Her Attractive," *New York Times*, December 22, 2012.

79. Alissa J. Rubin, "Painful Payment for Afghan Debt: A Daughter, 6," *New York Times*, April 1, 2013.

— Afghan tradition allows the groom's family to pay a "bride price," in this case, the forgiveness of the $2,500 debt. If this is an acceptable traditional practice, are Westerners imposing their sense of morality when they say it is wrong? Is a "bride price" fine as long as it does not involve children? If Westerners become involved in denouncing bride price, are they being paternalistic toward Afghan women?

— Is the use of women as property universally wrong under all circumstances regardless of traditions and cultures? Are ethics and morality a construct of specific people groups, or do they transcend cultures and traditions regardless of time periods? If certain moral truths apply to everyone, everywhere, always, who gets to determine what is universally right or wrong?

— Before Naghma was handed off to her husband to repay a debt, an anonymous donor stepped forward and paid the loan.[80] This story has a happy ending, but how many unknown Naghmas are being sold as property, and what can be done about it? Even though her trade was considered illegal under Afghanistan's Elimination of Violence against Women law, the law can be enforced only if the one abused or her relative files a complaint. How can the Naghmas of the world be safeguarded without the end product appearing paternalistic or seen as an imposition of a Western sense of morality? Or is Western morality superior? Why or why not?

4. Beatriz of El Salvador, already a mother of a toddler and someone who believes that abortions are almost always wrong, is experiencing a high-risk pregnancy that ultimately could kill her. The fetus she is carrying is not viable, suffering from anencephaly, with almost no chance of surviving. Although the doctors are urging her to abort the fetus, El Salvador prohibits abortions under any circumstances.[81] She and her doctor could face up to eight years in prison if he performs the abortion. She awaits the decision of the Salvadoran Supreme Court to determine her case. The Salvadoran Roman Catholic Church has argued that the fetus's malformation should not be met with a death sentence. "This case," according to the Episcopal Conference of El Salvador, "should not be used to legislate against human life."[82]

— Is the church right? Does the life of the unborn trump the life of the mother? Should the matter of life and death remain only in the hands

---

80. Alissa J. Rubin, "Afghan Who Agreed to Trade His Daughter to End a Debt Says It Was Paid," *New York Times*, April 2, 2013.

81. Other Latin American countries with total bans on abortions are Chile and Nicaragua.

82. Karla Zabludovsky, "A Salvadoran at Risk Tests Abortion Law," *New York Times*, May 28, 2013.

of God? Or is the church imposing its religious views upon the people, some of whom may not believe in God? Still, if abortion is indeed murder, as the church claims, should the church then do everything in its power to uphold this universal claim?

— On May 29, 2013, El Salvador's highest court, in a 4-1 ruling, denied Beatriz's request for an abortion. Beatriz's lawyer described the ruling as "misogynistic," claiming, "Justice here does not respect the rights of women."[83] Is her lawyer correct in her assessment? Why or why not? Travel abroad is not possible because the trip could kill her. So what other options are available to her?

— Although abortion is not an option because of the court's decision, Salvadoran Health Minister María Isabel Rodríguez stated that at the point when Beatriz's life is in danger, doctors can "induce birth" via an abdominal or vaginal birth. Less than a week after the court decision, a cesarean section ended her high-risk pregnancy.[84] Did doctors unable to perform abortions terminate a pregnancy without technically violating the law? The fetus was placed in an incubator and provided fluids, expiring within five hours. Is this a creative way around the law, or is it a result of decisions concerning women's bodies being beyond the control of women? Is this a victory for women rights, or a quick fix in one particular case?

---

83. Karla Zabludovsky and Gene Palumbo, "Salvadoran Court Denies Abortion to Ailing Woman," *New York Times*, May 29, 2013.
84. Karla Zabludovsky, "A High-Risk Pregnancy Is Terminated, but Was It an Abortion?" *New York Times*, June 4, 2013.

Chapter 16

Private Property

Step 1. Observing

Until the present day, land and its ownership were part of nearly every social, economic, or political issue. While the ownership of land is still important for creating, sustaining, and maintaining wealth, in the new world order wealth can be created apart from land. Under the present system of neoliberalism, the importance of property has diminished, since the means of production need not necessarily be owned. For example, the source of Microsoft's billions is cyberspace rather than physical space. Capital need not be connected to a particular workforce or tied to a specific physical location. With a few keystrokes on a computer, an entrepreneur from New York, sitting at a café in Rio de Janeiro, can transfer billions in assets from Paris to Tokyo within microseconds. In such a world, wealth tied to a particular piece of land is losing its importance. Why, then, explore the ethical ramifications of private property? Because it is still land that sustains all of life, and the primary obstacle in preventing the vast majority of the world's dispossessed from living a more humane existence is the lack of control over the land—physically, politically, and economically. Hence the question before us is this: What are the socioeconomic consequences of land ownership upon the world's dispossessed?

For most of us, land appears to be neutral. Yet the ownership and the use of land lie behind much of the political, social, and economic violence that tears apart the world today. While land, in and of itself, is not the root of evil, it has been used as an instrument to foster injustice. The commodification of land—making it into something that can be bought and sold—turns it into a source of power over others and can also turn it into an idol, something to be worshiped. How, then, can the use of land become a redemptive source of justice?

Historically, in Greece and Rome property did not belong to an individual; instead, individuals, grouped in families, belonged to the land. Originally, the family was attached to the family altar, and the altar was attached to the soil. Even if the family perished, the land endured. Consequently, an intimate relationship was formed between the family (not the individual) and the soil. The property was improved not for the lifetime of a single person but for all generations. The past and the future were connected through the

313

soil. Land was used inclusively, and it represented the wealth and well-being of the overall community. How, then, could land be valued and exchanged in the marketplace (de Coulanges 1980, 54–55, 62)?

The modern construction of Western society, particularly a system based on neoliberalism, relies on an exclusive use of land. Individual self-interest remains supreme. The land is valued for its physical location and its resources rather than as the source of all life. The person with the most land or with land in the most ideal location is often the wealthiest individual in a community or the member of the community with the most power. This individual pursuit for the most profitable use of the land contributes to a negation of community and communal values and shows a lack of concern for the general welfare. This approach to land valuation is a clear obstacle to justice and is the very antithesis of the biblical mandate concerning our use of land as God's stewards.

Step 2. Reflecting

One of the fundamental purposes of neoliberal governments, which usually operate in an individualistic and capitalist society, is to protect private property and preserve an open-market economy. In many places and at different times in U.S. history, the Christian faith has been artificially linked to a laissez-faire economic philosophy. This connection has then been used to create ethical truths concerning freedom and rights, often allowing the dominant culture to prosper freely, even at the expense of others. The application of freedom and rights to human dignity has often been missing from the equation. Property rights have also become a battle cry in any serious conversation about correcting the wealth disparities within the United States. César Chávez explained how property rights can be used to mask oppression:

> When the racists and bigots, the industrialists and the corporation farmers were not shedding our blood, they were blocking our way with all kinds of stratagems. We have heard them all—"Property Rights," "States Rights," "Right to Work." All of these slogans, as you will have noticed, and as you will still notice, have been uttered in ringing tones of idealism and individual freedom. But that is the special genius of those who would deny the rights of others and hoard the fruits of democracy for themselves: They evade the problems and complex challenges of equal justice by reducing them to primitive oversimplifications that plead for nothing else but the perpetuation of their own special, exploitative interests. (Dalton 2003, 67–68)

The danger in hiding behind a "property rights" slogan is that when wealth is concentrated in the hands of a few, democracy is threatened if the privileged few use their property to control the direction and policies of the society. And this often happens. In short, economic power leads directly to political power. The fight then waged is not for the land itself, but over who will have the right to use, enjoy, and gain from it. This is why land use should be subject to theological discussion.

American economist Henry George defined "land" as follows:

> The term land necessarily includes, not merely the surface of the earth as distinguished from water and the air, but the whole material universe outside of man, for it is only by having access to land, from which his very body is drawn, that man can come in contact with or use nature. The term land embraces, in short, all natural materials, forces, and opportunities, and, therefore, nothing that is freely supplied by nature can be properly classed as capital. A fertile field, a rich vein of ore, a falling stream which supplies power, may give to the possessor advantages equivalent to the possession of capital, but to class such things as capital would be to put an end to the distinction between land and capital, and, so far as they relate to each other to make the two terms meaningless (1951, 38–39).[1]

Our modern concept of property considers it as a thing to be claimed and possessed. Property represents personal liberty over against external powers and/or the means by which one's needs are satisfied, produced, or distributed. The lure and promise of property are liberty and security; the property holder thus dominates the one without property, who as a result is also without liberty or security (Meeks 1989, 99–125). Or, as Frantz Fanon wrote, "For a colonized people the most essential value, because the most concrete, is first and foremost the land: the land which will bring them bread and, above all, dignity" (1963, 44). Over time, land moved from being part of the natural environment to being one more commodity that could be used for domination. The misuse of land has become throughout history a primary source of massive oppression and misery.

Mexican theologian Enrique Dussel maintains that private real property has three origins: one works for it, or steals it, or inherits it. If one works for

---

1. Henry George (1839–1897) was a North American economist and social philosopher who rooted a doctrine of land in ethics rather than economics. While living in San Francisco, he argued that the Western economic boom that he witnessed resulted from the development of the railroads. Nevertheless, a paradox existed. While this "boom" created an unparalleled increase in wealth, most people remained trapped in widespread poverty. George concluded that the industrial development occurring during his lifetime concentrated wealth in the hands of the few who controlled land. When the value of land rose, so did their fortunes. Yet their wealth was not the result of their efforts but rather was due to the increase in the population and the development of the economy. His teachings ceased to be taken seriously because he did not hold an advanced degree during a time when economics was becoming a specialized profession.

it, the amount of land acquired is relatively small. If much property is owned, then undoubtedly it was stolen, he says, sometimes without one's realization. Stealing it causes the dispossessed to be impoverished and/or killed (1978, 25). When property is inherited by one's children, the original sin of stealing and murder is transmitted to the next generation, which, through complicity with their progenitors' acts, continue to benefit from land ownership.

Most modern principles of land ownership are based on the laissez-faire economics of Adam Smith. Smith argued that pursuit of economic self-interests within the context of a competitive society benefits all persons. Thus, no restraints should be placed on the accumulation of land. Land ownership by individuals is a fundamental if not sacred building block of civilization, and to suggest the resumption of land as common property is paramount to advocating a regression toward some premodern, uncivilized existence. Yet Smith's model creates problems. For example, the privileged will be in an economic position to acquire immense portions of land. Through their holdings, they can impose laws upon those who need land for basic subsistence. In exchange for the use of the land, tenants must recognize the supreme authority of the landlord, whether the landowner is an individual, a multinational corporation, or a civil government. When society is constructed on the fundamental principle of private ownership, the state must protect property by enacting laws against trespassing and theft.

Franz Hinkelammert reminds us that the unconditional recognition of the right to private property deprioritizes all other rights, leading to global disenfranchisement and dispossession. Protecting private property is maintained at the expense of rights "to satisfy basic needs in food, shelter, medical attention, education, and social security" (1986, 120). In effect, property rights trump human rights. The act of jumping over a fence to pick up a fallen apple rotting on the ground is a convictable trespassing and theft offense, even if the motivation of the offender was to feed her or his hungry child.

Contrary to Smith, Catholic social teaching maintains that private property cannot be held to the detriment of the poor. Private property must also serve the common good. While Catholic social teaching views the right of people to own property, it limits property rights with the human right to take care of one's family. Because those who have an excess supply have a moral responsibility to share with those who are destitute, it is not considered wrong when the poor, who have no other recourse but to take from those with a surplus for the common good of feeding those who are dying from hunger, steal. Guillaume d'Auxerre, thirteenth-century bishop of Paris, along with other theologians living during the plagues and famine of the twelfth century, insisted that the poor had a right to steal what they needed in order to survive; they were not considered to be sinning if they engaged in "starvation theft."

English philosopher John Locke (1632–1704), considered to be the father of classical political liberalism, is responsible for advancing certain "self-evident natural rights," one of which is the exclusive use of real property. He viewed property as an institution of nature, not a social convention based on human laws (1952, 17). Property became the third of the inalienable rights, along with "life and liberty." Locke argued for the right of each person, based on self-preservation and personal interest, to keep whatever property he or she possessed, despite the means utilized in its acquisition or an individual's ability to use all of its resources. Locke first limited the accumulation of property to what would not spoil, rust, rot, or decay (1952, 23). However, with the introduction of a cash economy, previous limits were no longer applicable. Eventually, money became the common denominator for land, as well as for labor. While the fruits of the land might spoil, money as a commodity does not. Wealth, accumulated in the form of gold or silver (money), became unlimited (1952, 29), and so did the accumulation of land.

The state, constructed to preserve the rights of the individual to life, liberty, and property, is duty-bound to ensure these inalienable rights (1952, 5–6). And the state is needed by the landholders to guarantee their property interest. The sacredness of property was reaffirmed in the young U.S. republic, reserving the right to participate in the political discourse to those white males owning property. Rather than the traditional right to property being derived from the power to rule, the Federalist Papers inverted this concept to reflect a right to rule in order to protect said property. Land became owned by "legal" individuals possessing a title that conferred rights protected by the state's judicial system. Still, land equality remained a seditious idea to be quashed because it created the possibility that the wealthy might lose their privilege. The goals of the young republic were fully identified with the interest of the landholders (Madison 2001, 48).

Missing from most analyses of the Western concept of private property is how the property was acquired in the first place. Most of our modern Western understanding of private property is based on Locke, an international slave trader[2] who worked as a business manager for a colonial landholding corporation that held interests in North America. Eventually he moved beyond being a mere colonial bureaucrat to owning a minority share in the Carolina province along with a seat in the colonial legislature of the Carolina territory. As Tink Tinker reminds us, Locke's ethical philosophy justified the international theft of indigenous people's land via a façade of legal and moral

---

2. Locke was part owner in a slave-run plantation, Bahamian Adventurers, and a slave acquisition and selling firm, Royal Africa Company.

propriety. God, according to Locke, wanted the English to take the "vacant" lands of North America. Even though indigenous people lived on the land, their failure to develop it amounted to a forfeit of any legal rights to it. The original inhabitants did not own the land on which they lived, because in the "state of nature" it was owned by all. The superior English succeeded because the indigenous people failed to labor upon the land (agriculture), thus developing and transforming it into private property. Labor conducted upon the land makes it private, and those who simply used the land for eons held no claim. Thus, the taking of indigenous land was philosophically justified (Tinker 2011, 56). According to Locke, who had a vested interest in the colonial venture,

> God and his reason commanded him to subdue the earth, i.e., improve it for the benefit of life, and therein lay out something upon it that was his own, his labour. He that in obedience to this command of God, subdued, tilled and sowed any part of it, thereby annexed to it something that was his property, which another had no title to, nor could without injury take from him. (1952, 31)

The strong economic positions of the elite led to the control of all aspects of political life. When private property (and free markets) secures the liberty of the wealthy class, with the help of the government, it is generally secured at the expense of a marginalized class that becomes increasingly alienated. The interests of the common person (specifically those who are poor and of color) become subordinated to the interests of this ruling class. Questioning the ruling class becomes paramount to revolution or treason. Even though there is a guise of universal participation in government, the wealthy class is instrumental in deciding by its political contributions who become governmental officers. This holds true whether the property owners are individuals or corporations. In return, the governmental officers protect the power and privilege of the wealthy class.

When John Locke first commodified land, he reduced its importance to nothing more than a unit of capital. He overlooked the rights of the land itself. In other words, he failed to see land as a gift of nature; instead, it was viewed as passive and worthless until the active principle of human labor was applied to it (1952, 26). By and large, economists have ignored the importance of land. It is merely one commodity among many rather than a precondition of economic life or the giver and sustainer of life. All living creatures share a common heritage in the land. While labor and capital remain reproducible, the land and its resources (such as fossil fuels and minerals) are exhaustible, as is seen in many parts of the world today.

Wealth-building through the use of land falls short of biblical standards.[3] Biblical texts clearly emphasize that all land is the sole possession of God.[4] As ultimate creator and sustainer, God alone possesses absolute property rights. The biblical regulations concerning the Sabbatical Year, gleaning, Jubilee, and interest were attempts to keep the land available to all and to avoid great extremes of wealth and poverty. The biblical concepts of gleaning and Jubilee were not utopian dreams or abstract principles from which to derive systems of ethics; rather, they provided a valid economic structure designed to ensure an equitable distribution of resources. When these concepts were flagrantly ignored, they roused the prophets to call upon the people to repent.

Step 3. Praying

Both the evolutionist and the biblical literalist agree that land preceded the advent of human beings. Land was not produced or created by humans; rather, it preexisted as a gift of the Creator. But, the land also has rights over its inhabitants. The book of Leviticus dictates, "When you come into the land which [God is] giving you, the land shall keep a Sabbath for Yahweh" (Lev. 25:2). According to Hebrew Bible scholar Walter Brueggemann, "Sabbath in Israel is the affirmation that people, like land, cannot be finally owned or managed" (1977, 64). The "right" to use the land is limited by humane, ecological, and economic concerns.

God's sole ownership of land makes personal possession impossible: "The land shall not be sold in perpetuity, for the land is [God's], and you are but aliens and tenants" (Lev. 25:23). To live on the land requires obedience to the Lord, who is in fact the land(lord). Improper land stewardship defiles the land. Safeguards provided by the biblical texts established justice and prevented land ownership from unjustly stratifying the population.

The idea of the rights of the land itself ensures a just distribution of its fruits. By biblical law, one was not allowed to reap to the very edges of the field or pass through a second time to glean missed produce. The overlooked grain remained for the poor and the aliens (Lev. 19:9–10). In addition, the law of Moses forbade the selling of land for profit. Land was to be the inheritance of the family (Lev. 25:23–24). When property was purchased, absolute

---

3. For some time, papal encyclicals have wrestled with issues of property rights. Unfortunately, their historic allegiance to "landed" interests has caused a credibility gap in their attempt to define land for the common good. Pope John XXIII, while affirming the right of private ownership in Mater et Magistra (1961), extends this right to all classes through equitable distribution. Property is to be shared among all because it has a social destiny. Pope Paul VI's Populorum Progressio (1967) questioned the exclusive claim to property by some individuals while others lack necessities, and Pope John Paul II's Laborem Exercens (1981) balanced the rights of private property with the Christian responsibility for other members of society. Likewise, ecumenical movements among predominantly Protestant churches have provided insight into ways of reestablishing an inclusive use of land.

4. God's ownership of land can be noted in Exod. 9:29; 19:5; Deut. 10:14; 26:10; Ps. 24:1; 50:12; 1 Cor. 10:26.

ownership was never transferred to the new owner. Instead, the land was returned to the original owner in the Jubilee Year (Lev. 25:13); if land had been sold due to financial difficulties, the property could be reclaimed (Lev. 25:25–28).

Nevertheless, the story of King Ahab, Queen Jezebel, and Naboth tells how the land was misused by the rich and powerful to the detriment of the marginalized. According to 1 Kings 21,

> [Naboth] had a vineyard in Jezreel, near the palace of Ahab the king of Samaria. And Ahab spoke to Naboth saying, "Give me your vineyard so it can be a garden of green herbs for me. . . ." But Naboth said to Ahab, "Far be it from me, by Yahweh, that I should give the inheritance of my fathers to you. . . ." [Ahab told Jezebel his wife these things, and she said to Ahab], "Do you now rule over Israel? . . . I will give you the vineyard of Naboth. . . ." [Jezebel then had Naboth stoned by bearing false witness against him], and when Ahab heard that Naboth was dead, Ahab rose to go down to the vineyard . . . to take possession of it.

This view of land as a commodity to be acquired by whatever means necessary to increase personal wealth at the expense of the dispossessed produces injustices. The prophets frequently condemned their own communities for their avarice for land. During times of economic crisis, the biblical distribution of land rights was sometimes ignored as some people purchased the "inheritance" of their weaker neighbors and in the process created an urban elite profiting from the conversion of subsistence farming to exportable cash crops. The prophet Isaiah denounced this practice: "Woe to those touching house to house, bringing near field to field until no end of space, and you are made to dwell alone in the middle of the land" (Isa. 5:8). Likewise, the prophet Micah proclaimed, "Woe to those plotting wickedness. . . . They covet fields and seize them and houses, and carry them off. And they oppress people along with their inheritance" (Mic. 2:1–2).

Another biblical example of the oppressive effects of ownership of land appears in the account of Pharaoh's appropriation of all the land at the expense of the Egyptians' economic welfare: "And Joseph bought all the land of Egypt for Pharaoh, because each one of the Egyptians sold their fields, because the famine was severe upon them. The land became Pharaoh's. As for the people, he reduced them to servitude from one end of Egypt to the other" (Gen. 47:20–21). It is interesting to note that Joseph, a patriarch of the faith, is responsible for creating this oppressive economic structure by redistributing the land from the hungry to the well-fed. In short, the biblical text declares that the right to land is subordinate to the rights of the disenfranchised to earn a just living and the rights of the land itself. Human beings are given biblical rights to be stewards of the land for the purposes of providing basic needs for sustaining life.

As we have already seen, two types of claims can be made on property. Biblical texts champion inclusiveness, the belief that the land should be openly available. This pattern of land usage liberates both the individual and society from the perpetual grip of capitalism and neoliberalism. The land is held in stewardship for God so that the owner and his or her neighbors can obtain the basic necessities of life. Property serves the livelihood of all in the community rather than becoming the form of their subjugation. Such is the paradigm established by Leviticus. This paradigm of land ownership was also employed in the early Christian church, where all believers shared their possessions (including their real property) according to each person's needs (Acts 2:44–45). This biblical concept has its roots in the wilderness experience of Israel when the bread (manna) provided by God was sufficient to meet each person's daily needs (Exod. 16:18). When accumulated in excess, it spoiled. The inclusive use of land can be used to atone for injustice and to restore broken relationships.

The concept of the Trinity, one of the most important teachings of the Christian church, is a doctrine of a God whose life is an inclusive life of sharing. Tertullian's classic formula "one substance and three persons" introduced the Greek word *oikonomia* into theological discourse. This one God exists according to an inner order, the sharing of *substantia* (substance). *Substantia*, the legal terminology used by Tertullian, also meant "property." Hence, the Trinity can be understood as three persons, equal in power, sharing one *substantia*, one property (González 1990b, 111–15). This "economic" doctrine of the Trinity models a social order that avoids the socioeconomic consequences of exclusiveness.

Diametrically opposed to this inclusive claim on property is our modern Western form of land ownership, whose roots lie in Roman law. One of Rome's enduring contributions to Western civilization is its construction of the concept of land. Ownership constituted the right to use, to enjoy, and even to abuse the land. It was the function of the state and the backbone of Roman law to protect private property rights (González 1990a, 14–19). The title to property was exclusive. Nowhere in nature does this concept exist. It is a social construction designed to protect the appropriation of land by a single person. When this happens, the world's marginalized generally are left to barter for a small piece of land, often no longer fertile, in order to raise the bare necessities of life. This arrangement contributes to the fragmentation of our covenant with our God, our neighbor, and our land.

The Mexican revolutionary slogan coined by Emiliano Zapata, "La tierra es de quien la trabaja" ("The land belongs to those who work it"), best captures the biblical concept of land ownership. Many of the early church leaders condemned massive private property held by the rich in favor of land held for the common good. Among the church's greatest exponent for common property was Ambrose (ca. 340–397), who wrote,

> The land was made to be common to all, the poor and the rich. Why do you, of the rich, claim for yourselves alone the right to the land? . . . When you give to the poor, you give not of your own, but simply return what is his, for you have usurped that which is common and has been given for the common use of all. The land belongs to all, not to the rich; and yet those who are deprived of its use are many more than those who enjoy it. . . . God our Lord willed that this land be the common possession of all and give its fruit to all. But greed distributed the right of possessions. Therefore, if you claim as your private property part of what was granted in common to all human beings and to all animals, it is only fair that you share some of this with the poor, so that you will not deny nourishment to those who are also partakers of your right (by which you hold this land). (González 1990a, 191)

Adolfo Pérez Esquivel, a 1980 Nobel laureate, calls for neither the exclusive use of land nor the abolition of land ownership. Rather, he maintains that the land should be distributed according to need. Speaking against the backdrop of South American economies, where cash crops grown for export contribute to a deficiency in food crops, he challenges the notion that land title obtained through purchases is more legitimate than property earned through need and toil. The people who work the land for their sustenance hold a nobler title than the *patrón* who "never sowed a solitary seed" (1983, 99). Enrique Dussel agrees, stating that all people have a natural right to whatever is required to live, be it calories, clothing, or housing. The excess of the unjust accumulation of real property is responsible for subjugating those who have none (1978, 50).[5] This is consistent with the biblical messianic dream expressed by Isaiah: "They shall build houses and live in them; and they shall plant vineyards and eat their fruit. They shall not build and another live in them, or plant and another eat" (Isa. 65:21–22).

Step 4. Case Studies

1. Richard Robinson Jr., a member of the Ojibwe people, remembers how his grandfather, a hospital janitor, looked forward to retiring and return-

---

5. Dussel views private property as an offshoot of original sin, which, for him, is colonial domination. I maintain the opposite: it was avarice for land and its resources that led to colonial domination, thus making land accumulation the original sin and colonialism its offshoot.

ing to his land. But Robinson's grandfather quickly learned that "his" land was no longer his. The Bureau of Indian Affairs told him he had signed the land over to the United States in exchange for a few thousand dollars. "He swore until he died that he never received a check and never signed any papers," said Robinson. "He was dead certain."[6] Robinson's grandfather's story is a common one concerning what once was Native American land, before the relentless westward push of white settlers and railroads. Prior to the Mexican-American War of the 1840s, if Europeans wanted indigenous people's lands, they either fought for it or raised local militias to decimate the original inhabitants. Others chose the "peaceful" means of signing treaties. After the Mexican-American War, with the creation of a standing army, the signing of treaties was substantially reduced. Would-be settlers made powerful lobbying groups pressuring Washington to seize native lands for them. But what do you do with the displaced persons?

After the armies stole lands, the original inhabitants were consigned to reservations. A bureaucracy was created (eventually becoming the Bureau of Indian Affairs) with the mission overseeing the relocation of the indigenous people. Determining that the indigenous people were incompetent of handling their own affairs, reservation land was and continues to be held in trust for them. The U.S. government manages some 56 million acres for the tribes and oversees more than 100,000 leases on those lands. In addition, the government also manages about 2,500 trust accounts for more than 250 tribes.

Holding the lands of Native Americans in trust makes it impossible for them to sell their allotted parcel of land or use it as collateral to begin businesses or send their children to college. Little economic incentive exists to work or improve the land. On March 10, 2006, the U.N. Committee on the Elimination of Racial Discrimination ruled that the U.S. government violated native peoples' land rights; furthermore, Washington has run afoul of an international antiracism treaty. In 2003 a similar finding was issued by the Inter-American Commission on Human Rights, an organ of the Organization of American States. Like most Native Americans, Robinson rejects the argument that their dispossession from their tribal lands was some past event. Although several Christian denominations have apologized to Native Americans for the conquest of their land, there is a lack of recognition that the taking of native lands constitutes an ongoing theft. Native Americans do not believe that the

---

6. Stephanie Strom, "Indians Fight to Regain Lands Lost to Railroad," *New York Times*, December 25, 2002.

apology is sufficient. Referring to apartheid, Archbishop Desmond Tutu said, "If you take my pen, what good does an apology do, if you still keep my pen?" (Kidwell, Noley, and Tinker 2001, 170).

— Does the sin of land theft constitute a sin that continues to be passed down to each succeeding generation? How are the social and economic hardships of Native American nations today linked, if at all, with how Native Americans have been historically treated?

— Once Euroamerican Christians apologize, should Native Americans simply "get over it" because it happened in the past? If not, what specifically should Christians do? What responsibility, if any, do Euroamerican Christians who continue to profit from the lands stolen from the Native Americans have toward them?

— If the U.S. government is unable to produce an authentic bill of sale from Robinson's grandfather, what is due Robinson? Does it matter if a bill of sale does exist? Why or why not?

— In 2012 the U.S. government, in response to over a century of accusations by tribes of doing a poor job of keeping track of the tribal funds that it maintains and of not being diligent in collecting fees from companies that hold leases on reservations, agreed to pay forty-one tribes $1.023 billion for past mismanagements.[7] Some, within poor reservations, have become multimillionaires. Is this adequate compensation? Does this absolve Europeans of all complicity with centuries of land theft? Should the U.S. government continue to hold Native Americans' land in trust for them? Why?

2. Dinavance Kamukama sits under a tree on the grounds of Uganda's largest AIDS clinic and weeps.[8] Anti-AIDS drugs offer hope as powerful medicines changed AIDS from a death sentence to a chronic disease in wealthier countries. But Kamukama is hopeless, for she is unable to obtain the life-saving medicine. And she is not alone. For every 100 people placed on treatment, according to the U.N. AIDS-fighting agency (UNAIDS), 250 are newly infected. The $10 billion donated annually to control the epidemic falls short of the $27 billion a year needed.[9] Kamukama, who has had the disease since birth, lives in the region most heavily affected by HIV. In 2010 about 68 percent of all people living with HIV resided in Sub-Saharan Africa, a region that accounts for only

---

7. Timothy Williams, "U.S. Will Pay a Settlement of $1 Billion to 41 Tribes," *New York Times*, April 20, 2012.
8. Donald G. McNeil Jr., "At Front Lines, AIDS War Is Falling Apart," *New York Times*, May 9, 2010.
9. Ibid.

12 percent of the world's population. This region also represents 70 percent of all new HIV infections. Since 1998, at least a million people living in the Sub-Sahara have died annually of AIDS-related illnesses (UNAIDS 2011, 6–7). Most of these deaths occur because of a lack of access to low-cost anti-AIDS drugs, and the United States has played a role in limiting access.

U.S. demands for tougher review standards for generic copies of patented AIDS drugs prevent the use of cheaper versions of the drugs in the anti-AIDS program in Africa. U.S. officials say that they are concerned about the safety and effectiveness of the generic drugs. However, critics charge that present generic copies have been successful. The administration of President George W. Bush was accused of seeking to protect the profits of large U.S. drug companies, some of whose executives contributed to Bush's reelection campaign. "The Bush project is to ensure the dominance of big pharmaceuticals in poor countries," said Sharonann Lynch, leader of Washington-based NGO Healthgap, at the time. According to activists, up to four times as many Africans could have been treated with life-extending drugs if the United States permitted purchase of the generic equivalents.[10] When President Obama was elected, he made strong statements supporting the rights of countries to buy these affordable generics. Nonetheless, the Office of the U.S. Trade Representative negotiated a different type of free-trade agreement that aggressively protects pharmaceutical monopolies by discouraging generic production.[11]

Dominance over the African drug industry is maintained through the intellectual-property rights held by the pharmaceutical companies. Intellectual-property laws and regulations ensure that royalties are paid to creators of intellectual property. By having the Office of the U.S. Trade Representative lower the standards of what can be patented, generic production is discouraged, in spite of Obama's rhetoric. According to the World Bank, it is estimated that global intellectual-property rules result in the yearly transfer of $41 billion from poor countries to corporations in the top six industrial nations (Kumar, Tripathi, and Tiwari 2011, 579). The World Trade Organization (WTO) is saddled with such regulations as special-interest groups attempt to protect their interests. Jagdish Bhagwati, an economics professor at Columbia University, claims, "This is not a trade issue. It's a royalty-collection issue. It's pharmaceuticals and software throwing their weight around."[12]

---

10. "U.S. Trying to Block Generics in Africa, Say AIDS Activists," *Africa News*, March 29, 2004.
11. Tina Rosenberg, "A Trade Barrier to Defeating AIDS," *New York Times*, July 26, 2011.
12. Tina Rosenberg, "The Free-Trade Fix," *New York Times Magazine*, August 18, 2002.

— Do corporations have a right to protect their royalties from countries with the capability to reproduce their products? Should such corporations pursue copyright violators through the WTO? Is the ultimate purpose of medicine to provide healing to Kamukama, or to increase the pharmaceutical's corporate bottom line?

— The major obstacle to poor nations developing and providing cheap generic AIDS drugs for their inhabitants is intellectual-property rules that ensure that the pharmaceutical creator of the medicine continues to be compensated. Is this system just?

— The world's largest provider of cheap generic drugs is India, exporting about $10 billion of medicine a year. In April 2013 the Indian Supreme Court ruled for the right of local companies to make the cheaper drugs. But brand-name pharmaceutical companies argue that the profits that they reap are essential to their ability to develop and manufacture innovative medicines. The very effective leukemia treatment drug Glivec, costing about $70,000 a year, is generically reproduced in India as Gleevec for about $2,500 a year.[13] Is it fair that Indian firms are profiting at the expense of brand-name pharmaceutical companies? Did the pharmaceutical companies already profit from the development of new medicines? If the poor of the world cannot afford the cost of brand-name medicines, are they simply condemned to illness and death? Are the profits made by brand-name companies being reinvested in the creation of newer drugs, or are they going to bonuses for CEOs?

3. Papa John's CEO John Schnatter declared shortly after the reelection of President Obama that the cost of implementing the Affordable Care Act for his company would force him to increase the price of his pizzas by 10 to 14 cents (even though an independent analysis conducted by *Forbes* placed the cost at 3.4 to 4.6 cents per pizza). Papa John's cost of providing healthcare at $5 to $8 million annually against total revenue of $1.218 billion represents a .4 percent to .7 percent increase in the company's total expense. Ironically, Papa John's, in a promotional stunt, announced in September 2012 the giveaway of 2 million free pizzas. The cost of 2 million free pizzas represents $24–$32 million in revenue.[14] Schnatter also threatened to scale back employees' schedules to less than thirty hours a week to qualify for the health insurance exception, whereby he

13. Gardiner Harris and Katie Thomas, "Low-Cost Drugs in Poor Nations Get Lift in Court," *New York Times*, April 2, 2013.

14. Caleb Melby, "Breaking Down Centi-Millionaire 'Papa' John Schnatter's Obamacare Math," *Forbes*, November 12, 2012.

could avoid paying for the healthcare.[15] He backed off his threats in an opinion piece that he wrote for the *Huffington Post* after a public outcry led to a drop of Papa John's stock values. Meanwhile, John Schnatter lives in a forty-thousand-square-foot castle megamansion with a twenty-two-car garage, a golf course, a drawbridge, an office for valet parking, a car wash, and even a motorized turntable to move limousines.[16] His total compensation package for 2011 was $2.75 million.[17] By comparison, his typical delivery driver earns about $6 to $7 per hour, not including tips.

The value of personal property such as a megamansion often does not exist within the commodity itself, for such value is secondary. Rather, the conspicuous consumption of a commodity mainly seeks recognition by others of the consumer's higher social standing. Hence, conspicuous consumption fails to satisfy any particular need of the consumer; instead, it is the display of commodities, in and of itself, that enhances the reputation of the consumer (Veblen 1953, 21–80).

— Is conspicuous consumption moral? Does a person have a right to spend money on any commodity that he or she chooses to own, even when the sole purpose of owning that commodity is to flaunt a higher social standing? Should people be allowed to accumulate luxury items while their neighbors go hungry? If so, is it a governmental responsibility to address this? If not, are there any ways to create a more balanced society?

— What responsibility do CEOs have to their corporation, their stockholders, the community at large, and the poor? Should Schnatter employ every legal means possible to increase his company's profits? Even if it means reducing employees' weekly work schedules to under thirty hours in order to avoid having to provide healthcare?

---

15. Steven Greenhouse and Reed Abelson, "The Cost of Change: Small Employers Weigh Impact of Providing Health Insurance," *New York Times*, December 1, 2012.

16. http://homesoftherich.net/2008/12/the-house-that-papa-johns-built.

17. http://www.forbes.com/profile/john-schnatter-1.

Epilogue

As mentioned in the preface, the thoughts, ideas, and methodologies appearing within this book were forged within the "privileged" classrooms where I have taught. I recall one incident at the end of the semester when a student said, "Every issue we discuss, no matter how clear-cut it may have appeared to be, seems always to boil down to issues of race, class, and gender. Are there any issues void of these three perspectives?"

Although I said nothing, I really wanted to respond, "Welcome to my world!" For those from the margins of society, race, class, orientation, and gender matter each and every day. The privilege of whiteness and maleness lies in not having to deal with these characteristics in order to survive within society. These factors represent the norm. White men, and white women to a lesser degree, can be good Christians without ever needing to consider how this culture privileges their very existence. And when they are made aware of how structures are designed to benefit them, some become angry at the marginalized when they attempt to raise consciousness. I have consistently heard from colleagues who have used this book in their class that students either love it or hate it. No one is ever simply neutral.

Ethics for the Christian must become the means to dismantle structures that privilege one group at the expense of another. Christian ethics also is the path by which God is known, by which justice is created, by which liberation for the oppressed is chosen. Nevertheless, Christian ethical discipline continues to be formed and shaped by those who benefit from the present structures of power. The ethical perspectives discussed throughout this book have avoided discussion of the moral deliberation of the powerful, the privileged, and the intellectuals in favor of the ethics that resonates among the oppressed, the disenfranchised, and the marginalized.

In order for a system of ethics to be Christian, it must be forged contextually within the margins of society, specifically within the faith community. Such an ethics, by its very nature, serves as a critique of the reasoning employed by ethicists from the dominant culture, whose so-called objectivity, in the final analysis, remains situated in a culture of privilege, a context that is either consciously or unconsciously justified.

This book has attempted to hold the dominant culture accountable for failing to address how race, class, and gender are embedded in Christianity. Christian ethics has ignored and continues to ignore its complicity with oppressive structures, refusing to take responsibility for creating a morality that does not adequately address the concerns of the marginalized. The benefactors of the status quo, in order to maintain their privilege, create certain principles that attempt reform without changing the very way in which power is constructed. For this reason, doing ethics from the margins is not simply an interesting ethical perspective, nor is it an extension of Eurocentric ethics. Rather, to do ethics from the margins is to participate in a Christian social ethics that fully considers (1) the privilege of power, (2) the causes of supposed superiority, and (3) the rules by which power is maintained. Only then can Christians expose and debunk the obstacles preventing all of God's creatures from living the abundant life.

Bibliography

Abell, John D. "Defense Spending and Unemployment Rates: An Empirical Analysis Disaggregated by Race." *Cambridge Journal of Economics* 14 (1990): 405–19.

———. "Military Spending and Income Inequality." *Journal of Peace Research* 31, no. 1 (1994): 35–43.

Acevedo-Garcia, Dolores, et al. *Unequal Health Outcomes in the United States: Racial and Ethnic Disparities in Health Care Treatment and Access, the Role of Social and Environmental Determinants of Health, and the Responsibility of the State*. New York: U.N. Committee on the Elimination of Racial Discrimination, 2008.

Amnesty International. *United States of America: Death by Discrimination—The Continuing Role of Race in Capital Cases*. London: Amnesty International, 2003.

———. *Iraq: Beyond Abu Ghraib; Detention and Torture in Iraq*. London: Amnesty International, 2006.

Anderson, Sarah, et al. *Executive Excess 2001: Layoffs—Tax Rebates—The Gender Gap*. Washington, DC: Institute for Policy Studies and United for a Fair Economy, 2001.

———. *Executive Excess 2011: The Massive CEO Rewards for Tax Dodging*. Washington, DC: Institute for Policy Studies, 2011.

Aquino, María Pilar. "Theological Method in U.S. Latino/a Theology: Toward an Intercultural Theology for the Third Millennium." In *From the Heart of Our People: Latino/a Explorations in Catholic Systematic Theology*, edited by Orlando O. Espín and Miguel H. Díaz, 6–48. Maryknoll, NY: Orbis Books, 1999.

Arendt, Hannah. *The Human Condition*. Chicago: University of Chicago Press, 1958.

Augustine. *The City of God against the Pagans*. Edited by T. E. Page et al. Translated by William Chase Greene. Vol. 6. Cambridge: Harvard University Press, 1960.

Bacon, David. "World Labor Needs Independence and Solidarity." *Monthly Review* 52, no. 3 (2000): 84–102.

Baker-Fletcher, Karen. *Sisters of Dust, Sisters of Spirit: Womanist Wordings on God and Creation*. Minneapolis: Fortress, 1998.

———. "Spirituality." In *Handbook of U.S. Theologies of Liberation*, edited by Miguel A. De La Torre, 117–28. St. Louis: Chalice, 2004.

Barlett, Donald L., and James B. Steele. *The Betrayal of the American Dream*. New York: PublicAffairs, 2012.

Barth, Karl. *The Word of God and the Word of Man*. Translated by Douglas Horton. London: Hodder & Stoughton, 1928.

————. *This Christian Cause: A Letter to Great Britain from Switzerland*. New York: Macmillan, 1941.

Baum, Katrina, et al. *Stalking Victimization in the United States*. Washington, DC: U.S. Department of Justice, Bureau of Justice Statistics, 2009.

Baxandall, Phineas, and Dan Smith. *Picking Up the Tab, 2013: Average Citizens and Small Businesses Pay the Price for Offshore Tax Havens*. Boston: U.S. Public Interest Research Group, 2013.

Bayer, Patrick, Shamena Anwar, and Randi Hjalmarsson. *The Impact of Jury Race in Criminal Trials*. Durham, NC: Duke Population Research Institute, 2011.

Becker, Patricia C., ed. *A Statistical Portrait of the United States: Social Conditions and Trends*. 2nd ed. Lanham, MD: Bernan, 2002.

Belasco, Amy. *The Cost of Iraq, Afghanistan, and Other Global War on Terror Operations since 9/11*. Washington, DC: Congressional Research Service, 2012.

Bell, Daniel M. *Liberation Theology after the End of History: The Refusal to Cease Suffering*. New York: Routledge, 2001.

Bhabha, Homi K. *The Location of Culture*. New York: Routledge, 1994.

Blackman, Allen, et al. *Health Impacts of Power-Exporting Plants in Northern Mexico*. Washington, DC: Resources for the Future, 2011.

Blank, Rebecca M. "Presidential Address: How to Improve Poverty Measurement in the United States." *Journal of Policy Analysis and Management* 27, no. 2 (2008): 233–54.

Blount, Brian K. *Then the Whisper Put on Flesh: New Testament Ethics in an African American Context*. Nashville: Abingdon, 2001.

Boff, Clodovis. *Theology and Praxis: Epistemological Foundations*. Translated by Robert R. Barr. Maryknoll, NY: Orbis Books, 1987.

Boff, Clodovis, and George V. Pixley. *The Bible, the Church, and the Poor*. Translated by Paul Burns. Maryknoll, NY: Orbis Books, 1989.

Boff, Leonardo. *Cry of the Earth, Cry of the Poor*. Translated by Phillip Berryman. Maryknoll, NY: Orbis Books, 1997.

Boff, Leonardo, and Clodovis Boff. *Salvation and Liberation: In Search of a Balance between Faith and Politics*. Translated by Robert R. Barr. Maryknoll, NY: Orbis Books, 1984.

Bogusz, Christine, et al., eds. *The Budget and Economic Outlook: Fiscal Years 2010–2020*. Washington, DC: Congressional Budget Office, 2010.

Bonino, José Míguez. *Doing Theology in a Revolutionary Situation*. Philadelphia: Fortress, 1975.

——. *Toward a Christian Political Ethics*. Philadelphia: Fortress, 1983.

Bonney, Roland, and Marian Stamp Dawkins. "The Future of Animal Farming." In *The Future of Animal Farming: Renewing the Ancient Contract*, edited by Marian Stamp Dawkins and Roland Bonney, 1–4. Oxford: Blackwell, 2008.

Bourdieu, Pierre. *Outline of a Theory of Practice*. Translated by Richard Nice. Cambridge: Cambridge University Press, 1977.

Bowen, William G., and Sarah A. Levin. *Reclaiming the Game: College Sports and Educational Values*. Princeton, NJ: Princeton University Press, 2003.

Bravve, Elina, et al. *Out of Reach 2012: America's Forgotten Housing Crises*. Washington, DC: National Low Income Housing Coalition, 2012.

Brubaker, Rogers. "Rethinking Classical Theory: The Sociological Vision of Pierre Bourdieu." *Theory and Society* 14 (1985): 745–75.

Brueggemann, Walter. *The Land*. Philadelphia: Fortress, 1977.

Brunner, Emil. *The Divine Imperative*. Translated by Olive Wyon. Philadelphia: Westminster, 1947.

Bullard, Robert D. "Anatomy of Environmental Racism." In *Toxic Struggles: The Theory and Practice of Environmental Justice*, edited by Richard Hofrichter, 25–35. Philadelphia: New Society Publishers, 1993.

——. *Dumping in Dixie: Race, Class, and Environmental Quality*. Boulder, CO: Westview, 1994.

Bullard, Robert D., Glenn S. Johnson, and Angel O. Torres. *Environmental Health and Racial Equity in the United States: Building Environmentally Just, Sustainable, and Livable Communities*. Washington, DC: American Public Health Association, 2011.

Bullard, Robert D., et al. *Toxic Wastes and Race at Twenty, 1987–2007: A Report Prepared for the United Church of Christ Justice and Witness Ministries*. Cleveland: Justice and Witness Ministries of the United Church of Christ, 2007.

Burns, Crosby, Kimberly Barton, and Sophia Kerby. *The State of Diversity in Today's Workforce: As Our Nation Becomes More Diverse So Too Does Our Workforce*. Washington, DC: Center for American Progress, 2012.

Bush, George W. "Remarks to the United States Chamber of Commerce." Speech given at the Chamber of Commerce's Hall of Flags, Washington, DC, April 16, 2001.

Butler, Smedley D. *War Is a Racket*. New York: Round Table Press, 1935.

Calvin, John. *The Institutes of the Christian Religion*. Translated by Henry Beveridge. 2 vols. Grand Rapids: Eerdmans, 1983.

Cannon, Katie. *Black Womanist Ethics*. Atlanta: Scholars Press, 1988.

——. *Katie's Canon: Womanism and the Soul of the Black Community*. New York: Continuum, 1995.

————. *The Womanist Theology Primer: Remembering What We Never Knew; The Epistemology of Womanist Theology*. Louisville: Women's Ministries Program Area, National Ministries Division, Presbyterian Church (U.S.A.), 2001.

Carnevale, Anthony P., and Stephen J. Rose. *Socioeconomic Status, Race/Ethnicity, and Selective College Admissions*. New York: The Century Foundation, 2003.

Catalano, Shannan. *Intimate Partner Violence in the United States*. Washington, DC: U.S. Department of Justice, Bureau of Justice Statistics, 2007.

Catalano, Shannan, et al. *Female Victims of Violence*. Washington, DC: U.S. Department of Justice, Bureau of Justice Statistics, 2009.

Catherine of Siena. *The Dialogue*. Translated by Suzanne Noffke. New York: Paulist Press, 1980.

CELAM. *La iglesia en la actual transformación de América Latina a la luz del concilio*. Vol. 2, *Conclusiones*. 2nd ed. Bogotá: Secretariado General del CELAM, 1968.

Centers for Disease Control and Prevention. "Adverse Health Conditions and Health Risk Behaviors Associated with Intimate Partner Violence." *CDC Morbidity and Mortality Weekly Report* 57, no. 5 (2008): 113–40.

Chang, Jeani, et al. "Homicide: A Leading Cause of Injury Deaths among Pregnant and Postpartum Women in the United States, 1991–1999." *American Journal of Public Health* 95, no. 3 (2005): 471–77.

Chávez, César. "Farm Workers at Risk." In *Toxic Struggles: The Theory and Practice of Environmental Justice*, edited by Richard Hofrichter, 163–70. Philadelphia: New Society Publishers, 1993.

Child Trends Data Bank. *Late or No Prenatal Care*. Bethesda, MD: Child Trends Data Bank, 2012.

Cobb, John B., Jr. "Liberation Theology and the Global Economy." In *Liberating the Future: God, Mammon and Theology*, edited by Joerg Rieger, 27–42. Minneapolis: Fortress, 1998.

Cohen, Thomas H., and Tracey Kyckelhahn. *Felony Defendants in Large Urban Counties*. Washington, DC: U.S. Department of Justice, Bureau of Justice Statistics, 2006.

Cone, James H. *Black Theology and Black Power*. New York: Seabury, 1969.

————. *God of the Oppressed*. New York: Seabury, 1975.

————. *A Black Theology of Liberation*. 20th anniversary ed. Maryknoll, NY: Orbis Books, 1990.

————. *Speaking the Truth: Ecumenism, Liberation, and Black Theology*. 2nd ed. Maryknoll, NY: Orbis Books, 1999.

Coleman-Jensen, Alisha, Mark Nord, and Anita Singh. *Household Food Security in the United States in 2012: Economic Research Report #155*. Washington D.C.: U.S. Department of Agriculture, 2013.

Cool Foods Campaign. "Another Take: Global Warming and Your Food." In *Food, Inc.: How Industrial Food Is Making Us Sicker, Fatter and Poorer—And What You Can Do about It*, edited by Karl Weber, 119–22. New York: Public Affairs, 2009.

Cooper, Alexia, and Eric L. Smith. *Homicide Trends in the United States, 1980–2008: Annual Rates for 2009 and 2010*. Washington, DC: U.S. Department of Justice, Bureau of Justice Statistics, 2011.

Cooper, Lisa, et al. "The Associations of Clinicians' Implicit Attitudes about Race with Medical Visit Communication and Patient Ratings of Interpersonal Care." *American Journal of Public Health* 102, no. 5 (2012): 979–87.

Cooper, Mary H. "Income Inequality." *Congressional Quarterly Researcher* 8, no. 15 (1998): 339–59.

Correll, Joshua, et al. "The Police Officer's Dilemma: Using Ethnicity to Disambiguate Potentially Threatening Individuals." *Journal of Personality and Social Psychology* 83, no. 6 (2002): 1314–29.

Costanzo, Mark. "The Death Penalty Is Discriminatory." In *The Death Penalty: Opposing Viewpoints*, edited by Mary E. Williams, 173–75. San Diego: Greenhaven, 2002.

Crawford, Neta C., and Catherine Lutz, eds. *The Costs of War since 2001: Iraq, Afghanistan, and Pakistan*. Boston: Watson Institute for International Studies at Brown University, 2013.

Dalton, Frederick John. *The Moral Vision of César Chávez*. Maryknoll, NY: Orbis Books, 2003.

Daly, Lois K. "Ecofeminism, Reverence for Life, and Feminist Theological Ethics." In *Feminist Theological Ethics: A Reader*, edited by Lois K. Daly, 295–314. Louisville: Westminster John Knox, 1994.

Daly, Mary. *Beyond God the Father: Toward a Philosophy of Women's Liberation*. Boston: Beacon, 1973.

Death Penalty Information Center. *National Statistics on the Death Penalty and Race*. Washington, DC: Death Penalty Information Center, 2012.

de Coulanges, Numa Denis Fustel. *The Ancient City: A Study on the Religion, Laws, and Institutions of Greece and Rome*. Baltimore: Johns Hopkins University Press, 1980.

de la Cruz, Juan. "Ascent of Mount Carmel." In *John of the Cross: Selected Writings*, edited by Kieran Kavanaugh, 41–154. New York: Paulist Press, 1987.

De La Torre, Miguel A. *Reading the Bible from the Margins*. Maryknoll, NY: Orbis Books, 2002.

———. "The Challenge of Lazarus." *Celebration* 31, no. 3 (2003a): 99–100.

———. *La Lucha for Cuba: Religion and Politics on the Streets of Miami*. Berkeley: University of California Press, 2003b.

————. *Santería: The Beliefs and Rituals of a Growing Religion in America.* Grand Rapids: Eerdmans, 2004.

————. *A Lily among the Thorns: Imagining a New Christian Sexuality.* San Francisco: Jossey-Bass, 2007.

————, ed. *The Hope of Liberation in World Religions.* Waco, TX: Baylor University Press, 2008.

————. *Trails of Hope and Terror: Testimonies on Immigration.* Maryknoll, NY: Orbis Books, 2009.

————. "Beyond Machismo: A Cuban Case Study." In *Sexuality and the Sacred: Sources for Theological Reflection,* edited by Marvin M. Ellison and Kelly Brown Douglas, 221–40. 2nd ed. Louisville: Westminster John Knox, 2010.

————. "Mad Men, Competitive Women, and Invisible Hispanics." *Journal of Feminist Studies in Religion* 28, no. 1 (2012): 113–25.

De La Torre, Miguel A., and Edwin David Aponte. *Introducing Latino/a Theologies.* Maryknoll, NY: Orbis Books, 2001.

Deloria, Vine, Jr. *Custer Died for Your Sins: An Indian Manifesto.* New York: Macmillan, 1969.

DeNavas-Walt, Carmen, Bernadette D. Proctor, and Jessica C. Smith. *Income, Poverty, and Health Insurance Coverage in the United States: 2010.* Washington, DC: U.S. Census Bureau, 2011.

Dobuzinskis, Caroline. *Statement from IWPR President Dr. Heidi Hartmann on the 50th Anniversary of the Equal Pay Act.* Washington, DC: Institute for Women's Policy Research, 2013.

Dovidio, John F., and Susan T. Fiske. "Under the Radar: How Unexamined Biases in Decision-Making Process in Clinical Interactions Can Contribute to Health Care Disparities." *American Journal of Public Health* 102, no. 5 (2012): 945–52.

Dube, Arindrajit, T. William Lester, and Barry Eidlin. *A Downward Push: The Impact of Wal-Mart Stores on Retail Wages and Benefits.* Berkeley, CA: UC Berkeley Labor Center, 2007.

Duhart, Detis. *Violence in the Workplace, 1993–99.* Washington, DC: Bureau of Justice Statistics, 2001.

Durkheim, Emile. *The Division of Labor in Society.* Translated by George Simpson. New York: Collier Macmillan, 1933.

Dussel, Enrique. *Ethics and the Theology of Liberation.* Translated by Bernard F. McWilliams. Maryknoll, NY: Orbis Books, 1978.

————. *Ethics and Community.* Translated by Robert R. Barr. Maryknoll, NY: Orbis Books, 1988.

————. *The Invention of the Americas: Eclipse of "The Other" and the Myth of Modernity.* Translated by Michael D. Barber. New York: Continuum, 1995.

Ebert, Franz Christian, Raymond Torres, and Konstantinos Papadakis. *Executive Compensation: Trends and Policy Issues.* Geneva: International Institute for Labor Studies, 2008.

Editor's Desk. *Unemployment Rates by Race and Ethnicity, 2010.* Washington, DC: U.S. Bureau of Labor Statistics, 2011.

Ehrenreich, Barbara. *Nickel and Dimed: On (Not) Getting By in America.* New York: Henry Holt, 2001.

Ehrenreich, Barbara, and John Ehrenreich. "The Professional-Managerial Class." In *Between Labor and Capital,* edited by Pat Walker, 5–47. Boston: South End Press 1972.

Eisenhower, Dwight D. "The Chance for Peace." Speech given to the American Society of Newspaper Editors, Washington, DC, April 16, 1953.

Eisenhower Research Project. *The Costs of Wars since 2001: Iraq, Afghanistan, and Pakistan.* Providence: Brown University, Watson Institute for International Studies, 2011.

Epstein, Lee, William M. Landes, and Richard A. Posner. "How Business Fares in the Supreme Court." *Minnesota Law Review* 97, no. 2 (2013): 1431–72.

Fanon, Frantz. *The Wretched of the Earth.* Translated by Constance Farrington. New York: Grove, 1963.

Feinberg, Joel. *Rights, Justice, and the Bounds of Liberty: Essays in Social Philosophy.* Princeton, NJ: Princeton University Press, 1980.

Feith, Douglas J. *War and Decision: Inside the Pentagon at the Dawn of the War on Terrorism.* New York: HarperCollins, 2008.

Fieldhouse, Andrew, and Ethan Pollack. *Tenth Anniversary of the Bush-Era Tax Cuts.* Washington, DC: Economic Policy Institute, 2011.

Finer, Lawrence B., and Mia R. Zolna. "Unintended Pregnancy in the United States: Incidence and Disparities, 2006." *Contraception* 84, no. 5 (2011): 478–85.

Fischer, Brendan, and Blair Bowie. *Election Confidential: How Shady Operators Used Sham Non-profits and Fake Corporations to Funnel Mystery Money into the 2012 Election.* Boston: Center for Media and Democracy, and U.S. Public Interest Research Group, 2013.

Foshee, Vangie A., et al. "The Safe Dates Project: Theoretical Basis, Evaluation Design, and Selected Baseline Findings." *American Journal of Preventive Medicine* 12, supplement no. 5 (1996): 39–47.

Foucault, Michel. *Madness and Civilization: A History of Insanity in the Age of Reason.* Translated by Richard Howard. New York: Pantheon Books, 1965

———. *The Foucault Reader.* Edited by Paul Rabinow. New York: Pantheon Books, 1984.

————. *Technologies of the Self: A Seminar with Michel Foucault*. Edited by Luther H. Martin, Huck Gitman, and Patrick H. Hutton. Amherst: University of Massachusetts Press, 1988.

Freire, Paulo. *Pedagogy of the Oppressed*. Translated by Myra Bergman Ramos. 20th anniversary ed. New York: Continuum, 1994.

Friedman, Milton. *Capitalism and Freedom*. Chicago: University of Chicago Press, 1962.

Fukuda-Parr, Sakiko, ed. *United Nations Development Programme Human Development Report 2003*. New York: Oxford University Press, 2003.

George, Henry. *Progress and Poverty: An Inquiry into the Cause of Industrial Depressions and of Increase of Want with Increase of Wealth*. 50th anniversary ed. New York: Robert Schalkenbach Foundation, 1951.

George, Susan. *Food Strategies for Tomorrow*. San Francisco: Hunger Project, 1987.

————. "A Short History of Neoliberalism." Paper presented at The Conference on Economic Sovereignty in a Globalising World. Bangkok, Thailand, March 24–26, 1999.

George, Susan, and Fabrizio Sabelli. *Faith and Credit: The World Bank's Secular Empire*. Boulder, CO: Westview, 1994.

Giani, Luise, and Elke Ahrensfeld. "Pedobiochemical Indicators for Eutrophications and the Development of 'Black Spots' in Tidal Flat Soils in the North Sea Coast." *Journal of Plant Nutrition and Soil Science* 165, no. 4 (2002): 537–43.

Gilligan, Carol. *In a Different Voice: Psychological Theory and Woman's Development*. Cambridge, MA: Harvard University Press, 1982.

Glenn, Jerome C., Theodore J. Gordon, and Elizabeth Florescu. *2012 State of the Future*. Washington, DC: The Millennium Project, 2012.

Gnanadason, Aruna. "Toward a Feminist Eco-Theology for India." In *Women Healing Earth: Third World Women on Ecology, Feminism, and Religion*, edited by Rosemary Radford Ruether, 74–81. Maryknoll, NY: Orbis Books, 1996.

Goldsmith, Pat Rubio. "Schools or Neighborhoods or Both? Race and Ethnic Segregation and Educational Attainment." *Social Forces* 87, no. 4 (2009): 1913–41.

Gómez, A. M. "Sexual Violence as a Predictor of Unintended Pregnancy, Contraceptive Use, and Unmet Need among Female Youth in Colombia." *Journal of Women's Health* 20, no. 9 (2011): 1349–56.

González, Justo. *Faith and Wealth: A History of Early Christian Ideas on the Origin, Significance, and Use of Money*. San Francisco: Harper & Row, 1990a.

————. *Mañana: Christian Theology from a Hispanic Perspective*. Nashville: Abingdon, 1990b.

Gottschall, Jonathan A., and Tiffani A. Gottschall. "Are Per-Incident Rape-Pregnancy Rates Higher Than Per-Incident Consensual Pregnancy Rates?" *Human Nature* 14, no. 1 (2003): 1–20.

Greider, William. "A New Giant Sucking Sound." *The Nation* 273, no. 22 (December 31, 2001): 22–24.

Griffiths, Brian. "The Challenge of Global Capitalism: A Christian Perspective." In *Making Globalization Good: Moral Challenges of Global Capitalism*, edited by John H. Dunning, 159–80. Oxford: Oxford University Press, 2003.

Grimmett, Richard F. *Conventional Arms Transfers to Developing Nations, 1994–2001*. Washington, DC: Congressional Research Service, 2002.

Grimmett, Richard F., and Paul K. Kerr. *Conventional Arms Transfers to Developing Nations, 2004–2011*. Washington, DC: Congressional Research Service, 2012.

Grosz, Elizabeth. *Jacques Lacan: A Feminist Interpretation*. London: Routledge, 1990.

Gruenstein Bocian, Debbie, Keith S. Ernst, and Wei Li. *Unfair Lending: The Effect of Race and Ethnicity on the Price of Subprime Mortgages*. Washington, DC: Center for Responsible Lending, 2006.

———. *Foreclosures by Race and Ethnicity: The Demographics of a Crisis*. Washington, DC: Center for Responsible Lending, 2010.

Guerino, Paul, Paige M. Harrison, and William J. Sabol. *Prisoners in 2010*. Washington, DC: U.S. Department of Justice, Bureau of Justice Statistics, December 2011.

Gustafson, James M. *Christ and the Moral Life*. New York: Harper & Row, 1968.

———. *Theology and Christian Ethics*. Philadelphia: United Church Press, 1974.

———. *Can Ethics Be Christian? An Inquiry*. Chicago: University of Chicago Press, 1975.

Gustafson, James M., and James Laney, eds. *On Being Responsible: Issues in Personal Ethics*. New York: Harper & Row, 1968.

Gutiérrez, Gustavo. *The Power of the Poor in History: Selected Writings*. Translated by Robert R. Barr. Maryknoll, NY: Orbis Books, 1984.

———. *A Theology of Liberation: History, Politics, and Salvation*. Translated and edited by Sister Caridad Inda and John Eagleson. 15th anniversary ed. Maryknoll, NY: Orbis Books, 1988.

———. "Liberation Theology and the Future of the Poor." In *Liberating the Future: God, Mammon and Theology*, edited by Joerg Rieger, 96–123. Minneapolis: Fortress, 1998.

Guttmacher Institute. *States Enact Record Number of Abortion Restrictions in 2011*. New York: Guttmacher Institute, 2012.

———. *2012 Saw Second-Highest Abortion Restrictions Ever*. New York: Guttmacher Institute, 2013.

Haines, John, and Laurel Staley, eds. *Risk Management Evaluation for Concentrated Animal Feeding Operations*. Cincinnati: U.S. Environmental Protection Agency, National Risk Management Laboratory, 2004.

Hall, Daria, and Natasha Ushomirsky. *Close the Hidden Funding Gaps in Our Schools: K–12 Policy*. Washington, DC: The Education Trust, 2006.

Hamilton, Cynthia. "Environmental Consequences of Urban Growth and Blight." In *Toxic Struggles: The Theory and Practice of Environmental Justice*, edited by Richard Hofrichter, 67–75. Philadelphia: New Society Publishers, 1993.

Hartung, William D. *And Weapons for All*. New York: HarperCollins, 1994.

Hauerwas, Stanley. "Some Theological Reflections on Gutierrez's Use of 'Liberation' as a Theological Concept." *Modern Theology* 3, no. 1 (1986): 67–76.

Heen, Mary L. "Ending Jim Crow Life Insurance Rates." *Northwestern Journal of Law and Social Policy* 4, no. 2 (2009): 360–99.

Hegel, G. W. F. *The Phenomenology of Mind*. Translated by J. B. Baillie. New York: Harper & Row, 1967.

Hegewisch, Ariane, and Maxwell Matite. *Fact Sheet: America's Women and the Wage Gap*. Washington, DC: National Partnership for Women and Family, 2013.

Hegewisch, Ariane, Claudia Williams, and Vanessa Harbin. *Fact Sheet: The Gender Gap by Occupation*. Washington, DC: Institute for Women's Policy Research, 2012.

Henderson, Errol Anthony. "Military Spending and Poverty." *Journal of Politics* 60, no. 2 (1998): 503–20.

Heyward, Carter. "Christ." In *Handbook of U.S. Theologies of Liberation*, edited by Miguel A. De La Torre, 16–30. St. Louis: Chalice, 2004.

Hinkelammert, Franz J. *The Ideological Weapon of Death: A Theological Critique*. Trans. Phillip Berryman. Maryknoll, NY: Orbis Books, 1986.

———. *Cultura de esperanza y sociedad sin exclusión*. San José, Costa Rica: Departamento Ecuménico de Investigaciones, 1995.

———. "Liberation Theology in the Economic and Social Context of Latin America: Economy and Theology, or the Irrationality of the Rationalized." In *Liberation Theologies, Postmodernity, and the Americas*, edited by David Batstone et al., 25–52. London: Routledge, 1997.

———. "Globalization as Cover-Up: An Ideology to Disguise and Justify Current Wrongs." In *Globalization and Its Victims*, edited by Jon Sobrino and Felix Wilfred, 25–34. London: SCM, 2001.

Hinn, Benny. Sermon televised on *Trinity Broadcasting Network*, November 6, 1990.

Hobbes, Thomas. *Leviathan*. Oxford: Clarendon, 1909.

Hodson, Gordon, John F. Dovidio, and Samuel L. Gaertner. "The Aversive Form of Racism." In *The Psychology of Prejudice and Discrimination: A Revised and Condensed Edition*, edited by Jean Lau Chin, 1–13. Santa Barbara, CA: Praeger, 2009.

Hopkins, Dwight N. *Shoes That Fit Our Feet: Sources for a Constructive Black Theology*. Maryknoll, NY: Orbis Books, 2000.

Hoxby, Caroline M., and Christopher Avery. "The Missing 'One-Offs': The Hidden Supply of High-Achieving, Low-Income Students." Washington, DC: National Bureau of Economic Research, 2012.

Huang, Ganlin, and Jonathan London. "Mapping Cumulative Environmental Effects, Social Vulnerability, and Health in the San Joaquin Valley, California." *American Journal of Public Health* 102, no. 5 (2012): 830–32.

Hungerford, Thomas L. "Taxes and the Economy: An Economic Analysis of the Top Tax Rates Since 1945." Washington DC.: Congressional Research Service, 2012.

International Energy Agency. *IEA Statistics: CO_2 Emissions from Fuel Combustion Highlights*. Paris: International Energy Agency, 2011.

Jackson, Jesse. *Legal Lynching: Racism, Injustice, and the Death Penalty*. New York: Marlowe, 1996.

Jiang, Xing, "Letter from China." *The Nation* 274, no. 8 (March 4, 2002): 23–25.

John Paul II. *The Gospel of Life*. New York: Random House, 1995.

Johnson, Tiffani J., et al. "Association of Race and Ethnicity with Management of Abdominal Pain in the Emergency Department," *Pediatrics* 132, no. 4 (October, 2013): 851–58.

Jones, Major J. *Christian Ethics for Black Theology*. Nashville: Abingdon, 1974.

Kahlenberg, Richard D. *A Better Affirmative Action: State Universities that Created Alternatives to Racial Preferences*. New York: The Century Foundation, 2012.

Kahn, Katherine L. "Health Care for Black and Poor Hospitalized Medicare Patients." *Journal of the American Medical Association* 271, no. 15 (1994): 1169–74.

Kammer, Charles L., III. *Ethics and Liberation: An Introduction*. Maryknoll, NY: Orbis Books, 1988.

Kearns, Rick. "U.S. Navy Tests Create Health Risks in Viéques." *Hispanic* 12, no. 9 (1999): 12–16.

Kennedy, Paul. *The Rise and Fall of the Great Powers: Economic Change and Military Conflict from 1500 to 2000*. New York: Random House, 1987.

Kidwell, Clara Sue, Homer Noley, and George E. "Tink" Tinker. *A Native American Theology.* Maryknoll, NY: Orbis Books, 2001.

King, Martin Luther, Jr. *Stride toward Freedom: The Montgomery Story.* New York: Harper, 1958.

———. *Strength to Love.* Philadelphia: Fortress, 1963.

———. *Why We Can't Wait.* New York: New American Library, 1964.

———. "Pilgrimage to Nonviolence." In *A Testament of Hope: The Essential Writings of Martin Luther King Jr.* Edited by James Melvin Washington. New York: HarperCollins, 1986a.

———. "The Trumpet of Conscience." In *A Testament of Hope: The Essential Writings of Martin Luther King Jr.* Edited by James Melvin Washington. New York: HarperCollins, 1986b.

Kost, Kathryn, and Stanley Henshaw. "U.S. Teenage Pregnancies, Births and Abortions, 2008: National Trends by Race and Ethnicity." New York: Guttmacher Institute, 2012.

Kozol, Jonathan. *Savage Inequalities: Children in America's Schools.* New York: Crown, 1991.

Kumar, Ranjeet, R. C. Tripathi, and M. D. Tiwari. "A Case Study of Impact of Patenting in the Current Developing Economies in Asia." *Scientometrics* 88, no. 3 (2011): 575–87.

Kwok, Pui-lan. *Introducing Asian Feminist Theology.* Cleveland: Pilgrim, 2000.

Labor Council for Latin American Advancement and Public Citizen. *Another America Is Possible: The Impact of NAFTA on the U.S. Latino Community and Lessons for Future Trade Agreements.* Washington, DC: LCLAA and Public Citizen, 2004.

Lacan, Jacques. *Écrits: A Selection.* Translated by Alan Sheridan. New York: W. W. Norton, 1977.

Ladd, Helen F. "Education and Poverty: Confronting the Evidence." *Journal of Policy Analysis and Management* 31, no. 2 (2012): 203–27.

LaDuke, Winona. "A Society Based on Conquest Cannot Be Sustained: Native Peoples and the Environmental Crises." In *Toxic Struggles: The Theory and Practice of Environmental Justice*, edited by Richard Hofrichter, 98–106. Philadelphia: New Society Publishers, 1993.

Landau, Saul. "The End of the Maquila Era." *The Progressive* 66, no. 9 (2002): 24–26.

Lioz, Adam, and Blair Bowie. *Billion-Dollar Democracy: The Unprecedented Role of the Money in the 2012 Election.* Boston: Demo and U.S. Public Interest Research Group, 2013a.

———. *Election Spending 2012: A Pre-Election Analysis of Federal Election Commission Data.* Boston: Demo and U.S. Public Interest Research Group, January 2013b.

———. *Election Spending 2012: A Post-Election Analysis of Federal Election Commission Data.* Boston: Demo and U.S. Public Interest Research Group, January 2013c.

Locke, John. *The Second Treatise of Government.* Edited by Thomas P. Peardon. Indianapolis: Bobbs-Merrill, 1952.

López, Ann Aurelia. *The Farmworkers' Journey.* Berkeley: University of California Press, 2007.

López, Mark Hugo, and Michael Light. *A Rising Share: Hispanics and Federal Crime.* Washington, DC: Pew Research Center, 2009.

Luther, Martin. *Luther's Works.* Vol. 46, *The Christian in Society III.* Edited by Helmut T. Lehmann and Robert C. Schultz. Philadelphia: Fortress, 1967.

———. *Luther's Works.* Vol. 1. *Lectures on Genesis, Chapters 1–5.* Edited by Jaroslav Pelikan. St. Louis: Concordia, 1995.

MacDorman, Marian F., and T. J. Mathews. *Understanding Racial and Ethnic Disparities in U.S. Infant Mortality Rates.* Washington, DC: Center for Disease Control and Prevention, 2011.

Madison, James. "Federalist Paper #10." In *The Federalist,* by Alexander Hamilton, John Jay, and James Madison, edited by George W. Carey and James McClellan, 42–48. Indianapolis: Liberty Fund, 2001.

Maher, Timothy. "Environmental Oppression: Who Is Targeted for Toxic Exposure?" *Journal of Black Studies* 28, no. 3 (1998): 357–67.

Malcolm X. "The Leverett House Forum of March 18, 1964." In *The Speeches of Malcolm X at Harvard.* Edited by Archie Epps. New York: William Morrow, 1968.

McCann, Dennis P., and Charles R. Strain. *Polity and Praxis: A Program for American Practical Theology.* Minneapolis: Winston, 1985.

McConnell, D. R. *A Different Gospel: Biblical and Historical Insights into the Word of Faith Movement.* Peabody, MA: Hendrickson, 1995.

McKay, Alexander, and Michael Barrett. "Trends in Teen Pregnancy Rates from 1996–2006: A Comparison of Canada, Sweden, USA and England/Wales." *Canadian Journal of Human Sexuality* 19, nos. 1–2 (2010): 43–52.

McMahon, Shawn, Yunju Nam, and Yung Soo Lee. *The Basic Economic Security Tables for the United States.* Washington, DC: Wider Opportunities for Women, 2011.

Meeks, M. Douglas. *God the Economist: The Doctrine of God and Political Economy.* Minneapolis: Fortress, 1989.

———. "Economy and the Future of Liberation Theology in North America." In *Liberating the Future: God, Mammon, and Theology,* edited by Joerg Rieger, 44–59. Minneapolis: Fortress, 1998.

Michalos, Alex C. *A Pragmatic Approach to Business Ethics.* Thousand Oaks, CA: Sage Publications, 1995.

Mireles, Ricardo Castillo. "Chinese Maquiladoras Threaten Mexico." *Transportation and Distribution* 43, no. 11 (2002): 26–28.

Mitchem, Stephanie Y. *Introducing Womanist Theology.* Maryknoll, NY: Orbis Books, 2002.

Moltmann, Jürgen. "Political Theology and Theology of Liberation." In *Liberating the Future: God, Mammon and Theology,* edited by Joerg Rieger, 60–80. Minneapolis: Fortress, 1998.

Moorman, Jeanne E., et al. "Current Asthma Prevalence—United States, 2006–2008." *CDC Morbidity and Mortality Weekly Report* 60, supplement no. 1 (January 14, 2011): 84–86.

Morgan, Edmund S. *American Slavery, American Freedom: The Ordeal of Colonial Virginia.* New York: W. W. Norton, 1975.

Morrison, R. Sean, et al. "'We Don't Carry That'—Failure of Pharmacies in Predominantly Nonwhite Neighborhoods to Stock Opioid Analgesics." *New England Journal of Medicine* 342, no. 14 (2000): 1023–26.

Mosher, William D., and Jo Jones. "Use of Contraception in the United States: 1982–2008." *Vital and Health Statistics* 23, no. 29 (2010): 1–42.

Moskowitz, Gordon B., Jeff Stone, and Amanda Childs. "Implicit Stereotyping and Medical Decisions: Unconscious Stereotype Activation in Practitioners' Thought about African Americans." *American Journal of Public Health* 102, no. 5 (2012): 996–1001.

Murphey, David. *What Do We Know about the High School Class of 2013?* Bethesda, MD: Child Trends, 2013.

Mutiangpili, Jhoana. *Government Sector Outsourcing: Transforming Public Service with Outsourced IT Services.* New York: Tholons' Services Globalization, 2010.

National Partnership for Women and Family. *Fact Sheet: African American Women and the Wage Gap.* Washington, DC: National Partnership for Women and Family, 2013a.

———. *Fact Sheet: Latinas and the Wage Gap.* Washington, DC: National Partnership for Women and Family, 2013b.

Nelson-Pallmeyer, Jack. *School of Assassins: Guns, Greed, and Globalization.* Maryknoll, NY: Orbis Books, 2001.

Niebuhr, H. Richard. *The Responsible Self: An Essay in Christian Moral Philosophy.* New York: Harper & Row, 1963.

Niebuhr, Reinhold. *The Nature and Destiny of Man.* Vol. 2, *Human Destiny.* New York: Scribner, 1943.

———. *Moral Man and Immoral Society: A Study in Ethics and Politics.* New York: Scribner, 1960.

No More Deaths. *A Culture of Cruelty: Abuse and Impunity in Short-Term U.S. Border Patrol Custody.* Tucson, AZ: No More Deaths, 2011.

Nunez-Smith, Marcella, et al. "Institutional Variation in the Promotion of Racial/Ethnic Minority Faculty at US Medical Schools." *American Journal of Public Health* 102, no. 5 (2012): 852–58.

Obama, Barack. "Remarks by the President on International Tax Policy Reform." Speech given at the White House, Washington, DC, May 4, 2009.

O'Brien, Barbara, and Catherine M. Grosso. *Report on Jury Selection Study.* East Lansing: Michigan State University College of Law, 2011.

(OECD) Organisation for Economic Co-operation and Development, Social Policy Division, Directorate of Employment, Labour and Social Affairs. *Child Poverty.* Paris: OECD Family Database, 2011.

Ong, Paul M., and Michael A. Stoll. *Redlining or Risk? A Spatial Analysis of Auto Insurance Rates in Los Angeles.* Ann Arbor, MI: National Poverty Center Working Paper Series, 2006.

Orfield, Gary. *Reviving the Goal of an Integrated Society: A 21st-Century Challenge.* Los Angeles: Regents of the University of California, 2009.

Ortega, Bob. *In Sam We Trust: The Untold Story of Sam Walton and How Wal-Mart Is Devouring America.* New York: Random House, 1998.

Owens, Ann. "Neighborhoods and Schools as Competing and Reinforcing Contexts for Educational Attainment." *Sociology of Education* 83, no. 4 (2010): 287–311.

Pedraja, Luis G. "Trinity." In *Handbook of U.S. Theologies of Liberation*, edited by Miguel A. De La Torre, 46–58. St. Louis: Chalice, 2004.

Picone, Christopher, and David Van Tassel. "Agriculture and Biodiversity Loss: Industrial Agriculture." In *Life on Earth: An Encyclopedia of Biodiversity, Ecology, and Evolution*, edited by Niles Eldridge, 99–105. Santa Barbara, CA: ABC-CLIO, 2002.

Pérez Esquivel, Adolfo. *Christ in a Poncho: Testimonials of the Nonviolent Struggles in Latin America.* Edited by Charles Antoine. Translated by Robert R. Barr. Maryknoll, NY: Orbis Books, 1983.

Phillips, Kevin. *The Politics of Rich and Poor: Wealth and the American Electorate in the Reagan Aftermath.* New York: Random House, 1990.

Pimentel, David, and Marcia Pimentel. "Sustainability of Meat-Based and Plant-Based Diets and the Environment." *American Journal of Clinical Nutrition* 78, no. 3 (2003): 660–63.

Pixley, George V. *On Exodus: A Liberation Perspective.* Translated by Robert R. Barr. Maryknoll, NY: Orbis Books, 1987.

Pristoop, Eli. "Appendix." In *The Funding Gaps, 2006.* Washington, DC: The Education Trust, 2006.

Public Religion Research Institute. *Survey: Americans Divided between Principle and Practice on Affirmative Action, Divided on DOMA*. Washington, DC: Public Religion Research Institute, 2013.

Raboteau, Albert J. *Slave Religion: The "Invisible Institution" in the Antebellum South*. New York: Oxford University Press, 1978.

Raines, John. "Making Global Capitalism More Just by Imposing an International Transaction Tax." Lecture given at the Indonesian Consortium for Religious Studies, Yogyakarta, June 20, 2012.

Ramsey, Paul. *Christian Ethics and the Sit-In*. New York: Association Press, 1961.

Rand, Michael. *National Crime Victimization Survey: Criminal Victimization, 2007*. Washington, DC: U.S. Department of Justice, Bureau of Justice Statistics, 2008.

Rawls, John. *A Theory of Justice*. Cambridge, MA: Belknap Press of Harvard University Press, 1971.

Rejón, Francisco Moreno. "Fundamental Moral Theory in the Theology of Liberation." In *Mysterium Liberationis: Fundamental Concepts of Liberation Theology*. Edited by Ignacio Ellacuría and Jon Sobrino. Maryknoll, NY: Orbis Books, 1993.

Renzulli, Linda A., and Lorraine Evans. "School Choice, Charter Schools, and White Flight." *Social Problems* 52, no. 3 (2005): 398–418.

Roberts, Mary Louise. *What Soldiers Do: Sex and the American G.I. in World War II France*. Chicago: University of Chicago Press, 2013.

Rollin, Bernie. "The Ethics of Agriculture: The End of True Husbandry." In *The Future of Animal Farming: Renewing the Ancient Contract*, edited by Marian Stamp Dawkins and Roland Bonney, 7–20. Oxford: Blackwell, 2008.

Rosales, Mauricio. *Livestock Policy Brief 03: Cattle Ranching and Deforestation*. Rome: Livestock Information, Sector Analysis and Policy Branch, Animal Production and Health Division of the Food and Agriculture Organization of the United Nations, 2011.

Rousseau, Jean-Jacques. *The First and Second Discourses*. Edited by Roger D. Masters. Translated by Roger D. Masters and Judith R. Masters. New York: St. Martin's Press, 1964.

Ruether, Rosemary Radford, ed. *Women Healing Earth: Third World Women on Ecology, Feminism, and Religion*. Maryknoll, NY: Orbis Books, 1996.

Runge, C. Ford, and Benjamin Senauer. "How Biofuels Could Starve the Poor." *Foreign Affairs* 83, no. 3 (2007): 41–53.

Rutkow, Lainie, and Joshua T. Lozman. "Suffer the Children? A Call for United States Ratification of the United Nations Convention on the Rights of the Child." *Harvard Human Rights Journal* 19 (2006): 161–90.

Sabin, Janice A., and Anthony G. Greenwald. "The Influence of Implicit Bias on Treatment Recommendations for 4 Common Pediatric Conditions: Pain, Urinary Tract Infection, Attention Deficit Hyperactivity Disorder, and Asthma." *American Journal of Public Health* 102, no. 5 (2012): 988–94.

Sanders, Cheryl. *Empowerment Ethics for a Liberated People: A Path to African American Social Transformation.* Minneapolis: Fortress, 1995.

Santelices, Maria Veronica, and Mark Wilson. "Unfair Treatment? The Case of Freedle, the SAT, and the Standardization Approach to Differential Item Functioning." *Harvard Educational Review* 80, no. 1 (2010): 106–34.

Santelli, John S., et al. "Explaining Recent Declines in Adolescent Pregnancy in the United States: The Contribution of Abstinence and Improved Contraceptive Use." *American Journal of Public Health* 97, no. 1 (2007): 150–56.

Sarkozy, Nicolas. Speech given at the Fortieth World Economic Forum, Davos, Switzerland, January 27, 2010.

Sawyer, Pamela J., et al. "Discrimination and the Stress Response: Psychological and Physiological Consequences of Anticipating Prejudice in Interethnic Interactions." *American Journal of Public Health* 102, no. 5 (2012): 1020–26.

Schecter, Arnold, and John D. Constable. "Commentary: Agent Orange and Birth Defects in Vietnam." *International Journal of Epidemiology* 35, no. 5 (2006): 1230–32.

Schluger, Neil. *The Acute Respiratory Infections Atlas.* Atlanta: World Lung Foundation, 2010.

Schubeck, Thomas L. *Liberating Ethics: Sources, Models, and Norms.* Minneapolis: Fortress, 1993.

Schulman, Kevin A., et al. "The Effect of Race and Sex on Physician's Recommendations for Cardiac Catheterization." *New England Journal of Medicine* 340, no. 8 (1999): 618–25.

Seager, Joni. "Creating a Culture of Destruction: Gender, Militarism, and the Environment." In *Toxic Struggles: The Theory and Practice of Environmental Justice,* edited by Richard Hofrichter, 58–66. Philadelphia: New Society Publishers, 1993.

Secretariat of the Commission for Environmental Cooperation. *Hazardous Trade? An Examination of US-Generated Spent Lead-Acid Battery Exports and Secondary Lead Recycling in Mexico, the United States and Canada.* Montreal: Commission for Environmental Cooperation, 2012.

Segundo, Juan Luis. "Conversion and Reconciliation in the Perspective of Modern Liberation Theology." In *Signs of the Times: Theological Reflections,* translated by Robert R. Barr, edited by Alfred T. Hennelly, 37–52. Maryknoll, NY: Orbis Books, 1993.

Shiva, Vandana. "Let Us Survive: Women, Ecology and Development." In *Women Healing Earth: Third World Women on Ecology, Feminism, and Religion*, edited by Rosemary Radford Ruether, 65–73. Maryknoll, NY: Orbis Books, 1996.

Shute, Sara. "Sexist Language and Sexism." In *Sexist Language: A Modern Philosophical Analysis*, edited by Mary Vetterling-Braggin, 23–33. Totowa, NJ: Littlefield, Adams, 1981.

Singh, Amrit. *Globalizing Torture: CIA Secret Detention and Extraordinary Rendition*. New York: Open Society Foundation, 2013.

(SIPRI) Stockholm International Peace Research Institute. *SIPRI Yearbook 2012: Armaments, Disarmament and International Security*. Stockholm: SIPRI, 2012.

Smith, Adam. *An Inquiry into the Nature and Causes of the Wealth of Nations*. Edited by R. H. Campbell, A. S. Skinner, and W. B. Todd. Vol. 1. Oxford: Clarendon, 1976.

Sobrino, Jon. *Christology at the Crossroads: A Latin American Approach*. Translated by John Drury. Maryknoll, NY: Orbis Books, 1978.

———. *Jesus the Liberator: A Historical-Theological Reading of Jesus of Nazareth*. Translated by Paul Burns and Francis McDonagh. Maryknoll, NY: Orbis Books, 1993.

Steinfield, Henning, et al. *Livestock's Long Shadow: Environmental Issues and Options*. Rome: Food and Agriculture Organization of the United Nations, 2006.

Taylor, Mark Lewis. *The Executed God: The Way of the Cross in Lockdown America*. Minneapolis: Fortress, 2001.

Taylor, Paul, et al. *Wealth Gaps Rise to Record Highs between Whites, Blacks, and Hispanics*. Washington, DC: Pew Research Center, 2011.

Teninty, Ellen. "The S&L Crisis: Time to Strike Back." In *Ethics in the Present Tense: Readings from Christianity and Crisis, 1966–1991*, edited by Leon Howell and Vivian Lindermayer. New York: Friendship Press, 1991.

Thandeka. *Learning to Be White: Money, Race, and God in America*. New York: Continuum, 1999.

Tinker, George. "Spirituality and Native American Personhood: Sovereignty and Solidarity." In *Spirituality of the Third World: A Cry for Life; Papers and Reflections from the Third General Assembly of the Ecumenical Association of Third World Theologians, January, 1992, Nairobi, Kenya*, edited by K. C. Abraham and Bernadette Mbuy-Beya, 119–38. Maryknoll, NY: Orbis Books, 1994.

———. "John Locke on Property." In *Beyond the Pale: Reading Ethics from the Margins*, edited by Stacey M. Floyd-Thomas and Miguel A. De La Torre, 49–60. Louisville: Westminster John Knox, 2011.

Towery, Britt. "Torture and We're Number 1?" *Christian Ethics Today* 71, no. 4 (2008): 19–20.

Townes, Emilie. *In a Blaze of Glory: Womanist Spirituality as Social Witness.* Nashville: Abingdon, 1995.

Trimiew, Darryl M. *Voices of the Silenced: The Responsible Self in a Marginalized Community.* Cleveland: Pilgrim, 1993.

———. "Ethics." In *Handbook of U.S. Theologies of Liberation,* edited by Miguel A. De La Torre, 101–9. St. Louis: Chalice, 2004.

Trussell, James. "Contraceptive Failure in the United States." *Contraception* 83, no. 5 (2011): 397–404.

Turner, Margery Austin, et al. *Housing Discrimination against Racial and Ethnic Minorities, 2012.* Washington, DC: U.S. Department of Housing and Urban Development, 2013.

Tutu, Desmond. "South Africa's Blacks: Aliens in Their Own Land." In *Ethics in the Present Tense: Readings from Christianity and Crisis, 1966–1991,* edited by Leon Howell and Vivian Lindermayer. New York: Friendship Press, 1991.

UNAIDS (Joint United Nations Programme on HIV/AIDS). *UNAIDS World AIDS Day Report: 2011.* New York: United Nations, 2011.

UNDP (United Nations Development Programme). *New Dimensions of Human Security.* New York: Oxford University Press, 1994.

———. *Fighting Climate Change: Human Solidarity in a Divided World.* New York: Palgrave Macmillan, 2007.

———. *The Real Wealth of Nations: Pathways to Human Development.* New York: Palgrave Macmillan, 2010.

UNFAO (United Nations Food and Agriculture Organization). *The State of Food Insecurity in the World, 2012.* Rome: Food and Agriculture Organization of the United Nations, 2012.

U.S. Department of Defense. *Department of Defense Annual Report on Sexual Assault in the Military: Fiscal Year 2012.* Washington, DC: Department of Defense, 2012.

U.S. Department of Health and Human Services. *An Evaluation of Environmental Biological and Health Data from the Island of Vieques, Puerto Rico.* Washington, DC: U.S. Department of Health and Human Services, 2011a.

———. *Federal Register Notice* 76, no. 13 (2011b): 3637–38.

U.S. Department of Labor. *Current Employment Statistics—CES (National).* Washington, DC: U.S. Bureau of Labor Statistics, Division of Current Employment Statistics, 2013a.

———. *Employment, Hours, and Earnings from the Current Employment Statistics Survey—National.* Washington, DC: U.S. Bureau of Labor Statistics, Division of Current Employment Statistics, 2013b.

———. *Industries at a Glance Manufacturing: NAICS 31–33.* Washington, DC: U.S. Bureau of Labor Statistics, Division of Current Employment Statistics, 2013c.

————. *Occupational Employment and Wages, May 2012*. Washington, DC: U.S. Bureau of Labor Statistics, Division of Current Employment Statistics, 2013d.

U.S. Department of State. *Trafficking in Persons Report*. Washington, DC: Department of State, 2012.

U.S. Energy Information Administration. *Country Analysis Brief: China*. Washington, DC: U.S. Energy Information Administration, 2010.

————. *Rising Asian Demand Drives Global Coal Consumption Growth*. Washington, DC: U.S. Energy Information Administration, 2011.

Veblen, Thorstein. *The Theory of the Leisure Class*. New York: New American Library, 1953.

Velasquez, Manuel G. *Business Ethics: Concepts and Cases*. 4th ed. Upper Saddle River, NJ: Prentice Hall, 1998.

von Rad, Gerhard. *Old Testament Theology*. Vol. 1, *The Theology of Israel's Historical Traditions*. Translated by D. M. G. Stalker. New York: Harper & Row, 1962.

Walker, Alice. *Living by the Word: Selected Writings, 1983–1987*. San Diego: Harcourt Brace Jovanovich, 1988.

Wang, Wendy, Kim Parker, and Paul Taylor. *Breadwinner Moms: Mothers Are the Sole or Primary Provider in Four-in-Ten Households with Children; Public Conflicted about the Growing Trend*. Washington, DC: Pew Research Center, 2013.

Warren, Karen. "Feminism and Ecology: Making Connections." *Environmental Ethics* 9, no. 1 (1987): 3–20.

Warrior, Robert. "Canaanites, Cowboys, and Indians: Deliverance, Conquest, and Liberation Theology Today." *Christianity and Crisis* 49 (1989): 261–65.

Welch, Sharon D. *A Feminist Ethic of Risk*. Minneapolis: Fortress, 1990.

Wessler, Seth. *Race and Recession: How Inequity Rigged the Economy and How to Change the Rules*. New York: Applied Research Center, 2009.

West, Cornel. *Prophesy Deliverance: An Afro-American Revolutionary Christianity*. Philadelphia: Westminster, 1982.

Wiener, Ross, and Eli Pristoop. "How States Shortchange the Districts That Need the Most Help." In *The Funding Gaps, 2006*. Washington, DC: The Education Trust, 2006.

Williams, Delores S. "Black Women's Surrogacy Experience and the Christian Notion of Redemption." In *After Patriarchy: Feminist Transformation of the World Religions*, edited by Paula M. Cooey, William R. Eakin, and Jay B. McDaniel, 1–14. Maryknoll, NY: Orbis Books, 1991.

————. *Sisters in the Wilderness: The Challenge of Womanist God-Talk*. Maryknoll, NY: Orbis Books, 1993.

Williams, Preston N. "An Analysis of the Conception of Love and Its Influence on Justice in the Thought of Martin Luther King Jr." *Journal of Religious Ethics* 18, no. 2 (1990): 15–31.

Williams, Robertson. *Who Benefits from Tax Expenditures?* Washington, DC: Tax Policy Center, Urban Institute and Brookings Institute, 2011.

Wilson, William Julius. *The Truly Disadvantaged: The Inner City, the Underclass, and Public Policy.* Chicago: University of Chicago Press, 1987.

———. *The Bridge over the Racial Divide: Rising Inequality and Coalition Politics.* Berkeley: University of California Press, 1999.

Winant, Howard. *The New Politics of Race: Globalism, Difference, Justice.* Minneapolis: University of Minnesota Press, 2004.

Wolf, F. Ron. "God, James Watt, and the Public Lands." *Audubon* 83, no. 3 (1981): 58–65.

Wolfensohn, James D. "The Challenge of Globalization: The Role of the World Bank." Address to the Bundestag at Berlin, Germany, on April 2, 2001.

Woodson, Carter G. *The Mis-Education of the Negro.* Washington, DC: Associated Publishers, 1933.

Wright, Beverly Hendrix, and Robert D. Bullard. "The Effects of Occupational Injury, Illness, and Disease on the Health Status of Black Americans." In *Toxic Struggles: The Theory and Practice of Environmental Justice,* edited by Richard Hofrichter, 153–62. Philadelphia: New Society Publishers, 1993.

Wright, Erik Olin. *Classes.* London: Verso, 1985.

Yang, Seung Ai. "Asian Americans." In *Handbook of U.S. Theologies of Liberation,* edited by Miguel A. De La Torre, 173–84. St. Louis: Chalice, 2004.

Yip, Fuyuen Y., et al. "Unhealthy Air Quality—United States, 2006–2009." *CDC Morbidity and Mortality Weekly Report* 60, supplement no 1 (January 14, 2011): 28–32.

Index